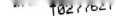

Human Geography

by Kyle Tredinnick

A Wiley Brand

Human Geography For Dummies®

Published by: **John Wiley & Sons, Inc.**, 111 River Street, Hoboken, NJ 07030-5774, www.wiley.com

Copyright © 2024 by John Wiley & Sons, Inc., Hoboken, New Jersey

Media and software compilation copyright © 2024 by John Wiley & Sons, Inc. All rights reserved.

Published simultaneously in Canada

For general information on our other products and services, please contact our Customer Care Department within the U.S. at 877-762-2974, outside the U.S. at 317-572-3993, or fax 317-572-4002. For technical support, please visit https://hub.wiley.com/community/support/dummies.

Wiley publishes in a variety of print and electronic formats and by print-on-demand. Some material included with standard print versions of this book may not be included in e-books or in print-on-demand. If this book refers to media such as a CD or DVD that is not included in the version you purchased, you may download this material at http://booksupport.wiley.com. For more information about Wiley products, visit www.wiley.com.

Library of Congress Control Number: 2023952212

ISBN 978-1-394-20827-2 (pbk); ISBN 978-1-394-20829-6 (ebk); ISBN 978-1-394-20828-9 (ebk)

SKY10064238_010824

Contents at a Glance

Contents at a Glance

Table of Contents

Introduction

As I write this, we're presently looking at a shockingly high number of major world issues — the Russian Invasion of Ukraine; Israel and Hamas in the Gaza Strip; climate change; reverberating impacts of the COVID-19 pandemic; sectarianism and fanaticism in multiple governments around the world; and poverty and inequality in many places. All of it — let me say that again, all of it — can be better understood by geography. And because these things can be understood by geography, then maybe geography can help begin correcting some of the many issues out there. Maybe, just maybe, if everyone had a little more understanding of what is actually going on, there wouldn't be so much of this craziness going on.

As my biographical information on the cover says, I am a geographic educator. My career is devoted to teaching others about geography. Human geography is, by far and away, my favorite subject to teach. All of the issues I listed at the beginning of this introduction can be contextualized by human geography to help make sense of them. Sometimes, it feels like you can see into the inner workings of a problem to make those problems just a little less daunting.

What I especially love about this subject is its ability to connect with anything and anyone. In my experience, people love learning about new things and places. It's one reason travel logs are so plentiful; you can learn about the world from someone else's point of view from the safety of your own couch. Human geography, however, empowers you to write your own story. Your story can be a geographic story that's not just about collecting superlatives. Geographic exploration is about much more than checking things off so you can post pictures on social media. Your story will have a deeper meaning. You will also connect what you find to the collective of what others have seen and done. That's one of the great things about learning: You learn things you never even thought you would, and then you can contribute to the world's body of knowledge so that others can learn from you. Sometimes, we don't know what we don't know until we know!

We're constantly being cued about how and what to think. Only by learning for yourself can you really truly figure things out. For example, about a month into living in China, a couple of us took a trip to Tiananmen Square in the heart of Beijing's governmental center. While being a couple of goofy-looking tourists amidst the throngs of people celebrating China's National Day, a man who wasn't Chinese came up to us and asked if we were Americans. My friend is Canadian, so he quickly corrected the man, saying we were from the US, Canada, and Malaysia. To which he replied, "I'm Iranian; I don't want to kill you!" Once we stopped laughing, we talked about how our respective governments and media cue us to dislike and mistrust one another. I genuinely enjoyed talking to Hamid, the engineering student from Iran.

And that connects to one of my overarching goals for this book: to start building your own perspectives of the world. And human geography gives you the context and framework to do just that.

About This book

Human Geography is a collection of subdisciplines dealing with the location and distribution of human systems worldwide. I usually sum it up as: "Why people live where they live, and how do they live?" though that is a vast oversimplification of the subject. As a discipline, we generally divide the subject between population, migration, urbanization, agriculture, industry, development, culture, and political organization. That is a lot to fit into one book. We will refer to these as the main subdisciplines of human geography.

When most people think of geography, they generally assume it is about memorizing place names and locations or making maps. Those things are part of this subject but only minimally. Nowhere in this book will you find a quiz to test your knowledge. It is important, but the field of human geography reaches much deeper than memorizing place names and locations. Instead, we seek to understand how those subdisciplines are present, distributed, and compared from one location to the next.

This book is arranged thematically, not chronologically or regionally. Many geography classes are set up regionally, where the teacher goes region by region and talks about the different geographic, physical, and human features before talking about the superlatives and moving on. While that is an interesting way to learn what there is to see and do worldwide, you can find deeper meaning by learning it thematically. In this book, I'll introduce a concept, then give you an example, and invite you to come up with an example of your own where you can apply it. I'm hoping you'll think about the content and try to apply it to better understand the world around you. Then, through the examples, you'll be able to see how where you're living is connected to other parts of the world.

I tried to connect my personal experiences (like meeting Hamid) to explain how it is possible to connect with the materials personally. This does not mean you have to travel all the way to Beijing. You could just visit a part of town you've never been to or even drive home by taking a different way to see what you can see. I'm selfishly hoping this book will inspire you to explore more wherever you are!

How This Book Is Organized

Human geography is a multi-dimensional field of study comprising multiple areas of interest and concern. As one of the social sciences, human geography seeks to better understand how people are living in different parts of the world. With so many applications for human geography, it is possible to find connections to any area of interest. This book will begin demystifying the field of geography by describing how geographers study the world in the following areas.

Part 1: Introduction to Human Geography

Part 1 will look at the history of the field of geography in general and the study of human geography specifically. The chapters in this part will look at historical and philosophical developments in the field and how they've directed the study of the human world from a spatial perspective. There will also be a discussion of some of the overarching ideas, known as the Five Themes of Geography, that help guide our study of the world.

Part 2: The Geography of Human Habitation

By looking at the geographic phenomenon of population, human migration, and clustering of populations in urban areas, we can understand some trends in human populations. Where are they living? Why are they living there? How has their living there been affected by the physical characteristics of the land? We'll answer these questions in the chapters in this part.

Part 3: The Spatial Organization of Human Systems

How humans distinguish themselves from one another can be done by creating intricate cultures and rigid political divisions. These are both topics that human geographers are interested in because they can be measured over space and time to come up with a clear picture of what makes groups of people unique and how they divide themselves from one group to the next. The chapters in this part look at the principles and examples of cultural and political geography.

Part 4: The Spatial Organization of Human Economic Systems

The structure of economies and how people provide for themselves is of great interest to economic geographers. They can do this by examining the relationship between humans and the cultivation or utilization of the land to provide wealth. This can come either in the form of food production by different agricultural systems or the mining and collection of resources to produce goods in industrial systems. These are large contributing factors that help better understand the levels of development and how humans interact with the land. Part 4 explains agricultural, industrial, Land Use, and Developmental geographies.

Part 5: The Part of Fives

The final part of this book, The Part of Tens, breaks down how you could use your knowledge of human geography in the job world and apply what you've learned in this book to the real world.

Foolish Assumptions

Going into this book, I assume you are not a dummy but just want to learn more about the topic. Human Geography is not a required subject in most of the world. Subjectively, I think it's a terrible shame that human geography is not required learning everywhere since it's so helpful. So, I'm going to assume you've never taken a human geography course before and are learning this stuff for the first time. However, the thing about a lot of this content is that you probably are already familiar with a lot of it; you just didn't know there were terms and concepts connected to it. You might be reading this book to help you with a class or because of your general interest. Either way, I wrote the book to be accessible to all, no matter how old you are.

I'm also going to assume you have an Internet device nearby. There is only so much I can explain in a book this size, so I'll sometimes recommend looking up content to expand your understanding beyond what you read here. Almost all the topics I discuss can be much more complicated than what I have the space to cover in this book. Some topics can get complex to the point that people have devoted entire academic careers to understanding one part of them. For this reason, I use a lot of open-ended wording and avoid definitive explanations. I often point out exceptions and encourage you to find your own. You may be able to come up with some off the top of your head or with a quick Internet search.

Conventions Used in This Book

To help you navigate through this book, I use the following conventions:

>> *Italic* is used to emphasize and highlight new words or defined terms.

>> **Boldfaced** text indicates keywords in bulleted lists or the action part of numbered steps.

>> Monofont is used for web addresses.

>> Sidebars, which look like text enclosed in a shaded gray box, consist of information that's interesting to know but not necessarily critical to your understanding of the chapter or section topic.

Icons Used in This Book

Throughout the book, I have used many examples to clarify specific points or direct you to other means of thinking. Here are the icons you'll see throughout the book and how I use them.

TECHNICAL STUFF

This is pointing to some really specific stuff that I happen to think is really cool. These vocabulary terms and concepts specific to geography or examples help drive a point home. Either way, I highly recommend reading these since they're often the "bacon bits" in the salad of the subject.

WARNING

Believe it or not, human geography does deal with some very controversial things. Students sometimes come up to me in tears when the materials we've discussed in class don't align with what they previously knew. I use the warning symbol to occasionally point out these controversial topics where there can be varied opinions and understandings.

REMEMBER

You have a lot to remember when reading about the world. This icon alerts you to important information you don't want to forget because it can often make the entire process of understanding human geography go much more smoothly.

TIP

Life is rarely straightforward. When you see this icon, you'll find a strategy to help you get the most out of your understanding of human geography.

Beyond the Book

Find out more about Body Language by checking out the bonus content at www. dummies.com. You can locate the book's Cheat Sheet by visiting the Dummies site and typing this book's title into the search field to find the Cheat Sheet. In the Cheat Sheet, you'll find more about human geography.

Where to Go from Here

If you want to and have the time, you can read this book from cover to cover. This book gives you a great view of how much, how, and where to save money for education. But if you don't have the time or the interest, you may choose to hop around from topic to topic, skipping those that don't apply to you and paying more careful attention to those that do. That's one of the great things about *For Dummies* books. You can get in and get out wherever and whenever you choose. If the information you need to understand a certain topic is covered elsewhere, the text will direct you, so you don't need to worry that you're missing basic information by skipping over a portion of the book.

1

Introduction to Human Geography

Chapter **1**

Welcome to Human Geography

uman geography. What is it? Obviously, that's why you're here! The easiest answer I can give you is that it's about why people live where and how they got there. The field of human geography is filled with topics you're probably already familiar with, and you just didn't know there was an academic study that tries to understand the trends and patterns of human systems over space. Human geographers look for the distribution of human systems (economic, political, social, and environmental) and how they impact — and are impacted by — their physical location on the Earth's surface.

Originally, I aimed to teach high school history at a school near where I grew up. Through a weird series of events, I eventually moved to Omaha, Nebraska, to pursue a master's in geography at the University of Nebraska–Omaha and then a Ph.D. in geography from the University of Nebraska–Lincoln.

Via my training and experience, I have gotten many opportunities to travel, and my background in geography has helped add meaning to the things I have encountered along the way. Geospatial technology professor Nicholas Chrisman says,

"Geographers never get lost; they only do accidental fieldwork." This is one of my favorite quotes because it's a nice way of embodying the field as one of discovery — intentionally or accidentally.

Human geography opens many new possibilities to understand the world from a new perspective. I'm sure I occasionally drive my wife nuts as we travel because I'll stop to photograph a seemingly insignificant thing. I'll take a photo, check around for anything else of interest, and mutter something like "agricultural geography" before we're on our way again. Where one person may only see people working out in a field, a human geographer may see subsistence farming and top-ics for discussion in agricultural geography.

I hope this book will help you grow as a geographer and use the terms and con-cepts within this book to understand the world around you. Also, I hope you will be encouraged to get out and explore. Whether exploring your own neighborhood, city, state, country, or even another faraway place, geography is about the world; that is where you'll be able to connect these topics best. Getting out and applying what you learn will make it all the more enriching (see Figure 1-1).

FIGURE 1-1: Get out and explore. You never know what a new perspective will get you.

Important Context for Learning Human Geography

I would argue that geography is among the most misrepresented and misunderstood subjects. Many people's perceptions about the subject are that it is about simply memorizing place names and locations. As I'll cover later, this is the most basic baseline knowledge you'll get about geography. Human geography is a social science that studies people; people are also studied in other social sciences (history, sociology, anthropology, political science, economics, and psychology). Instead of studying people from a historical or structural perspective, human geographers examine many of the same topics from a spatial perspective. We're interested in culture, economic systems, political systems, and so on, but we're more focused on how those things are distributed. We'll cover some of these structures in depth. However, much of this book will focus on how things in one area are similar or different from other areas. For example, we won't get any detail about the tenets of Islam — that is best saved for a theologian — but we will look at how religions like Islam spread over time and space.

When we teach social sciences in grade schools, the purpose is for students to develop their critical thinking and reasoning skills. I use the Assertion, Reasoning, Evidence (ARE) method, which involves making assertions like "English is the most widely spoken language in the world" and then explaining your reasoning for that assertion. This reasoning might include noting the number of native English speakers, the number who speak it as a second language, and countries where learning English is required in school. You might then support this reasoning with evidence, such as a series of maps showing the percentage of people who speak English fluently by country and then comparing that to other languages. The evidence is crucial in building up the argument because unless you're already an expert who has published papers, you're not a reputable source.

When it comes to the social sciences, it's not what you claim or your opinions. It's what you can support.

REMEMBER

Throughout this book, I've given you some background to show you why I'm a reputable source, but I'll be the first to tell you that I don't know everything about human geography. One of the disheartening things about studying is that the more you study, the more you realize you don't know.

REMEMBER

As a side note, this book does not contain every kernel of knowledge about human geography. In fact, there are many parts of the book where I encourage you to refer to other areas for their depth or expertise.

An important part of human geography is the continual search for knowledge and the checking and rechecking of that knowledge's validity. For example, let's say you're trying to learn more about the prevalence of English across India. If your sources are all from one perspective, say the Indian perspective, you might only have part of the story. That is why it is important to supplement that research with sources from somewhere else, perhaps Britain, which can be used to corroborate the information you already have. Better yet, this is where geography gets really fun. The best way to learn about India is to go to India and learn for yourself. With the world changing as fast as it does, many commonly held truths are no longer valid.

I have tried writing this book in as broad and timeless a manner as possible and have tried to avoid writing too many things that would otherwise become outdated. All this is to say that geography, like many other subjects, allows you to evaluate information and assess its reputation.

TECHNICAL STUFF

Contrary to how some people use it, "research" is not just reading some stuff on the Internet. The important components of doing actual research are developing a hypothesis, collecting data, analyzing the data, drawing conclusions, and then submitting them for review from others knowledgeable about the topic. Reading stuff on the Internet will not make you an expert about anything. In human geography, we use the research method to expand our knowledge about topics and contribute to the field's knowledge bank.

Geography: Where things happen

Saying that everything happens somewhere is kind of a cop-out that gives a free pass for anything to be considered within the realm of geography, but it's not far off if you do it right. The geographic perspective differs from the other social sciences' distinct focus on space, where "space" combines the physical location on the Earth's surface and the interacting human and physical characteristics.

LOCATION, PLACE, AND SPACE

Throughout this book, you'll hear "space" referred to in several ways. Location, place, and space refer to the same general idea with subtle, nuanced differences:

- **Location.** Location refers to an actual physical place on the Earth's surface.
- **Place.** Place refers instead to the human and physical characteristics of that location.
- **Space.** Space connects the ideas of place and location.

Most of these differences can be used interchangeably. However, I have reserved the discussion of "place" for Chapter 3, "The Five Themes of Geography."

TECHNICAL STUFF

Another nuance I tried to explain as much as possible is how to refer to an area as a political entity. In geographer-speak, the word "State"(note the capitalized usage) can be used interchangeably with the word "country" because both refer to a politically designated land area that works at the national level and interacts with other states as an equal. A "state" (note the lowercase usage) is a subdivision of a State that has a lesser, more regional designation of political control that interacts with other states and is not on the same level with States. So, "State" refers to a country, and "state" refers to the smaller subdivision of a State (similar to a province). A State would be something like the United States of America. A state, however, would be like the state of California within the United States. I use this convention throughout the book for consistency, so I felt it necessary to introduce it early on.

TIP

While we're on the topic of naming conventions, in geography-speak, a nation is not synonymous with a country or State.

In Chapter 4, "The Philosophies of Geography," we'll talk about the different perspectives of space that geographers have used throughout the history of the discipline. There will be a specific emphasis on the "sense of place" idea that gets into the characteristics and the meaning we attach to different spaces. As we go through the topics in this book, I repeatedly redirect the focus on concepts to their connections to spaces and places. This is very much about contextualizing concepts in their physical locations to understand them in what we call the "spatial perspective." Through the spatial perspective, geographers try to understand how human and natural features interact. In human geography, we focus heavily on human features, though natural factors remain very significant.

Why Learn Human Geography?

I am very biased when discussing why learning human geography is important, but that should be unsurprising. Having taught almost every social science at the high school level, I can confidently say that human geography is my favorite subject because the students "get it" and can connect with the materials, making it easy to have engaging discussions about the different topics in the subject. With human geography especially, just about everything that goes on in the world can be placed into one of the subdisciplines of human geography.

TECHNICAL STUFF

As I write this chapter, the Russian War on Ukraine is still very much ongoing. I often bring up this war through this book, given its multiple connections to population and migration geography, cultural geography, and political geography; it even has implications in agricultural, developmental, and urban geographies. I don't use this war in every example, but I could have done so pretty easily.

Geography: A practical science

That gets me to my first point: Human geography is a practical science with many applications. It's not a super-abstract field with a lot of hard-to-comprehend topics. The content of human geography can be seen around you every day. Even the more complex stuff, like geographic models, maps, and different theories, are still fairly comprehendible because geography relies so much on real-world examples.

I like to take my students on walks around the school or even have them look at pictures to see how many geographic concepts they can connect to what they see. We look for things like advertisements, architectural styles, and city structure — things that can all be connected to ideas found in the study of human geography. That's one of the reasons I strongly believe you've made a good choice learning more about human geography: It makes the world around you make sense.

Throughout the book, I offer multiple suggestions for connecting the content to real-world situations. Or I offer suggestions for seeking out more information through experiences. I even devote Chapter 22 to places you could visit to see different human geography ideas and hint at what you may want to look for.

Human geography also tries to understand issues and problems from a spatial perspective to address those issues. A whole set of human geography philosophies encourages geographers to be activists and try to correct social and environmental concerns once armed with their expertise and understanding. This is what makes human geography such an enriching subject. It can empower you to take better stances on topics you care about.

Much of this can be achieved through a geographic study utilizing the geoinquiry process. By developing a solid research question (utilizing the root questions of "Where?" "Why there?" "Why care?" and "What can be done?"), geographers can then collect and organize data — analyzing it to identify trends and patterns — and then develop an action plan to address issues. Geography should rarely be about research for research's sake; it should always have a goal. Geography is a framework through which we can learn more about the world around us and fix problems.

Drawing your mental map

Growing up in the 1980s and 1990s, I was taught many things about Russia as the evil antipode of the United States. Then, I made the seemingly crazy decision to go there and see for myself. I traveled the width of the country by rail, and never once did I encounter an evil supervillain with a weird name and a complex plan to rain evil down upon me. Instead, I encountered a multitude of people just going about their day who became increasingly easier to connect with and understand with a bit of *piva (beer)*.

By interacting and immersing myself in another culture, I could reprogram my thinking. Like anybody else, most Russians are just going about their daily lives and trying to get by. The same could be said for just about any group of people worldwide. The media, government, and people often try to cue you as to how you're supposed to think.

REMEMBER

Remember that the actions of governments do not necessarily represent the will of the people they represent. There are many cases throughout history where whole populations become lumped in together despite many being in opposition. Russia is a great example. Much of the narrative in the media is about the Russian people against Ukraine, but remember that at the start of the war, some of the largest demonstrations against the war took place in Russian cities like St. Petersburg and Moscow. It is important to look deeper for nuanced differences and variety. Human geography allows you to think for yourself and come to your own conclusions.

A *Flâneur* is a French phrase (and one of my favorite words) for someone who leisurely strolls without much purpose — one of my favorite activities when traveling somewhere new. By mapping with your feet, you can expand your understanding of the world and broaden your thinking of the human forces surrounding you. Human geography offers a convenient method to contextualize what you see and put it in such a way as to add further meaning. A bus stop turns into a force of urbanization. The shops you encounter along the way are representations of the New International Division of Labor. Even the route you take is a product of your spatial thinking processes. All of this is made possible by learning about human geography. That's pretty neat if you ask me. Just make sure you bring good walking shoes!

One of my goals for you is to expand your mental map of the world further and start metaphorically coloring it with your enriched understanding of different topics connected to human geography. I have tried to incorporate my experiences to aid you as you embark on this task. One of the things that you'll have to come to grips with is that this is a continual process, and you'll constantly need to edit and refine your mental maps. As I did when I was in Russia, I throw out all my perceptions of a place and replace them with an entirely new schema gained through empirical experiences and conversations.

This is increasingly important because of the rise of technology. With all the world at our fingertips, we've somehow lost our connection to it. I've had students who, when asked how they get home from school (in terms of what roads and direction they go), have absolutely no idea since they have their noses shoved in their phones the entire time they're sitting on the bus. Human geography encourages you to take a look around, experience the world for yourself, and build your own mental maps.

Roadmap for This Book

When you arrive at a place you've never been before, it is often necessary to pick up a map to figure out where you're going. Just like with this book, consider human geography a place you've never been before, and the following section will function as the map to help guide you along the way. Although, in theory, you can start just about anywhere in your study of human geography, I would not necessarily recommend that approach when reading this book because the topics are interconnected, just like with our world. I have built this up in a manner where I try to connect the topics as much as possible to concepts in other chapters. I use a lot of foreshadowing to make connections to content yet to come, but in later chapters, I won't go into depth into some areas I've already covered in previous chapters. As much as possible, when I refer back to topics, I include a chapter reference pointing you to the right place to go. That's why it is theoretically possible to start wherever you like, though you might have to do a bit of searching around.

General sequencing

My original training was in history, so when I inherited my first human geography class, I struggled at first to set up the class. The most common structure to approach the class is to start with the theories and concepts of geography, then go into population and migration, then cultural geography, political geography, agriculture and rural land use, urban geography, and finally industrial and economic geography. I take a bit of a different approach that aligns more with a world history perspective of societal development.

Human geography subfields

This book's Introduction briefly touched on how this book is organized, but I think broadening that discussion a little here will help you get more from the chapters after this one. This book is broken into five parts, as described below:

>> **Part 1 — Introduction to Human Geography:** Along with this chapter, the introductory part covers some overarching theories, philosophies, and

concepts that drive the study of human geography. We'll cover the history of geography in general and human geography in specific, from its origins until modern practice. The field of geography has frequently reasserted and reinvented itself to meet the needs of society. This is covered in Chapters 2 and 4. Chapter 3 covers the quasi-universal approach to studying a place from a geographic perspective that puts what you see in a geographic perspective. These first four chapters are highly theoretical and will be recalled frequently throughout the rest of the book, especially Chapter 3.

» **Part 2 — The Geography of Human Habitation:** In this part, we'll get into the content of human geography itself. We start with a discussion about how geographers approach the study of where people live and how they move around. We do this by combining population, migration, and urban geographies. Population geography relies heavily on collecting and analyzing demographic information to understand the characteristics of the people who live in an area. Much of this part is spent on the different statistics that are kept and how they can be useful. From there, we will get into migration geography — the processes and motivations for people's movements across space. We also look at historical and present examples of human migration to establish trends and patterns. Paired with the ideas of population and migration, we round out this part with urban geography.

» **Part 3 — The Spatial Organization of Human Systems:** Cultural and political geography are discussed in this part. Rather than looking at different cultural practices or governmental structures, we spend most of these chapters on how geographers approach these topics. Cultural geography looks at specific patterns and how culture has spread throughout history. We'll also discuss case studies, especially language and religion, as examples of how culture spreads and why. The later chapters in this part are devoted to understanding the political organization of space and how humans have gone about arranging ownership of different parts of the world. We'll look at several types of government and how they're distributed and have spread throughout the world. Culture and government are more abstract philosophies and ideas, so they're linked here.

» **Part 4 — The Spatial Organization of Human Economic Systems:** Again, just like with government and culture, we won't spend much time defining different economic structures. There are subjects purely devoted to that. With this, we will start with agricultural geography and understand the types of farming that take place and how that is connected to the physical environment. As with industrial geography, we'll look at the connection between physical space and the development of different industries. Much of that often depends on the availability of natural resources, so we'll focus on how resources impact economic structure. Agriculture and industry play a significant part in how comfortably people live, so that is why developmental geography is tied in. Development focuses on how we can measure that and how developed different parts of the world are. We'll look at the physical and human factors that have led to differences in the levels of development for areas historically and presently. We'll round out this section with a look at the effect of industry and development on the natural environment and how humans are taking measures to balance the human and physical worlds.

» **Part 5 — The Part of Tens:** To conclude the book, we'll look at how you can use your newfound knowledge of human geography. Chapter 21 looks at careers that use human geography content knowledge and skills, including government, business, and teaching. Chapter 22 looks at places you can go to connect human geography concepts to the actual landscape. Human geography has almost infinite applications as a practical science, so these two chapters should give you a good place to start.

Whatever your motivation for learning human geography, one of the things that is so great about the subject is there really is a way to connect nearly any topic area to the field of human geography. Hopefully, you'll learn some new things or even just get a better idea of ways to start expanding your knowledge about the world around you from the perspective of human geography.

Chapter 2

The History of Human Geography

One of my favorite geographers is Halford Mackinder from the United Kingdom. As a product of his time, he most definitely had his faults, notably guiding the British crown's politics and subjugating more than one-quarter of the world's population at the time. His theories (which we'll discuss later in this book) were used to justify Imperialism and further worked to extend the dominion of the British Empire.

Beyond Mackinder's advocacy that helped lead to the establishment of geography as an academic subject, one of the other things I like about him is his approach to geography. Early in his career he joined an expedition to climb Mount Kenya because he thought that's what geographers were supposed to do. The underlying spirit of adventure that drove Mackinder embodied the very origins of the field of geography.

Like many academic areas, men from Western Europe and the United States dominated the field's early history. The academic field of geography is mainly rooted in the United Kingdom and Germany. Notable early geographers like Alexander von Humboldt, Carl Ritter, and Friedrich Ratzel established theories that can still be applied and studied to explain the world even today. The field has grown since then to include people of all backgrounds. For example, the International Geographical Union ties geographers together from all around the world.

The history of geography is filled with the spirit of adventure and the push to far-off places. Seeking out new experiences and reaching for new goals led geographers to all corners of the globe, sometimes with disastrous results. Geography acts as the vehicle to help us fill voids of knowledge and better understand the world around us. Geography helps us understand the past, explains the present, and plans for the future. The same sense of discovery that defined the origins of the field is still present among the geographers of today.

Throughout the history of geography, the goal has always been the same: to explain the world from a spatial perspective. Understanding the connection to space makes us unique. Geography's main contribution to the social sciences is its spatial approach to understanding humankind. Understanding humans is the primary goal of all social sciences. It's just our perspectives that differ. History studies the human experience through a historical perspective. Political science studies the human experience by trying to understand the relationship between power and sociology through a social perspective. Geography distinguishes itself through its focus on space.

A Brief History of Geography

Understanding how the field of geography developed helps us understand human geography as it is now. This chapter provides a very brief look at the history of geography as an academic and practical science in general before delving into human geography in particular. This chapter also helps dispel some misconceptions about the field and maybe even about the Earth itself. This chapter is not meant to be a comprehensive history of the field; doing so would take far more than the allotted pages here. It will also not be exclusive to human geography since the specific discipline of human geography has not been around all that long, given the extensive and distinguished history of geography.

REMEMBER

Geography. What does the term mean? Many people might guess the study of the Earth, but that would be geology. Geography translates into "Earth writing," learning and writing about the Earth. Consequently, writing is an essential skill for geographers.

Map movers and makers

The creation of maps is tied to much of geography's earliest history. The term *geography* is credited to the Greek geographer Eratosthenes (276–194 BCE), but the practices of geography reach back further than that. To guide our discussion, we will view the history of geography using a couple of key maps.

Mapping in its oldest form

Maps are thought to be some of the oldest forms of human visual communication. Cave drawings dating back tens of thousands of years, containing intricate pictographs and depicting scenes of hunts and other important events, are considered guides — not on how to hunt but on how to get to the hunting grounds. The communication of geographic information has always been vital to the continued survival of humankind.

Though not many representations of these sorts of visuals still exist today, the earliest maps are believed to trace back to the earliest parts of human history. The maps drawn on caves are only the ones for which we have a record. Even before that, a simple series of lines drawn in the dirt with a stick could have sufficed to show the location of important sites to the earliest humans. Along with the maps of terrestrial areas, some drawings are meant to be celestial — mapping the stars for navigation, perhaps? Even before that, the importance of mental maps should not be discounted. Our earliest hunter-gatherer ancestors were guided by generational knowledge passed down through the spoken word and experience.

The true nature of these drawings is speculative, but given the importance of knowing the location of things for human survival, it is not a far reach to assume many of these drawings could be the earliest forms of maps.

In the South Pacific, Polynesian navigators used specialized stick maps to sail the ocean swells between the far-flung islands. These rare and unique maps served the needs of the people very well. It is said a knowledgeable way finder could navigate home using these charts while lying in a boat (where they could feel the swells). While the knowledge may not come in a form we're familiar with, it's no less valuable. Indigenous and local knowledge can be just as important and more comprehensive than the knowledge generated by a researcher or maps made with fancy computer programs. Geographic knowledge can come in all shapes, sizes, and mediums, but it all contributes to the field's general body of knowledge.

Mapping the world as we've known it

Thanks to the widespread development of computer mapping — collectively known as Geographic Information System (GIS) — thousands (if not millions) of maps have been made throughout human history. I don't have the space necessary to cover the entire history of mapping, but I want to go over a few examples that relate well to the history of geography.

The oldest known map in existence is a 2,800+-year-old map made of clay from the Mesopotamian region during the Babylonia era (see Figure 2-1). This map relates to one of the earliest uses of geography, simply keeping track of where things are. Early maps like this were important for establishing ownership and determining taxable lands. As empires looked to expand, they needed to know where to expand. Many people still assume geography is largely about identifying and mapping the locations of things. However, modern maps have that information sorted out (though it often needs to be revised as our understanding of areas and regions improves).

FIGURE 2-1: The Babylonia Clay tablet map by Bruno Meissner. (Image source: public domain.)

In Europe, the first true cartographer is thought to be a Greek mapmaker by the name of Anaximander. His Greco-centric world map (at least as he knew it) from around 550 BCE contained a roughly outlined Mediterranean region, then giant blobs representing the remaining unknown portions of Asia, Europe, and Africa (Libya). One of the other significant features of Anaximander's map is that he represented the Earth as a flat cylinder (thus originating the idea that the Earth was flat). Given that paper and animal skins break down over time, the map itself is lost, but writings about the map survive and have helped develop re-creations (like the one in Figure 2-2).

The idea that the world was flat survived among the scientific and academic communities for just a few years until Greek philosopher Pythagoras (you might be aware of his theorem) and later Aristotle theorized a spherical Earth. Eratosthenes confirmed the Earth was spherical about 2,000 years ago by using the difference in shadows cast at two different locations on the same day. Using angles, Eratosthenes calculated the circumference of the Earth at 24,390 miles. His calculation was surprisingly close, given that the Earth's actual circumference is 24,855 miles along the meridians.

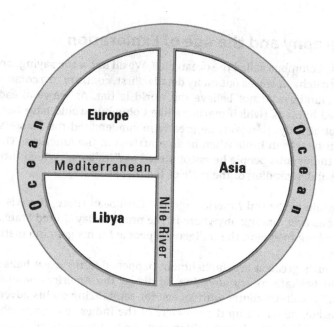

FIGURE 2-2:
Re-creation of
Anaximander's
world map

TECHNICAL
STUFF

While Eratosthenes did get surprisingly close, some gaps in his understanding prevented an even more accurate estimate of the world's circumference. The largest is that the Earth and is not a perfect sphere. Instead, Earth is a geoid: a shape created by the Earth's rapid rotation, causing it to bulge near the Equator. Not accounting for the oblong shape is one of the reasons why Eratosthenes's calculations were off. The Earth rotates at a speed of about 1,000 miles per hour. We get 24 hours in a day because Earth's circumference is about 24,000 miles, and the Earth spins at about 1,000 mph.

While we're discussing meridians — or lines of longitude — Eratosthenes came up with those, too (not to mention lines of latitude). That's not bad for a guy who had no idea that the continents of North America, South America, Australia, and Antarctica existed. (To be fair, most people of the time had no idea that other continents existed.) One important thing to note about geography that is especially relevant when talking about these early geographers is that geography is a continually evolving field. Our understanding of latitude and longitude has continually evolved to what it is today.

Far from being a field purely set in Europe, cartographers worldwide went through similar processes of making and understanding representations of the spaces around them. Traditions of mapmaking can be found everywhere, including an especially rich tradition in parts of Asia (with mapmakers like Da Ming Hun Yi Tu from China), Ottoman geographer Piri Reis, and Muslim cartographer Muhammad al-Idrisi.

Geography and the Age of Exploration

In 1492, Columbus sailed the ocean blue. We all know the saying, and while it may be very catchy, it leaves out many details. First, contrary to a common misconception, Columbus did not believe the world is flat. As we've already established, educated humans (which mariners like Columbus would have been) had figured that out already. However, he greatly misunderstood the planet's true size and thought he was in India when he first arrived in the Americas. Thus, he referred to the Indigenous people he encountered as "Indians," which further highlights his misunderstanding of the scale of the planet.

Also, while in Central America and the Caribbean (note, there is no evidence of Columbus ever landing anywhere in the present-day United States), he spent his time looking to exploit the Indigenous people for his gain, no matter the cost.

TECHNICAL STUFF

Columbus's greatest accomplishment happened in the great halls of Europe, and I would hesitate to say anything he did in the Americas would be considered "great." A self-promoter with an eye for capitalizing on his adventures as much as possible, he talked up the wonders of the Indies to anyone who would listen. Even until his death, the guy still thought he had found an all-water route to India and the "spice islands." His most captive audience (besides those he literally held captive) were the kings and queens of Europe looking to extend their own wealth and glory.

Columbus represented a new wave of European exploration into the "unknown" in search of riches, acumen, and a chance to add to the kingdom (both Earthly and divine). Europeans like Prince Henry the Navigator and Vasco de Gama preceded Columbus in terms of daring long-distance voyages into the unknown. The Viking Leif Erickson led an expedition that also happened to find its way to North America (almost 500 years before Columbus, if anyone is keeping score), but the Viking settlement in Vinland (because they found some wild grapes) was short-lived at best.

In the sagas of the European exploration (I am not calling it "discovery," given that millions of Indigenous people already lived in the Americas), names like Samuel de Champlain, John Cabot, Ponce de Leon, and Amerigo Vespucci go down in history with their exploits. Rather than go into depth with the tales of their voyages, successes, blunders, and implications, we will focus on their contributions to building geographic knowledge.

To do this, I'm actually going to give credence to a map that otherwise is frequently the source of contempt: the 1569 world map developed by Gerardus Mercator. Mercator's map was primarily used for sea navigation using *dead reckoning* to determine what was directly east or west of any other location on the planet. The primary focus is not to accurately show the size of places, only the latitude. In Figure 2-3, you can vaguely make out the shape of the Americas. The voyages of exploration and discovery were meant to fill in all the parts of the map and build up our knowledge of the world. The "fabled" southern continents of Australia and Antarctica would not become known to Europeans until the 18th and 19th centuries, respectively.

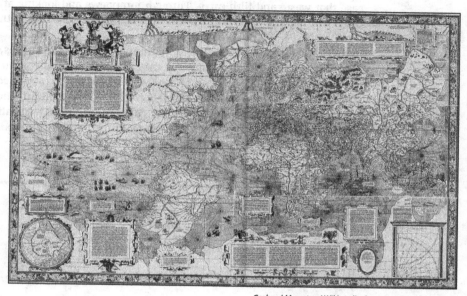

FIGURE 2-3: Mercator's 1569 World Map. (Image source: www.alamy.com.)

Gerhard Mercator / Wikimedia Commons / Public Domain

REMEMBER

Explorers can't really "discover" a place that is already known to the people who live there. They might discover a place previously unknown to them, but it's already known to the people who already live there. One exception is Antarctica, which was discovered in the truest sense in 1820 by a pair of Russian explorers, Fabian Gottlieb von Bellingshausen and Mikhail Lazarev, on the ships Vostok and Mirny, respectively.

The expansion of geographic and scientific knowledge meant potential wealth and glory, so between the 1400s and the mid-1900s, much effort was put into this endeavor. Captain James Cook, for example, was bankrolled by the British government for three such expeditions. He was the first European to have traveled to many islands across the Pacific, like New Zealand, and the first European to Eastern Australia, before being killed while trying to kidnap a Hawaiian chief during his third voyage.

The last map I want to highlight was created just as geography became an academic subject and started revealing its capabilities as more than just pointing out where things are. In 1854, a cholera epidemic struck the city of London. Physician

John Snow had identified the Broad Street Pump (something highlighted later in this book) as the epidemic's main culprit.

Before modern sanitation systems, much of human and animal waste filth worked its way into the ground — you know, where the groundwater is. The waste had a way of working its way into where said groundwater, infecting it with the bacteria and disease that waste and filth carry. Through interviews and looking at what connected those who got sick or died, Snow was able to identify the pump as the likely culprit.

Rather than taking his evidence in written form to city authorities, Snow made the map (shown in Figure 2-4) showing the clear correlation between cases (signified as black dots) and the location of the Broad Street Pump (signified with an X). He used the map to convince city officials to close off the pump, and magically, the epidemic abated. The way that Snow communicated and visualized geographic information revolutionized the field of geography and further extended the foreseeable applications of the study.

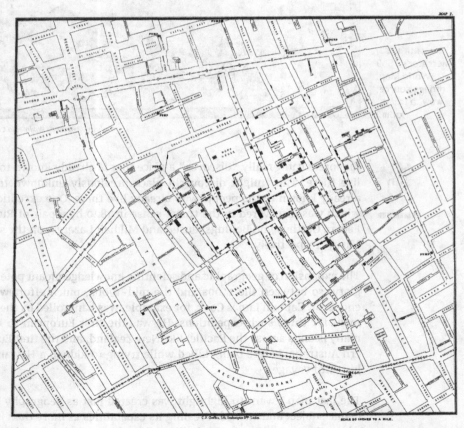

FIGURE 2-4:
Dr. John Snow's 1854 cholera map of London. (Image source: public domain)

John Snow / Wikimedia Commons / Public Domain

Geography and academia

Though the discipline of geography has been around for quite some time, the academic study of the subject hasn't. Its major origins trace back to the 1800s in the United Kingdom and Germany (or at least what would eventually become Germany). Relying on the work of early figures like Bernhardus Varenius, Immanuel Kant, and Friedrich Ratzel, the subject entrenched itself at academic institutions around Germany. Much from the effort of our friend Halford Mackinder, the subject gained a distinguished place at the University of Oxford in the United Kingdom and established itself as a subject of study there. It was not until 1903 that the subject of geography reached the shores of the United States when the University of Chicago established it as a division of its geology department.

The university level has driven the field of geography ever since. Much of the modern field of geography has been influenced by ideas originated by researchers and geographers at the university level. Geographers have occasionally undergone existential crises, causing them to reflect on what the nature of the field should be. We'll examine this a bit further later in this chapter.

Geography as an essential subject

Ask any geographer about the value of geography; they'll probably have a long, pre-prepared spiel about the subject's merits because the subject's disciplines have long had to justify its importance. Geographers have advocated for its teaching since geology became an academic subject. The study of geology has shifted and adapted as necessary, but its status has remained precarious, largely because it straddles the line between the social and physical sciences, sometimes leaving people asking whether it is a science or humanity (as if it's not possible to be both). Unfortunately, many people's perceptions of the subject come from their limited exposure to it during their school years.

Geography has been a core subject in primary and grade schools in public education systems since the mid-1700s. At the lowest levels of schooling and during the earliest phases of the subject, the focus was on mapwork (drawing and labeling maps) and the rote memorization of place names, locations, and geographic superlatives (such as biggest rivers, largest cities, and so on). In the geographic education community, we call this "sailor's geography" because it was the kind of geography most necessary for navigation.

In the United States, the earliest widely distributed texts were developed by Jedidiah Morse from Yale University in the late 1700s and early 1800s. Morse's text focused on a regional approach to geography from an American point of view with an eye on promoting the ideals of the young republic. In the 1850s, the philosophy toward geographic education shifted to a more physical geographic approach because of the influence of Princeton University geographer Arnold Guyot. His views were inspired by his fellow Swiss countryman Johann Pestalozzi and German geographer Carl Ritter.

Harvard University geographer William Morris Davis further veered geography in the direction of physical geography in the 1890s. He saw geography as being tied to geology and the use of fieldwork being integral. Davis published a widely distributed textbook in 1902 titled *Elementary Physical Geography* that further helped alienate geography from the other social sciences by likening geography to the physical sciences. This alienation created a bit of an identity crisis for geography and made it vulnerable to other disciplines looking to siphon away students — made abundantly clear when Harvard University dropped geography as a discipline in 1948.

TECHNICAL STUFF

A combination of factors caused Harvard to drop geography. Along with pressure from the geology department, the university's president criticized geography as not being "rigorous" enough. A 1939 book, *The Nature of Geography: A Critical Survey of Current Thought in the Light of the Past*, by University of Minnesota/University of Wisconsin geography professor Richard Hartshorne, attempted to get American geographers to evaluate the nature of the field, but geography didn't start regaining its position in American schools until the 1980s. Much credit must be given to University of California, Berkeley geographer Carl Sauer for his writings emphasizing the need to keep humans central to the discussions of geography. Sauer, William Pattison, Richard Hartshorne, and Carl Ritter formed the basis of human geography. Developments in Geographic Information Sciences and Technology (GIS&T) and the dogged efforts of academic and professional organizations have continued the fight for geography. Although they succeeded in reinstituting geography at Harvard University in the 2000s, many geography departments around the United States face the dangers of cuts even today.

Through the efforts of individual geographers, university geography departments, and geographic organizations (especially the National Geographic Society, National Council for Geographic Education, and Association for American Geographers — now the American Association of Geographers), the National Geography Standards and Five Themes of Geography were formed and still guide many US geographic teaching philosophies for school-aged children today.

One significant area of growth for human geography has actually come at the high school level. In 2001, a monumental shift in geographic education took place when the College Board offered the Advanced Placement (AP) Human Geography course. In the first year of the exam, only about 3,000 students took the test. Now, more than 275,000 students take the test each year, making it one of the most commonly taken tests offered in the AP lineup.

I have left out many geographers and philosophical underpinnings for brevity. We'll briefly touch on some philosophical approaches to geography in Chapter 4, but please remember that thousands of geographers have contributed theories and ideas to the field. Within each human geography discipline, subdisciplines and specialty areas expand geography's research areas across a vast spectrum. For example, the American Association of Geographers has 69 specialty groups, spanning everything from Africa to wine, beer, and spirits.

Throughout geography's history, one thing that has remained constant is the spirit of exploration and discovery that drove figures like Halford Mackinder to climb Mount Kenya. Nowhere else has that been more prevalent than in the British Royal Geographical Society and the National Geographic Society of the United States. Both organizations, founded in 1830 and 1888, respectively, focus on supporting efforts to learn more about the world. *National Geographic* remains one of the most popular mediums for communicating geographic knowledge. However, *National Geographic's* focus on biological and environmental science has led to widespread criticism within the geographic community for its disconnect with geography, especially content related to human geography.

TIP

To understand the true nature of geography as a field of study, I would recommend the following sources:

» American Association of Geographers https://www.aag.org/

» National Council of Geographic Education https://ncge.org/

» American Geographical Society https://americangeo.org/

» National Geographic Society https://www.nationalgeographic.org/society/

Modern Geographies: Not Just Maps!

When I meet someone and they ask what I do for a living, my response is always the same; "I'm a geographer." Their response is usually the same as well — something like, "Oh, I love maps!" before discussing how they'd like to attempt learning all the names and locations of places around the world. I love the enthusiasm, but I liken that discussion to telling an English teacher that you love the alphabet. Remember, geography translates to "Earth writing." In this analogy, the place names and locations are our alphabet. We use them to piece together sentences of the human experience and tell the story of human existence over space. We use maps to do this, but maps aren't our only tools.

Geospatial technologies: We all do it!

In the 1950s and 1960s, geography as an academic study underwent another shift: the quantitative revolution, an effort to heighten the credibility and prestige of the discipline by focusing the subject on the collection and analysis of spatial data. Through the infusion of the scientific method and building models and theories based on quantitative data, geography attempted to rebrand as a serious field science, whether physical or human geography, correlating with the rise of computers as a technology (originally first centralized in universities).

The parallel development of computers and quantitative methods in geography helped develop a third major track of focus to join physical and human geography pathways, the geospatial technology pathways.

Geospatial technologies use technology — especially computers and mapping software — to collect, organize, visualize, and analyze geographic information. The geospatial technologies use GIS and Geographic Positioning Systems (GPS). You're probably most familiar with GPS. When you open the map app on your phone and navigate to the closest gas station, GPS identifies where you are (using your latitude and longitude coordinates) and where the closest gas stations are. You may not know that a whole bunch of geographic data is all working together to get you there. When represented on maps as different pieces of geographic information, we refer to these as "layers." So, to get you to the gas station, the GPS data works in conjunction with a layer of streets to help you navigate along the streets, not driving through people's yards.

TIP

GIS For Dummies, by Michael N. DeMers (Wiley) focuses on the geospatial science side of geography, and *Geography For Dummies*, by Jerry Mitchell (Wiley) covers geography from a broad breadth. This *Human Geography For Dummies* book now extends the discussion of content related to the field that is otherwise briefly covered in *Geography For Dummies*.

What is really nice about GIS is that the data can be updated instantaneously when tied to servers where the data is stored and sent out. Weather data, traffic, and even demographic information can be pulled from databases and presented on maps in real time. Ever watch election night coverage as they updated their big maps with the results? That's GIS. When the power goes out after a big storm, the city needs to identify where to send their trucks. That's GIS. Some cities even use GIS apps to have citizens update the location of potholes (with pictures) at the end of winter so that crews can be routed to fix them.

TECHNICAL STUFF

GIS relies on location data to make the point and polygon raster and vector layers that appear on the maps. GPS has been made readily available for public use. Relying on satellites, GPS was only available for military and government purposes initially. After the accidental downing of Korean Air Flight 007 over Soviet airspace because of navigational errors, the United States government made the technology available to all (though the US military still uses a different, more precise GPS than the civilian version).

Everything is geography, and geography is everything

One of the things that I enjoy most about geography is that just about anything can be studied as part of the field. I particularly enjoy being an education geographer because I can jump around between physical geography, human geography, and geospatial technologies. Human geography is still my favorite, though. My focus areas are political geography and developing educational materials to connect political topics to a geographic lens. For example, these topics could help us understand US election trends from a geographic perspective or contextualize the Russian invasion of Ukraine in a geopolitical framework.

I especially love to travel because it is through applying geographic concepts to new locations that you develop an intimate understanding of a location by being able to know it better. Geography makes that possible.

Human geography is primarily divided between population geography (the study of demographics and the characteristics of people), migration, cultural, economic, geography (which can include development, industry, and agriculture), and urban and political geography. This book is organized around those major subfields of human geography, but just know that the field is contributed to by an even larger number of bodies of knowledge. We'll talk about some of them in Chapter 4. Geographies focusing on historically marginalized groups (like women, racial groups, Indigenous geographers, and non-Western contributors) are contributive fields that are getting increasing attention. The field of human geography is expanding and welcomes the contributions of many new voices.

TIP

This book is meant to introduce human geography but is not a comprehensive look at the subject. The more you dive into the subject, the more you'll discover that is yet to be discovered. So, while the subject's past already contains the contributions of many interesting characters, the future is likely to hold much the same!

- » **The physical and human characteristics of a place**

- » **Different forms of regions and organizing similar places**

- » **How movement changes the cultural landscape**

- » **How humans are connected to the physical world**

Chapter **3**

The Five Themes of Geography

Think of where you live for a moment. What makes it unique? What makes it similar to other places? What are its defining characteristics? What makes it similar or dissimilar to other places? Geographers deal with these types of questions when trying to understand and contextualize a place. This is all part of "reading" an area's cultural landscape and trying to understand the geographic forces that have influenced it.

The cultural landscape was heavily emphasized by geographer Carl Sauer, who stressed the importance of understanding human activity to understand a place's geography. The Five Themes of Geography were then developed to frame the study of geography and establish and understand the cultural landscape. Introduced in 1984, the Five Themes examine the connection between humans and the physical environment, the physical environment and humans, and individual humans and each other.

Mostly designed as an educational tool, the Five Themes of Geography are a helpful way of breaking down an area of land and systematically examining the different physical and human geographic ideas present there. It can be especially helpful when studying geography from a world-regional perspective where you're going area by area and studying, but it can be just as helpful in human geography.

REMEMBER

As you read this book, remember the Five Themes of Geography because they apply throughout. When I talk about location, *place*, regions, movement, or human-environment interactions, it'll be in the context of the Five Themes of Geography. A deeper understanding of human geography further enriches these themes since it provides an academic framework for understanding and making sense of the landscape. A bus stop will be just a bus stop when viewed outside the context of *place*. However, when you understand urban geography, a bus stop represents a mass transit system and urbanization processes.

REMEMBER

As we go through the Five Themes, think of where you live and see how you can link the concepts discussed here to your own world.

TIP

You've already been introduced to *State* versus *state*, and you'll be introduced to more terms later, such as *diffusion*, *distribution*, *growth pole*, and many others, that have very specific meanings in the field of human geography. As you read, make sure you're paying special attention to the vocabulary because some terms may differ from what you're used to.

Place and Making Sense of It

I recently went to Kenya, and the person I stayed with had some neighbors over who wanted to hear about where I lived since they didn't know much about Omaha. Located on the equator and high in elevation, Nairobi has a fairly mild climate with average temperatures around 60°F. With rainy and dry seasons, the city's agreeable climate can make it a very pleasant place to visit. They asked whether Nebraska gets cold. At the time, Omaha was experiencing a cold snap of temperatures plunging to the double-digit negatives and snow, contrasting the usual blazing hot, sunny, and dry summers. They also wanted to know other things about Omaha, such as what the city is like, what most people do to make a living, whether there are many trees or mountains, and what I do for fun.

In a geographic sense, they were trying to establish their understanding of the context of Omaha using the concept of *place*. These are the human and physical characteristics that distinguish one place from another. For example, let's look at the Central Siberian city of Listvyanka, an urban locality in the Irkutsky District of Irkutsk Oblast, Russia, to frame the concept of *place* (see Figure 3-1). We will use Listvyanka in this chapter to learn how to "read" the cultural landscape to understand an area's physical and human features.

FIGURE 3-1: The city of Listvyanka on the shores of Lake Baikal

WARNING

The term *place* is used frequently throughout this book. It can be tricky in geography because it can sometimes be used simply to talk about an actual place, but most frequently, it is discussed as the physical and human characteristics of that location. This can be confusing since the word *place* does not necessarily carry this meaning in everyday speech. *Place* is one of those terms that changes based on the context of how it is used. As much as possible, I used *place* to connect to the Five Themes. Otherwise, I frequently used *space* or *location* to refer to an actual area.

Physical: How a land defines a place

One way *place* can be described is through the physical attributes that distinguish it. For Listvyanka, the cool waters of Lake Baikal and the bright green forests of the taiga (subarctic forest) rising up the hills and mountains ringing the lake are the most defining features. The birch and aspen trees complement the many species of conifers to create a lush green landscape that contrasts the bright blue of the lake and sky. The wind coming off the frigid lake adds a cooler feel to the lakeside town, even at the height of summer.

Human: How a people define the same place

Similarly, the human characteristics of *place* are defined by the manufactured attributes that distinguish a place. In Listvyanka's case, it is the brightly colored wooden buildings. Being there in summer, I could only imagine how much the buildings would stick out next to the frozen lake during the height of the snows of winter in Siberia. Looking like a combination of log cabins and Swiss chalets, the buildings on the side of the lake look like they wouldn't be out of place in any mountain town in the Alps or the Maine seashore. What *did* stand out somewhat — as opposed to the nearby city of Irkutsk — was the lack of stone buildings. All buildings are made of wood, metal, and very little brick or stone. Wood is the primary building material because of its abundance in nearby forests. Much of it looks very weathered, but the shops selling locally made goods and the smell of smoked omul (a small fish in the trout and salmon family) hint at the town's touristy feel. The boats visible on the lake hint at the fishing industry, but the throngs of buses coming in highlight the village as more of a destination for visitors.

Location, Location, Location

One thing you must do when trying to understand a place is establish where it is in the world. There are two ways to go about this using the Five Themes: absolute and relative location. Think about telling someone where you live when you want them to come visit versus telling someone where you live who has literally no idea about your location. When describing where I live to people in other countries, they shockingly rarely know where Omaha is, so I will use that as my example for this discussion (see Figure 3-2).

Absolute location: No question about it

When dealing with the exact location of a place, you can use a place's coordinates (latitude and longitude) or an address. We'll use Omaha City Hall at 1819 Farnam Street, Omaha, Nebraska, 68183, as the central location. In this example,

>> The street number 1819 indicates it is located between 18th and 19th streets, with the main door facing Farnam Street.

>> Omaha tells us the city, and Nebraska communicates the US state (to distinguish between the seven other states that have a city named Omaha).

>> The 68183 zip code tells which part of the city the address is located in.

FIGURE 3-2:
Downtown Omaha, Nebraska in winter finery

Alternatively, we can use the latitude and longitude coordinates to communicate where Omaha City Hall is located:

>> The DMS (degrees, minutes, seconds) of 41°15′25.95″ North and –95°56′25.43″ West.

>> The fact that it is positive 41° tells us it is in the Northern Hemisphere. If it were -41°, it would be in the Southern Hemisphere.

>> Using the same reasoning, the –95° tells us it is in the Western Hemisphere.

Relative location: Depends on where you stand

Absolute location can be very helpful, but it is almost too much information for someone just trying to figure out where something is located generally. In that case, relative location (describing where something is in relation to other things) can be most helpful. If I were telling someone where Omaha is located, I would tell them it is located fairly close to the middle of the United States (the contiguous 48 states, at least) or about a seven-hour drive west of Chicago, Illinois. With relative location, you're trying to describe the location in relation to things people will most likely know. If I were telling someone where the Omaha City Hall is located, I would tell someone familiar with Omaha that it is located on the western side of downtown.

TECHNICAL STUFF

The psychology of relative location actually connects to the concept of gender. Psychological studies have been done on how people of different genders talk about location, specifically when giving directions. Men are more likely to give directions and explain location using cardinal directions (North, South, East, West), and women are more likely to give directions referring to the location of landmarks (such as "take a right at the school").

Regions Connect Us

Geographers are constantly trying to see how one place connects to another. By looking at *place* characteristics, we can establish commonalities and determine how areas are unique or different. Geographers work with several regions that can fit different organizational structures that we're studying or trying to establish. Within the Five Themes, the regions are perceptual/vernacular, functional, and formal.

Perceptual/vernacular: It is what you think it is

One of my favorite class discussions with my students is to have them figure out what classifies as the "Midwest" in the United States. We get into some pretty heated debates about which states do and don't belong in the region to the point that the discussion spills over into other classrooms, leading other teachers to get me their input. Here in Omaha, for example, there is a lot of debate about whether Nebraska is part of the Midwest or part of the West. Or, we make up a completely different region called the Great Plains. That is the whole point of a perceptual/vernacular region; it depends on who you're talking to. It is a region discussed in common usage (vernacular) that changes based on people's perceptions of the region.

Functional: It's how we use it

This is one that I'll want you to remember and be able to come back to when we're talking about *threshold* and *range* in later chapters. The functional range is the area being serviced or serviced by a particular entity. Think of a city — any city — and where the grocery stores are located. Each grocery store has a region that it effectively services. Because food is essential, most people will not want to travel too far to purchase it, so they'll go to the closest grocery store. Each grocery store will have a fairly small functional region in urban areas. In rural areas, each grocery store will service a much larger geographic area and thus will have a larger functional region. Other ways to think of functional regions are to think about where your closest hospital, school, shopping mall, or even airport is and what other areas are serviced by that same business.

TECHNICAL STUFF

An easy way to look at functional regions is to look at the fan bases of different sports teams. For example, in Omaha, Nebraska, we're split between the Minnesota Vikings and the Kansas City Chiefs for football teams. That means we usually can pull the games up on local television or radio stations.

Formal: We can measure it

One of the tricky things in this book is distinguishing different parts of the Americas. As physical entities, there are the regions of Central America, South America, North America, the Caribbean, the Lesser Antilles, and the Greater Antilles. There are many ways to break the Americas into physical or cultural regions. One of the easiest ways to distinguish the Americas is by using the idea of a formal region. Using measurable statistics, we could look at the main languages people use.

With measurable statistics, we could separate the Americas between Anglo-America and Latin America and include most countries (understanding, of course, that there are large numbers of people whose main language does not fit into either of those categories, but that's part of the point). We can identify that more than 50 percent of the inhabitants in these countries speak a Latin-based language like French, Spanish, Portuguese, or English. (Anglo, by way of much of history, refers to the English.) From that, we could split off the United States, Canada, Belize, Guyana, Jamaica, and a handful of others that have English as a primary language from other countries. We can further look at exceptions, like the territory of Aruba, where the main language is Dutch, or large sections of the Americas, where an Indigenous language like Quechua or Inuit is spoken.

Movement and Spatial Connections

Another big thing that human geographers are interested in is looking at how places are connected and how that influences their social, political, cultural, economic, and even environmental development. With movement, we're really looking to establish the relationship between distant places. It has historically been that nearer places have more relationships with each other than far places, but with new technologies, that is not always true anymore. This concept is connected to *distance decay*, which will be covered later.

Communication: The world is smaller now

It used to be that when someone moved away, you'd have to rely on letters or infrequent phone calls to stay in touch. Then along came the Internet and improvements in cellular technology, drastically changing the communication landscape. Video calls using platforms like Skype, Zoom, or FaceTime make it so you can talk as if they're right there with you. Kids play video games and chat with their friends just as they always have, but they'll do it from the comfort of their homes. They can play against people worldwide in different time zones (especially given how late some students will stay up playing these games).

One of the most popular applications in the world, WhatsApp, has made cross-country communication easier than ever before. No longer is it necessary to fight with changing SIM cards everywhere you go. Just hop on the new cellular network and use your WhatsApp to use your phone just as you would at home to call and text. The changes in communication can be marked on the cultural landscape to see the spread of ideas and the increasing cooperation between places that have come with better communication.

Transportation: A global supply chain

Over a winter break, my wife and I went to Kenya, a journey that literally would have been noteworthy in newspapers for its complexities and difficulties about 150 years ago; we accomplished the trip in 4 flights spanning 24 hours.

Airplanes, cars, ships, and even drones have increased in massive leaps and bounds, making it possible to quickly and easily (relatively, of course) ship yourself or goods worldwide. I shipped burlap bags of stuff to my parent's house when I moved back from China, and it only took a couple of weeks (via ships and trucks). Journeys across the Atlantic that used to take weeks now take about 6-7 hours. This has opened businesses to what we'll refer to as the *new international division of labor*, which has built up connections between far-off places because of their abilities to conduct commerce and trade with one another. Through transportation, the cultural landscape has also been affected by the availability of goods and products from all parts of the world.

Migration: Helping us come together

We'll spend a couple of chapters looking at the geographic phenomenon of movement, so we won't spend much time on it here. Within the context of the Five Themes, when studying an area, you would look at how the area has been affected by people coming or going. You'd look at the demographic and cultural composition as a product of the physical relocation of people into and out of an area. As I said, we will spend chapters on this because this is in and of itself its own subdiscipline of human geography.

Human-Environment Interaction

Humans like to attempt to control the world around us. Mega engineering projects like dams hold back rivers, and bulldozers carve away literal mountains to get at the resources below. The Earth is always good at humbling us and proving that we don't control it as much as we may think we do. The fifth and final theme looks at the relationship between humans and the physical world. This is presently one of the most dynamic of the Five Themes because decisions regarding them have to be made in real time to meet the demands of an increasingly changing landscape.

Adaptations: How we make it work

While living in downtown Saint Paul, Minnesota, I always thoroughly enjoyed walking from one end of the central business district to the other without ever having to go outside. What we nicknamed the "gerbil tubes" — the skyway system — is an example of how people adapted to living in such a cold environment. On the other hand, Northern Europe is struggling to adapt quickly enough. In a region with historically mild temperatures (even in summer), increasingly common heatwaves are turning deadly. Temperatures regularly breaching 100°F in countries like Germany, France, or the United Kingdom that do not have extensive histories with high heat have caused them to adapt quickly (see Figure 3-3). Modernizing buildings with air conditioning is becoming increasingly necessary as the Earth heats up. It is adaptations like this that geographers focus on to see how humans have changed their behaviors to be able to live where they do.

Resources: How we use the Earth

A common theme in this book is how people use the planet as a source of the things they need to live their lives. Whether it's things within the Earth, the soil, things that grow in the soil naturally, or things that eat the things that grow in the soil, there are thousands of different ways humans use what occurs naturally around the globe. Water, oil, and physical space are perhaps some of the highest-profile goods. However, take any product you use and think of all the resources that went into making it. Those resources are the result of geography, and the economic geography chapters later in this book focus on how those resources can be used to support human populations.

FIGURE 3-3:
People dodging the heat in Cologne, Germany, in the relief of shade, sun hats, and gelato

Impact: Living with our actions

You might've heard the expression, "You've made your bed; now lie in it." This expression is just as true for the relationship between humans and the environment as for personal relationships. If you've spent years denuding hillsides of the vegetation that holds them together, can you really be surprised when the whole hillside collapses in a mudslide? People often are only to gain wisdom in hindsight to see how their actions led to negative results. Climate change is another example of this type of situation. The idea of impact refers to how geographers will examine how people are affected by their environmental actions. This area is of great concern as the climate heats up and the adverse impacts of climate change are becoming more apparent. This topic will come up quite a bit and is one of the greatest growth areas for study in human geography.

REMEMBER

Human geography is diverse, but the Five Themes help tie ideas together under a framework that helps make the world make sense. They will be connected frequently throughout this text, so I emphasized and explained them here. Words like *region*, *location*, *place*, *movement*, and *interaction* may not have any special emphasis in common speech, but they have great significance in human geography.

Chapter 4

The Philosophies of Geography

The philosophies of geology help us understand the intellectual framework through which knowledge is generated. Academic geographers will usually lend their ideas to one or more of these philosophies and use them as a framework for their own work, often leading to multiple interpretations of the same general idea, depending on which perspectives they employ.

Within every academic subject, there are intellectual discussions about what the subject really is and its purpose. Geography is no different. How an academic geographer thinks about geography is very different from the average person's. To the average person, geography is about memorizing place names and locations. However, an academic geographer may perceive geographic study as a means of uncovering more truths about the world. They may see it as a vehicle to address social inequalities or global environmental concerns. It can be perceived as a mechanism to collect, analyze, and display data using methods impossible in any other discipline.

One of the cool things about the geographies (human, physical, and geospatial) is that most graduate and undergraduate students must pick a specialty but are usually required to take at least a class or two in the other specialty areas. So, no matter what area of geography you focus on, you should have at least some understanding of the other fields.

The differing philosophical approaches bind the study of geography. In this chapter, we will look at some of the different philosophical areas and connect them to human geography to understand its uses beyond just learning about the world. As a social science/humanity, geography is a bit different than the physical sciences (biology, physics, chemistry, and so on) because the methodology is a bit different. Sometimes, this leads to questions about geography's place among the sciences — another thing many philosophies look to address.

Putting Humans Back Into Geography

As we already learned in Chapter 2, during the second half of the 1800s and early 1900s, geography was shifted toward physical geography. Another trend in the early 1900s was the focus on *regionalism*. As we saw in Chapter 3, regions are an important part of the study of geography and a helpful means of comparing one place to another.

REMEMBER

Before we get too far, one thing to note is that some regions are also social constructs (meaning they only exist because humans more or less decided they exist). When we talk about regions from this sense, we see that we're trying to come up with theories about what a region is and then develop supporting evidence and examples.

TIP

Geography as a field is traditionally divided between physical geography and human geography. Geographers will usually frame their studies regionally (looking at the effect of geographic concepts within that region) or thematically (looking at a geographic concept and then seeing how that concept compares in different regions). Geographic information science and technology (GIST) has developed as a third branch that lends itself to physical and human geography. GIST uses technology, especially Geographic Information Systems (GIS — computer mapping software) to understand spatial distributions.

One early scholar supporting regionalism was French geographer Paul Vidal de la Blanche. He actively worked to define the different regions of France and tried to determine how they compared to one another. By looking at the different human and physical characteristics, Vidal tried to define regions based on how people use the land. The heavy connection between the physical landscape and human interactions led Vidal to focus on *genre de vie (kind of life)*. This focus effectively established humans as the center of the regional focus — not something that could easily be removed from the landscape study.

Richard Hartshorne was another geographer who, in the mid-1900s, questioned the purpose of regionalism in geography. What Hartshorne essentially landed was much less practical than Vidal's attempt to define the regions but was the loftier idea of trying to understand the phenomenon as a whole. He wanted to take a more holistic view and look at large human ideas, say culture, and see how different regions reacted to them differently. This method is better suited to examine the interrelation among places but then identify the uniqueness of one area versus another. In doing this, regions have to be understood as the sum of all parts, and the study of humans is an important piece of this. While Hartshorne's and Vidal's understanding of regions took a more academic purpose, a geographer's perspective of regionalism in the budding Soviet Union greatly impacted the organization of that new State. Nikolai Baransky used his closeness to Vladimir Lenin to make economic geography one of the prominent influences in the centralized State economy as much as he could. He envisioned 21 "rational regions" based on the available natural resources, the working skills of the population, and the culture/history of the region. Each region would specialize in producing a particular resource or product, which would then contribute to the national whole. Think of *The Hunger Games*, where each district has its own specialization, and the whole region is devoted to raising and preparing people to work in that economic sector.

REMEMBER

As discussed previously, a *State* is the same as a country in geographic terms. A *state* is a smaller region within a country. Many early geographers spent considerable time discussing the makeup and role of a State since there were many questions about the purpose of governments and how they should interact with governments in other States.

One of the biggest criticisms of regionalism is that it leads to overgeneralizations. Regions are much more diverse than how they are perceived and presented from a regionalist point of view. As a social construct, regionalism almost romanticized regions as something other than they actually are. Like the fantastical presentation of the Dixie South in the United States as a place of values and honor, other groups don't view that region similarly.

TECHNICAL STUFF

These two philosophical ideas (and the debates they have sparked) have existed for much of the academic lifetime of the subject of geography. We'll examine them further in depth in Chapter 18, but the origins of these concepts are traced to their philosophical underpinnings. For example, geographer Ellen Churchill Semple argued on behalf of determinism, and Carl Sauer argued for possibilism. Environmental determinism is the idea that the environment plays the largest role in economic and cultural development, so underdeveloped areas can only advance so far because of their environments. Possibilism rejects this idea and instead says that people can advance to great levels despite the environmental constraints of their physical location. Humanists, regionalists, Marxists, spatial scientists, and really all modern geographic perspectives reject determinism in favor of possibilism.

Humanistic geography

Humanistic geography emerged in the 1970s and attempts to refocus geography on the scientific revolution (discussed in the next section). Influenced by the work of people like David Ley, Anne Buttimer, and Yi-Fu Tuan, humanistic geography argues that humans' actions are the result of their own doing, not the result of some mysterious force.

Much inspired by the work of David Levy, humanistic geography recognizes that humans are self-aware, rational, diverse, and creative individuals. A wholesale rejection of environmental determinism, humanists favor looking at the individuality of places on a local scale (to the extent possible) to understand a place's identity. From a humanistic mindset, the study of geography emphasizes the perspective of experience. As to how geography as a whole should be approached, this is difficult because it will differ based on your perspective. For example, if you take an individual building in a downtown area, you could study its architecture, its uses throughout history, or the economic or political forces that led to its construction. For a person who lives there, however, that's home. Their view of the building will differ from that of an outside academic. That's why location is so important for human geographers to keep the human experience central to our understanding of places.

One of the important concepts that came out of the humanistic movement is the idea of the sense of place. This is the idea that trying to understand a locale from individual and shared perspectives is important. There has long been a focus on the importance of understanding the significance of locations, but this brings it to a more local level and tries to understand the significant characteristics and essence of that place. From an outsider's perspective, a neighborhood may be just a collection of houses with a couple of roads. However, for the people who lived there, it represents where they learned to ride a bike; a tree might have been where they built a rope swing as a kid. The sense of place is the meaning we attach to locations that allow humans to connect with them. An outsider will never connect with a location like someone who lives there does. It is important to go into human geography knowing that each person will connect with a place differently and have different perspectives and opinions about it.

Post-modernism and the search for "truths"

Imagine that a researcher went through the process of conducting a research study on the religious composition of three different cities in France and found them to be heavily Protestant. They used solid research designs and published their findings in research journals; their findings were well received. A couple of years later, another researcher returned to France's cities to expand the research study. When they arrived, they found very few Protestants; instead, they found the areas heavily populated by recent immigrants who were Muslim. Does this mean that the first researcher lied, or their research was invalid? Absolutely not! From a post-modernist idea, this is not at all surprising or unexpected. That is because, from a post-modernist perspective, geographers deal in multiple truths, not a single one. What I mean by that is that geographic studies will not develop scientific laws that are mutually applicable to all areas at all times. Instead, geography develops truths — things true in that place, with those people, and at that time. From these truths, we can develop generalizations to evaluate their applicability elsewhere and make comparisons.

Post-Modernism is a 1980s reaction to modernism that sought models and theories that could be applied in one area just as easily as another. The analogy used when I was originally learning about this in graduate school was cookie-cutter architecture that was otherwise soulless without any connection to the actual physical location. The square concrete apartment blocks served the appropriate function of housing people, and the designs were copied and pasted throughout the country. Post-modernism, by contrast, would take local needs, tastes, and style into account and make a building that fits the locality more than a generic building.

A post-modernist approach was heavily incorporated into this text because it is very difficult to deal with absolutes in human geography. There will almost always be individual exceptions and differences that prohibit being able to say things are a certain way in a certain place. It may be mostly true, but in all likelihood, there are exceptions. All this even applies to post-modernism, which is often discussed as a philosophy centered in Los Angeles. While this may be true for one of its major theorists, Edward Soja, the exception is that one of the other major writers, David Harvey, is from the UK and has very little to do with the Los Angeles area.

A Quantitative Approach

As mentioned in Chapter 2, a major shift happened in 1948 in the field of geography. Heralded by the closing of the Harvard University Geography Department, the quantitative revolution was a mindset shift about the approach to geographic research. This has been a blow that geography has been trying to recover from ever since.

TIP

As part of the methods training of a geographer, they often have to take research classes and more specialized qualitative or quantitative statistics methods courses. For more information on the research methods, I would suggest checking out *Statistics For Dummies*, by Deborah J. Rumsey (Wiley).

To combat this, geography departments embarked upon an effort to re-establish the field and shift the focus of study to better align with the other physical sciences. This included the efforts to develop scientific laws instead of making broad descriptions of regions. There was a focus on making models and representations of geographic relationships that could be applied to multiple areas. The focus on incorporating math, especially statistics, sought to elevate the position of geography by using the same levels of computation and analysis of other disciplines.

One of the guiding ideas of the scientific revolution that has taken place in geography comes in the form of Auguste Comte's ideas on positivism. This is the idea that knowledge that can be experienced is the most valid and applicable. In geography, this translates to the focus that geographic knowledge should be from the observable reality, can withstand the peer review process, and reflects that scientific knowledge is fluid and changeable. Since there will always be exceptions, especially in geography, trying to avoid absolutes is also an important concept. This is why statistics become such an important part of the process because correlation can be measured and established. With sound scientific principles, one of the main goals of the quantitative approach has been to improve the perceptions of geography among the scientific community.

The quantitative revolution revisited many of the models from previous eras. Like Christaller's Central Place Theory or transportation theories like Weber's Least Cost Theory, geographers like August Lösch and Edward Ullman applied quantitative methods to add further depth to the models. The quantitative revolution has also been especially popular with physical geography and the study of landscapes. Geomorphology (the study of the changing of the Earth) has especially gravitated toward the scientific processes of the quantitative revolution since they're fairly easily able to develop theories and models within the framework related to their studies. Because that is more about physical geography and not as much about human geography, we won't get into that.

TECHNICAL STUFF

Christaller's Central Place Theory and Weber's Least Cost Theory are older theories that are discussed more in depth later in this book. The Least Cost Theory looks at the location of different industries in relation to the location of raw materials and the market to determine where to place production facilities. Central Place Theory looks at the locations of cities of different sizes and how they depend on and interact with each other.

There has been plenty of opposition to the quantitative revolution both within geography and externally. Much of it concerns the appropriateness of quantifying human actions and interactions. One of the major benefits of using quantitative methods is that it puts geographic concepts into a commonly understood language (statistics) that can be presented to policymakers to advocate for change.

Spatial science and GIS: Understanding the human landscape

An area where the quantitative revolution has been especially helpful as an off-shoot is in the growth of Geographic Information Systems (GIS). There has long been heaps of data available from organizations like the US Census Bureau (among other governmental agencies), the World Health Organization, various branches of the United Nations, and nonprofit organizations like the Population Reference Bureau. GIS has made it relatively less complicated to collect spatial data, organize it, visualize it in map form, and analyze connections. Processes that used to take hours of computation can now be done in a few seconds or minutes by the computer software.

Geographers who work with GIS must be well-versed in different statistical calculation methods and the appropriate applications of each. Maps are still one of our best tools for visualizing spatial data, but it needs to be done in such a way that is easily readable and accessible to our readers. GIS lets us take data (historical data, all the way to future predictions, everything in between, and even in real time) and apply cartographic principles to make engaging and readable geographic representations.

GIS has revolutionized how we can get students to interact with actual geographic data. Instead of just coloring in maps, students can easily access data and start making web-based maps. The skill of GIS is heavily in demand by employers. Human geography provides ample opportunities for students to use quantitative methods to display and analyze geographic relationships while learning a highly valuable skill.

TECHNICAL STUFF

Geographers have advocated for incorporating more quantitative methods into primary and secondary-level geography courses (mostly high school). They want students to go through the process of collecting and analyzing spatial data to make space-based decisions. One of the ways this has occurred is through the incorporation of more GIS into classrooms. The Environmental Systems Research Institute (ESRI), the largest mapping company in the world, has donated millions of dollars of software to K-12 schools around the world to help facilitate the teaching of geography using GIS.

Geography for All: Marginalized Groups

There is frequent criticism of the work of academics and universities that they are disconnected from the realities of the world and just spend their time researching for the sake of researching with little contribution to everyday humans. The so-called "ivory tower" analogy refers to the disconnect between research and application. In the 1960s, the United States and much of the world experienced a lot of social change, including the Civil Rights, American Indian, and Feminism movements. Massive social problems like inequality, social justice, poverty, gender norms and sexuality, and racism were all very much in the national conversation. Along with the social issues, environmental topics like pollution, the distribution of resources, and the destruction of habitat were part of a national discussion. There was much debate among academics and college campuses around the world about the end goal of geographic study.

Marxist geographies and the push for change

Geographers like David Harvey, William Bunge, and Neil Smith were among those who called for a revolution in how geography was taught. Inspired by the ideologies of Karl Marx, geographers tried to push the subject in the direction of being able to understand and address these social issues. Whether this was the publication of new papers utilizing Marxist perspectives or taking a more direct approach and leading tours into blighted areas of cities like Detroit, geographers started taking it upon themselves to understand and expose areas of inequality. Predictably, this faced a lot of criticism; labeling anything "Marxist" is bound to get quite a few people wound up. Marxist geographies were meant to be a reaction to the shift toward spatial science and a redirecting of humanists to focus on specific topics.

TECHNICAL STUFF

Even within the subject, the Marxist perspective is heavily attacked for taking stances on political, social, and economic issues. Understandably, the ones who often complain the most about it are those who benefit most. A Marxist geographer will note how human landscapes result from the actions of those in power to preserve their power. They can influence political, cultural, and social forces against any perceived threat, especially if this threat is meant to overthrow their power in favor of a reorganization of social structure and space.

Marxist geographies were especially applied to the field of urban geography, where a lot of the inequalities could be very easily observed. Understandably, a Marxist perspective was also readily applied to economic geography. Rather than purely getting into the mechanisms of Marxist ideologies, geographers focus on the resulting landscapes created by the processes of inequality. Rather than just looking at space as the places where things happen, space is perceived to be the result of human processes.

More simply put, a run-down neighborhood does not just happen. It is that way because of the unequal distribution of resources. Henri Lefebvre specifically cites the economic doctrine of capitalism as the creator of these spaces of inequality.

Because the wealthy can decide where and how they will use space, they impose their economic wills, and the people living there reap the benefits or disadvantages. This creates conflict spaces between areas with opportunity versus places that don't. A perpetual conflict between the needs of the people and the wants of those in power to remain in power.

From a geographic perspective, in the Marxist struggle between the "haves" and the "have-nots," the haves have the literal high ground by controlling and reproducing their space of power (a group's ability to control and maintain a location, place, or region, and replicate that power across time and space), while the have-nots are at the whims of those in control.

One of the most applicable areas of study related to the production of space is the Weber Least Cost Theory of Industrial Location (that will show up in Chapter 18). In this theory, the capitalistic forces weigh the pros and cons of where to establish manufacturing centers based on the availability of the production factors (land, labor, capital). However, Marxist geographies apply to all parts of the landscape, even to the "natural" landscape. Smith focused on the expression and manifestation of space in rural areas. One of the more interesting arguments he comes up with is that even the natural protected areas are a human landscape because of the conscious choice not to extend control over them. This extension of the understanding of human control over landscapes helps lead to the development of the ideas of political ecology and the human impact on the natural environment. With this understanding, we can incorporate ideas like pollution, climate change, and land degradation into the realm of human geography.

Feminist geographies: Adding perspective

You've probably noticed that up to this point, there have been very few women or non-westerners mentioned among the geographers talked about. While within the academic community, the field might have been dominated by white men from Europe and North America, that does not mean there were no female geographers from different racial groups. Gillian Rose, an early feminist geographer, argued that examples of women in geography exist, but they just need to be looked for.

One way to widen the scope of who a geographer is is to broaden the description of what is included within the field of geography. When travel narratives are included as one specific possibility, the field suddenly opens up to include many women travelers who wrote in their memoirs about their experiences. By doing this, we could add the travel accounts of women like Isabella Bird and Mary Kingsley to the history of geography. If James Cook's travels to Hawaii contribute to the geographic body of knowledge, why shouldn't Bird's journey in the 1870s? One of the major differences as to why women have been excluded is that they often were not traveling in any official capacity on behalf of a university or government. Both realms have historically (and arguably even today) been dominated by men who have acted as gatekeepers of what counts as geographic study (and what doesn't).

TIP

The work and research of Janice Monk, a geographer at the University of Arizona, is devoted to the task of expanding our understanding of the breadth of women's contributions to geography and geographic education.

The field of Feminist geography has risen as a sort of offshoot of Marxist geography. The general premise of the field is that women experience space differently than men. By broadening the study to include a gender focus, the whole of geographic knowledge is enriched by including a specific focus on how people of different genders will experience events differently. The depth of knowledge about how the world works is expanded by broadening the study scope. In labor geography, for example, the focus is often on paid wage-earning careers that still tend to be male-dominated in most parts of the world. This discounts the importance of the informal economy and the contributions of women through their making and selling of artisanal crafts or selling of products in a more market-styled economy.

TIP

This also ignores women's unpaid domestic labor, arguably as demanding and vital to supporting the economic structure as paid labor.

The connection to Marxist geography comes with the criticism of patriarchal structures. Since the 1980s, there has been a focus among feminist geographers to understand the power dynamics between men and women as a means of equalizing the relationship and value of contributions. A specific line of study, the self-proclaimed *radical feminists*, see societal structures put in place as a means of preserving the dominance of men over women.

This common struggle against patriarchy is what unifies women globally. Only by understanding the nature of patriarchy better (from a spatial geographic perspective in this case) can the situation be improved for women. One of the best ways to do this is by including women in academic levels of geography so that there is more focus on issues that concern or include women. Within this spectrum, geographers like Ester Boserup and Vandana Silva have looked at things like transportation networks and development, specifically how women experience them differently than men. Bus services are also built that benefit men's movement to and from work, but not for women who need to do domestic errands. When this area is finally studied, it can be better understood, and something can be done to correct these imbalances at long last.

Within feminist geography, there have been a couple of specific focus areas that the field has focused on — such as the geography of fear of space. Child safety is one of the best ways to talk about this. There is a lot of talk about "indoctrination" and the inclusion of certain books that are part of a "woke" agenda. You would think that that is the largest danger facing our students. However, I see that about a third to half of my female students have some form of self-defense mechanism on their key chains (mace, whistles, alert buttons, and so on). Few males seem to worry much about walking to their cars at night, but it can be a constant concern for women. How gender affects how you interact with the landscape is the geography of fear, as geographers like Rachel Pain have examined.

While we're talking about landscape, we focus on how the landscape is portrayed — the feminine attributes are given to different natural elements (such as Mother Earth) and how that affects people's feelings about an environment. The Soviet/Russian State has formalized this in its propaganda during World War II and beyond. When the message was about protecting the country's innocence, the Soviet Union was called the "motherland." When they evoked patriotism and duty to defend, it was in the context of serving the "fatherland."

The field of feminist geography is definitely one that has been growing and will continue growing as more women enter the field and the definition of *geography* is expanded to include the work of women that has previously been excluded.

The geography of marginalized communities

Thousands of groups could be included in discussions about how different groups interact with space, including Black, Indigenous people, and LBGTQ+ geographies. Much as feminist geographers have pushed geography to expand its scope of study and understanding beyond gender, including marginalized geographies has led to the inclusion of topics that otherwise had been excluded. Beyond that, including multiple perspectives enriches the field by allowing new ideas and points of view that change the way of thinking about topics. Westward expansion by the United States and Canada became colonialism when viewed from the Indigenous perspective. Segregation is the restriction of movement in Black geographies. Demographics and the study of a population turn into the denial of rights and exclusion from equal treatment based on gender and sexuality.

Within Black geographies, there is a lot of focus on the connection between space and race. Trying to identify some of the lasting impacts of policies like segregation and redlining led to some really interesting studies on how African Americans are still impacted by systemic racism. Geographer Carolyn Finney looks at this topic more specifically by examining the relationship between African Americans and natural areas. Because of restricted mobility during segregation that frequently created a hostile environment in outside areas, there are lower levels of Black people who participate in activities like camping, hiking, boating, and rock climbing than White people.

TECHNICAL STUFF

Much focus in this area has been on a guide for African American motorists and where they could actually stay as they traveled across the United States during the time of segregation, nicknamed the "Green Book." This guide has been an extensive and invaluable resource for studying the access to different locations and regions for African Americans. It is an interesting study into the relationship that different people have with places based on their race. Black geographies examine is how a person's race affects their perceptions or connections to a place.

Urban geography and development have also been of particular interest to Black geographers as they examine the organization of city infrastructure and the allocation of resources to areas of the city as connected to race. More than just these topics, Black geographers focus on how topics of race and ethnicity can be incorporated into just about every dimension of human geography. By doing so, just like with Feminist and Marxist geographies, they can better understand levels of inequality to be able to address it better.

TIP

Indigenous geographies have even more recently been generating attention a Indigenous peoples have been increasingly in the national discussion. Questions of land rights and names have perhaps been the most visible. Renaming of locations (such as Mount McKinley being reverted to its original name, Denali) have led to controversies and discussions over toponomy and the differences in the perspective of *place.*

Indigenous land rights are heavily incorporated into political geography discussions and the creation and subsequent relationships between Indigenous places and non-Indigenous peoples. The connection between land and people has been included in this to further discuss the sense of place and the significance of locations for different people. For example, the Black Hills of South Dakota are seen as a fun vacation destination for non-Indigenous people, but for the Lakota who originally inhabited the area, the Black Hills are the center of their civilization with many ties to their creation story and culture. The understanding of meaning has been significant in Indigenous geographies and will expand as the study of geography expands among Indigenous communities.

TECHNICAL STUFF

Another thing that should be understood is that Indigenous geographies do not only apply to the Americas. In every permanently inhabited continent (even Europe), there are active disputes (some that even involve military conflict) over the rights of Indigenous peoples. However, Many of these disputes are reserved for legal battles in courtrooms and ballot boxes. For example, on October 14, 2023, Australia passed the Australian Indigenous Voice Referendum that guaranteed a voice to Indigenous Aboriginals and Torres Strait Islander people on parliament issues related to them.

2

The Geography of Human Habitation

» How population and growth are affected

» Visualizing demographic information

Chapter **5**

Where Are the People?

With human geography, remember that the people are the primary focus of study — where they are, how they're distributed, where they're not and why, and even where they've been. In this chapter, I'll introduce you to how geography studies human populations. Throughout the chapter, we'll keep a spatial focus. We will delve a bit into where they've been over time without going too far into world history.

Writing about these topics is a challenge because they cover a lot of ground, and there are many examples I could use. I've settled on a few examples to avoid bogging you down in the details, but I encourage you to look for other ways to apply the concepts you'll learn here.

The world's size and diversity make generalizations difficult because exceptions exist to any sort of rule. Where population geography is concerned, generalizations are especially difficult because migration creates many nuanced regional differences. For example, while China is a unified country, the State itself recognizes 56 minority groups in addition to the Han Chinese ethnic majority. Most countries are similarly diverse, so classifying and mapping out populations is an especially difficult task.

Establishing Terms

One thing I must do right away is establish some of the terms that geographers use to talk about different human population groups. Before breaking down the complexity of each term, I will provide a simplistic — not necessarily technical — definition for each. Let's start by discussing ethnic groups.

A *nation* is a group of people who share a heritage, have perceived similarities, and can trace their lineage to a specific part of the world. Most governments use ethnicity as a means of understanding who their people are.

A nation is very similar to ethnicity but with ties to a specific homeland. Nation can be one of the most difficult terms to define because geographers use the word differently than others do. Colloquially, a nation is synonymous with *country* or *State*, but its definition differs in academic speech.

TIP

We'll spend a considerable amount of time in Chapter 13 talking about a nation, but for now, know that a nation is a group of people with a common culture, history, and heritage whose linkage with each other is based on a common homeland.

The United States is a *country* (or *State* in geographers speak) made of many nations. Native American tribes (or American Indians — the preferred term varies from tribe to tribe and even person to person) are great examples of true nations within the Americas. The Navajo, for example, have their own unique culture and heritage that is very much tied to their physical location in what is now the Southwestern states of Arizona and New Mexico. (The Navajo's historic homeland was originally much larger.) The experience of Navajo people is very different than that of other groups, so it is difficult to talk about them in the same sense.

REMEMBER

Nations usually have political aspirations (discussed in more detail in Chapter 13).

Brazil, for example, is a complex country where about half of the population is traced back to European or White descent. Less than 10 percent comprises African, Asian, or Indigenous heritage. The other 40 (or so) percent have multiple ethnic backgrounds. In the United States, ethnicity is divided between people of African, Asian, European, and Pacific Islander descent and people whose ancestry is linked to the Americas. Each ethnic group's experiences differ greatly from that of the other groups. There are even vast differences within each group. Racial groups are somewhat similar and are sometimes accidentally used interchangeably with ethnic groups. Race is a social construct, meaning it exists because society agrees that it exists.

Race is based on *perceived* physical differences and common physical attributes. While race usually focuses on skin color, some physical attributes are thought to be tied to race. *Comedy Central* comedian Trevor Noah's narrative of growing up as the child of a Black mother and a White (Swiss, to be exact) father in *Born a Crime* does a great job of detailing the complexities of race. Among the Black South African community, Trevor talks about being perceived as mixed or even White. Among the white community, he was perceived to be Black or mixed.

TECHNICAL
STUFF

Race can very much depend on each person's opinions. Race is only skin-deep and is based on physical appearance. Ethnicity is traced through location and can be better understood in DNA, which looks at your genomic structure and compares the similarity of your unique combination of genes with that of others to find the physical location where you have the most commonalities.

Gender is another demographic characteristic frequently of interest to demographic and population geographers. A key distinction must be made between gender and biological sex. Biological sex is based on the biological and physiological makeup of an individual. Gender is the societal norms and expectations attached to biological sex. Perceptions of gender and what that means for an individual can vary from culture to culture and even from person to person. Geographers are primarily interested in understanding the makeup of a group of people. Qatar, for example, has a drastically higher number of men than women of working age because of the high rates of migration of guest workers from India.

Demography and the Study of Human Populations

One thing that makes population geography so fun is that you can connect with most of the terms discussed in this chapter, no matter where you are in the world. The study of demographics tries to understand the makeup and characteristics of the people living in an area.

Arithmetic population is a basic statistic that is vital to the understanding of demography. Population is determined by figuring the number of people in a given area. People rarely stop to think about this, but population is inherently a geographic concept because it uses a unit of land to set the measurement's boundaries. You can't simply say, "Give me the population." You must set the population's geographic parameters, making scale important.

For example, if you were examining the population of Sydney, Australia, you need to be specific about the scale. Australia, as a whole, has a population of about

25.6 million people, 5.3 million of which live in Sydney. Before you get too specific, you might see that the New South Wales population — the state in which Sydney is located — is about 8.16 million. However, Sydney is broken up into multiple parts, and if you change your scale of analysis to be even more local, you'll start seeing a different picture of the city's population composition. The Sydney central business district's population is 16,000–17,000, revealing more about the city's population dynamics. From here, we can start looking at some of the city's suburbs and other neighborhoods and their population changes over time to better understand how the population has changed and shifted.

We'll further discuss how cities are defined in Chapter 9.

Population is just one of the things that demographers collect when they're looking at population. An almost infinite number of statistics can be collected and analyzed to get a clearer picture of who lives in an area, including age, gender, race, income, size of household, and even the level of education of each family member.

Much of this is done through the completion of a Census by the government. The Census is a systematic counting and data collection process that almost every national government completes regularly, giving it a better idea of who the people are in an area and the services the government needs to provide there. If a government learns the population has doubled since the last Census, it had better put a plan in place to build more roads in and out of the area and build more schools and medical facilities.

Completed every 10 years, the United States Census has an additional duty beyond just understanding the population's characteristics (see Figure 5-1). The Census is used for establishing the political districts as well. A state can lose or add government representatives, depending on what has happened to its population. In 2020, the number of representatives in the Upper Great Lakes region states (New York, Pennsylvania, West Virginia, Ohio, Michigan, and Illinois) and California was decreased and reallocated to Montana, Colorado, Oregon, Florida, North Carolina, and Texas (which got two seats).

I would highly recommend doing some further research on the Census that covers the area where you live and trying to answer the questions they're asking. For each question, try to figure out why it would be helpful for the government to have that information. Many early Censuses had the added goal of establishing tax rates based on income, so try to think of how else the government benefits from knowing its people.

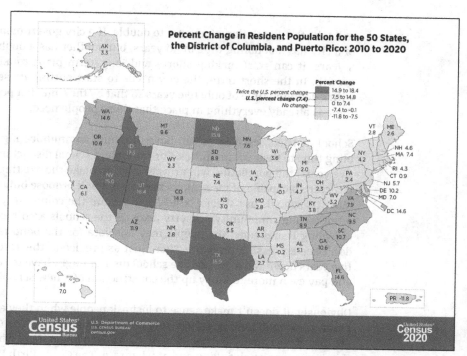

FIGURE 5-1:
Changes in population from 2010 to 2020. (Photo Credit: US Census Bureau.)

Population growth indicators

One of the main goals of the Census is to understand population changes and try to plan for the future. Demographic statisticians use many indicators to track trends and patterns in population growth and decline over space.

REMEMBER

I cannot get into all the indicators and statistics that demographers use because there are so many. Each one tells a different story about the population. Instead, we will break down a couple of key indicators.

Planning for the future: Doubling time

If an area's population doubled and the government had not properly made preparations, just think about all the issues that area could have. Traffic jams, overcrowded schools, long hospital wait times, insufficient police and firefighters, and an inadequate electrical grid would be much worse without planning. Quite a lot is on the line, so governments consider which areas are growing or predicted to grow.

That's why one of the most important statistics for any government to know is the doubling time. Exactly like it sounds, this is the amount of time in years that it will take the population of an area to double. If a city government knows one area of a city has a doubling time of 30 years, but another has a doubling time of only 5 years, it can start making short- and long-term plans to address population growth. In the short term, the city needs to start putting its service in the area with a doubling time of only five years so that by the time that population doubles, there is already everything in place that those people need.

School districts, especially, can have difficulty communicating the idea of doubling time to their communities. For example, a school district might know that in five years, the population will grow enough to make the existing education infrastructure incapable of meeting its needs, so it will propose building a new school. Most US schools use special bonds that require the community to vote on them, often raising community property taxes. If the schools aren't experiencing overcrowding issues now, the people may not vote for the bond issue because they don't see a pressing problem. Then, just as predicted, the schools are overfilled five years down the road, and the school district might have to rush to pass a bond and pay even more to hurry up the construction of a new school.

Obviously, it doesn't make sense to just ask people when they expect their population to double. Demographers rely on information from the Census and public records of new births and people passing away to understand whether the population is growing or shrinking and at what rate. The Crude Birth Rate (CBR) and the Crude Death Rate (CDR) will begin to give a clearer picture of just that. The CBR is the average number of live births for every 1,000 people. The CDR is similar, though it measures how many people pass away instead. You can't just go by the total number of births or deaths since that will depend on the population in an area — and you can get totally unmanageable numbers. In 2021, the Illinois Department of Public Health reported about 28,909 births and 22,882 deaths in Chicago. That translates into roughly 8.3 deaths per 1,000 people and 10.5 births per 1,000 people, which is much more manageable!

The Total Fertility Rate (TFR) and the Life Expectancy Rate (LER) are the two main statistics we can use to help understand what the CBR and CDR will do. TFR is the average number of children a woman is expected to have during her childbearing years. As of 2022, Portugal has the lowest TFR, with an average of 1.25 babies per woman. Niger remains the highest with 6.86 per woman. This could be especially concerning for Portugal since this number is below the replacement rate:

>> If the TFR were 2.1, the two parents would be replaced by their two children, meaning the population would not grow.

>> If the TFR were above two, the parents average more than two children, meaning the population would grow.

>> If the TFR is below 2, the parents do not have enough children to replace them when the parents die, meaning the population will shrink.

The TFR tends to be significantly lower in More Developed Countries (MDCs) where women have better access to education and have their own careers. In Less Developed Countries (LDCs), where women typically have more societal pressure to remain at home, the TFR tends to be higher.

Life expectancy is the other useful statistic, particularly for the CDR. Changes in medical technology and improvements in the quality of life — from access to better food, clean water, and healthy living conditions — can influence life expectancy. Natural disasters or wars may lead to temporary dips, but pandemics like COVID-19 can cause shifts in life expectancy. According to the US Centers for Disease Control (CDC), COVID-19 added to the background mortality rate, causing a decrease in the overall life expectancy by more than two years. From 2014 to 2021, Johns Hopkins University reported that average life expectancy dropped to 76.1 years in 2021 after being as high as 79 years. Japan and Singapore have the highest average life expectancy at 85 years. The small State of Lesotho in Southern Africa has the lowest average life expectancy at about 53 years.

These numbers help us calculate the natural increase rate (NIR) — or rate of natural increase. This number helps us understand the percent growth an area can expect to grow or shrink. In Chicago's case, it would be calculated by subtracting the CDR from the CBR (10.5–8.3) to get 2.2, which we divide by 1,000 to get 0.2 percent. So, based on 2021's numbers, Chicago was expected to grow 0.2 percent based on its NIR. That's not very fast at all, but that is for the entire city (not even including the suburbs). At that rate, Chicago's population would not double for nearly 350 years. Now, before thinking you understand it all, just remember demographers must consider many things.

Along with the NIR, many other things can influence how quickly an area grows — one of the most influential being the net migration rate (NMR), which is calculated the same way as the NIR except that it looks at the number of people who move into an area as well as the number of people who move out.

Population momentum refers to an increase in population that occurs when the total fertility rate drops. Even though each woman might have fewer children, more women are having children. Also, people might live longer, so the total population continues to grow because more people have babies (but not necessarily more babies per woman), and then the babies live longer.

TECHNICAL
STUFF

We'll deal more with migration in Chapters 7 and 8, but for now, just know that the NMR must be combined with the NIR to get the clearest look at what the population is doing. Most of North America (at least with Canada and the United States) and Western Europe have fairly low NIRs but high NMRs. Their migration rates contribute to their fairly consistent population growth.

Influencing population growth rates: Pronatalism

The average person probably does not consider the population growth rate daily, but it is a fairly important number, considering that much of our societal and economic growth depends upon it. A steady supply of workers supports most countries' economies. If that supply runs up, massive structural changes can occur. The birthrate can go down for any number of reasons, such as

>> The economy is bad, and people can't afford to have many children.

>> War makes people not want to bring children into that environment (or the parents are separated as they go off to fight).

>> They simply don't want many children (or any at all).

Without a large supply of workers where there once was one, the supply of people to fill those jobs is lessened, and unemployment decreases. While this may sound good, businesses with many unfilled positions might see their productivity and profits decrease. Sometimes, a country will use pronatalist policies to encourage people to have more children.

Russia has had trouble maintaining its population growth, so many cities have instituted special sweepstakes to encourage people to have more children — often incentivizing them with winning money or even a car. This pronatalist policy has been in place since 2005 and has shown some signs of success. The contest is also commonly tied to some notion of a patriotic duty to have more children to support the State.

Similarly, Denmark doesn't have enough young people to contribute to the country's social programs that support its aging population. A Danish travel company launched the infamous "Do it for Denmark" program to help support population growth by encouraging couples to go on tropical vacations (with the help of grandparents who could help get them there with their own financial contributions).

Denmark has a particularly high dependency ratio: the number of people supported by working-age people. Specifically, the dependency ratio is the number of children (under 15) and elderly individuals (over 65) who are not working and rely on their parent's income or social support like welfare systems. In Denmark, the dependency ratio in 2022 was 57.60 percent, meaning there are more people of non-working age than working age. Denmark's welfare system — and similar systems in other countries — relies on the contributions of younger generations who pay into the welfare system with the hope that it will also support them when they reach retirement age.

However, longer life expectancy and lower CBRs in MDCs mean people live longer and have fewer kids, so more people are drawing from the social security systems longer, and fewer people are paying into it. This has led some countries to consider increasing the retirement age or removing social security and government welfare programs altogether. In 2023, France experienced widescale rioting after its government proposed raising the retirement age from 62 to 64. Americans should take note because some politicians have discussed raising Social Security eligibility from 65 to 69.

Influencing population growth rates: Antinatalism

An antinatalism policy is the opposite of a pronatalist policy. Sometimes, populations can grow faster than they can be managed. (We'll discuss how this can be determined in this next section.) If a population grows too quickly, governments and society might resort to antinatalist policies to decrease the population growth rate. Antinatalist policies might include increased access to contraception and family planning, or harsher methods could be used. Throughout history, governments have employed forced sterilization and abortion policies to prevent populations from growing any further. One of the less harsh policies (at least in theory) is India's government, which pays men to get vasectomies, incentivizing them not to have more kids. There are hints, however, that the vasectomies are not always voluntary.

The most famous examples of antinatalist policies are the laws China enacted to manage its population growth. Following some rather difficult transitions toward communal farming (discussed in Chapters 16 and 17), China's population began steadily (and then rapidly) rising in the 1960s and 1970s.

With an eye on its carrying capacity, which will be discussed in the next section of this chapter, China enacted the one-child policy in 1979. The policy restricted families to only one child and charged families fines for having more than one child (or even forced adoptions or abortions), leading to some interesting repercussions. First, the Chinese welfare system is for elderly people to live with their son, who is culturally obligated to care for them into their old age, leading some families to abort female babies and try again for a male. This preference for sons led to a vast disproportionality in male and female babies. An analysis of the demographic characteristics of people born between 1979 and 2015 (when the policy was relaxed to allow two girls) shows far more males than females — more than 35 million more male babies. The policy was remarkably successful in reducing the population growth rate and has since been repealed.

This policy also means that many Chinese men will never get married because there are not enough women. (Same-sex couples and marriages are not recognized by the Chinese government.) China's economy is also taking a hit because of its demographic shift and the COVID-19 pandemic. The strength of its economy was built by its large supply of laborers, but with the decrease in children and the population shift toward the middle class, the country is less capable of supporting the manufacturing needs to support the economy with lots of low-cost labor. Recognizing this, China shifted to a three-child policy in 2021, encouraging couples to have more children.

Hans Rosling, through his statistical analysis of global data on demographics and economic indicators like income, showed that women's education empowerment was the greatest contributor to slowing a population increase. Educated women are more likely to pursue careers and less likely to have as many children. More wage earners and fewer dependents help increase the overall family income.

TIP

For more on these statistics, I suggest checking out gapminder.org.

Population distribution indicators

Now that we understand the concept of population and the things that affect its rise and decline, we need to learn how geographers can use population numbers to understand trends and patterns. We've determined that population is the number of people in an area, but now let's examine the importance of that area.

We will use the concept of carrying capacity to frame this discussion. The carrying capacity is the number of people a particular land can support. Basic deductive reasoning tells us that fertile grasslands will support far more people than barren deserts.

The carrying capacity is determined in many ways — some of which are similar to species other than humans, and some dissimilar. Food, water, and shelter are the most basic needs. Certain daily caloric intake levels are necessary for humans to meet basic physiological needs. Agriculture is needed to supply the food to meet those daily calorie needs. Everyone universally needs food and water. The form it comes in and how much is needed will depend on each person's culture and physiological needs.

From there, things start getting more complicated, and more variation on a global scale occurs. Following are some things people need:

» Space to rest, prepare their meals, and generally base their lives. What peoples' homes look like and how much space each individual gets depends on the available space. In tightly packed cities, people usually have to make do with far less space than in the far-off suburbs or rural areas.

- » Sanitation systems to help try to keep them healthy.

- » Medical facilities to help diagnose and treat medical conditions.

- » Education systems to support the socialization of new members of society so they can make positive contributions to society once they become adults.

- » Transportation systems to help get them around.

- » Governmental structures provide order and protection.

- » Entertainment allows them to relax and enjoy life.

- » Sporting facilities and parks provide places for them to stay fit, active, and in good physical shape.

- » Retail outlets are needed for humans to purchase the goods they need (or just want).

- » Communication networks to help them stay connected and coordinate their activities.

Then, on top of all that, you need all the construction and supporting roles (laborers, bankers, lawyers, engineers, and so on) to make all the rest of the stuff possible. I'm sure I'm missing quite a lot, but this all should give you an idea of just how many things go into supporting just one person. If you think of all the different stores and services you need daily, weekly, monthly, or yearly, it all adds up pretty quickly!

With all that in mind, only so many people can be supported at any given time. Not enough, and there is a shortage. Economics 101 tells us that there is always a shortage. That's what economics is in the first place: studying how humans allocate scarce resources. However, if there's too much of a shortage, you can quickly run into some pretty large social problems — especially for the more basic needs like food, water, and housing.

Desperation can be one of the worst enemies of peace, which is the base understanding of carrying capacity. People need stuff, and an area can only provide so much stuff. Case in point: housing in California. There is a space shortage in many large cities, and home prices have shot up to reflect that shortage. In Los Angeles, if you wanted to buy a three-bedroom, two-bath house, you're most likely starting at around $1 million with no guarantee it'll be in a great neighborhood; it might need some serious repairs, and it's most likely not even going to be that big!

In Houston, Texas, by comparison, for $1 million, you can get a rather large, often fairly new, house in just about any part of the city you want. It's no wonder California's population is going down, and Texas's is going up.

Housing prices are not the only thing; the general cost of living is also much higher. With an out-of-control housing market, you must pay workers more so they can actually afford to live there. Remember: All roles are necessary. This will mean paying "unskilled" laborers higher wages, too, so they can support themselves. Don't like it? Try living in a city without grocery store workers, garbage collectors, and fast-food workers. I'll break it to you now: You can't. Human populations depend on all levels of workers. I would even argue that "lower" skilled laborers are needed more than the "high-value" professions.

Geography densities

Carrying capacity will stay at the forefront of our minds here as we look at the actual process of mapping populations to look for patterns and trends. We can just map raw population numbers, which will tell us some interesting information, but we need to equalize the data a bit more to look for commonalities between places. One of the best/easiest ways to do that is to convert population statistics into densities. Simply put, divide whatever you're analyzing by the area you're examining.

Population density is the most basic, and probably the most common, form of density that population geographers deal with. The academic term for this concept is *arithmetic population density*. It's really straightforward: the number of people divided by area, usually expressed as the number of people per square mile (or kilometer). Cities in North America (minus Mexico City) and Europe have no hope of contending with the megacities of Asia, South America, and even some of the rising cities of Africa when it comes to the sheer number of people in those cities.

New York City's population of about 8.5 million would be around China's eighth-largest city. Los Angeles, the US's second-largest city, has a population of just under 4 million, placing it around the 28th ranking in China (see Figure 5-2). However, if we convert those population numbers into density, we start getting more commonalities over space with fewer outliers that bunch up the data at the top.

We could look at several other densities, but again, for brevity's sake, we'll restrict it. The set of densities connected to agriculture is particularly helpful for understanding the carrying capacity . Agricultural Density and Physiological density are helpful tools to help us establish and understand the carrying capacity of an area. Agricultural density is found by taking the number of farmers and dividing that by the amount of arable land. Arable land is land that is actually usable for agriculture. Deserts, mountains, and swampy areas that are not suitable are removed from this calculation. If your agriculture density is too low, you don't have enough farmers to help the land reach its productive potential. If your agricultural density is too high, you've got too many farmers being supported by too little land, and they won't be able to support themselves.

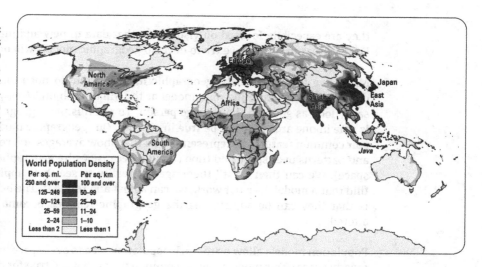

FIGURE 5-2:
Looking at this map with a simplified scale, you can see the tight concentrations and high populations, but if we had just done the total population, there would be massive concentrations in Eastern and Southern Asia with only little spikes here and there elsewhere.

World Population Density

Per sq. mi.	Per sq. km
250 and over	100 and over
125–249	50–99
60–124	25–49
25–59	11–24
2–24	1–10
Less than 2	Less than 1

Physiological density is the other agriculture-based density. This is the total population of an area divided by the amount of arable land, not just farmers. Areas with a high physiological density have a lot of people being supported by each acre (or hectare) of agricultural land. That puts a lot of stress and pressure on the agricultural land. Any bit of land that is unproductive or is taken out by a natural disaster puts even more stress on the other bits of agricultural land. The higher the physiological density, the more possible it is for an area to experience food insecurity.

TECHNICAL STUFF

Having enough high-quality fresh food to meet peoples' needs is one of the massive problems we face. Low physiological densities are good in this situation because there is plenty of farmland to support your population, and you might even be able to export any surplus to help the economy. Physiological density can be an especially helpful indicator for understanding the nature of the landscape. At first glance, the population of a State like Egypt appears to be pretty good. It has a fairly dense population density of about 292 people per square mile. Egypt's physiological density of 3,500 people per square mile reflects that much of the country is not farmable, and there is a lot of pressure on each square mile of farmland.

Modeling Population Patterns

Geographers are inherently visual people. We like looking at pictures of places and dreaming of going there. We look at data tables and say, "I bet I could map that." Some quantitative geographers focus on numbers, data sets, and tables, but even they are especially focused on visualizing that data in new and interesting ways. For this reason, I think we try to develop geographic models whenever possible.

Much like fashion models, geographic models often do not reflect reality. The dress that looks stunning on a model at the Milan Fashion Week will not necessarily look as good on the average person. To put this more geographically, what is true in one area may not be true in another. Our geographic models allow us to pair common features in representations that show averages and represent trends and patterns over space and time (though because we're geographers, it's mostly space). We can then "test" them against reality to see their applicability. If we find that a model does not work, we can adjust and refine it. The beauty of models is that they can be adjusted as the geographic realities become clearer or are altered.

Population models allow us to track population trends over space and time (again, mostly space). Our models look at commonalities that are true for different places that can display complex relationships. We will use quite a few models throughout the rest of this book, but in this section, I will introduce you to some of the most foundational models we use in understanding population dynamics.

DTM and ETM

The Demographic Transition Model (DTM) is one of the favorite models for those who teach this subject because it is such a straightforward model, and you can do so much with it. The primary relationship that the DTM (see Figure 5-3) is looking at is economic development and the impact that it has on the Crude Birth Rate (CBR), the Crude Death Rate (CDR), and the Natural Increase Rate (NIR).

REMEMBER

As we discuss the different stages of the DTM, remember that scale must be considered when reading these descriptions. I might say something like, "Denmark is a stage 4 or 5 country," meaning a country might be stage 4, with regions that are stage 2. The stage applies to the country on average, but there will be some fluctuation in the rural areas. Even the richest countries have poor areas, and even some of the very poorest countries have rich areas with high development.

>> **Stage 1:** In Stage 1 of the DTM, the CBR and the CDR are both extremely high and fairly equal. There is a lot of yearly fluctuation in both numbers because there's still a high risk of things like famine and disease. We'll talk more about that when we get to the Epidemiological Transition Model. In the Rostow model that you'll be introduced to in Chapter 18, these are the "traditional" societies with basic subsistence-based economies. No countries fit wholly into this category, but there most definitely are regions within some countries that do, particularly in the deep Amazon or jungles of Papua New Guinea.

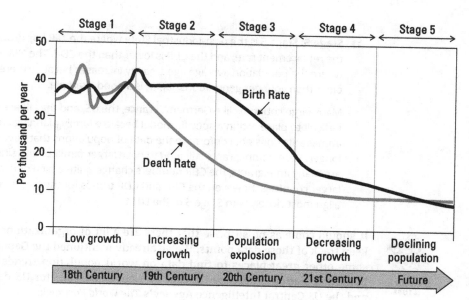

FIGURE 5-3:
The Demographic
Transition
Model (DTM)

>> **Stage 2:** In Stage 2 of the DTM, the CBR remains high, as contraception and family planning have not quite caught on yet. However, the introduction of medical technology and food stability means that the CDR has declined. Infant mortality rates drop, and more children survive into adulthood. As a result, the NIR starts to increase drastically. The population will start to increase, supplying a large supply of workers. This stage usually corresponds with the industrial development that coincides with foreign investment and the beginnings of the industrial era. A perfect example of this would be China before it implemented its one-child policy.

>> **Stage 3:** Stage 3 will start leveling out population growth as the CBR declines to eventually meet the CBR as education levels increase and families consciously decide to have fewer children. With improvements in medical technology, there is higher confidence that children will reach adulthood, so there is less need to have as many children. With the focus of the economy shifting from agriculture to industry, there is also less need to have multiple children to help with farm growth. Also, more women are entering the workforce, shifting their focus toward careers rather than taking care of kids at home. Angola is a great example of a State at this stage.

>> **Stage 4:** Stage 4 sees the CBR and CDR equalize but at a much lower level than had been experienced at Stage 1. Population growth has leveled out, and the NIR reaches close to 0. The Total Fertility Rate stabilizes near two children per woman and hovers right around the replacement rate. In stage 4, you see many late industrial states transitioning to service-based economies. A state like Argentina would fit in fairly nicely here.

>> **Stage 5:** Stage 5 is the post-industrial State where the TFR has dropped below the replacement rate, and the CBR is lower than the CDR. The NIR is negative, where the population average age steadily increases because there are more older than younger generations. Japan is a good example.

Many large countries like Germany, France, the US, and the UK are very difficult to place within a specific model because family planning among immigrants does not conform to the data of populations that have been there longer. Recent immigrants still tend to have larger families, and since there are many immigrants, the CBR numbers change quite a bit. For each of these larger countries, however, the CBR and CDR trends for the long-time residents align most closely with Stage 5 of the DTM.

TECHNICAL STUFF

It should come as no surprise that there are a lot of organizations out there that keep track of these data points. We've already mentioned the Gapminder site, but some other great places to find data on world population trends are the World Bank, Population Reference Bureau, US Census Bureau (for US data, of course), and the US Central Intelligence Agency's *The World Factbook*.

The Epidemiological Transition Model

The basic idea of the Epidemiological Transition Model (ETM) more or less aligns with the same basic structure of the DTM. Instead of looking at the connection between economic development and birth and death rates, the ETM looks at the connection between economic development and what people die from. It's weird to think, but the place where you are born actually has quite a bit of influence on what you'll die from.

That is a very morbid thought, but in a Stage 1 country, a disease of broken bone that would be easily treatable in a more economically advanced country can be fatal. The common flu, dysentery (from contaminated food or water), or infections from cuts and fractures are common causes of premature death. As you move up the ETM, the likelihood of dying from one of those things becomes greatly diminished (still possible) and transitions to lifestyle-based diseases like heart disease, cancers, and diabetes. In the most advanced stages of the ETM, even those are not necessarily fatal, and the degeneration of the body from old age becomes a leading cause of death.

Charting populations in pyramid form

Population pyramids are particularly helpful to population geographers and anyone interested in population trends.

Niger's population pyramid is a fairly bottom-heavy shape, reflecting a lower position on both the DTM and ETM (see Figure 5-4). Fewer than half of all people born there survive past 50 years old. The largest portion of the population is the very youngest, and very few people survive into old age. The distribution shows about 2.5 million boys and 2.5 million girls between the ages of 0–4 and only a couple of thousand people living to ages 80–84. At the older ages, there are more women than men.

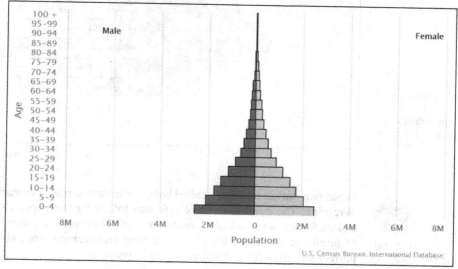

FIGURE 5-4: Niger's population pyramid. (Image source: *The World Factbook*.)

Singapore's population pyramid (see Figure 5-5) reflects a very high level in the DTM and ETM. People survive in great numbers into old age, but we can see other trends. Women are more likely to survive longer than men. This is because women are less likely to engage in self-destructive behaviors like heavy drinking or smoking (and instances of "hold my beer and watch this"). The declining birth rate means fewer and fewer children are being born, and the population growth rate is slowing down, if not already negative.

TIP

I suggest hopping on populationpyramid.net, where you can look at many different countries at different times. Look at the United Arab Emirates and see the impact of a heavy number of male foreign guest workers. Look at Germany in 1950, and you'll see the effect of World War II on fighting-age men (compare men and women between the ages of 20 and 70). Or look at the United States in 1950, and you'll see the post-war baby boom. The modern-day United States' population pyramid resembles a skyscraper with equal distributions of people at each age group that begin to taper off at the bottom. Population pyramids can also be drawn at different scales, such as local or city scales, to better understand trends in a particular area in a State.

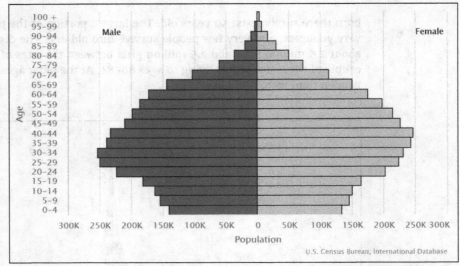

FIGURE 5-5:
Singapore's
population
pyramid (Image
source: *The World
Factbook*)

US Census Bureau, International Database

US Census Bureau / Public Domain.

TECHNICAL
STUFF

Rapid population increases called baby booms are sometimes visible in population pyramids. The most noticeable one was following the Second World War in the United States. A period of economic and social optimism, paired with the returns of hundreds of thousands of service men and women from abroad, created the perfect situation for . . . biology . . . to happen.

The resulting increase in births in the late 1940s and 1950s resulted in a large increase in the crude birth rate. Along with that, an increase in the standard of living helped lead to an overall increase in the NIR for the United States. Add in increased migration, especially from Eastern Europe, and the population had a recipe for a massive increase. The population increase was so drastic that the entire generation of people born in the 1940s to the 1960s are called Baby Boomers. Understanding population is important to planners and policymakers of all levels. Knowing what is happening with the population can help them make better decisions about what is needed where, and what resources are needed to support a growing population. As much as planners may like to try to control population growth, there are just too many demographic variables. Understanding population trends means being willing to dive into a number of statistics. More than that, you need to understand how statistics work with one another.

» **Population theories and population growth**

» **Why people don't live in certain areas of the world**

Chapter **6**

Where the People Aren't

Population is a big concept that helps drive the discussion of human geography since understanding people and where they're located is central to much of our work. Attaching meaning and significance to those places within the context of culture, political structure, city organization, and so on is where some human geography subdisciplines can help enrich our understanding of those populations.

The last chapter contained a lot of theory and general trends. This one will build off many of those concepts and apply them to human populations. We will try to understand where people are located and where they aren't, why they're not there, and what is happening with those populations. As you can see, this is a busy chapter.

In November 2022, the world's population is estimated to have surpassed 8 billion people — a major milestone considering that the world reached a population of 7 billion in 2011 and is expected to reach 9 billion by 2045.

TECHNICAL STUFF

For perspective, the Earth is 24,901 miles around the equator, where it is the widest. The average human takes 2,100 steps to walk a mile, meaning it would take the average human 52,292,100 steps to walk around the Earth at the equator. The average human would have to walk around the Earth roughly 152.98 times to take as many steps as there were humans in 2022. Get walking!

Obviously, the distribution of humans is not equal everywhere in the world. Of those 8 billion people, just more than one-third live in China and India, both of which have a population of about 1.4 billion as of 2023. To put that number in perspective. Europe's entire population of about 746 million is just under half of the population of China and India. In fact, you could combine the populations of Europe, South America, and Oceania and still be smaller than China's.

Understanding Population Trends

As we discussed in Chapter 5, "Where Are the People?" many things affect the population of an area. Carrying capacity reflects the maximum number of people that can be sustainably supported in a particular area, but most places are nowhere near their carrying capacities. As it stands, very few States have all the resources needed to sustain their population. Understanding carrying capacity can determine the stress on the available resources and the necessity to utilize other States' specialized production and comparative advantages. The forces of migration, which are described in Chapter 7, also play a significant role in why some areas have higher populations than others. Cultural factors, such as the influence of religion, education, or gender roles, can significantly impact the distribution of humans worldwide.

Determinism is the theory that the physical landscape plays a key role in a group of people's overall development and trajectory. For example, determinism would say if you live in the far North, you are hearty and hard-working because that's what it takes to survive. However, many hearty and hard-working individuals don't live in the far North.

TIP

Environmental determinism and possibilism are repeatedly brought up throughout this book, especially in Chapter 18.

Determinism was often used as a justification for colonialism and imperialism, indicating that Europeans were more fit since their environment more or less gave them the conditions needed to become that way. Determinism is highly criticized since it ignores political factors, such as colonialism and imperialism, that can have been far more influential in a State's present level of development than can be explained as a function of their physical location..

Beyond determinism, historian Louis Wright summarized the reasons why Europeans grew to dominate much of the world down to gold, glory, and gospel. Europeans found gold and trading markets, desired personal fame (see Christopher Columbus), and wanted to convert others to Christianity. This combination of gold, glory, and gospel pushed Europeans far beyond their borders to control much of the world. None of these advantages had anything to do with Europe being located in the rather pleasant temperate zone.

On the other hand, environmental possibilism reflects the reality that humans can develop and grow despite their environmental constraints. In fact, as history has often shown, sometimes, the only thing that holds back human progress is us.

The physical size of a space and its climactic conditions can most definitely influence the population but do not wholly define it. Many of Canada's coastal areas share the same physical characteristics as Western European countries, but Canada didn't build a global empire spanning multiple continents.

TECHNICAL STUFF

It should be noted that Canada *did* build a continental empire at the expense of the native First Nations of the northernmost regions of North America.

Let's look at some of the physical features that *affect the population's distributions*, as shown in the population density map in Figure 6-1. You saw this map in Chapter 5, but this time, we're looking at it to see where the people are versus where they're not.

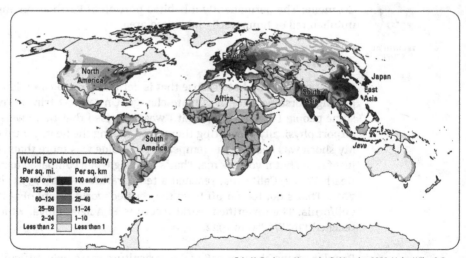

FIGURE 6-1: World population density

Erin H. Fouberg, Alexander B. Murphy, 2020 / John Wiley & Sons.

Ecumene and the "toos"

Beyond those factors that humans can control, there are a number of geographic factors related to the planet's physical geography that will also affect the distribution of humans around the planet. We can sort those factors into what we'll call the "Five Toos":

>> Too hot

>> Too dry

>> Too hilly

>> Too cold

>> Too wet

Using these principles to identify the uninhabited part of the world, we can better identify why humans live in the parts of the world that they do. Geographers use the Greek word *ecumene* to describe the parts of the inhabited world. A word that the ancient Greeks originally used to describe the parts of the world known to them that were inhabited, Asia, Europe, and Africa, we now apply the term to refer to all parts of the world that are inhabited.

Ecumene: The permanently inhabited portion of Earth as distinguished from the uninhabited or temporarily inhabited area.

Too hot

Let's start with too hot because that is definitely one I can relate to, and it is only getting worse because of climate change. On my last trip to Texas, I joked with some people I was meeting that I was surprised that there weren't people at the airport physically preventing them from fleeing the heat, yet they were still there! My shock was because the temperature outside was more than 110°F/43°C. That's just far too hot if you ask me. That's nothing when compared to some other places. Death Valley, California, reached a temperature of 132°F/55°C in the summer of 2023. That's not too far off from the verified world record of 134°F/56.7°C, also in California. The unverified world record is El Azizia, Libya, which claims to have reached 136°F/58°C in 1922.

Regular temps above 100°F make agriculture extremely difficult and cause many heat-related injuries (heat exhaustion or heat stroke) and can even lead to death. For this reason, if you are ever flying over the Arabian Desert and look out the window, once your eyes adjust to the blinding reflection of the sun off the sand, you will see miles and miles of not much beyond said sand. Most cities in or near deserts are in coastal areas that offer some relief. Even there, significant adaptations are needed to deal with the intense heat.

Areas around the desert regions of the Sonoran (the southwest United States and northern Mexico), Sahara (the northern third of Africa), the great Australian desert, and the Arabian peninsula/Middle East that regularly reach those dangerous levels are some of the most sparsely populated regions in the world. The Equatorial regions of Africa, South America, and Southern Asia that also sustain yearly hot, humid temperatures have many of their large population centers clustered near the coasts or highland areas where the ocean breezes of altitude provide some relief to the heat.

Too dry

Many places discussed in the "Too hot" section would also fit here. The largest *hot* desert in the world is the Sahara desert of northern Africa.

TECHNICAL STUFF

Fun fact: The largest desert in the world is in Antarctica. Yes, there is snow there, but much of it has accumulated over thousands of years and never melted. Deserts can be hot or cold.

A desert is any region that receives less than 10 inches (25 centimeters) of precipitation in a year. See Figure 6-2.

FIGURE 6-2:
The desert of Utah is not seen fit for human habitation, so it has instead been reserved for use as a protected park (Canyonlands National Park).

TECHNICAL STUFF

Here's another fun fact: According to the US National Oceanographic and Atmospheric Administration (NOAA), 1 inch of rain equals about 13 inches of snow. So, a desert could receive 12 feet of snow over the year and still be classified as a desert.

Antarctica fits in another category ("too cold"), but many deserts are dry but not too hot or too cold. The Atacama desert in west central South America, the Namib desert in Southwest Africa, and the Gobi desert of central Asia are regions with milder temperatures (because of their latitude or altitude) but still receive very little rainfall. All three regions are very sparsely populated, or even not at all!

Water is the most basic necessity that humans need to have to live. We can survive for weeks without food but only a few days without water. Plants also need access to at least some water to survive, especially the ones we depend on for food. In Figure 6-1 (shown earlier), if you look right around 25-35 degrees North or South Latitude, you'll notice that those areas with very little population are often deserts.

Too cold

As much as I like the cold and snow, I admit that parts of the world are just too cold. Like the areas that are too hot, places that are too cold make agriculture difficult.

Many live in the Earth's frigid regions. The predominantly native peoples of the high Arctic of Russia, Finland, Norway, Iceland, Greenland, Canada, and Alaska survive off a combination of fishing/whaling, reindeer herding, and food that has to be brought in from warmer regions. Think your grocery bills are high? A gallon of milk in the Canadian territory of Nunavut can cost you more than $8 US. Some people live in Antarctica, but many are scientists. Their supplies must be shipped in, and their waste is shipped out. In areas permanently covered by snow and ice, like Antarctica and the interior of Greenland, permanent inhabitation is impossible. There are some creative solutions to living in colder regions, like Iceland using its geothermal heat to provide ideal growing conditions in greenhouse-based vegetable farms, but it's almost impossible to have any sort of agriculture on the 2-mile-thick ice sheets at high latitudes.

Too hilly

Agriculture is very difficult in the world's mountainous regions. Life is made difficult simply by being able to find a place to live. Humans need oxygen to breathe. Above 9,000 feet, many people will find it difficult to breathe, given how thin the air is. The Hindu Kush/Altai/Himalaya regions of Asia, the Andes of South America, the Alps of Southcentral Europe, and the Rockies of the Western United States and Canada are perfect examples of places where the low populations can be attributed to the mountain terrain.

Some people can live in small communities or off-the-grid-style solitary living, but large cities are difficult since the mountains often provide ample barriers to connecting large settlements. Mountains may be very attractive to live next to because of the views; just look at the housing prices in Denver, Colorado.

However, cities' size decreases rapidly as you go from the "flatlands" into the "highlands." This is as true for other parts of the world as it is for Colorado.

Too wet

"Too wet" can be a little bit contradictory, seeing as how we've spent so much time saying you need precipitation and favorable temperatures to have agriculture, but even in the temperate zones, there is such thing as too rainy. A rainforest typically receives more than 80 inches (200 centimeters) of rain annually. Some rainforest regions can even receive drastically more than that.

With that much rain, the ground remains almost permanently saturated, and plants that aren't adapted to the moist conditions can literally rot away. Some crops like rice can thrive in such conditions, but even they have limits. Frequent flooding can also be a problem, carrying away people's homes and forcing them to move elsewhere. Bangladesh has experienced rapid urbanization, which coincides with increased flooding events of the Padma and Brahmaputra rivers. Farmers from the countryside leave their land, hoping for greater stability in the city that is not so much at the mercy of potential floods. The Amazon River in South America and the Congo River in central Africa are also well known for frequently spilling over their banks, leading to loss of life and property.

TIP

These migratory trends are discussed in Chapters 8 and 9.

Population distributions

We've looked at where the people aren't; now, let's focus a little bit more on where the people are. We're still working off the world population density map, and in this part of the chapter, we'll discuss some trends you'll see there.

Some like it hot

It's totally against my comprehension, but there are many large population centers well within the tropical zone (or at least just outside it). Megacities like Jakarta, Indonesia, Mexico City, Mexico, and Lagos, Nigeria, are between the Tropic of Cancer and the Tropic of Capricorn (the two lines of latitude establishing the "tropical zone").

One barrier to the further spread of human population centers in the planet's equatorial region is dense rainforests. Being too wet comes into play quite a bit in these regions, but some of the largest cities in the world have grown along the fringes of those forests. One of the main commonalities for the distribution of population centers in the tropical equatorial region is that they're near water. This also holds true in the hot desert regions of northern Africa and the Middle East.

Rivers like the Nile support the city of Cairo, Egypt. Baghdad, Iraq, sits between the Tigris and Euphrates rivers. The hot deserts push populations to the shores, with very few large population centers within the deserts themselves.

Setting up on the water's edge

A couple of years ago, NASA published satellite photos online in a very interestingly curated collection called "The Visible Earth." Taken by NASA satellites and space-based cameras, this satellite imagery was assembled in map form. NASA always does a good job of highlighting specific points of interest, such as one showing Africa at night.

Though the interior is rather dark, the dots of light (cities) are spotty enough along the coastal areas to make out the continent's shape clearly. Then, in the Northeast, there is a beacon of bright lights resembling a snake leading away from the coast and into the interior. A quick search of daylight imagery reveals tightly packed cities along the Nile River, complete with lush green farmland. These sorts of patterns are repeated around the globe.

Most of the world's oldest or most influential cities are located near major waterways, mostly linked to the advantages of transportation or access to sea-based resources: Moscow on the banks of the Moskva River, London, Thames, Tokyo, around the harbor, or Shanghai, where the Yangtze meets the East China Sea. There are many examples of large numbers of people congregating near oceans, rivers, and lakes. Just think at any scale, globally, nationally, or even locally. I'm sure you can think of many cities where the main point of focus is some body of water.

TIP

NASA's collection highlighting the "blue marble" on their visible Earth platform offers a very interesting look at the distribution of human population centers using satellite imagery. Check it out at https://visibleearth.nasa.gov/.

Many old German towns took advantage of the rivers for the possibilities of transportation and collecting tolls (see Figure 6-3). The castles overwatching the rivers were as much for protection as intimidation.

Temperate versus tropical

There's a fine line of finding a place that is not too hot or cold but also not too wet, dry, or hilly. That gives us a finite amount of space in the temperate mid-latitude areas of our planet. Yes, there are some massively dense areas of human population in the tropical zones, but in the temperate zones, there are quite a few regions with dense populations spread out over a larger area. These areas don't have as many huge population clusters, though there are still megacities in places like Buenos Aires, Seoul, Tokyo, and Beijing. Much of the population is more spread out but is still dense.

FIGURE 6-3:
Würzburg,
Germany, on the
shores of the
Main River

Look at much of Western Europe or Eastern North America. Heavy population distributions are found throughout most of both regions, especially when compared to Eastern Europe or Western North America. Eastern China, the Korean Peninsula, and Southern Japan also have heavy population clustering. There are also heavy concentrations in the Southern Hemisphere's temperate zone, especially around Southern Brazil, Northern Argentina, Southeast Australia, and Southern South Africa.

The tightly packed city of Shanghai has undergone rocketship-like speed in population growth. In fact, this skyline has actually drastically changed with even more mega skyscrapers since this photo in Figure 6-4 was taken in 2011.

Urban versus rural

As of 2023, the World Bank estimates that about 56 percent of the world's population lives in cities. That number is still rising and could reach 70 percent by 2050. In rural areas, one of the largest trends we're seeing, besides the declining populations, is the increasingly aging demographic composition. Younger people are primarily moving to the cities for education and career opportunities. Rural areas worldwide have a lot of difficulty keeping their younger people around.

FIGURE 6-4:
Shanghai, China

However, during the height of the COVID-19 pandemic, many younger (and even older) people moved to rural areas to set up their home offices where living costs were lower. Rural states like Wyoming have seen their populations affected by the migration of people trying to find land cheaper than in more traditional population centers. Especially during the COVID pandemic, people moved to areas like Wyoming to have beautiful views for cheaper prices (see Figure 6-5).

FIGURE 6-5:
Thunder Basin
National
Grasslands, in
Eastern Wyoming

Many also sought places with beautiful scenery, like lakes or mountains, to set up their home offices. Some young people find the transition to urban areas difficult and return to their rural hometowns. With a few exceptions here and there, we're seeing migration trends shift further in favor of rural-to-urban migration across much of the planet.

TIP

We'll discuss urban trends and migration patterns in Chapters 8, 9, and 10.

Using Demographics to Plan for the Future

As we've already discussed in Chapter 5, a steady handle on demographics is necessary to ensure that governments can plan for future trends. Governments do much of this through the collection and analysis of the Census, but this has to be a continual process to ensure that governments aren't caught off guard. Having too high of a concentration in any demographical statistical category can act as a sort of ticking time bomb that, if not properly planned for, can cause serious issues for a population. Too many men and not enough women? You've got a gender distribution time bomb like China. Too many older people and not enough younger people? Denmark and Japan understand that. Not enough jobs in the service industry to support a more educated population? That actually does a pretty good job of describing countries like the United States at times. Many people will go through the process of earning college degrees only to find out there are not any jobs available in their field and have to end up working in jobs outside their education.

Understanding the population is required before governments can use that information to improve their living conditions. History is dotted with examples of people rising up and replacing their governments with governments that would improve things. When basic needs (food, water, shelter, safety, and so on) aren't met, this process speeds up.

Managing population growth

Sometimes, when populations grow faster than governments can manage, the reasons are obvious; sometimes, they aren't. I'm guessing you know there are many people in India. I'm more or less assuming that many of you don't know that many people lack access to some of the most basic facilities. Think of where you live and what you might take for granted.

Toilets are one of those things we don't think about often but are very important in many ways. In India, the National Health Family Survey estimated that more than 730 million people do not have access to a toilet. Instead of proper sanitation — not only in India but elsewhere as well — human waste often ends up working its way into rivers or groundwater. A lot of toilet facilities increase the likelihood of drinking water contamination, which is responsible for tens of thousands of deaths every year. Since that particular report came out in India, the government has taken steps to improve access to sanitation, but there are many barriers. In slums and unplanned settlements, many governments are especially hesitant to provide services in what are not seen as legitimate settlements. However, if services aren't provided, slums can become hot spots for disease. Or, gangs can root themselves as they present themselves as the providers of services that the government is otherwise unwilling to supply.

While the shortage of public restrooms may not make the national radar, some events are so in your face that they can't be ignored. Unfortunately, it's sadly shocking to see the sheer number of events that should be newsworthy but do not even get air time on news networks. Occasionally, however, some events are impossible for the world to ignore. In 1993, a South African photographer named Kevin Carter traveled to Sudan to cover the famine happening there. He photographed a small girl suffering from hunger, with a vulture waiting behind her.

Carter won the Pulitzer prize for the photograph but died months later by suicide from guilt for the photo and not doing more to help her. The impact of the photo sparked a global conversation and response from the world community, who could not look away from the horrific effects of the famine. (It is believed the girl reached an aid station.)

With increased access to almost all parts of the world, we can face the trials and tribulations others are experiencing. This has fostered the development of the "world community," where the world has great potential to come together to address issues as they arise.

One of the issues that is becoming increasingly pressing, especially in the age of climate change, is water scarcity. Increased temperatures are taxing aquifers more than ever, and the effect is being felt in almost all parts of the world. We've already established that water is one of the most basic necessities. We can only speculate what awaits us in a world where water remains critically sparse. Based on what we've seen in previous examples where water has been involved (like between Egypt and Sudan or Kazakhstan and Uzbekistan), contestation over water can pit States against one another. None of the scenarios appear rosy, though. The importance of securing water and food supplies for the future of a people cannot be understated.

A population of many

When we ask ourselves what more must be done to prepare for the future, the only answer can be "more." Geographically speaking, the threat of overpopulation and the question of distributing scarce resources has been one of the worst nightmares for population geographers like Paul and Anne Erlich. So far, thankfully, their fears have not been fully realized. They most feared what would happen when the people's demands surpassed available supplies. When overpopulation is established, people will switch into desperation — wars, famines, diseases, and all the worst parts of all the worst Hollywood movies. It's shockingly sad to see what people are capable of when faced with desperation and opportunities to exploit it.

A good example happened in the 1990s in the East African country of Somalia when warlords vying for power took control of food supplies to force populations into submission. This strategy resulted in the deaths of hundreds of thousands of people.

World War II's origins are often partially attributed to Germany's desire to expand the available living space (what Adolf Hitler referred to as *Lebensraum*) and Japan's attempt to secure its industrial future by securing raw material supplies. Those weren't even pressing needs, but this perceived scarcity was enough justification in leaders' minds to prompt the largest and most destructive war in history.

REMEMBER

Many conflicts throughout history have their roots in issues concerning resources. The French Revolution followed years of bad harvests, making food scarcer. In World War II, the German Army was halted in Northern Africa and Stalingrad on its way to capture strategic oil reserves. Japan's campaign during World War II aimed to secure crucial raw materials needed to maintain its military and industrial capabilities. More recently, in 2022, much of Russia's motive for invading Ukraine has been attributed to Russia's desire to secure oil and natural gas pipelines to the West.

Population theories: Ideas to plan for the future

These concerns have long been on the minds of demographers, geographers, sociologists, politicians, and just everyday people. There have been many theories and approaches to understanding them, leading to many potential solutions for fixing them. There are a number of theories about overpopulation trends, so we'll touch on a few here, though this list is not exhaustive. Each attempt to answer, "What are the problems associated with population increases?" and "What will happen when overpopulation is achieved?"

Some people definitely have a more optimistic viewpoint and approach than others. And though they come from different fields, their understandings are all geographic in nature because they're trying to understand the connection between people and scarce resources.

The haves and the have-nots

The first is probably one of the most well known. Karl Marx (see Figure 6-6) was born in Germany and got himself run out of a couple of places before ending up in Manchester, England. In the 1800s, he worked to understand the population shifts occurring in England as an ongoing result of industrialization and urbanization there. Marx was really interested in the relative plight of the working class, even though they made up the majority of the population.

FIGURE 6-6:
An homage to Karl Marx in Chemnitz, Germany (formerly Karl-Marx Stadt)

Wealth was concentrated amongst a finite few, and their wealth was dependent upon the labor of others. Based on this, Marx said governments should do what will benefit the greatest number of people and that all laborers should be considered valuable because all labor is necessary for a smoothly functioning society. He even suggested that vast wealth shouldn't be concentrated among a select few while the rest are left to squabble over scraps. The basic tenets of socialism are based on the idea that wealth should be more evenly (if not equally) distributed and that government should benefit the majority instead of working for a select minority.

To achieve these ideas, Marx advocated for the world's workers to unite and overthrow the wealthy to secure a worker's paradise where each could contribute to their abilities, and in return, they received what they needed. Marx believed everyone should work in the way they are best able, and everyone should have access to the basic things they need, which is contrary to the capitalistic model, where each profession has a different societal worth and is paid accordingly. In Marx's model, a factory worker is just as valuable as a doctor, so it makes sense to have them paid similarly.

In a capitalistic model, the value of what the doctor provides is much more than that of the factory worker, and their pay reflects that. What both capitalism and socialism try to answer is how to address the distribution of scarce resources. With the understanding that all items are scarce — some more scarce than others — access to them will be tiered. In a capitalistic society — like what Marx observed — the wealthy had more access to goods than everybody else.

All of this is to say that Marx and others like Louis Blanc and Georg Wilhelm Friedrich Hegel — started coming up with ideas of socialism as an alternative to capitalism to help meet the needs of the general population. In the 1800s, common workers had no clean and comfortable life, and there was not even much of a middle class. So, Marx started advocating for common workers to be able to meet their basic needs, and if that was not possible, they should rise up and overthrow the people who were preventing that from happening. How goods and services should be distributed is still very much under debate. Increasingly, there are calls for things like healthcare and education to be human rights and should be readily available and accessible to all.

REMEMBER

There is much to debate about the merits and quality of service provided under each system. There is also something to be said about who benefits from each form of economic structure and to what lengths they'll go to further entrench their system into society.

Marx's viewpoint was further broadened within sociology to form the basis of the conflict perspective — the general idea being that society is based on conflict. In the distribution of goods and wealth scenario, a conflict perspective could be used to point out how conflict is created amongst the lower classes to distract them from the pilfering and hoarding of resources by those at the top of the class chain.

During World War I, at the end of the old era of Lords and formal positions based on birthright, one of the biggest dangers that Generals feared was soldiers talking with other soldiers. Marx would have wholeheartedly advocated for soldiers to talk with their compatriots on the other side to see that they had more in common than they did with their own officers. Class warfare was always one of the inevitable outcomes in Marx's mind. There are still some that are predicting class warfare. At least in my mind, more equitable access to goods and services seems to be a no-brainer as a means of trying to ensure that overpopulation (or not even in the case of overpopulation) is dealt with in such a way as to try to provide for all and not just the select few.

REMEMBER

What I covered here was just a very brief overview of the principles of the economic structures of capitalism and socialism. I recommend checking out *Economics For Dummies,* Third Edition by Sean Masaki Flynn (Wiley), for more information about these two systems.

A finger snap

In the multibillion-dollar Marvel franchise, the heroic warriors must square off against the villain Thanos. Thanos planned to wipe out half of all living species because he believed that the universe was over its carrying capacity and its over-population was creating misery. The obvious plot hole is that eliminating half of all living things, including the plants and animals humans depend on for food, the problem isn't being addressed. You'd just have half as many people being extra miserable. And this is definitely one example where the ends do not justify the means. We geography teachers were actually all over our super-cool and not-at-all-nerdy discussion boards talking about the connections between Thanos's and Thomas Malthus's theories.

Malthus was an English economist who came along slightly before Marx and was most interested in the rising population and its relationship to food production. Malthus noted that food production was growing at an arithmetic rate (1 to 2, 2 to 3, 3 to 4, and so on), but the population was growing exponentially (1 to 2, 2 to 4, 4 to 8, and so on). At some point, the population would exceed available food stores, and then we would be in a really bad situation.

Malthus called the point where the population caught up with available food pro-duction the "point of crisis." As Malthus explained, everything above that point would be misery because there would not be enough food to go around and sup-port the population.

Malthus suggested negative population checks to prevent reaching the point of crisis. These were measures meant to decrease population growth. In terminology we've used previously, negative population checks would be antinatalist policies. Things like restraint (people choosing to have fewer children), access to contra-ception and abortion, and even societal shifts like increasing women's access to education and careers could be used to decrease the population growth rate. All of these things would negatively affect the crude birth rate.

Positive population checks are another measure that Malthus noted would slow the natural increase rate (the difference between the number of live births and deaths, generally calculated over a year).

Don't let the name fool you; positive population checks are not good things. Positive population checks increased the crude death rate (or positively affected the CDR). War (World War II), disease (The Black Death and even COVID-19), and famine (Somalia) would've qualified as positive population checks from a statistical demographic standpoint. It should always be noted that each one of those "statistics" was a person who had a life as full and enriching as your own.

Malthus's intended message was that where population growth is concerned, antinatalist measures are sometimes necessary to prevent the horrific side effects of population increase.

Remember, the crude birth rate represents the number of live births per 1,000. The natural increase rate is the difference between the number of live births and deaths, which is generally calculated over a year.

Modernizing population growth theories

The ideas of Malthus and Marx have been expanded upon by demographers, geographers, economists, and cable news commentators (though I am not sure how much I'd trust these last ones). There have been many viewpoints on the subject, some more pessimistic than others.

Perhaps the most pessimistic of them, the words of caution offered by William Catton in his cornucopia theory warn of impending doom. A cornucopia is a mythical horn of plenty with limitless supplies, most often associated with Thanksgiving and a Hollywood movie of children murdering one another for the bemusement of social and political elites. (Neither of these are associated with the theory itself, but they help provide visuals.) Catton applied his cornucopia theory to how humans seemingly approached their relationship with the Earth. By observing how forests were being denuded, animals were harvested to extinction, carbon is being burned and released into the atmosphere, and land cultivated to the point it is no longer productive, it is not hard to envision why Catton had reason for despair. The problem is that our over-usage will eventually catch up with us. We need to be wise to understand our limits before we recognize that it is too late. That's what Catton was cautioning about as he applied his theory to the study of ecology and our relationship with the natural world around us.

Neo-Malthusian theories expand on Thomas Malthus's ideas by approaching resource usage from a more realistic perspective. Basically, Neo-Malthusians took Malthus's ideas and expanded them to all types of resources. Oil, housing, healthy environments to live in, humans need all of these. As they become increasingly scarce, competition for them increases. They'll point to things like Germany's directed attacks at the oil fields of the Soviet Union and Japan's attacks to secure raw materials as proof that countries will go to just as desperate measures to secure raw materials as they will for food. To understand the needs of a people, you need to consider far more than just food, especially in the modern era.

Another economist, Ester Boserup, held a bit more of an optimistic perspective of the future of humankind. Boserup was a 20th-century Danish theorizer looking at agriculture production. She did quite a lot throughout her long career, but we will focus on her work there since it is most relevant to our discussion here. She directly analyzed Malthus's ideas and recognized many of the same assertions that he was making. Her viewpoint, however, is that he greatly misrepresented human ingenuity. She cited pivotal developments in human history that seemingly came in the nick of time and avoided disaster. Boserup placed quite a lot of emphasis on the importance of technology.

We'll talk more about the Green Revolution in Chapter 16, but to give you a quick rundown, let me set the situation for you. India has endured a number of famines throughout its history, either due to environmental factors or imperialist reliance on cotton development, which does not do a lot of good when food stores dwindle. Famine seemingly came in cycles, carrying away thousands (if not millions) whenever it struck. Then, in the 1960s, a series of technological agricultural developments, collectively known as the *Green Revolution*, were introduced in India.

The effect was profound. India has shifted from cyclical famine to a food exporter of plenty. Sure, there are still periods of decreased supply, but the introduced technology has helped avert the continued patterns of famine. Beyond food, programs like the desalinization of seawater to convert it to usable drinking water or the conversion to green energies to break our reliance on dwindling fossil fuels are seen as examples of technologies that could help us divert from paths to future ecological population growth caused disasters.

It is still yet to be seen which theorizer is the most correct or whether a combination of those ideas is the solution. Regardless of whose ideas you subscribe to, there is a need to understand the trends and patterns of population growth to better plan for the future. Demographics are an important part of this, but so is understanding people's movements. The next chapter examines that topic further.

Chapter 7

Where the People Are Going

Humans move around . . . a lot! This is as true today as it's been at any other point in history. Whether moving within the same town or region or to another country, the patterns and reasons why people move are fairly timeless.

People from the United States tend to be among those who move the most. On average, someone from the United States will move 11 times throughout their life (closer to 17 times if you're like me), while people in many European countries average 4 moves in their lives. People move for many reasons — to start a new job, attend school, or be closer to family — and are subject to moving nearly any distance. Whatever the reason, the migration processes are bound to affect all of us at some point or another. Given how many times I've moved in my life so far, I consider myself a bit of an expert in the migration processes.

The statistics on migration can be very spotty, but it should come to no surprise that a lot of the numbers that are tracked are kept by moving companies. These numbers can be especially hard to come by for most countries unless there is an official designation for the migrants (refugees or internally displaced peoples, but we'll get into that more later). Many moving companies here in the US report that about 20-30 million people move within the country each year.

In this chapter, we'll be examining some of the terminology that geographers use in relation to migration and some of the trends and patterns in where people move presently and throughout history.

Trends and Patterns of Human Migration

The word "migration" sounds like something that should be used in the context of a nature documentary about a flock of birds. From a geographic perspective, however, it merely refers to the semi-permanent or permanent movement of people across space. Migration can be internal — within a country — or international. It should come as no surprise that internal migration is much more common than international migration, mainly because of the politics of migration. Usually, there are very few, if any, barriers that prevent migration within the same country. The usual limiting factors are finding housing and employment, though some countries, like China, have political hurdles that complicate migration processes.

When I was working in Shanghai and Beijing, most of my students were either Chinese students from outside the region or international students whose parents were there as time-contract workers. This allowed me to experience a couple of different types of migrations, including the Chunyun, the largest annual migration of humans globally. The international students could not really attend public schools where instruction was done in Chinese, so private schools like ours were the only option. My Chinese students were there for different reasons entirely:

>> Their parents wanted their children to go to a private school.

>> Our school offered a more direct path for them to attend a university in the United States, Europe, or Australia.

>> They had moved to the city (Shanghai or Beijing) from elsewhere in China. High school enrollment was based on where you were born. For example, if you were born in Hefei in the Anhui province, your public school placement was there. Because of the population constraints and the difficulties of accommodating the children of so many internal migrants, it was very difficult, if not impossible, to switch public schools. Instead, families who moved provinces would have to enroll their children in private schools like I worked in. I had very few students from the city I worked in. Instead, they came from cities like Xi'an, Nanjing, and Fujian and even as far away as the Inner Mongolia Autonomous Region.

Because of this policy, China has a large population of migrant workers who live in a large city, but their families live back in their hometowns. The educational aspect is part of this, but so is the influence of the cost of living. Cities in China are considerably more expensive than rural villages — to the point of being cost-prohibitive. It is cheaper if only the main wage earners travel to work in the cities, where there are sometimes dormitories provided for guest workers that are much cheaper than apartments. This policy creates one of the most interesting migration cases in the world. Every year during the Spring Festival Chinese New Year holiday, a large portion of the country's migrant workers return to their hometowns.

During the multi-week holiday, anywhere between 200 and 305 million people travel within the country in the world's largest annual migration. For the two years I lived in China, I avoided traveling within the country since the roads, train stations, and airports were absolutely jam-packed with people. I took the Chinese New Year holiday as an opportunity to travel outside the country since the international terminals were much less busy. The intense travel period has come to be known as *Chunyun*. One of the more infamous features of this heavy travel period is the intense multi-day traffic jams that travelers must endure. Yes, you saw that correctly: *multi-day traffic jams*. As I said, it is a good opportunity to travel outside the country, especially when you consider the main way to celebrate the holiday in the evenings is to shoot off fireworks at all hours of the night. It definitely made trying to fall asleep a difficult task.

We need to distinguish between immigrants and emigrants. Both are types of migrants, but they describe very particular aspects of migration. An emigrant is someone who has left a country or area. An immigrant is someone who moves into an area from somewhere else. They're titles that are completely situational and depend on perspective. So, let's say that someone migrates from Pakistan to Australia. They would be an immigrant in Australia and an emigrant from Pakistan. We'll use these terms in this chapter to talk about specific migration trends and relationships, so it's important to understand their differences.

While living in China, I became more familiar with another geographic concept connected to migration: the community of expatriates. An *expatriate*, or "expat" as often referred to, is someone living outside their native country. Many people who move away from their homelands do not intend for their new location to become their permanent home. So, they'll build up a community based on their shared experience of being foreigners and experience a bit of home. Some bars and restaurants specifically cater to expats, serving food and drinks that remind them of home — usually at prices much higher than could be paid at a local place, though the taste of home is often worth the expense. Having some comfort food, watching hometown sports teams on television, or even just playing a game of pool can be well worth it after a long week living in a foreign place. One of my particular favorites was joining in on a Sunday morning soccer meet-up at the British International school, which was part of the British expat community's process of making Shanghai feel a little more like home. (Sunday morning soccer, er, football, is a common pastime in the UK).

The life of an expat regularly led to some interesting experiences, and sometimes, it was a case of experimenting together (see Figure 7-1).

FIGURE 7-1: Some sort of songbird egg for dinner in Hangzhou, China

The experience of expats differs depending on where they're from and where they've moved to. Sometimes, they can integrate without much difficulty. My experience in China as a blond, very obviously American person made it impossible to blend in. Expat communities offer a chance to blend in when they're otherwise unable to.

TECHNICAL STUFF

If you really want to be technical about naming a group of people from a particular background in an area outside their homeland, one of the terms you could use is *diaspora*, which is often used to refer to large populations displaced from their homelands and clustered elsewhere. Expats could be considered a form of diaspora, but one of the historical examples of a large diaspora was the Jewish diaspora during the 8th century BCE. Subsequent conquests of the Judea region by the Assyrians, Babylonians, and Romans, followed by a continued struggle between Christian and Muslim empires, led to the dispersion of Jewish inhabitants over the Mediterranean region and Eastern Europe. They were "othered" in many regions because they were seen as outsiders who had migrated there and were frequently singled out for persecution.

Migration now

It's just impossible to talk about all the current forms of migration. Instead, I will explain some more recent trends and patterns, many of which are connected to massive strife — a historically large driver of migration.

TIP

Chapter 8 discusses migration's push and pull factors.

Migration trends toward Europe

One of the most monumental developments in migration history is the Schengen Zone, established as part of the European Union (EU). The Schengen Zone had a limited existence before the Eurozone was established in 1999, but since its initial creation, it has expanded to include much of Western and Central Europe. The Schengen agreement established something previously unheard of — open borders between member States. Since the inception of the modern Nation-State after the Treaty of Westphalia in 1648, one of the most basic definitions of what made an established country was the control over the flow of people across its borders. True, there have been varying amounts of the ability to regulate migration in and out of a country, but completely opening the country to migration from outsiders is a very rare concept. Granted, you need to be from a Schengen country in the first place, but if you are, you have the right to free movement (to live, work, or study) within the whole of the Schengen Zone.

TIP

The European Union comprises 27 member states: Austria, Belgium, Bulgaria, Croatia, Republic of Cyprus, Czech Republic, Denmark, Estonia, Finland, France, Germany, Greece, Hungary, Ireland, Italy, Latvia, Lithuania, Luxembourg, Malta, Netherlands, Poland, Portugal, Romania, Slovakia, Slovenia, Spain, and Sweden. Notably, the United Kingdom withdrew from the EU in 2020 in what became known as *Brexit*.

This has actually helped dramatically decrease the number of Europeans looking to migrate to the Americas or elsewhere. Many European States also offer tax-funded education to their nationals free of any additional costs as long as they can pay for housing.

So, why would Europeans choose to come to the United States, where they would have to pay out of pocket for their college education while they could get a quality college education anywhere within the Schengen Area for no additional costs? The easy answer: They don't because of the Erasmus Learning Agreement (OLA) that allowed Eurozone nationals to migrate anywhere within the zone for schooling.

University towns like Utrecht, Cologne, and Uppsala see students from around Europe move there to pursue their education, leading many institutions to shift their manner of instruction because of this. Some will have a limited selection of classes not exclusively taught in the country's native language (Spanish in Spain's schools, French in France's schools, and so on), but English as a *de facto* universal language is becoming increasingly common. Many institutions offer entire English study programs to be as accommodating to as many students as possible.

What is kind of funny about all of that is that the largest English native-speaking country, the United Kingdom, has now left the Eurozone. The Republic of Ireland remains the only native English-speaking country in the zone. However, while traveling around the Eurozone, it might surprise you that people in countries that *are* part of the EU are not native speakers. I remember going to Sweden and talking to someone I thought was from Wisconsin, but they were native Swedish. Their accent was just very similar to that of a Wisconsinite.

HOW WAS BREXIT CONNECTED TO MIGRATION'S IMPACT ON THE BRITISH ISLES?

The United Kingdom left the European Union partly because of the EU's migration policies. Europe has been experiencing a mass influx of refugees who have been making it to the shores of Britain. The Eurozone established the Common European Asylum System in 1999.

Recognizing that most asylum seekers who reached Europe were primarily entering the Southern States like Italy or Greece, the EU wanted to distribute the responsibility of managing asylum seekers throughout the Eurozone equally. Each country was meant to take on a portion of asylum seekers. Factions within the United Kingdom opposed this policy, citing fears about the origins of these asylum seekers (primarily those coming from the Middle East or Africa) to develop support for the British Exit from the European Union. Brexit, as it has come to be called, officially went into effect on January 31, 2020, with no official agreement between the United Kingdom and EU on how that would actually work. Seemingly overnight, the free movement agreements were wiped out, making the negotiation process especially complicated when establishing a new relationship between the UK and the EU. This has been especially frustrating for the Republic of Ireland and British Northern Ireland. They share a relatively small island but are divided between two countries whose relationship can best be described as complicated.

These complications have renewed talks of the Republic of Ireland absorbing Northern Ireland to help uncomplicate the issues brought upon them by Brexit, which is regarded as a problem for the UK region of England. Another region in the UK, Scotland, has made rumblings about whether it should be more connected to England and the rest of the UK or the EU. These rumblings are especially centered on the strength of the UK's economy compared to that of the Eurozone's economy. Scotland and England have not always been the best of friends. Historically, Scotland has been buddies with France in what they call their *Auld Alliance*. Ireland's and Scotland's migratory interests had long been a moot point because they were in the Eurozone, allowing free movement within Ireland and between the UK and France, rendering their major concerns irrelevant. Migration complications have reignited some questions about whether Scotland and Northern Ireland should remain in the UK.

The politics of migration

These examples from the UK and the EU just go to show how much political factors affect the processes of migration. Political decisions can help facilitate or hinder the flow of immigrants into a country. In fact, just like with Brexit, the question of migration can lead to a change in the political landscape. President Donald Trump came to power in 2016 based largely on his anti-immigration rhetoric. President Trump received a lot of attention for his strong opposition to immigration from Africa, Central and South America, and the Middle East while promoting migration from European countries like Norway.

President Trump also took issue with chain migration because it offered a possible avenue for people to "skip the line" of the normal migration processes to the United States. The US offers a family reunification pathway through which US citizens can use their status as citizens to help their family members migrate to the US more quickly. What is somewhat perplexing about Trump's criticism of the program is that Melania's (his wife) parents could migrate to the United States using the same family reunification program he was criticizing.

TIP

Chain migration describes the kind of migration that occurs after migrants from a particular place follow other migrants to a particular destination.

To be fair, the United States' southern border is where most of the encounters with undocumented migrants are taking place. Yes, some of the migrants attempting to cross the Southern border are from Mexico, but if you look at the numbers, the recent trend has been more people have actually been moving back to Mexico from the United States than are coming to the US from Mexico. More recently, many migrants have been coming from economically and politically unstable countries in South or Central America. States like El Salvador, Guatemala, and Venezuela with intense economic or political collapse (often resulting in increased gang activity) have resulted in thousands of people making the dangerous trek toward the US.

TIP

I encourage you to read up on the source of any political or economic unrest that causes people to leave. Here in the US, for example, we hear a lot about people who want to come here without paying much attention to why they want to leave their homelands. In some cases, their reasons for leaving are connected to conditions in their home countries that the US government partially created. We'll talk more about refugees and asylum seekers later because these are special political designations and will get much attention in Chapter 8.

Many of these migrants ultimately want to end up right back where they started — back in their home countries — even though those places aren't safe for them. Many migrants, out of desperation, end up leaving their home countries and risking the trek through scorching-hot deserts and thick forests. Along the way, they risk dangerous animals, extreme temperatures, perilous trails, and those who would take advantage of them. Human trafficking is a big problem since they are traveling without proper documents. It is extremely common for criminal organizations to pick them up and essentially force them into modern forms of slavery. That's before they even get to the US border and encounter all the difficulties involved in making the crossing, legally or illegally. Still, thousands of people attempt this trek every year, though the true number is unknown because of the difficulty of tracking something that is happening clandestinely.

Much the same can be said for the Southern border of Europe. Instead of a river or border wall to cross, migrants from war-torn countries like Syria, Afghanistan, and Northeast Africa attempt to make their way across the Aegean Sea between Türkiye (Turkey) and Greece. Also, many try to cross the Mediterranean Sea into Southern Italy. We'll discuss these cases later, but millions of people have been moving this way since about 2001.

Figure 7-2 shows a sign in London's Luton Airport with instructions for newly arrived migrants from Ukraine. The migration process for most refugees or asylum seekers can be quite chaotic. In some cases, they're fleeing for their lives with only what they can carry. Without being able to plan for their migration, they may arrive in a country like the United Kingdom without having researched the process of claiming refugee status. Signs like these help direct incoming refugees where to go to start the process.

FIGURE 7-2:
A sign in London's Luton Airport with instructions for newly arrived migrants

Ethnicity and migratory patterns

In Chapter 13, we will look at the processes of establishing borders. One of the more unfortunate side effects of establishing borders is the division of ethnic groups into different political entities, dividing historically connected communities and leading to the development of some rather interesting migration case studies.

In Central Africa, the Maasai are one such group that is divided because of the establishment of the modern states of Kenya and Tanzania. The Maasai are a nomadic herding group that runs their cattle over the grasslands of Eastern Africa. Kenyan and Tanzanian policies toward the Maasai have created difficulties for them. The Maasai people have historically migrated to different pastures and open areas across East Africa. Recently, however, Kenya and Tanzania have been trying to adopt policies meant to further constrict the practice to get the Maasai to accept a more sedentary life, which has been met with much resistance. However, it is still common to see the Maasai moving their herds along the side of the road and even into the national parks in search of grazing lands.

A similar sort of conflict has played out in many parts of the world. The struggle between Indigenous rights and traditions and the formation of modern nation-states has almost universally led to the suppression of Indigenous rights. We'll talk about some of the patterns from a historical context in the next section, "Migration in the past," but these are still very relevant issues. The Sami people of Northern Europe still rely on migratory reindeer herds as a way of life. There are far fewer complications between Norway, Sweden, and Finland because they allow free movement of the Sami people. Russia, however, is a different story. Norway and Finland share borders with Russia, and they're not on the best of terms with one another. The Russians charge Norway a couple thousand-dollar fine for each Sami reindeer that wanders into Russian territory. To limit these fines, Norway has constructed a "reindeer fence" along its Russian border to prevent the accidental movement of reindeer into Russian territory.

Migration in the past

There is simply no way to discuss every significant migration event throughout history. Instead, I'm just going to point out a couple of case studies to highlight how other geographic forces have affected migration patterns over time. Migration has been occurring as long as humans have been, well, human. We started as nomadic hunter-gatherers and were that for most of our history until the Neolithic agriculture and the development of agriculture (something we'll discuss in Chapter 16 when we discuss agricultural geography). The establishment of cities and agriculture transitioned most cultural groups to be more sedentary. While some ethnic and cultural groups still retain their nomadic migratory life-styles, they're quickly dwindling. Groups like the San of Namibia and the Chukchi of Russia still retain some of their nomadic migratory patterns to keep their traditional culture alive.

Figure 7-3 shows a historical marker for the Fort Laramie–Fort Robinson Trail near Harrison, Nebraska. The marker explains the conflict between the westward expansion of the United States and the Native inhabitants of the land. Fort Laramie was established to protect the flow of migrants from the East into the Great Plains. They were often taking up land traditionally owned by Native American tribes, who were often threatened by the arrival of migrants. These forts later served as points for the allotment of resources to the Native Americans restricted to reservations who no longer were able to continue supporting themselves using their traditional migratory hunting patterns.

FIGURE 7-3:
A historical marker for the Fort Laramie-Fort Robinson Trail near Harrison, Nebraska

Indigenous Peoples: Restricted movement, restricted culture

Early in the colonization process of the Americas, it became very evident to the European (and subsequent continental) empires that the Indigenous peoples would not easily hand over their homelands. The United States has relied on a process of establishing Indian Reservations, while Canada has relied on Indian Reserves. The general idea of both is about the same. Land was set aside for the Indigenous peoples to be able to live in return for payment or some other negotiated settlement.

In the United States, a great deal of coercion and outright deception was used to force the Native peoples to sign over the rights to their lands.

Before the reservations, many tribes spread themselves over vast portions of what is now the United States and Canada. The United States' concept of Manifest Destiny and the desire to hold dominion over the lands between the Atlantic and Pacific Oceans led them to establish a series of treaties with different tribes to create reservations in return for payment and other stipulations. The reservations were an attempt by the United States government to constrict the nomadic tribes to comparatively tiny areas and begin the process of "Americanizing" them. Sometimes, farm equipment was specifically included in the treaty terms as a means of helping the tribes establish United States–style agricultural practices instead of the hunting and gathering that many tribes were still practicing.

REMEMBER

It should be noted that not all peoples of the Americas were nomadic. Large cities like Cusco (in modern-day Peru), Tenochtitlan (modern-day Mexico City), and Cahokia (outside modern-day Saint Louis, Missouri) rivaled even some of the European cities at their height. Crops were cultivated by many of the tribes through-out the Americas. Many tribes had their lands severely constricted by encroaching settlers, heightening the conflict between them and the native peoples. In 1830, President Andrew Jackson authorized the Indian Removal Act to relocate American Indians from east of the Mississippi to unsettled lands in the west. The Trail of Tears was the infamous culmination of the Indian Removal Act in which the Chero-kee were forcibly removed from the lush forests of the Southeast United States to the deserts of what is now Oklahoma. Andrew Jackson remains a controversial fig-ure, with many Native people still refusing to use the $20 bills that bear his likeness.

Some tribes, especially those in the Great Plains region, relied on huge tracts of land to support their populations. Tribes followed animal herds, especially bison, and usually spent their winters off the prairies if possible. The establishment of reservations put an end to the practice, along with the wholesale slaughter of the bison herds. Famine and disease impacted some of the tribes so harshly during the transition to a sedentary lifestyle that some of them famously rebelled. Leaders like Crazy Horse, Little Crow, and Geronimo led rebellions against the reservation system. Ultimately, tribes were constricted to the reservations, and their migra-tory patterns were so disrupted that it arguably led to the irreparable extinction of many tribe's livelihoods. However, many of the tribes are still in legal battles with the United States government over the terms of the treaties. These battles can often end up in the Supreme Court, where tribes actually have had some degree of success in upholding their legal rights.

TIP

There is a great resource on the Internet at native-lands.ca that shows all the original homelands of Indigenous peoples worldwide. I frequently use this site in my classes when discussing the distribution of historical populations and the incompatibility between modern borders and ethnic groups.

An empire divided: India and Pakistan

In 1947, the establishment of the States of India and Pakistan began as the British dissolved their imperial hold over the area. While it was initially well received, it quickly dissolved into the reality of trying to settle the populations of the two newly formed states, making an understanding of demographics crucial. Pakistan was established as a predominantly Muslim State, while India was set up as a Hindu-majority State. The problem is that there was no easy dividing line since the populations were so closely intermixed.

Also, religious and ethnic minority groups were mixed in, so there was no easy solution for dividing the lands to reflect the composition of the populations. So, when India and Pakistan were formally created, there was a bit of a grace period to allow the Muslim population of India to migrate to Pakistan and the Hindi to migrate to Pakistan. Shockingly (said totally sarcastically), a chaotic situation erupted when millions of people tried to move at once with little pre-warning.

There are no official counts of how many people migrated when the partition of India and Pakistan was made in August of 1947, but the best estimates are between 14-18 million people migrated because of the partition. The chaotic nature contributed to many difficulties (to put it lightly) in the transfer process. An estimated 1 million people died during the transition period, either from hardship or violence. This whole process fostered unease that continues to this day between the two countries. India and Pakistan have been involved in many conflicts with each other, which is especially concerning since they both have nuclear weapons. Much of the continued tension between the two States is due to the status of some of the border regions, particularly Jammu, Kashmir, and Punjab. Also, there are concerns about how Muslims have been treated in India and the status of non-Muslims in Pakistan. The borders have been tense and made more (or less, depending on how you want to look at it) complicated with the establishment of East Pakistan (now called Bangladesh) in 1955.

Even with the best intentions, the situation devolved and has been the source of ongoing questions of demography stemming from the constriction of migration due to the establishment of borders. Tensions are still high between India and Pakistan and between India and Bangladesh — even to this day.

The Great Famine as a push factor: Escaping hunger

Between 1845 and 1852, disease struck the potato crops of Ireland. Potatoes had been imported to Ireland from the Americas and served as an abundant and cheap food source that many of the island's poorest populations relied on. Because potatoes grew rather well in Ireland, they were planted in great abundance. As the main crop, Ireland practiced a sort of monocropping where much of the caloric intake of the Irish people relied on this one crop.

When the Phytophthora infestation struck, it spread quickly through the crops, essentially causing the potatoes to rot and die. Without the main food source, the island descended into a famine known as the *Great Famine* or the *Irish Potato Famine*. An estimated 1 million people died during the famine, which is significant given that the island's population was only about 8.5 million in 1845.

With deaths from the failing potato crops rising so quickly, many people left the island, hoping to escape the famine. About 1 million people left Ireland during the Great Famine, primarily moving to England, which was easier since it was all the dominion of Great Britain at the time. The Republic of Ireland would not be formed until later in the 20th century, somewhat because of the potato famine, because Irish people never fully forgave England for not doing more during the Great Famine. Along with England, many Irish people traveled to the United States. Boston was a main port of entry for many of the newly arrived immigrants, many of whom decided to stay there, establishing a heavy Irish identity that remains today.

Processes of Migration

Migration comes in all distances and scales, but many forms can be bunched based on some commonalities. Sometimes, migration occurs because of family, jobs, or even climate. All the same, the different migration patterns follow semi-predictable patterns to the point that geographers have come up with terms (or theories) linking different types of migration.

Migration patterns

Because migration is such a common part of being a human, many of you will have a lot of firsthand experience with many of the terms used in this chapter. Migration is a deeply personal experience, so I will discuss these concepts in a way that is specific enough to understand but vague enough not to be so specific that it narrows your thinking.

Distance decay: Closeness brings togetherness

The concept of distance decay is really quite simple. The basic idea is that interaction decreases as physical distance increases. In geography, we deal with many theories and models but not many laws, so introducing a law is always exciting. Tobler's First Law of Geography states that near things are more related than far things. So, things closer to one another will have more commonalities with one another than they would with an area much further away. These commonalities will largely depend on the forces of migration and the interaction of people between spaces. People will interact more with people who are closer to them. I'm sure most of us can think of at least one friend we lost touch with when one of us moved. This is connected to distance decay: People will most likely stay in better contact with people located closer to them. If people are separated, there is less opportunity to remain in contact.

In the realm of migration, this is a fairly straightforward application. Migration between near places happens more frequently than migration between far places. Using this logic, there should be more migration transactions between Toronto, Ontario, and London, Ontario, in Eastern Canada than between London, Ontario, and Victoria, British Columbia, in the far western part of Canada. These interactions are affected by the size of cities, but these will be further discussed in Chapter 9 when we talk about the Gravity Model. The basic concept of the Gravity Model is that larger cities have more "pull" than smaller cities. People are more likely to migrate to larger cities than smaller cities.

Step migration: Working toward a final destination

Step migration is the idea that migration happens in steps. People migrate in a series of moves to reach their final destination. On a small scale, this could be that people ultimately want to work their way into a nice, big house in the suburbs but must live in apartments and starter homes first. Step migration can also happen over multiple years. During the Westward Expansion phase of American history, many European settlers had the ultimate goal of making their way to the Great Plains to take advantage of the farmland there. First, however, they might have migrated to an Eastern seaboard city like Montreal, New York, or Boston. Some might have ended their process there, while others migrated almost immediately to the Plains. Still others delayed and finally made their way after a couple of years.

The steps may not always be known ahead of time by the person migrating. They may have no idea where they're ultimately going to end up. Or, it is possible they had a plan and stuck to it. What is so difficult about this concept is that life has a habit of getting in the way of our plans and changing our direction for better or worse.

Guest workers: Working for the chance to go home

I will lump together two terms — *guest worker* and *time-contract worker* — because of how well-connected they are to one another, and they're really of the same spirit. In essence, both refer to the migration of people to complete a job. Time-contract and guest workers are similar in that they are both economic migrants.

TIME-CONTRACT WORKERS

A time-contract worker has a set deadline — perhaps a project in another city that will only take a year — leading them to move for the duration of the contract and then move to the next location. That's how I ended up in China as a time-contract worker, where the duration of my visa depended on how long I would be working there. When I decided to move back to the US, I did not have that much time after the school year ended, and my visa ended, allowing me to stay in the country. That is how many time-contract gigs go. You're there to complete a job; once the job is done, your reason for being there is also done.

A very common form of time-contract worker is a military deployment. Members of the armed forces move around frequently, both internally and internationally. When on foreign deployments, they're there to complete a job. Once the job is done or their deployment ends, they are rotated back home or to a different deployment. The US military used to use indefinite deployments. Now, it restricts deployments to about a year and a half.

GUEST WORKERS

Guest workers move to a different area to work but not necessarily setting up permanent residency. For example, let's say you live in an area that is not doing as well economically, but they still need to be able to support themselves and their family, so they move to try to make some more money in a different area. They'll often send a lot of the money back to their original hometowns to help support their families there or build up their savings. These are called *remittances*. In 2022, the World Bank estimated that about $647 billion US dollars were transferred as remittances globally.

For example, some Turkish people migrated to West Germany after World War II. Germany's population greatly reduced due to the war, especially younger men. The country needed workers to help rebuild the economy, so it invited guest workers from Turkey. People from Turkey migrated to other countries in Europe as well, but the majority ended up in Germany. Ethnic Turks now make up the largest immigrant community in Europe. The problem is that Germany has citizenship by blood, not by birthright, meaning you don't receive the full benefits of being born in Germany if your bloodlines are not German. In fact, there are ethnic Turks whose families have been in Germany for multiple generations and still don't have German citizenship. They're still treated as guest workers. They can live and work there but are still treated as outsiders in many ways. It has led to many questions, especially since the next generation of migrants are coming to Central Europe from places like Syria, Afghanistan, and Ukraine.

This is not at all unique to Germany, however. Throughout much of the history of development and the demographic shifts of States, highly developed countries have frequently had to rely on the low-paid labor of migrant workers (as dishwashers, custodians, factory workers, construction laborers, and so on). As States progress upward in the Demographic Transition Model (from Chapter 5), there is still a need for lower-wage laborers. When the Natural Increase Rate drops, countries will often lessen restrictions on immigration to increase the supply of workers who are usually only offered opportunities in lower-wage careers. Economically speaking, this is usually a boost for the population of native workers, who are often propelled into managerial middle-class positions overseeing the newly arrived migrant workforce.

Chain migration: Getting the family back together

Let me paint a scenario here for you about a repeating situation worldwide. Jens is a boy born near Bonn in Western Germany in about 1880. He was having a rough go of finding good work, and little agricultural land was available. He received information saying that Argentina was looking for workers and that plenty of land was available to set up his own farm. He checked it out and boarded a ship to Buenos Aires, Argentina. Upon his arrival, everything that he ever imagined appeared to be true. Plenty of land was available, the city was vibrant and growing, and land opportunities were seemingly endless. He wrote back home to his friends and family, told them about the terrific opportunities, and encouraged them to head that way. Some take him up on it.

When his friends and family moved to Argentina, they didn't choose a random place. Obviously, they moved close to Jens since he was already there and could help get them settled. The German people who moved to be close to Jens also wrote home to their friends and family to encourage them to move there as well. Soon, a whole crew of German people moved to Buenos Aires. They set up their own shops, schools, churches, and even political organizations. The city, or at least their section, took on the flavor of the "old country" and became a little Germany.

What I just described was the process of chain migration. It's not scary at all; it's just a process through which one person (or a small group) moves to a new area and then encourages others to follow them. This creates a chain linking two places by the flows of migration. Although the situation above was fictionalized, the process is not. There is a very large German presence across South America, specifically Argentina, because of this very similar experience. This is how ethnic enclaves (discussed in Chapters 9 and 13) are created. They're little pockets within cities or regions with high concentrations of people from a particular migrant community.

Beyond the Germans, these processes played out for most ethnic communities at one point or another. The Chinese are particularly famous for migrating and congregating to form new communities among the emigrant populations. The Chinatowns found in most major cities worldwide have a unique feel that goes back to the expats who originally clustered there. Italians in New York, Irish in Boston, Scandinavians in Minnesota, Polish in Chicago, and the chain migration processes have influenced the formation of the cultural landscape at almost every scale.

In Britain, the post-war era of chain migration was marked by the docking of the HMT Windrush (see Figure 7-4). Full of migrants from the Caribbean, especially Jamaica, the migrants on the Windrush is a stark example of the beginning of a chain migratory pattern. Once established, the people who had arrived on the HMT Windrush encouraged their friends, family, and others from the Caribbean to migrate to the UK.

FIGURE 7-4: A monument to the HMT Windrush in London's Waterloo Station

More recently, chain migration has been an influential force for many people:

>> People from Northern and Western Africa ended up in France.

>> India and Pakistan communities established strong connections to the United Kingdom (along with many other communities from the old Empire).

>> Japanese people migrated to Brazil. (Yes, you read that right. Brazil is home to the largest community of people of Japanese descent outside Japan.)

In the United States, chain migration has become controversial because of the family reunification method of migration. The waiting list to migrate to the United States is years long because of its quota system, which will be discussed in the next chapter. The process is drastically sped up if you have a family member in the US who is a citizen, and the move would be for reunification. Recently, a large influx of children attempting to migrate to the United States has occurred because their parents want their children to establish citizenship first so the parents can then join them legally. Family reunification operates very similarly to chain migration, but since it's now a political fighting point, you might start hearing about it more often. Just remember that it has been going on for years and years.

Cyclical migration: What moves out eventually comes back

To this point, we've been talking about migration as an A-to-B kind of thing where B represents where someone is ultimately meant to end up. A-to-B-to-A migration occurs with time-contract and guest workers. With step migration, it occurs in an A-to-B-to-C form.

Now, let's discuss the cyclical migration patterns best described as A-to-B, B-to-A, A-to-B, and so on. These can occur over a year, multiple years, or even within a week or a day.

Migration does not have to be a movement from one residence to another. One of the most common forms of migration is the cyclical migration patterns in commuting to work or school. Some people's commutes are as short as from their bedroom to their home office space (those lucky people!). Some commutes can take multiple hours per day. Still others have commutes that would be too long to make in a single day, so they commute on Monday morning (or Sunday night) and then return home on Friday. It is relatively short compared to many of the other forms of migration we've discussed, but commuting is a form of cyclical migration all the same.

Another form of cyclical migration is the seasonal patterns of movement that people go through during a year. These are semi-nomadic people who move because of weather changes. This can be for leisure or livelihood. One of the first examples is the seasonal farm workers who migrate from place to place depending on agricultural cycles. These workers may spend one week in one place helping with the harvest of watermelons, then move to another place to help with the wheat harvest, before heading back to their starting place to help in an orchard before starting the cycle all over again the next year. This is actually a fairly common pathway for people who want to see quite a bit of Australia. They'll spend time migrating from place to place and then restart the cycle as long as the work holds up.

Nomadic herders are another great example of cyclical migrators who will have their summer grazing and wintering grounds. They'll move their herds (or follow them) from each place yearly, as they have been doing for generations. This is especially true in the Northern Tundra, the Central Asian Steppe, and the Tropical Grasslands of the Equatorial region. In tropical areas, the migratory patterns follow the rains instead of seeking to escape the heaviest snows. A special form of herding migration occurs in the mountains, where farmers will move their herds up or down in elevation throughout a season or even daily. This form of migration is called *transhumance* and is especially practiced in the mountainous regions of South America.

The last major form of cyclical migration is mostly popular with retired people. This is the migration between more temperate areas in the summer and warmer tropical or subtropical areas during the winter. Mimicking the migratory patterns of seasonal bird species, this form of migration is rightly referred to as *snowbirding*. The "snowbirds" flock to places like Florida, Alabama, Arizona, or California in the United States, where they can escape the harshest parts of winter and enjoy their retirement in a nice, warm place. Then, during the summers, they can return to their hometowns to be with their friends and families. It's kind of a best-of-both-worlds situation.

Ravenstein's Laws of Migration

While Karl Marx was making his observations in central England in the mid-19th century, another member of the German diaspora was also developing theories based on observations. Instead of living and working conditions, Ernst Ravenstein developed his Laws of Migration based on people's movements and migratory patterns.

TIP

I encourage my students to see if they can find examples of these laws in news articles concerning different forms of migration present in current events. Try it!

Following are Ravenstein's Laws of Migration:

1. Most migration takes place over short distances, which connects to the ideas of the distance decay model. A closer migration relationship exists between near places than between far places.

2. Most migration takes place in steps. Not surprisingly, this connects to the step migration discussion earlier in this chapter. Ravenstein observed that most migrants gradually made their way to their final destination and rarely moved directly to where they wanted to end up eventually.

3. The further people move, the more likely they will migrate to an urban area. If you're moving from India to England, you're not as likely to end up in a rural cottage in Yorkshire as you would in London. Much of this has to do with the location of economic opportunities for migrants and the processes of chain migration.

4. As migrants move into an area, this will create migration in the opposite direction. It definitely won't be the opposite and equal reaction of Newtonian physics, but as people move to the United States from the Middle East, there will be people who move to the Middle East from the United States as awareness increases. In fact, I know quite a few people who have migrated to places like Dubai to teach students there and help prepare them to move to the United States.

5. I would be interested to see how well this holds up anymore, but in Ravenstein's observations, he noted that rural people were more likely to migrate than urban dwellers. At least in my experience, I would highly question this being true today because it seems people in cities must move frequently because of shifting rent prices or because they want to be closer or farther from work.

6. In my earlier Germany-to-Argentina example, I purposefully used the German male name Jens because it connects to Ravenstein's observation that people who move long distances are more often male. Within the country, however, he noted that women were more migratory.

7. This one should come as no shock and hopefully a bit of relief, but more migrants are adults. Some adults will still move if they have children, but it certainly adds many complications to moving with children. That is why it is quite common for people in the United States to move as soon as their last child moves out because it is much less complicated.

8. Ravenstein said cities grow more by the processes of migration than by the rate of natural increase. I don't question this one, at least in the United States or Western Europe, because a lot of demographic data supports it.

9. When the going gets tough, the tough get going is how the saying goes. And with it, so goes the patterns of migration. When times are bad, migration trends downward, but migration will tick upward when the economy is good. And that is because of the final observation.

10. Migration is primarily due to economic reasons. Think of it this way: People move for jobs (clearly economic), education (so they or their children can get better jobs), or cost of living (so they can stretch the value of their money). These are just a couple of reasons, but all are economically based.

Chapter 8

Why the People Are Going

In Chapter 7, we established the basics of migration; in this chapter, we'll discuss two types of migration: voluntary and involuntary:

» **Voluntary:** Voluntary migration occurs when people have a lot of say in why they're migrating. For example, perhaps they are migrating to improve their situation, though that's almost universally true in any kind of migration.

» **Involuntary:** Involuntary or forced migration is caused by dire circumstances beyond the control of the migrants forced to emigrate. Staying put is not an option since doing so could mean severe hardship or death.

I've divided this chapter into these two categories and will use other migration examples not discussed in other chapters. I'll also connect what we discuss in this chapter with the examples in Chapter 7.

REMEMBER

While reading this chapter, remember that real people are attached to the ideas. Many people are affected by things like slavery, famine, or war and have been forced to seek safety outside their homelands as refugees or asylum seekers. These people had/have lives as enriching as anyone else's. It's easy to get lost in the numbers, but remember that each migrant had their own family, friends, hopes, and dreams.

One story that comes to mind is of a child who became known as the "Red-Shirt Boy." In September 2015, photos of this young Syrian boy's body began circulating on the Internet. He'd washed ashore near the Turkish resort of Bodrum while trying to make his way across the Mediterranean Sea to Greece — just another of the thousands of people who have met such a fate trying to escape war, extreme poverty, terrorism, persecution, famine, and any other number of reasons. Eventually, we learned his name was Alan Kurdi (Shenu) and that his mother and brother had also died. Worse still, they were victims of human traffickers who take advantage of those desperately trying to escape war-torn Syria by charging exorbitant prices for a spot on a patchy, overfilled boat with low chances of reaching safety. Alan's father survived and shared their story, humanizing Alan. Another photo of Alan emerged — a happy young boy in the same red shirt on a playground. The story sparked a huge international response as many countries sought to aid refugees trying to reach the stability of European States. Conflicts elsewhere and political pandering have caused public attention to shift, but the struggles of these people just trying to live their lives go on.

WARNING

There is a lot of discussion about the taking and sharing of images like that of the red-shirt boy. On the one hand, they can help convey the seriousness of the situation. On the other hand, there is something to be said about respecting the dignity of people by not sharing photos of their strife and death. I have elected not to share images of Alan. Much controversy surrounds Western media, which widely distributes photos of human suffering when taken in places like Asia, Africa, or Less Developed Countries (LDCs) but blurs similar images if taken in Europe or North America. As Alan's story has shown, migration is a human story and a tale of movement and relocation. Behind each statistic is a person. Please remember that.

Going by Choice

We will discuss why people migrate using this acronym: ESPE (economic, social, political, environmental). When discussing migration by choice, we will operate under the assumption that if people don't choose to migrate, they'll still be able to continue living in relative order. They may not be as comfortable as they'd like and suffer hardships, but it is not necessarily paramount for them to remove themselves from their present location. Someone who moves to get a better job is moving voluntarily. Even if their job does not necessarily pay that much, as long as they can still subsist, their movement is a voluntary migration. In popular media, the term "economic migrant" is commonly used as a catch-all phrase. In academic speech, however, the term does not work for describing migrants who involuntarily move for economic reasons. This is an important distinction to make and can only be assessed on a situation-by-situation basis.

Reasons for migration

When examining migration, we need to understand why migrants emigrate from an area; we refer to these reasons as *push factors*. We also need to understand what brings immigrants to an area, so not surprisingly, we refer to these as *pull factors*. Both push and pull factors are highly individualized and are specific to each person or group. What may be a push factor for some people may be a pull factor for others. Many people I knew who moved away from Minnesota treated the cold, snowy winters as a push factor motivating them to move. However, the winters are one of the things I miss most about living up north, and the thought of consistently hot weather fills me with absolute dread.

Often, people choose to migrate for a combination of factors, not necessarily just one. What may be a push factor for some may be a pull factor for others.

REMEMBER

Economic push-pull factors: For the reward!

As German geographer Ernst Ravenstein noted in his theories on migration (see Chapter 7), most migration occurs for economic reasons. High-wage-earning jobs are one of the reasons why places like Canada, Western Europe, Australia, and the United States are high up on the list of desirable places to move. Even if those jobs aren't perceived that way by the current inhabitants of those places, workers of those jobs might make vastly higher amounts than people working similar jobs in other countries.

TIP

While working in China, I was making an admittedly low income compared to the average wage of a teacher in the United States, but because the cost of living was much lower, I had a few luxuries I couldn't afford here in the United States. Most of us expats had an aiye — which translates to "auntie" — who served as a weekly maid because we could afford one. We ate out a lot since restaurants were cheap (and our kitchens were not usually much more than a hot plate and microwave). We also traveled a lot, with most of us jetting away to far-off locations on our longer breaks thanks to our expendable income. When I transferred back to the United States, I got a laughably small raise and could no longer afford any of those things I had grown accustomed to while living in China.

Much of the rural-to-urban migration occurs because economic opportunities in the cities are unavailable in the rural areas. As we'll discuss in Chapter 18, factories are predominantly located in urban centers for easy access to the workforce there. In rural areas, the supply of laborers is smaller, so a factory is less likely to be located there.

Along with the direct influence of a new job, other economic factors can lead to people migrating. If the cost of living is really high, that might persuade people to move to a different area. For this reason, many retired people on fixed incomes from More Developed Countries (MDCs) move to places like Costa Rica or Thailand. They might not be able to afford as much on their pension or retirement funds as they could in an LDC or even a lower MDC. Urban areas are also attractive for migration because even though their living costs are higher, they usually have a better education infrastructure than rural areas.

So, while schools may not seem economical, they will eventually lead to better economic opportunities (or even better economic opportunities for their children), so I've included schooling in this section. Of course, this also means that places without well-developed educational or economic infrastructure will act as a push factor that encourages people to move to other areas where those opportunities exist.

Cost of living, availability of jobs, and educational infrastructure are some main reasons spurring migration, but other economic-based push and pull factors exist. Some states or countries will have a low income tax rate designed to attract workers with the promise that their take-home pay will be much higher. Housing costs — part of one's cost of living — should also be mentioned since people often find themselves moving to places based purely on the fact that they can afford a house or apartment where they're headed.

Social push-pull factors: For the family!

Social migration mostly refers to a move designed to bring one closer to their friends or family, and the degree to which this is a push-pull factor depends on the person. Also, people sometimes migrate for social reasons because they want to be closer to people their age, part of ethnic or cultural groups, or closer to entertainment venues.

Friends and family are a fairly straightforward explanation for social migration. In Chapter 7, we talked about chain migration, which would be classified as a social migration pull factor to a particular area, especially given the chain is started by one person who is often followed by friends and family. In terms of push factors, if all of your friends and family move out of the area, you'll probably start thinking about moving because the main connection you had to that area is no longer there. When moving abroad, migrants will often seek enclaves of emigrant people where they'll have cultural connections with others. I discussed expat communities in Chapter 7.

Political push-pull factors: For the ideals!

Moving for political reasons can fall under the auspices of a borderline forced migration. Within federalist states (where states or provinces have a degree of self-rule and whose political structures can reflect the beliefs of the local populations more directly), some people will move between states or provinces to live in an area where the government better reflects the individual's beliefs.

On a larger scale, there are people whose primary motivation for migration is to be part of new governmental systems. When the Soviet Union was formed (before the horrors of the Stalinist purges), many people migrated to the USSR to take part in the grand experiment of creating a "socialist utopia." Similarly, as the Islamic State of Iraq and the Levant (ISIL, sometimes referred to as the Islamic State of Iraq and Syria or ISIS) was formed, some people migrated to the Middle East to participate in its attempted formation. The horrors of that organization were also made very public, and eventually, many people who had joined the organization became disillusioned. Because ISIL has been classified as a terrorist organization, there have been debates on whether people who joined should be allowed to be repatriated, even if there is no proof they had done anything that would be classified as terrorism.

Another form of migratory trend is connected to the ideas of nationalism and the desire to establish a state based on the identity of the people. As these States establish themselves, they may use the nationalistic pull factors of irredentism to encourage people to move there. One example of this is the Zionist movement in Israel. The Israeli State formed in the 1948 was meant to be a homeland for Jewish people. Since then, the State of Israel has actively encouraged people of Jewish ethnicity to move to the region, creating tensions because the newly arrived migrants often displace the Palestinian residents of the area to create Israeli "settlements." These tensions, along with competing interests of other regional players (like Iran, the US, and Saudi Arabia), have led to frequent military conflict between the Israeli State and different Palestinian factions. In October 2023, Hamas (a terrorist organization from the West Bank) attacked Israeli cities near the border. This provocation resulted in Israel launching the largest military operation against Hamas since the organization took power in the West Bank in 2006.

When communities of people are displaced, they often seem to relocate to places near other refugees from their homelands. These communities of displaced peoples will often try to maintain their cultural connections with one another and continue advocating for their rights. The Jewish diaspora is one of the most famous examples. For thousands of years in Europe, Northern Africa, and the Middle East of Asia, the Jewish people have frequently been persecuted and forced to disperse. These communities of dispersed peoples have advocated for the establishment of a Jewish homeland (Israel) to try to put an end to the diaspora and reunite the ethnic community.

Elsewhere around the world, some people choose to migrate because of governmental corruption. Those in the middle and upper classes have the means to migrate and so will often choose to move to a different country where perceived governmental corruption is lower, leading to a brain drain, since many of the country's educated doctors, lawyers, business people, and academics migrate away from the area. Alternatively, this creates a brain gain for the areas they're moving to as they take their skills and knowledge. This process has led to patterns of underdevelopment since the people who could help a country develop are instead migrating and helping the development of other areas.

Environmental push-pull factors: For their health and well-being!

In May 2020, an international team of scientists released "Future of the Human Climate Niche," a paper that discussed the implications of climate change on where people live in the world. They contend that the zones where people can live are shifting further from the tropics as the tropical and subtropical regions get increasingly hotter and dryer.

In the United States, southern states are experiencing more frequent hot weather days and humid conditions, making life more and more uncomfortable. We are already seeing people displaced because of the effects of climate change, including in the United States. People are displaced as sea levels rise, precipitation patterns shift, and flooding becomes more common in some areas. Bangladesh in Southern Asia Dhaka has grown shockingly as frequent floods have rendered much of the countryside too unmanageable to continue trying to farm. We'll discuss climate refugees later in this chapter.

Otherwise, humans have always had their climate and landscape preferences. In biogeography, we talk about the tolerance range of species and the climate conditions in which they can thrive. We are a highly adaptable species and can live just about anywhere (within reason, as we'll talk about with climate refugees), but preferences can drive them to a specific area. Wickedly cold winters can act as a push factor for some, but so can unbearably hot summers. Mountains can be a huge attraction for people who enjoy outdoor activities like hiking or skiing. Just look at the housing prices in places like Denver, Colorado, compared to houses in nearby Kansas City, Missouri. Humans are also attracted to water for transportation, its peaceful nature, and boating or fishing. Beach towns can also attract people who enjoy the ocean views or water activities. The Midwestern regions of the United States have long been a pull factor because of its favorable climate for agriculture. Desert cities like Phoenix, Arizona, have even used their hot, dry air as a pull factor to attract people who have respiratory ailments.

Again, many environmental push-pull factors are highly preferential (unless bad enough to become a forced push factor) and vary from person to person. Some people like the hustle and bustle of a city, while others like the calm and slower pace of the countryside. Then, there is the happy medium of suburban areas. What works for one person may not work for another.

Immigration laws and barriers

With so many people in the world, it makes sense many people want to emigrate for one reason or another, but carrying capacities and limited space means not everyone who wants can do so. That is why many countries will rely on selective migration policies to filter who *can* migrate.

Quotas: Establishing who can come from where

Countries often establish quotas to level the playing field for those who want to immigrate. A quota is a maximum (or minimum) limitation on how many people can immigrate from a certain area of the world. The Chinese Exclusion Act, passed by the Congress of the United States in 1882, is a common example of a quota of Chinese laborers who could migrate to the United States being set at zero per year (for 10 years). In the 1920s, measures were enacted to restrict immigration from all parts of the world except Western Europe. Following public pressure (see Figure 8-1), the Immigration Act of 1924 (also known as the Johnson-Reed Act) formerly established the US Quota system.

Later, during the height of the COVID-19 pandemic, many countries severely limited the number of people who were able to travel to their countries (either as tourists or migrants) in an attempt to slow the diffusion of the disease and manage the process of quarantining and keeping tabs on those who still chose to migrate. Some countries, like New Zealand, fully shut off the ability to visit the country unless they were New Zealand citizens and a few other exceptions (emphasis on "a few"). Other states, like Australia and South Korea, have required recent newcomers to quarantine in specified hotels (or dormitories) until they are clearly COVID-free. This often involved paying for the accommodations and being kept in your room while your meals were delivered.

FIGURE 8-1: A political cartoon about the changing immigration quota system in 1921. (Photo source: US Library of Congress.)

Library of Congress Prints and Photographs Division

However, under normal circumstances, countries usually operate under a system that determines how many entry visas will be issued yearly based on demographic analysis or governmental policy decisions. Of those, a certain number will be allotted to different areas of the world to better distribute who receives those entry visas.

In the United States, there is quite a long waiting period for people wanting to migrate. In some regions, the waiting period could be years or even decades because the United States operates under a merit-based system through which preference is given to those with higher education, language skills, job creation capabilities, and personal wealth. Low-skilled laborers, or even just regular economic migrants with just a bachelor's degree, will not be given a lot of preference, so they may have to wait for a long time. Some may try to migrate earlier by claiming refugee or asylum status, for which a different quota exists. That is why the US maintains an entire court structure just to be able to determine whether people claiming refugee or asylee status have justifiable claims.

Undocumented migration: Victims of the system

If the quota is restrictive and asylum or refugee status cannot be established, some people may try to migrate without proper legal authorization. The more common term for this is "illegal immigration," but we'll save that term for cable news channels. Instead, we use the *undocumented migration* terminology. Typically, these migrants will migrate using legal mechanisms (under tourist or temporary work visas) and fail to return to their home countries when their visas expire.

REMEMBER

How undocumented migrants are talked about very much connects to political agendas. Supporters of limiting migration will often use the terminology of "illegal migrants" or "illegal aliens." The politically neutral terminology is "undocumented migrant."

Understandably, the numbers of undocumented migrants in the United States vary since those undocumented immigrants are not utilizing typical governmental procedures, but some estimates indicated as many as 75 percent of undocumented migrants arrive via airplane. Beyond flying, many undocumented migrants risk perilous journeys across harsh landscapes and rough seas to reach their destinations. Because undocumented immigrants have no official status, some people seek to take advantage of them, and some migrants even end up victims of human trafficking and modern-day slavery.

REMEMBER

The whole idea of building some sort of wall to prevent the flow of all undocumented migration in the United States is fairly laughable unless you're planning on building that wall 45,000 feet tall or blocking airline traffic.

The battles over undocumented migration have influenced the political status of more than a handful of States worldwide. They're often used as political fodder for fights over who should and shouldn't be allowed to migrate (like can be seen in Figure 8-2). Undocumented migration is often a sign of a broken immigration system with requirements that are too restrictive for legal immigration, so people are forced to rely on methods that aren't necessarily legal. Let me qualify that a bit since that is quite a statement. There have been a few cases where the quotas have been changed with little to no explanation other than "there are too many." The way to fix a broken immigration system is to offer more pathways to legal immigration. However, This is contentious since many arguments are thrown around both ways. I would encourage you to look at the raw data and studies on the impact of immigration in terms of fostering economic and social development.

FIGURE 8-2:
An anti-immigration rally in Eastern Bharat (India) against immigration from Bangladesh. (Image Source: public domain.)

Own work / Wikimedia Commans / Public Domain

Family reunification: A fast lane to ease separation

Let me preface this discussion by saying yes, some people take advantage of the system. Do they represent the vast majority of people? Absolutely not. There are some examples of people flying to the United States while very pregnant to be able to take advantage of the birthright citizenship process to use their child's citizenship status as a means of getting citizenship for themselves. It happens, but that is not a true measuring stick for everyone trying to gain migratory status through chain migration. But where this is related to the wider discussion of quotas and selective immigration is that applications for migration for family reunification are typically given preference over other visa applications. This narrows the pool for available spots even further but helps reunite families that had otherwise been separated by the processes of migration. As we've already discussed, These social pull factors are an important means of helping families re-establish themselves when one member moves away. Again, this can be a very slow process. It's not like a person moves and immediately uses their position to help move their family there. They would typically have to go through the naturalization process first, through which they work to become a citizen of the country. Only once a naturalized citizen can they use their status to begin the family reunification process. That itself can also be a rather lengthy process.

Going with No Other Choice

A personal pet peeve of mine is when people accidentally (or even purposefully) mix up their understanding of an involuntary migrant as being just another form of economic migrant. Far too many news stories talk about people trying to make their way to the United States or Europe because they're trying to make a better life for themselves. Leaving out the part about how they're being forced to do so under fear of persecution or death adds an important piece to the story of why they're migrating. I would wager that most news stories about migration have little to nothing to do with voluntary migration and are more about involuntary migrants. Many people crossing the deserts of the Southern United States or the Mediterranean Sea to get to Europe probably would not be doing so if they had literally any other choice.

The news likes to focus on these stories because it's a compelling, hot-button issue. Notice the lack of stories about the heaps of people whose visa applications were accepted and who flew to their new country on a commercial airline. That's not much of a contentious issue. So, please keep that in mind as we talk about involuntary or forced migration that occurs because people have no other options. And again, please remember these are human stories we're talking about here, not just data points.

Refugees, asylum seekers, and IDPs

Before getting too far into this discussion, we must discuss the difference between refugees and asylum seekers. Before we even do that, we need to clarify that both are official governmental designations usually established by a State's government, an intergovernmental organization like the United Nations, or a nongovernmental organization like the Red Cross.

» **Refugees:** Refugees are people who have been displaced from their homelands and seek sanctuary elsewhere.

» **Asylum seeker:** An asylum seeker is someone who has already gotten out of their homeland and seeks to stay in the country they have arrived at with legal protection.

The United Nations High Commission for Refugees estimates the number of refugees, asylum seekers, and other forcibly displaced people to be in the realm of 110 million people in 2022. Since then, with the renewal of hostilities in Israel and the West Bank, that number is expected to climb when 2023's statistics are released. Figure 8-3 shows that many refugees come from Sub-Saharan Africa and South Asia.

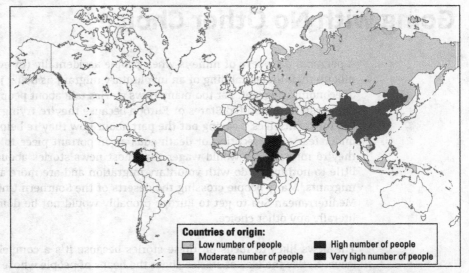

Countries of origin:
☐ Low number of people   ■ High number of people
▨ Moderate number of people   ▨ Very high number of people

FIGURE 8-3: Refugees and asylum seekers by host country in 1997. (Source: Institute for National Strategic Studies [INSS].)

For example, someone from Guatemala who has made their way into the United States after leaving the country due to fear of gang violence as a result of political instability is an asylum seeker. They've made their way into the United States, most likely as an undocumented traveler. Once there, they are apprehended by United States Border Control. They would then need to establish themselves as an asylum seeker and argue their case to a federal judge. They must convince the judge that they're in mortal danger and cannot possibly return to their homeland until the political situation improves.

If the judge is convinced, the asylum seeker's status is approved, and they're granted temporary residency (sometimes with a pathway to citizenship and sometimes not), they can work and reside in the United States. If the situation in their home country improves, many asylum seekers will try to return home, but if they've already established themselves in their new country and possibly had children while asylees (who are US Citizens), that situation gets very complicated very fast.

If they cannot convince the judge they're in danger, they risk being deported back to their country of origin or a different country. (In this case, it would most likely be Mexico since that is the country they entered the United States from.) In the earlier example about young Alan, who died on a Grecian shore while he and his family tried to immigrate from Syria to Europe, his family was trying to make their way to Greece because they would have been able to claim asylum status once they got there.

Establishing refugee status can be quite a bit more difficult and take considerably longer (upwards of 7 or more years). A refugee is someone from an area of persecution or plight or looking to be resettled in another country. Usually, they're looking to be resettled in a country like Canada, Germany, the United States, or Australia. They, too, must establish their status as a refugee, usually with an aid organization like the Red Cross. Sometimes, when there is open conflict, organizations like the United Nations will step in and declare anyone coming out of the war zone seeking sanctuary is automatically granted refugee status — as was the case in 2021 with Ukrainian refugees fleeing the Russian invasion.

While refugees might ultimately want to end up in Western Europe or North America, the vast majority end up in the next closest country. Some Syrian refugees have been able to make their way to Europe or North America, but most still reside in refugee camps in neighboring Turkey and Jordan. They'd like to end up in the West because, along with more economic opportunities, those countries have considerably more resources to provide for refugees.

Darfuri refugees from Western Sudan have predominantly ended up in the Eastern Deserts of Chad (which is exactly to the West of Sudan). The refugee camps in Chad have minimal resources, with few access points for running water, and are largely dependent upon foreign aid organizations and foreign governments to supply even the most basic needs for the refugees. Refugees in these camps seeking resettlement must often undergo intense vetting that spans multiple years, which includes background checks, interviews, and more background checks. While their application is being processed, they must continue living in the camps.

If their application is accepted, they'll be flown to a completely foreign place and resettled. They'll usually be put up in an apartment and given a few weeks of assistance for food and basic necessities. From there, they'll have to navigate the process of getting work and acclimating to a new culture. Eventually, they'll have to pay back quite a bit of the assistance, including the flight costs (at least in the case of many US programs).

The acclimation process can be difficult, especially because they are viewed as outsiders and often vilified in people's minds because of misleading news or a lack of knowledge about each other's cultures.

REMEMBER

The US media often identifies attacks carried out by "Muslim terrorists" but rarely specifically mentions religion when non-Muslims carry out attacks. This has contributed to rising Islamophobia. Also, people from predominantly Muslim areas are labeled "dangerous." Sometimes, politicians will go out of their way to specify that people who are actually trying to immigrate as refugees or asylum seekers are "rapists, murderers, or thieves." Blanket migration bans have even been put into place, including on refugees, to stem the flow of "terrorists." This places one more barrier in front of people trying to escape a dangerous situation and live their lives.

TECHNICAL STUFF

One of the things that I have experienced firsthand as an educator is the toll that refugee camps have on many refugees. It can be difficult to teach refugee students because they may not have a lot of training on how to be students. They often want to do well at school, but they can get lost and frustrated because of their lack of experience with the language and schooling in general. That said, I can confidently say the hardest-working student I ever had was an Afghani refugee. No offense to my other students, but she still stands out with her experience (or lack thereof) and how highly she achieved.

Refugee/asylee and IDP push factors

The reason why people will try to flee their homelands also fits under the ESPE model we discussed earlier in this chapter. Remember that we're primarily discussing push factors with refugees and asylum seekers. Many people have an "anywhere but here" mentality regarding pull factors. Of course, people have places they'd ideally like to end up. In fact, if you talked to many refugees, they would say that they would ideally like to end up right back where they started, as long as the conditions that forced them to relocate in the first place have resolved themselves.

REMEMBER

I have worked with quite a few students who were refugees, and many of them have gone into degrees like emergency management, nonprofit administration, or public policy–related careers, hoping to one day return to their home countries and be part of the solution.

Following is a breakdown of some push factors:

>> **Economic:** In this case, we're talking extreme cases of poverty or economic plight to the point that providing for their families is, by all intents and purposes, impossible. This can sometimes be environmentally linked as well. If floods or intense droughts have made agriculture impossible, people may have to migrate to find work. This was the case during the Dust Bowl in the United States in the 1930s, as pests and large dust storms destroyed farms. Today, many people in Bangladesh are finding themselves having to move as repeated floods have destroyed the livelihoods of many rural farmers. These sorts of situations will unfortunately become more common as the effects of climate change become more severe. Economic desperation can be particularly dangerous because when people don't have access to basic necessities like food, water, shelter, and medical supplies, an economic situation can quickly become political. Adolf Hitler took advantage of hyperinflation and

economic depression in the period following World War I to rise to power by vilifying and "othering" Germany's Jewish population. The scapegoating of the Jewish people provided a convenient means of uniting Germany under his horrific cause, which ultimately resulted in the deaths of untold millions of people.

>> **Social:** Regarding push factors, the "othering" of groups of people can lead to persecution. Stateless nations (discussed in Chapter 1), like the Kurds in the Middle East, can endure harsh treatment, as they did at the hands of Saddam Hussein. Social othering can also lead to open conflict, like the case in Rwanda in the 1990s. During that conflict, the social competition between the Hutu and Tutsi ethnic groups, which Hutu leaders fabricated, erupted into active genocide against the Tutsi. In less than 100 days, about 800,000 people were killed, and another 2 million people fled the country. The refugees from this conflict spilled into nearby Uganda and the Democratic Republic of Congo. The refugees further ignited ethnic strife there and intensified an ongoing civil war in the region of Katanga for the better part of 60 years.

>> **Environmental:** Increasing emphasis has been placed on tracking the increasing number of environmental refugees. These people are forced to migrate due to increasingly unlivable climate or environmental conditions. Conditions that are too hot (increased droughts and increasing average temperatures) and too wet (heavy and violent storms, flooding, or rising sea levels) are the main culprits. Already, there are cities in the United States, particularly in Alaska, Louisiana, and Virginia, where people have been forced out of their homes since the ocean has otherwise swallowed them up. The streets of Miami, Florida, flood on a sunny day. Many insurance companies will no longer provide home insurance in much of Florida because of the state's increasingly volatile weather patterns. More frequent hurricanes and flooding make the process of insuring homes not sustainable due to increasingly frequent payouts. In other parts of the world, increasing global temperatures decrease agricultural output. When that happens, famines and diseases (especially made worse by malnutrition) will become increasingly common. When food insecurity increases, so will desperation. And when desperation increases, so does conflict. Therefore, in 2021, US Secretary of Defense Lloyd J. Austin III declared climate change was a top priority to secure the country's future and prosperity.

TECHNICAL STUFF

In the 1990s, the US determined that the difference between asylum status in the US and being returned to Cuba was determined if you were caught. Cuban refugees who could land on the shores of the US could claim asylum status. If they were caught at sea, they were returned to Cuba. This led to tens of thousands of Cuban refugees trying their luck in a risky game. The boats on which they attempted the journey were inadequate for crossing the strait between Cuba and Florida. Unfortunately, many refugees drowned attempting to make the journey. President

Barack Obama ended the policy, instead looking to coordinate efforts with the Cuban government to try to ensure the safety of those trying to immigrate to the US as refugees.

Internally displaced peoples (IDPs)

Another special classification to discuss is people forced out of their homes but not necessarily out of their countries. These internally displaced peoples (IDPs) can be forced out for the same reasons as any other refugee or asylee. A current example is in Pakistan, where an estimated 8 million people were displaced from their homes in 2022 due to flooding in the Indus River valley (that also killed an estimated 1,700 people). In Ukraine, an estimated 6 million people have fled the country. Another estimated 8 million people have fled the Eastern Ukraine to seek the relative safety of the Western Ukraine. The United Nations High Commission for Refugees estimates more than 57.3 million IDPs worldwide in 2022. The Internal Displacement Monitoring Centre (established in 1998 by the Norwegian Refugee Council in Geneva) estimates that number even higher at 62.5 million people. These people place additional strains on governments that need to help them acquire food, jobs, and places to live. If these people are a marginalized community, fewer resources might be allocated to them. Minorities are often targeted for persecution because of their status as being from Stateless nations and their political marginalization.

A Stateless nation is a group of people who do not have a country of their own. Often, they're minority groups dispersed throughout many countries.

Forced labor

When most people think about the topic of slavery, I assume the Transatlantic Slave Trade or 19th-century slavery is what most comes to mind. Unfortunately, the geography of slavery did not end in 1865 with the passage of the 13th Amendment to the US Constitution. In fact, the last country in the world to ban slavery was the West African country of Mauritania in 1981. We're not going to get much into the history of slavery here, but throughout history, the institution of slavery has very much been connected to differences in things like race, ethnicity, social class, or even debt. Slavery in the United States was at first based on the African slave trade but shifted exclusively to a matter of race. During the time of the Roman Empire, people could be sold into slavery to pay off a debt or captured into slavery by force of conquest. In both situations, once a person was enslaved, they were almost completely at the will of their enslaver, and their migratory patterns were decided for them. Enslaved African people sent to the Americas to be used as forced laborers migrated against their wills.

TIP

For a history of slavery in the US, I would recommend *Black American History For Dummies*, by Ronda Racha Penrice (Wiley), *World History For Dummies*, by Peter Haugen (Wiley), or *U.S. History For Dummies*, by Steve Wiegand (Wiley).

With the Transatlantic Slave Trade, which took place between the 1650s and 1800s, millions of people were taken from West Africa and forced to migrate to the Caribbean, Eastern South America, and the Southern United States for enslavement. Slavery as a process is much older than this particular example, but this is the most recent and widely known example of the systematic enslavement and forced migration of large numbers of people.

In the modern era, slavery still affects millions of people. As it is no longer an act supported in any official capacity of legality tracking, it can be quite difficult to quantify. Young women, in particular, are targeted for human trafficking to be sold into sex slavery. Populations of undocumented migrants are also frequently targeted because of their lack of status and the decreasing likelihood that any law enforcement agency would investigate their whereabouts. Another population that is not as frequently discussed in the context of human trafficking is Native American women in the United States. Because of the limited funds and overstretched forces of tribal police agencies, many cases of missing Indigenous women also never go uninvestigated.

In parts of Southern Asia and Central Africa, women are also trafficked as child brides who are often forced to move away from their homes at a young age, usually in return for a dowry payment to the girl's parents.

Between all of these sources of modern slavery, estimates of the number of people forced into slavery are about 50 million. About 40 percent of that number are girls forced into marriages, and a quarter (of the original 50 million) are children. It is a global issue that multiple organizations are working to correct, with varying amounts of success.

Chapter 9

Where the People Are Concentrated

Worldwide, more people live in cities than don't. Regional variations exist, but we live in an increasingly urban world. Today, the fastest urban growth rates are occurring in the world's Less-Developed Countries (LDCs), leading to interesting environmental, social, and political developments.

This chapter explains general trends in urban growth and why cities attract migrants. Often, people move to cities for the same economic, social, political, and environmental push-pull factors that bring migrants to urban areas. We won't get into those push-pull factors here; instead, we'll focus on city-specific reasons driving migration.

Urbanization and urban geography are intricate and robust fields of study with many potential career options, including urban planning, emergency management, public health, and social services. These careers rely heavily on Geographic Information Systems (GIS) and geotechnologies to understand how the city is growing, model the organization of city services, and plan for future urban growth.

Defining the Urban Area

How do we define a city? By population? By population density? By function? By character? Cities act as perceptual regions, meaning while they have formal boundaries, they usually don't end at those boundaries. Think of a large city in your area and ask five people to explain what is and isn't part of the city. You'll probably get five different answers. And what may be a city in one person's mind may not be in another's.

For example, when I was teaching in Shanghai — one of the largest cities in the world — if I told my students I would be traveling to Hangzhou over the weekend, they would refer to Hangzhou as a cute little village that is much quieter and more relaxing than Shanghai. Never mind that Hangzhou has a population topping 10 million people! This just goes to show that "cities" themselves can be perceptual as well. What may be a cute "village" in one area might be considered a massive metropolis elsewhere.

TECHNICAL STUFF

Fun fact: With a population of about 10 million people, Hangzhou would be the third-largest city by population in the United States — not quite the quiet little village my students led me to expect. So, realizing how a city can be defined, we will go with the heavily concentrated population centers or economic, political, and/or cultural importance.

Drivers of urban growth

In urban geography, a couple of foundational theories help guide the study of urban areas and are fairly universal in their application. The theories and concepts we'll discuss in this section are meant to bring in some ideas of how cities interact — or, more specifically, how people within cities interact. One of the things about cities is that they almost interact like organic beings with a sense of energy and liveliness that helps attract people in the first place. Urban geography is the study of humans coalescing and contributing their energy to the growth of the urban area, leading to cities forming their own identities and building their own character. We will look at the contributing factors to growth and identify the formation of cities in this particular section.

The Gravity Model: Pulling cities together

We'll start with the Gravity Model since this is something we've already talked about quite a bit (and will continue to discuss). For urban geographers, a city acts like its own planet with its own physical gravitational pull. The larger the city, the larger the pull. Distance plays a role in this, as much as in astrophysics. The largest philosophical understanding in which we frame human geography is the relation to space.

In the Gravity Model, big cities have larger pulls than smaller cities. Near cities have more pull between each other than far cities. When we talk about "pull," in this case, we're talking about a city's ability to attract people to migrate for economic development, educational opportunities, and even entertainment options. Bigger cities can attract people from further away, but cities located near each other can have a lot of interaction with each other. For example, many interactions exist between Austin, Texas, and nearby Houston, Texas. Houston interacts with big cities like Los Angeles and New York since they're all very large cities.

If you ever want to see the Gravity Model at work and see the interaction between cities, go to your closest airport with commercial flights and look at the flight board. Because Austin is a smaller city, it only has two weekly direct flights to Omaha, Nebraska. However, because Houston is a much larger city, it has a lot more pull factor, meaning there are multiple daily flights between Omaha and Houston.

TECHNICAL
STUFF

In this book, we will use the tiered definitions of cities as described by Walter Christaller. A city is the largest urban unit with the highest concentration of people but also the highest concentration of goods and services. A town is the next level and still has high population densities but lower total populations than a city. A town has a diverse economic market but less selection or diversity in goods and services than a city. A village has an even smaller number of people, and the village market will only supply the most basic goods and services. A hamlet is the smallest urban unit. With few people, there may not even be a permanent market.

Central Place Theory: Foundational framework

When Walter Christaller established his Central Place Theory in 1933, he couldn't have known how foundational his theory would be in urban geography. Christaller's theory (see Figure 9-1) was based on the ideal spatial distribution of cities and surrounding nodes of villages and towns. Interestingly, Christaller worked for the Nazi German government, planning urban settlements for after the war, and then eventually worked for the Communist government of East Germany. Still, he is a highly respected urban geographer.

Figure 9-1 shows that Christaller imagined a series of hexagons surrounding each city, with towns on each node. Around each town, smaller hexagons represented villages. Hexagons around each village represent where the hamlets are located. (Hexagons are used because they allow interlocking of the surrounding hexagons without overlapping.) Christaller's theory also helps us understand and demonstrate the importance of spatial distributions in deciding how far they're willing to travel for goods and services.

Now, let's introduce the ideas of range and threshold.

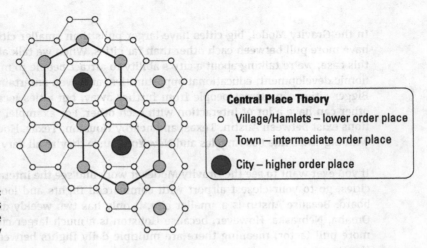

FIGURE 9-1:
Christaller's
Central Place
Theory

Central Place Theory

○ Village/Hamlets – lower order place

◐ Town – intermediate order place

● City – higher order place

RANGE

Have you ever needed to buy a product — something simple like a bag of flour — and stopped at multiple places like a nearby gas station or convenience store before finally giving in and driving further to a grocery store, where you eventually found the item? That is because people need low-order goods (basic necessities) more frequently and will want to travel the least distance possible to buy them.

Many gas stations and convenience stores stock basic foods and household items like batteries, so people don't have to travel further to a large grocery store. People are more willing to travel further away for goods they don't need as frequently, like clothing. Even less frequently needed items, like cars, can be found even further away since people will be more willing to drive further for something they buy infrequently. Luxury car dealerships might be located even further away.

REMEMBER

Small markets are found in hamlets, where they can meet people's daily needs. Once you move up to the village level, you will see shops with items like clothing that are still needed but more infrequent (along with larger stores for daily needs like groceries to meet the daily needs of a larger population). Then, in the towns, larger stores are found, along with car dealerships, that people need even less frequently. Finally, in the cities, you'll find even bigger stores (interspersed with small "neighborhood shops") and niche markets, like luxury car dealerships.

THRESHOLD

If a luxury car dealership were located in a village, it probably would not last very long because a certain number of customers is needed to sustain a business. A small neighborhood market selling basic foodstuffs will have a small threshold. Even a small population needs to eat, so that small neighborhood market will have frequent customers. Hamlets with very small populations may not even be able to support a market if the customer base is not large enough to keep it in business. A large city will still have only a few people who can support a business selling high-priced goods, like luxury cars, so only one dealership may serve the whole city. If a second luxury car dealership were to open, the customer base would be halved, and both dealerships might fail.

Even cities like Omaha, Nebraska, are not big enough to support a Ferrari dealership, so potential customers would have to travel to Kansas City, Minneapolis, or Chicago to buy their Ferrari. Professional sports teams need a large fan base, especially if ticket prices increase or the team isn't very good. Professional sports teams have a very high threshold. Semi-professional teams don't cost as much to operate, so they can be located in smaller towns or villages and stay afloat.

TECHNICAL STUFF

One of the best ways to connect to the ideas of range and threshold in the United States is by studying the meteoric rise of "dollar stores." These stores offer many of the same cheaper consumer goods as big box retailers like Walmart or Target but don't require nearly as high of a threshold to stay in business. In the 1990s and 2000s, stores like Walmart popped up all over the place, but that growth is now shadowed by dollar stores like Dollar General, Dollar Tree, Family Dollar, and Five Below. These stores can operate in very small towns or villages and draw people away from bigger stores that have to be more centrally located in cities or towns. If you live in the United States, a fun activity is to look at the location of big box stores (Target, Walmart, K-Mart) in your area and then check out the distribution of discount dollar stores to see the difference.

Urban pull factors: Drawing people to urban areas

Cities have an electric feel and can attract people to migrate to them in unique ways compared to other forms of migration. In this section, we'll specifically discuss urban area pull factors using the ESPE model.

>> **Economic:** The economic opportunities in cities are hardly rivaled in urban areas. In terms of the sheer volume of job opportunities and the increases in wage opportunities, rural areas are hard to match cities. Of course, it should be noted that the cost of living is considerably higher in urban areas than in rural areas, but there are more opportunities to make more money in urban areas than in rural areas. The Global Fortune 500 companies — as in the 500 largest companies in the world — are predominantly located in large urban areas like Tokyo, New York, Beijing, Seoul, and Shanghai. This is a kind of Catch-22 because the companies locate themselves close to the labor force (something we'll talk more about when we get to Weber's Least Cost Theory), and people locate themselves close to cities to be close to employers.

>> **Social:** Paris is known as "the City of Lights." New York is the "City That Never Sleeps." Detroit, Michigan, and Nashville have reputations for their music recording industries. Each city takes on a soul and culture of its own. Because of the modern architecture and diffusion of technology, it may feel like you walk in the same city everywhere you go, but they're all a little different. Younger people especially feel themselves drawn to cities. Nightlife, bars, restaurants, entertainment, and sports are harder to come by in smaller cities or more rural areas. The extent to which cities can draw people in depends on the person. Cities also attract people from diverse backgrounds, leading them to take on the character contributed by those who have moved there. London is an interesting city to visit because of the many cultures that contributed to its formation, though it has an identity all its own. This unique cultural mix continues to have a strong pull on people worldwide. Chinatown (as seen in Figure 9-2) is a great example. Even though you are still very much in London, the smells, sights, and sounds give it a different feel than the rest of Central London.

FIGURE 9-2: Chinatown in London. The Chinese lanterns and high density of restaurants serving Chinese food make it incredibly obvious when you enter Chinatown.

In previous chapters, we've mentioned chain migration as a process by which people who have migrated encourage their friends and families to move to the same area. As they migrate, they tend to congregate next to one another in cities. These accumulations of people can lead to whole neighborhoods or regions of a city taking on the identity of the migrant populations. In urban geography, this process is cited as the source of ethnic enclaves. These communities can be little bastions of culture completely different from the rest of the city. Some of the most common examples are the Chinatowns that can be found around the world created by migrant populations of Chinese people. The term *ghetto* is sometimes used to refer to ethnic neighborhoods since the process of ghettos was meant to describe a section of ethnic populations in different parts of the cities (through official and unofficial means). Unofficial things like housing prices could price new migrants out of large parts of the city, forcing them to migrate to parts where rents are cheaper. Redlining was a process used by the United States government to set guidelines and regulations for offering home loans. The process often resulted in the confinement of communities of African Americans to particular parts of the city with limited means of obtaining housing outside those areas. The term "the ghetto" was then applied to areas in which people of color were forced to live and eventually took on the added visualization of the decrepit part of town. Nazi Germany also used the system of ghettos in European cities to concentrate Jewish populations during the brutal processes of the Holocaust. Jewish people were forced out of their homes and forcibly relocated to the ghettos until they could be further moved into concentration camps.

>> **Political:** I always enjoy walking around the streets of Washington, D.C., because of its "official" feel. If you walk down K Street, you see the names of all the top movers and shakers and networks of lobbyists who use their acumen and charisma to influence the top politicians at the highest level of government. It is always interesting to eavesdrop on conversations as you walk past people on the streets because they are often about politics and sometimes from the perspective of people who know what they're talking about. National, provincial, and state capital cities have an air of importance that attracts people from around the world who are attracted to the epicenters of power. People interested in careers in politics, especially lawyers and those interested in public and foreign policy, are drawn to these political centers to have their own influence on the ebbs and flows of government.

>> **Environmentally:** Here is one where the push factors often outweigh the pull factors. Environmentally speaking, very few people will be attracted to a city's blacktop roads and smoggy air. There is something to be said for the human environment and people's attraction to large buildings, but from a natural standpoint, cities don't have as much going for them to act as a natural pull factor. Suburbanization is the growth of suburban areas (along the fringes or just outside core urban areas), often attracting people from densely popu-lated areas to less densely populated areas with more parks and cleaner

environments. Within cities, areas around parks (like New York's Central Park or London's Regent's Park) can have considerably higher rents because of their proximity to green spaces. People's attraction to green spaces and desire to live in urban areas influenced the development of the City Beautiful Movement in the late 19th and early 20th centuries. The development of city parks and broad boulevards of famous streets like the Avenue des Champs-Élysées in Paris became defining features of cities by combining urban and natural elements. It was a means of attracting people to the cities where they could have their cake (city life) and eat it too (natural scenery).

Types of cities

Human geographers have many ways of referring to cities of different sizes (both in population and influence). This section will cover some of those vocabularic-styled concepts. Scale is important. A city like Rapid City, South Dakota, may not be significant globally or nationally, but it is incredibly important for Western South Dakota (and the whole upper Great Plains region) at the regional scale.

Primate cities and the rank-size rule

First, we'll start with the most complicated one to make the rest of this easier. The concept of a primate city is not super complicated; it's just how you identify it. A primate city has a population of more than twice that of the next largest city in an area. This often translates into a primate city having an outweighing influence in politics, cultural attractions, and economic development. Paris is a good example. The metropolitan area has a population of around 12 million people. The next largest city, Marseilles, has a metropolitan population of about 1.75 million, which can be especially helpful for France since economic and political influence can be centralized. Although Paris is not one of the largest cities in the world, because it has such an overwhelming concentration of the French population, it can serve as a sort of beacon for French culture and political and economic influence. For example, while the Eifel Tower was originally built as a radio tower, it has grown to represent Paris's architectural and economic prominence on the world stage (see Figure 9-3).

The primate city concept gets a little complicated when paired with the rank-size rule, which ranks cities to the nth order (not a typo). The largest city is the first order; the second-largest city should be roughly half the size of the first-order city; the third-largest city should be roughly one-third the size of the largest city; the fourth should be one-quarter; and so on. If the first city is exponentially larger than the second-order city, that is a pretty good signifier that you're dealing with a primate city. Look at the cities in your own state/province and see if the largest city is a primate city or how closely the alignment of cities matches the rank-size rule.

Megalopolis: The city that keeps on keeping on

Look at a night map of the East Coast in the United States or the Rhine–Ruhr River Valley of Western Germany to get the best idea of this next concept — the Megalopolis. It sounds like the name of some fictional city in a comic book series or something, but in geographic terms, it refers to an area of continuous urban development linking multiple metropolitan areas.

The West Coast cities of Seattle, Washington, Portland, Oregon, San Francisco, or Los Angeles, California, are not megalopolises because they're all much too spread out with too much rural area between them. If you've ever had the unfortunate pleasure of driving Interstate 95 on the East Coast of the United States, I pity you and the traffic you had to endure. The famed BosNyWash Corridor is the quintessential example of a megalopolis. If you're driving north along Interstate 95 from Richmond, Virginia, to Bangor, Maine, to catch the fall colors, you had best prepare yourself. Along the route (assuming you stay on Interstate 95 the whole time), you will enter the metropolitan corridor just to the South of Washington D.C. (the "Wash" of BosNyWash) and be in a continuous urban landscape all the way through Boston (the "Bos"). Along the way, you will also pass through the metropolitan areas of Baltimore, Philadelphia, Newark, New York, New Haven, Providence, and many other urban areas.

Along Germany's Rhine River, you will find the urban areas of Bonn, Cologne, Dusseldorf, Essen, Duisburg, and Dortmund. This is mostly one continuous urban area.

On a global scale, those are the big ones, but on a more local or regional scale, you might identify other megalopolises.

Megacities and metacities: The biggest of the big

From the more complicated ideas of megalopolises and primate cities, we can shift to the comparative easiness of megacities and metacities. These concepts help us understand the scale of urban growth on a global level. A megacity is any city with a population of more than 10 million. We've identified Paris, France, as a megacity with a metropolitan population of 12 million people. However, placing Paris in the same category as the world's absolute largest cities is unfair when distinguishing the massive size of the world's largest metacities.

A metacity is a city with a population of more than 20 million. There are 37 megacities in the world. By 2050, Statista (www.statista.com) estimates the number of megacities will grow by another 14, but only two will be in Europe or the Americas (London and Chicago). The rest will be in Central Africa, the Middle East, and Southern and Eastern Asia.

TECHNICAL STUFF

Metacities are also classified as megacities, but not all megacities are metacities. According to Statista, as of 2023, there were only six metacities in the World. From highest to lowest population: Tokyo, Dehli, Shanghai, Dhaka, Sao Paolo, and Mexico City.

Gateway cities: Entry to a region

One of the most iconic landmarks in the United States is the Gateway Arch in Saint Louis, Missouri. Saint Louis' location at the confluence of the Missouri and Mississippi Rivers and proximity to the confluence of the Ohio and Mississippi Rivers make it an ideal place to start the overland trek into the Western United States. Saint Louis was considered the gateway to the West, making it a good regional example of a gateway city. On a more national scale, the Statue of Liberty welcomes migrants to the Port of New York, marking the gateway to the United States and Ellis Island. Internationally, Istanbul is the gateway to Europe from the Middle East or the gateway to the Middle East from Europe. Skagway, Alaska, was the Gateway to the Yukon territory and the Gold Fields of the Canadian and Alaskan subarctic on a local or regional scale. An otherwise tiny town, Skagway was a bustling boom town during the Alaskan Gold Rush for those seeking to find their riches in the harsh terrain of Alaska and the Canadian Yukon (see Figure 9-4).

FIGURE 9-4:
Skagway, Alaska

World cities: Beacons of urbanization

Megalopolises, metacities, and primate cities are fun and all, but another class of cities stands out from the rest. World cities are distinguished centers of commerce, global politics, and world-renowned centers for culture. Only the top of the top earns the distinction as a world city. These cities can often be debated as to their significance, but a couple cities in the world stand as undebatable to their importance. The first could not be any more obvious. The home of the United Nations, arguably the most important Stock Exchange in the World, the headquarters of countless influential businesses, and one of the most culturally iconic cities in the world, New York City stands in a class rivaled by few.

Among New York's equals are cities like Tokyo, whose influence over the whole of East Asia and the center for some of the most powerful technology companies in the world earns it the distinction of a world city. The cities of London and Paris once sat as the epicenter for multicontinental empires that spanned the whole globe. From their streets came economic, political, and cultural movements that influenced their respective holdings.

London and Paris still hold tremendous influence over their respective countries, previous domains, and the global system.

Moscow could be classified as a world city because of its influence over the expansive Russian and Slavic populations. With its influence in the Spanish-speaking world, Madrid could, too. You could argue similarly for a handful of other cities, like Dubai, Singapore, Sydney, Shanghai, or Hong Kong. Not too many people would contest you.

Sustainable cities: Going green in all the right places

One of the growing areas of study within urban geography is the class of sustainable cities. In fact, the United Nations has designated the focus on sustainable cities and communities as number 11 on its Sustainable Development Goals. How cities are working to develop sustainably depends on the city.

In Europe, cities like Copenhagen in Denmark and Amsterdam in the Netherlands are notorious for their emphasis on supporting biking infrastructure — so much so that many urban centers are restricting vehicle access to parts of the cities. Beijing has implemented restrictions based on license plates for who can drive and when. The push for public transit is reviving in many cities in the United States, leading some to bring back street cars to cities that had previously removed them.

Speaking of public transit, I once traveled to Bogota, Colombia, to see, among other things, the Transmilenio Bus System. Borrowing from a similar bus system in Curitiba, Brazil, the Transmilenio bus system operates like a subway. Operating on independent roads that cars aren't allowed to go onto, the Transmilenio has stations that look like train stops but operate at a fraction of the price of subways because it is above ground.

One of the biggest issues cities have to deal with is trash — where to put it and how to reduce it. Many cities are implementing systems whereby rods are inserted into landfills to mine out methane produced by trash decomposition. The methane is a usable fuel for vehicles, often used to power trash collection vehicles. Addis Ababa, the capital city of Ethiopia, actually burns its trash to fuel its power plants.

With the future becoming increasingly evident as the impacts of climate change settle in, countries worldwide are looking to reduce their own negative impact while also continuing development. Saudi Arabia has begun developing an ambitious green city called Neom, which is part of its plan for a post-oil world. (As one of the world's top mining and refining centers, Saudi Arabia's economy is highly dependent on oil.)

While not all the countries in the world may have the resources to take on such an ambitious project, there are other ways to make a green impact. Once referred to as the "Dark Continent" because little was known about it, Africa is certainly brightening up. Often skipping fossil fuels, many rural areas are going directly to solar because it is a readily accessible resource available in abundance in much of Africa and does not require complex electrical grids because rural electrification can happen locally.

In Europe and the Americas, electrical needs are increasingly being met by solar and wind.

TIP

Solar and wind power will be discussed in Chapter 20.

Urban Growing Pains

Urbanization is rarely a pretty process; sometimes, urban growth comes with some pain. This is another area where geographers can step in and understand the spatial extent of an issue and plan for the future.

Since the beginning of urban growth (a span that goes back over 10,000 years), there have always been questions about how to deal with the needs of a densely concentrated population, the environmental issues that cities have to contend with based on their location, and the waste that large numbers of people can generate. The earliest cities have evidence of sewer systems meant to whisk away excess rain and human waste. Even the mightiest city can be toppled if waste is not readily removed. Where waste piles up in cities, disease soon follows.

The city of Rome was not toppled by a great military battle. Attila the Hun merely had to block off the system of aqueducts that supplied fresh water to the city and let the accumulated filth and disease do the job for him. By the way, that was your excuse to think about the Roman Empire for the day.

Later, in 1854, Victorian London physician John Snow would effectively spawn the field of medical geography when he made his now wildly famous (at least in the not-at-all nerdy and totally cool community of geography nerds) cholera map, where he was able to pinpoint the origin of the outbreak to a single water pump (see Figure 9-5). The map helped stop the outbreak and led to a revolution in city sanitation that has helped save countless lives.

FIGURE 9-5:
The famous Broad Street Pump, now enshrined in front of the John Snow Pub in Central London

Urbanization and suburbanization

When World War I broke out in the summer of 1914, it took a while for armies to mobilize because many soldiers were dispersed away from the cities to escape the hot — and frankly, kind of disgusting — cities, where less-than-modern sanitation systems and lack of air conditioning gave many cities an unappealing aroma.

For centuries, people who have had the means have sought occasional refuge from the cities. Whether summer vacations to the countryside or a summer cottage in the Hamptons, people occasionally need a break from the hustle and bustle of the cities. When I was living in Saint Paul, Minnesota's central business district, I would occasionally drop everything and retreat to my uncle's cabin in the woods of Central Wisconsin just to escape the city a bit.

Psychologically, humans need space. Their crowdedness can leave humans feeling claustrophobic, so many seek the fringe area where they can still benefit from proximity to the cities but also enjoy a bit of breathing room (metaphorically and somewhat literally). If you look at the United States, Canada, and Western Europe, the trends in urban growth are trending down because as the middle class grows, many people seek out the wider spaces of the suburbs. This has led to the rise of edge cities, or urban centers that act like quasi-urban centers on the fringe of a larger metropolis. The suburbs, as they are known, are a reaction to urban growth and are used to check the growth of large cities by attracting development to the city's outer regions.

Effects of urbanization

Cities often grow at rates unforeseen to the government entity (if there is one) overseeing it. Even with the best demographic data collection and the most thorough reports on population growth trends, something like an economic depression or a natural disaster in rural parts of a region may send people flocking to the cities. When that happens, there might be difficulty providing for the needs of the new residents, resentment might grow between different communities, or the city might simply not have the resources to serve and protect all of its residents.

Food deserts: Meeting the needs of all parts of the city

Urban areas are defined by their heavy concentrations of people. Sometimes, however, too many people or businesses are located away from a particular urban area, leaving a portion of the population without stores selling fresh fruits, meats, and vegetables. There is usually a heavy correlation between communities of marginalized populations (especially people of color and minority populations here in the United States) and the presence of what are called *food deserts*.

An area without easy and ready access to healthy and nutritious food is called a food desert. That is not to say there is no food in a food desert. These areas might have access to prepackaged and heavily processed foods or fast food with limited nutritional value. Especially in the United States, eating healthy can be costlier, so higher-priced supermarkets may not be located in areas with lower average household incomes. This is a metaphorical kick in the teeth because, without access to fresh, healthy foods, people who live in food deserts are more likely to develop degenerative diseases like diabetes.

Food deserts don't only exist in urban areas. They also affect some rural communities since the lower populations may not meet the threshold needed for a grocery store. Their only readily accessible grocery stores may be convenience stores, gas stations, or discount dollar stores — none is known for having the freshest fruits and vegetables.

The negative effects of rural food deserts are especially felt on Native American reservations in the United States, where there are shockingly high levels of diseases like diabetes. (On some reservations, 30 percent or higher of the population has been diagnosed with diabetes.)

In other parts of the world, rural areas are not as affected by food deserts since the rural areas practice subsistence and small-scale commercial agriculture (instead of growing commercial grains and field crops as is done in the US). Every village you drive through in countries like Kenya, China, or Colombia has vendors selling freshly picked fruits and vegetables along the roadsides.

Community gardening — in both urban and rural areas — is one solution for food deserts. Cities like Detroit and New York have gained reputations for their urban gardening. New York, weirdly enough, has a thriving beekeepers association, who cultivate their products on the rooftops around the city. Detroit has utilized the open vacant lots, reminders of the effects of previous recessions that hit the auto industry hard, to develop neighborhood-based gardens where people can access fresh vegetables. Even on the reservations, the rediscovery of Native agricultural practices and cuisine is helping alleviate the food security issues by relying on Indigenous knowledge and practices. These creative solutions to urban areas' complex food security issues may help prove Danish economist Ester Boserup right. People *can* develop their way out of complex challenges.

Heat islands: Many hands make warmer cities

If you ask my students what they dislike most about Omaha winters, they may very well tell you about the "OmaDome" effect. Every time a mega snowstorm is headed our way, it seemingly splits itself around the city and reforms on the other side. The "OmaDome" effect has dashed their hopes for a snow day on more than one occasion.

Heavy storms will batter the suburban areas in the summers, but Saint Paul's Central Business District may only get some rain — partially because of the heat island effect. Imagine you're sitting in a room with just yourself, and the thermometer of the room is set at a comfortable temperature. Then, fill the room with people shoulder to shoulder. That room will heat up quickly with the heat created by all those bodies. The same principle holds true for cities, especially when you factor in the machines and cars that also create heat in a city. Then, on top of that, you have to factor in the city's structure. If you were to take a thermometer outside on a hot day and measure the temperature of the grass versus the blacktop, it shouldn't surprise you that the temperature of the road will be drastically higher than the temperature of the grass. On an urban scale, with the tightly woven network of paved roads and buildings with black shingled or tarred roofs, much of the sun's energy is absorbed and reemitted by the dark surfaces of the city.

TECHNICAL STUFF

Dark surfaces absorb the sun's energy, while light surfaces reflect it. Lighter surfaces can reflect the sun's energy back away from the Earth's surface. This is called the *albedo effect*. Blacktop pavement is one of the worst things you could have because it absorbs so much heat. You've probably seen videos of people frying eggs on city streets in the heat of a summer day (sometimes shockingly fast).

The cumulative effect of all of this energy being absorbed by city streets, along with the energy created by more bodies and vehicles in a small area, can often lead to cities being warmer than the surrounding areas. These little heat domes created by the heat can be enough to affect weather patterns by creating high-pressure centers that can cause storms to divert around them. The only way to combat this is by planting trees to shade the urban landscape. Heavy green tree cover is a heck of a lot better than blacktop. Los Angeles and other cities have painted some roads white to lessen their albedo effect and try to reflect more of the sun's energy.

WARNING

Please be mindful of walking your dogs on a hot, sunny day. While it may only be 85 degrees air temperature, the pavement temperature can easily be well over 100 degrees and can burn their paws.

Urban crime: Stick to the facts

If you watch too much cable news, you might think certain cities in the United States are lawless wastelands with out-of-control crime. Chicago is frequently cited as the real-life equivalent of Gotham city, where criminals run the city, and there is no Batman to save them. But you really should look at the numbers.

Yes, there is a lot of crime in any large urban center, but there are also many people. That is why the crime statistics always have to be adjusted and divided by the population (usually expressed as the average number of violent crimes per every 100,000 people). In that case, you actually have less of a chance to be a victim of a crime in Chicago than you do in some rural parts of Wyoming.

REMEMBER

This discussion is highly political, with Chicago frequently singled out because of its strict gun laws in an attempt to discredit their efforts. The geographic context reveals a more complete understanding of the hidden agendas. In Illinois, Chicago and East Saint Louis are the two large cities with the highest violent crime rates. Both cities border states (Indiana and Missouri, respectively) that have some of the weakest gun laws in the country. As I said, however, there is a lot of crime in urban centers, most simply because there are so many people in such a small area. If it seems like all they talk about on the news is another violent shooting or something in the "bad part" of town, maybe try turning off the news and realizing that news agencies make their money by getting people to watch the news and only focusing on the bad and not the good.

That is not meant to encourage going out and leaving your guard down. Often, one of the best ways to get into trouble really quickly is to be too relaxed and unaware of your surroundings. Cities attract a lot of people and have concentrated areas of poverty. As discussed in previous chapters, poverty can lead to desperation, and desperation can lead to people making rash decisions. However, cities like Acapulco, Mexico; Cape Town in South Africa; Guatemala City in Guatemala; and Port-au-Prince, Haiti, rightly have reputations due to high crime. In each case, poverty rates are high, and the government's ability to lessen crime is limited by the presence of informal settlements (described in more detail in the next section). Governments are in a bind because the slums are not official parts of the city. Officers don't enforce laws in the slums because those areas aren't recognized as established parts of the city. But there are people still living there that need help. Without government police, many slums are overrun with gangs and other criminal organizations. The high crime rates in these urban areas cause many people to flee the slums for the relative safety of cities in More Developed Countries (MDCs).

Informal settlements: The most natural form of urban growth

As mentioned in the previous section on crime, dealing with crime in informal settlements known as *slums* (or townships in South Africa or Favelas in Brazil) is difficult. These settlements pop up organically in cities worldwide and are homes to millions of people. With no official status, these informal settlements are usually built of piecework materials (whatever can be found or acquired), with very limited access to basic services like electricity, sanitation, and clean water.

Because they are unrecognized by city governments, there is little in the way of emergency services, and they often rely on community-based organizations like nongovernmental organizations (NGOs) for things like medical care and schooling.

These informal settlements are often a necessary part of the urban development process, as they provide access to the city's economic and educational opportunities that otherwise wouldn't be available because of the rent costs. However, there is a lot of debate about whether informal settlements are a springboard for opportunity or a trap for the poor.

Redlining, restrictive covenants, and de facto segregation

We've already talked about the development of ethnic neighborhoods through official and unofficial means in the previous chapter, but now, we will focus on the lasting effects. In the 1930s, redlining was used as a mortgage lending process that allowed lenders to restrict people from certain city areas from being eligible to be lent money. Redlining was done in conjunction with the development of the Federal Home Owners' Loan Corporation (HOLC), which used a color-coded system to assess risks for lending money.

In cities across the United States, neighborhoods were identified as low risk (green), medium risk (yellow), and high risk (red). Neighborhoods outlined in red (thus *redlining*) tended to be communities of people of color. Because of this decision, people living in these areas were restricted from moving to other parts of the city and buying houses in neighborhoods with reputations for good schools. Instead, they were confined to the redlined areas and were often served by lower-funded schools. This practice, along with the restrictive covenants that prevented people of color from buying homes in certain neighborhoods, led to the segregation of cities along racial lines. Even in the cities in the Northern United States, these practices led to them being some of the most segregated cities in the country.

This segregation was aided by the "white flight" phenomenon in which people of European descent (Caucasian Race) fled the cities to the suburban areas using lending programs that were restricted for people of color. That is one of the reasons why inner-city areas tend to have more people of color, and fewer people of color are in suburban areas — even today.

The effects of redlining were especially devastating with some of the other human developments. In 2021, US Transportation Secretary Pete Buttigieg was questioned and even openly mocked by his political rivals for asserting that the US interstate system was built upon a system of racism. Notice I said his political rivals, not academic geographers and urban planners. That is because he pointed out something more or less accepted as fact.

When the US interstate system was being developed in the post–World War II era, there were questions about where to build the new roads in urban areas. In cities across the United States, the overwhelming trend was that interstates were built through proportionally Black or Hispanic neighborhoods instead of through White neighborhoods. These new roads were not just taking out small areas. We're talking about parts of the city that were razed for constructing these new mega highways. 'What's more, the new interstates primarily benefited the suburban populations of car owners who commuted to work and were mostly White (due to redlining and restrictive covenants).

When the decision was made to build Interstate 94 connecting the downtown areas of Minneapolis and Saint Paul, the new road was routed right through the Rondo neighborhood, which was mostly African American. Rondo was a thriving community that was effectively halved, and the people dispersed to make way for the interstate.

Controlling urbanization

With so many issues cities face, managing them is quite a task. Thankfully, along with geographers, many professions are devoted to understanding the issues that cities face and working to address them both in the present and the future. A couple of methods can be used to contain or manage the growth of cities where needed, some of which are straightforward, and some are more controversial.

» **Infrastructure and urban planning:** One of the most direct forms of addressing the issues of cities is by constantly working to upgrade, maintain, and expand the city infrastructure — utilities (sewer, electricity, or water supply), transportation (roads and public transit), or services (police, education, fire, and medical) — before the migration process can overtake available infrastructure. In the case of infrastructure controlling urbanization, ensuring that all parts of the city are properly serviced can help avoid problems before they even start.

» **City limits and the restriction of city growth:** If you've visited a city and seen cranes and construction everywhere, there's a high likelihood that the city has expanded to its allowable city limits, and the only way to grow is up. City limits are one of the mechanisms to prevent sprawl or the seemingly endless extension of the city. Phoenix, Arizona, is one of the classic examples of sprawl. When flying into the city's airport, it can sometimes seem like you're flying over the city for quite a while before you actually land there. City limits are used to politically limit the city's jurisdiction to a physical area. Zoning is part of this, as cities will designate different areas of the city for different purposes (residential, commercial, industrial, or mixed). Within the already limited city, there are further limitations to how the land can be used for zoning. If a city has maxed out the amount of land they can utilize, it is time for them to build up instead.

» **New urbanism and the re-establishment of different parts of the city:** Go online and search for the benefits of gentrification, and you will find a good assortment of articles talking about how it breathes new life into otherwise neglected parts of the city or provides opportunities for the development of new trendy areas that can attract new people to the city. While you're at it, however, search for the negatives of gentrification, and you'll see many articles talking about how the process forces out the area's original inhabitants by increasing prices to the point it prices them out. This is not a debate that will be solved in this book, but just know that gentrification is a widespread process whereby older areas of cities are redeveloped for the middle class. (In Old English, the "Gentry" was the middle class.) Whether it is the destruction of hutongs (traditional urban housing blocs) in Beijing to make way for apartment buildings or renovating a run-down part of the city with new boutique stores and gastropubs, it may look different in different places but refers to the same urban process.

» **Bringing nature in with greenbelts:** At various times throughout history, there have been different attempts to establish natural areas within cities for the health of its citizens. In this case, however, the establishment of greenbelts has been utilized in one way or another for over a century to constrict the growth of a city through the establishment of protected natural areas. Along with the health benefits of trees and greenery, these green-belts provided more easily accessible natural areas where the city's residents can go and get away from the noise, if only for a moment.

» **Rural development:** One of the other methods to limit the amount of emigration from rural areas is through the promotion of rural development. This usually involves further infrastructure development or tax incentives meant to attract new businesses (and thus more jobs and opportunities). Increasing opportunities in rural areas decreases the pull factors of cities by offering similar services in the rural areas.

» **City growth and development models**

» **Cultural, political, economic, and historical influences on urban area growth**

Chapter **10**

Where People Live

I n the previous chapter, we looked at urbanization and its associated problems. In this chapter, we will examine the spatiality of urban areas. Looking for common connections to groups and classifying areas is especially relevant in urban geography because it allows us to compare one place to another more easily. When studying the growth of urban areas worldwide, much of the history of urbanization and some of its cultural, political, and economic influences become evident.

Urban models are not meant to be perfect representations of a particular urban area. Instead, they're meant to represent the traits of multiple urban areas against which we can "test" reality. We can look at actual city structures to see how closely they conform to the models. Urban geographers have developed and theorized these models throughout the field's history, so some will hold up much better than others. Some cities might conform pretty well to a model city, while sometimes, only parts of the city will conform. Questions like "To what extent?" "How well?" or "To what degree?" can be especially thought-provoking lead-ins to understanding how models are used to explain urban trends.

We will start at the smallest kinds of urban areas (hamlets and villages) and work our way up to town and city structures. When discussing smaller settlements, we'll look at some rural organization patterns for how space is organized in non-urban areas, which will help explain the structures that preceded urbanization and the urban patterns resulting from the subsequent human migration and urban development.

As we discuss each model, I suggest thinking about the area where you live and seeing to what extent each of the models applies to your community or nearby urban area.

Living in the Countryside

When driving along at ground level, you can see whether the road you're on is straight or curvy, but the landscape (especially trees) can prevent you from getting a wider sense of the area's overall organization. However, when you're at the 30,000-foot cruising altitude in an airplane, you can see some of these patterns more clearly. I always try to get a window seat to look for these patterns when possible.

Cadastral systems: Organizing large spaces

A cadastre is a comprehensive record establishing ownership boundaries of public and private lands. Surveyors and governmental planners rely on Global Positioning System (GPS) coordinates that can be input into Geographic Information System (GIS) programs to plot out the boundaries of different spaces when planning roads, utilities, or who owns what. Understanding the organization of land is one of the oldest applications of geography.

REMEMBER

Recall the ancient Babylonia map discussed in Chapter 1 and how it signified land ownership. This is of particular interest to governments because they can then determine taxation based on the amount of land owned by each individual. For each structure, I will let the figures do most of the describing and instead focus on discussing their distributions and development.

Metes and bounds: Organization by leaps and bounds

The metes and bounds system is one of the earliest means of organizing land, though many of the boundary demarcations didn't necessarily follow a standard pattern. Rather, metes and bounds rely on a system of landmarks, like roads, streams, buildings, or even large boulders. As Figure 10-1 shows, the boundaries seemingly don't follow any particular patterns. This form of rural organization is most common in older established areas, like the Eastern United States, but has been replaced in many areas because of the complicated nature of verifying boundaries and ownership. Because many claims were established centuries ago, legal and governmental intervention is sometimes needed to fully understand the extent of land ownership.

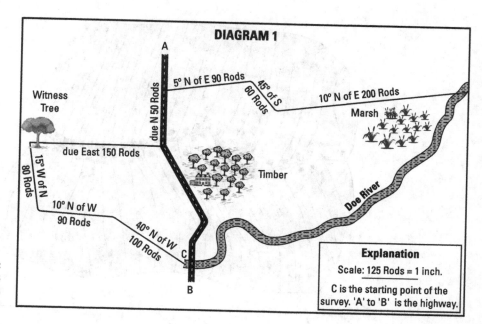

FIGURE 10-1:
The metes and bounds cadastral system

Long-lot system: The French way

Though not exclusively French, the long-lot form of cadastral organization is most often connected to the previously French-established colonies of New France (modern-day Québec in Canada) and Louisiana (see Figure 10-2).

The long-lot system can commonly be found along major transportation arteries — rivers or roads — worldwide. Long-lot organization leads to the creation of land plots that are much skinnier than they are deep. Just as Figure 10-2 shows, this allows each plot to have access to the road or river (for transportation or water access). On a smaller scale, you can also see long-lot examples in highly urban areas, where each house faces the road, has little space between houses, and long, skinny front and backyards.

Township and range system: Bringing order to the landscape

Over much of the United States, you'll notice a patchwork of square and rectangular land plots. By far, the township and range system is the most prevalent cadastral system across the US (see Figure 10-3), used over most of the country west of the Appalachian Mountains.

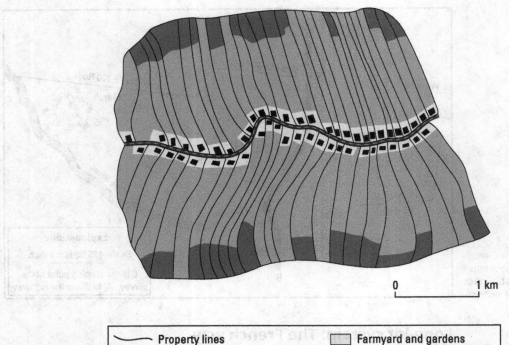

FIGURE 10-2:
The long-lot
cadastral system

Property lines
The central road
Farmhouse and other buildings
Farmyard and gardens
Fields, meadow, and pasture
Forest

0   1 km

Township System

6	5 Marsh	4	3	2	1
7	8	9	10	Lake 11	12
18	17	16	15	14	13
19	20	21	22	Timber 23	24
30	29 Marsh	28	27	26	25
31	32	33	Creek 34	35	36

FIGURE 10-3:
The township and
range system

Long-Lot System

Houses   Farmlands   Forests

1
2
3
4
road
5
6
7
8

Using the township and range system to divide land gets very technical, but it is based on an intricate series of townships — each 36 square miles and subdivided into 1-square-mile sections. This system was especially helpful in establishing areas before the large-scale immigration of people into the Western states during the American Westward Expansion.

The township and range system is a great example of an antecedent boundary, which is discussed further in Chapter 13. As part of the township and range system, particular plots are set aside for towns and schools, ensuring that each township would have access to basic services and rural centers of commerce.

Rural settlement patterns

Many of these concepts are discussed in the context of rural areas, but they apply — to an extent — in urban areas of all sizes. Figure 10-4 shows each of the rural village types.

Dispersed settlements: Out of the grid

Dispersed settlements are fairly straightforward because they are dispersed — spread out with considerable distance between houses — as the name implies. When driving through a dispersed settlement, you'll see a house here, a house there, a small cluster of houses there, and then maybe lots of open space until the next house. Dispersed settlements correspond with some of the least densely populated areas worldwide and are often affiliated with agricultural areas. The connection between city development and agriculture is discussed in Chapter 16.

Nucleated settlements: Come together

As the name implies, nucleated settlements are organized around a centralized nucleus and can be organized in myriad patterns based on the settlement's human and physical characteristics. How a village is structured (and why it's structured that way) heavily depends on the people's needs. If they depend greatly on each other to protect themselves or their animals, a round village or walled village might be the best form of organization.

TIP

These organizational patterns can apply to entire cities or just portions of cities. Many cities, especially those in the United States, started developing as rural villages but continued the same development pattern from infancy. Chicago started as a small, nucleated village along the shores of Lake Michigan and has grown to a large metropolitan area. However, it has maintained the grid pattern developed in its earliest history.

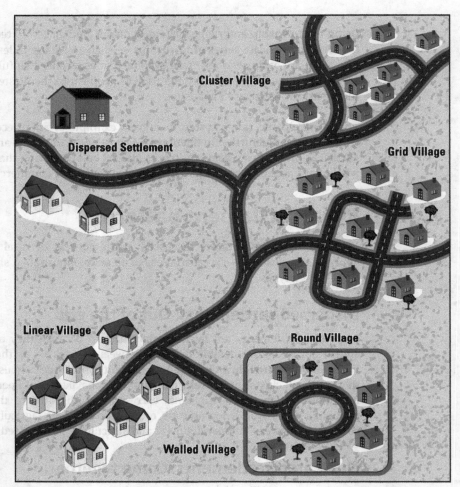

FIGURE 10-4:
Rural village types

Nucleated settlements come in several varieties:

>> **Linear villages:** Linear villages have ready access to a road or other transportation route like a river, and homes are close to one another. Just as with the long-lot survey, linear villages develop along transportation routes, primarily roads, in this case. Linear villages can be found in more rural areas, where the houses are organized fairly close to each other, and agricultural land is located behind them. These types of villages can be found literally worldwide because they create a sense of community similar to living in a village while allowing ready access to farmland.

>> **Grid villages:** Grid villages have multiple layers of people, some of which are not necessarily involved with agriculture and don't need ready access to fields. The organization of houses into a square or rectangular pattern is not revolutionary

and is very common. Its defining features change from place to place. In US Western states, grid villages are often organized around a central park (usually square). If that city happens to be the county seat, there will frequently be a county governmental building or courthouse in or near the central square. Many European, Central, and South American villages are organized in a central square that might double as pop-up markets. In Europe, a square's most common defining feature is a church or a civic building. During the Hellenic period, rapid diffusion of the grid village occurred throughout Western Asia, Northeastern Africa, and Southeastern Europe, corresponding with the growth of the Macedonian Empire of Alexander the Great. He grew one of the largest empires in history, actively seeking to spread Greek ideals and culture. Seemingly, everywhere his army went, his engineers and architects were not far behind. He established about 20 new cities, all bearing his name, that were meant to be central nodes for the diffusion of Greek culture and the administration of his vast empire, all built in a distinct grid pattern. The most famous city, still a major metropolis, is the city of Alexandria in Egypt.

» **Cluster villages:** Whereas the main feature of the grid village is its organization, the main feature of a cluster village is its seeming lack of organization. Whether because of the presence of physical features or the lack of centralized governmental planning, the city grows more organically. One of the most telltale signs of a cluster village is the presence of many intersections where more than two roads cross. The intersection of more than just two roads is one reason roundabouts are such a popular option in many villages across the United Kingdom; they're better for traffic flow than stop signs and stoplights in rural areas and allow for easy traffic regulation when multiple roads converge on a single intersection.

» **Round villages:** Round villages can widely be found across the Americas, Europe, Africa, and Asia. Often located in more historic or incredibly rural areas, round villages are more affiliated with agricultural areas. Like linear villages, round villages allowed people to live close to one another but still have ready access to farmland. Also, round villages allow livestock to be placed in the village's central area, protected by the buildings encircling them. This was especially helpful in areas where predators or thieves threatened the herds. The Fujian tulous in Southeast China are perhaps one of the most unique examples. Built as communal structures, they're interesting architectural pieces designated as significant cultural sites by the United Nations Educational, Scientific, and Cultural Organization (UNESCO).

» **Walled Village:** A walled village is any village built within the confines of a defensive wall. The villages were usually cluster, grid, or round villages surrounded by a wall to protect the inhabitants from outside threats. The historic remnants of the cities of Great Zimbabwe in Southern Africa are one of the most unique examples of the walled villages. The houses of Great Zimbabwe were built using sun-dried bricks in a circular pattern, protecting against both animal and human predators.

The walls may not have encompassed the entire village, but when an invading army was near, the villagers who lived outside the walls would be hurried inside and protected within the relative safety of the defensive structures. A specific exception is the Berlin Wall, which was begun in 1961 and was built to prevent its inhabitants from leaving. The Berlin Wall did just that until its toppling in 1989. Some cities, like Xi'an in central China, York in Northern England, and even Berlin, still have large sections of their original walls. Other cities, like New York City, have long since removed their walls but still have remnants of them built into their urban structure. In New York, Wall Street now marks the previous location of the city wall. Other famous cities, like Paris and London, also once had defensive walls. However, as the city grew, the usefulness of these fortifications lessened.

Big City Living

The nature and organization of cities have shifted throughout history as the role of cities and how people get around have changed. It is that very thing that American geographer John Borchert looked to conceptualize in 1967 when he came up with his model of urban evolution. Otherwise known as Borchert's Epochs, the model is meant to connect the changes in transportation technology to the change in urban structure. He used five distinct periods — called *epochs* — signifying the major revolutionary shifts that led to changes in urban structure:

» **Sail and Wagon Epoch (1790–1830):** The Sail and Wagon epoch is characterized by the heavy reliance on rivers and coastal areas for transportation, so cities were built up around areas with easy access to the sea.

» **Iron Horse Epoch (1830–1870):** The Iron Horse Epoch was characterized by expanding urban areas into previously disconnected parts of the country. Trains and steamboats extended the speed at which people could access interior cities (even those previously difficult to access because they were upstream).

» **The Steel Rail Epoch (1870–1920):** The Steel Rail Epoch further connected cities around the country as a national rail network, making travel between cities relatively easy. Rather than taking weeks, people could travel between cities in no more than a couple of days.

» **Auto-Air Amenity Epoch (1920–1970):** The Auto-Air Amenity Epoch saw the expansion of personal travel with the automobile, and the speed of travel between cities decreased with increasingly expanding airline networks. The increased availability of cars also changed the structure of individual cities. Cars allowed people with individual access to high-speed mobility, allowing them to live further away from city centers and travel between nearby urban areas.

>> **High-Technology Epoch (1970-present):** The final and most recent era, the High-Technology Epoch, represents changes that I'm sure not even Borchert could have predicted. Cities were connected by faster cars, planes, and trains, and travel times within cities were drastically reduced. I would also mark the significance of telecommunications and the ability for people to stay connected instantaneously. This telecommunications expansion allows people to work and interact regardless of where they are in relation to others.

While Borchert's theory is most applicable to the distribution of cities on a national scale, many theories deal with the organization of cities on a more local scale.

North American city models

In this section, we'll look at some of those patterns and discuss how cities are organized on a more local scale. First, we'll look at some of the models connected to North America, followed by other conceptualizations of urban centers in other parts of the world. See Figure 10-5.

These models are idealizations, so they won't perfectly apply. Their value is in their ability to identify trends and compare one city's structures to another.

Concentric city: Rings of development

The Concentric Zone Model was developed in 1925 by Ernst Burgess based on observations of the city of Chicago. The Concentric Zone Model is broken into five rings:

>> **Central business district (ring 1):** The model places the central business district (CBD) at the center of the city's development, representing the city's economic, cultural, and political core.

>> **Zone of transition (ring 2):** Directly around the CBD is the zone of transition, which comprises lower-income families and migrant populations who need ready access to the CBD but rely on public transportation.

>> **Zone of independent workers' homes (ring 3):** Primarily made up of blue-collar workers, these homes are more modestly priced, older, and more frequently rented than owned.

>> **Better residence zone (ring 4):** This zone comprises middle-class families who own their homes (through access to home mortgages).

>> **High-value commuter zone (ring 5):** This zone is located along the city fringe. High-value and large-footprint homes dominate this region.

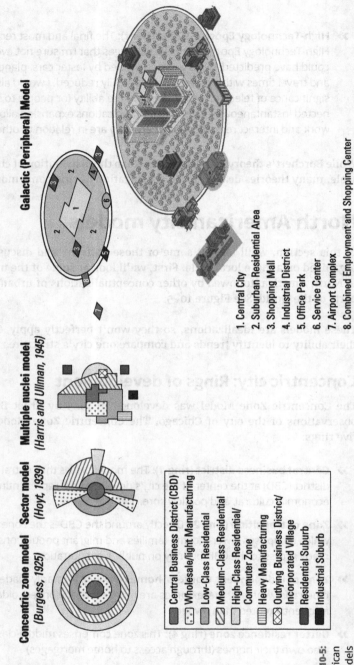

Galactic (Peripheral) Model

1. Central City
2. Suburban Residential Area
3. Shopping Mall
4. Industrial District
5. Office Park
6. Service Center
7. Airport Complex
8. Combined Employment and Shopping Center

Multiple nuclei model
(Harris and Ullman, 1945)

Sector model
(Hoyt, 1939)

Concentric zone model
(Burgess, 1925)

Central Business District (CBD)
Wholesale/light Manufacturing
Low-Class Residential
Medium-Class Residential
High-Class Residential/
Commuter Zone
Heavy Manufacturing
Outlying Business District/
Incorporated Village
Residential Suburb
Industrial Suburb

FIGURE 10-5:
North American
city models

TIP

Workers in zones 3–5 primarily rely on their own forms of personal transportation or commuter buses and trains that travel directly to the CBD.

Sector model: The times, they are a-changin'

In 1939, economist Hector Hoyt refined the urban model to reflect changes in transportation, corresponding with the Auto-Air Amenity Epoch by Borcher and the development of larger roads and railroads to move people into the urban core.

>> **Central business district:** Still marked as the CBD, this urban core remains unchanged in terms of being the main center for economic, political, and cultural developments. The sector model really changes the organization of cities because it reflects the development of wedges instead of rings connecting to the CBD.

>> **High-value commuter zone:** Recognizing that all groups want access to the CBD, the high-class residential zone now directly connects to the CBD.

>> **Better residence zone:** The middle-class residential zones now flank the high-value commuter zone.

>> **Transportation and industry wedges:** Running through the length of the model, from top to bottom, along the CBD are the transportation and industry wedges. The major roads and railroads produce noise and smoke, making the area less desirable to live next to, so growing industries are located along them instead.

The low-class residential areas also develop nearby since the undesirable location drives housing costs down to levels they can afford. The final middle-class residential areas develop along the city's fringes as cars become more available and new transportation networks increase the ease of commuting to work in the CBD.

Multiple nuclei and the rise of the suburbs

In many cities around North America, some areas are now wholly located well within the urban core that were fringe or even rural areas not 100 years ago. A good way to think of it is that many shopping malls were built where they are because there was a lot of open land available. This reflects the changing landscape of North American cities in the 1940s when Chauncey Harris and Edward Ullman theorized the Multiple Nuclei model.

The new model reflects a growing middle class and increased demand for suburban living. The development of new business districts in the suburbs allowed suburban dwellers easier access to higher-order goods without having to drive to the CBD. The city no longer has clearly defined progressions from low-class to middle-class to high-class residential areas. Instead, pockets of each develop, but the low-class residential areas remain fairly attached to the historic CBD.

New developments, like airports, also develop well outside the city where space is ample but still accessible by the developing interstate and highway system. This is the first of these models where urban development happens independently of the CBD. The city now has multiple nodes that foster localized development.

The peripheral and galactic city model: The subordinate becomes the peer

Over time, cities grew and evolved, just as they always have. That is why Chauncey Harris, one of the original creators of the Multiple Nuclei model, decided to develop the peripheral model based on observations from suburban Detroit. The model reflects the rising influence of areas that originally were located on the edge of the city (the periphery, if you will).

These fringe areas have developed further and operate as cities in their own right with CBDs of their own. Beltway interstate systems connect these peripheral cities, and arterial interstates connect the outer cities back to the original CBD core. The newly developed suburban cores seemingly orbit the city like planets in a solar system. The gravitational pull of the core CBD acts as the central star, holding metropolitan and nearby rural areas together and completing the galactic city analogy.

World city models

Recognizing that much of the world has had a very different experience than the United States and Canada, many efforts have been made to make region-specific models that more accurately represent the evolutionary histories of cities in other parts of the world.

Latin-American city model

In the 1980s, Ernest Griffin and Larry Ford developed an urban model that better reflects the development of cities in Central and South America (see Figure 10-6). The model's central feature is the historic market and CBD, which developed during the colonial era. This central "hub" acts as the nucleus of the Latin-American city, branching out "spokes" of transportation routes to connect outside areas to the CBD.

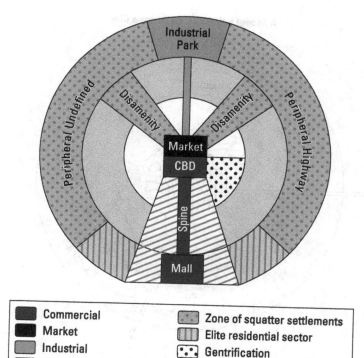

FIGURE 10-6:
The Griffin-Ford
Latin-American
city model

Legend:

Commercial	Zone of squatter settlements
Market	Elite residential sector
Industrial	Gentrification
Zone of maturity	Middle-class residential tract
Zone of In situ accretion	

More recently developed industrial and commercial centers (represented as the mall) developed on the city's periphery. The squatter settlements around the periphery and the zone of disamenity relate to the region's more modern trend of rural-to-urban migration and the importance of low-income wage earners in fueling urban development.

de Blij Sub-Saharan city model

Famous geographer Harm de Blij developed the de Blij Sub-Saharan city model (see Figure 10-7) for another portion of the world with a complex ethnic and colonial history. The model's main features are the ethnic neighborhoods, reflecting the complex demographic compositions of many urban areas across the continent.

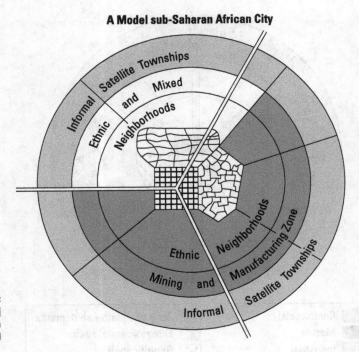

A Model sub-Saharan African City

FIGURE 10-7:
The de Blij
sub-Saharan
city model

The city's central nucleus is divided into a traditional CBD, a market area, and a colonial-era CBD. Just like with the Latin-American city model, the industrial development and mining areas develop along the city's edge with the informal settlements of slums/townships. The model has been criticized for excluding middle- and upper-class areas and minimizing the influence of the informal economy that does not conform to traditional ideas about industrial areas.

Islamic city model

Cultural influences can greatly impact the development of cities, especially evident in the Islamic/Southwest Asian city model (see Figure 10-8), where the city's central core is a great mosque, not a commercial center. Around the mosque, a bazaar (commercial vendors) is the central hub for commercial activity. A modern commercial center has developed along the main transportation corridors and on the city's outskirts, reflecting the more recent influences of outside businesses. Much of the newer development occurs outside the historic city wall and defensive citadel.

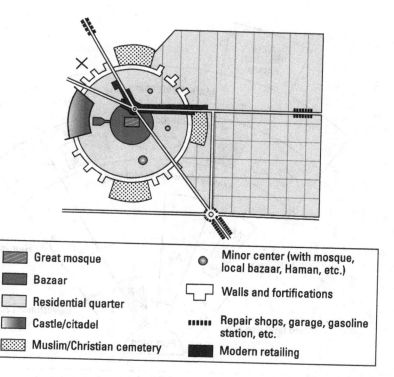

	Great mosque		Minor center (with mosque, local bazaar, Haman, etc.)
	Bazaar		
	Residential quarter		Walls and fortifications
	Castle/citadel		Repair shops, garage, gasoline station, etc.
	Muslim/Christian cemetery		Modern retailing

FIGURE 10-8:
The Southwest
Asia/Islamic city
model

Southeast Asia city model

Much of the growth of many of the largest cities in Southeast Asia can be attributed to the influence of colonialism and imperialism. During the imperial era, the port cities of Southeast Asia grew due to their usage by European powers to facilitate the withdrawal of natural resources from the region. For that reason, much of the city's growth is funneled toward the port. In Figure 10-9, the Western and Alien commercial zones were developed to cater to the business and trade needs of European and United States trade interests (the "Westerners"), and the predominantly Chinese interests (the "Aliens").

A more modern governmental zone has also developed close to the port to regulate the trade coming and going through the port area. The mixed land use areas combine low-, middle-, and even upper-class residential areas with interspersed commercial areas. Slums and newly developed middle- and upper-class suburbs form the buffer between the city's core and the rural area. Like many of the other city models, the industrial center is on the outside of the city, and for the same reason, most industrial growth has occurred recently.

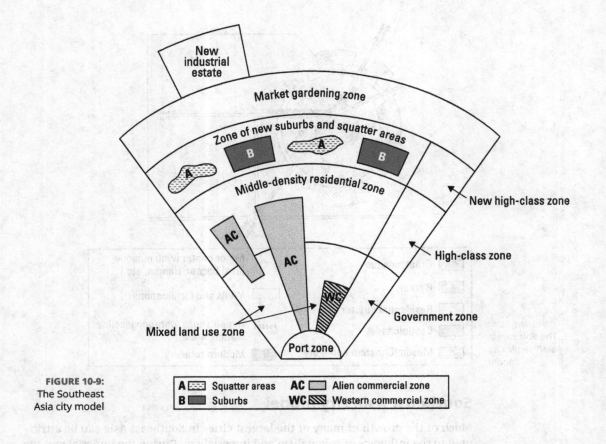

FIGURE 10-9:
The Southeast
Asia city model

A ▨ Squatter areas	AC ▢ Alien commercial zone
B ▦ Suburbs	WC ▨ Western commercial zone

Much of the growth of many of the largest cities in Southeast Asia can be attributed to the influence of colonialism and imperialism. During the imperial era, the port cities of Southeast Asia grew due to their usage by European powers to facilitate the withdrawal of natural resources from the region. For that reason, much of the city's growth is funneled toward the port. In Figure 10-9, the Western and Alien commercial zones were developed to cater to the businessmen in the needs of European and United States trade interests (the "Westerners"), and the predominantly Chinese marketers (the "Aliens").

A more modern government zone has also developed close to the port to regulate the trade-coming and going through the port area. The mixed land use area acts as a blue-collar traffic, and even upper-class residential areas with industry, retail, commercial areas. Slums and newly developed richer and upper-class suburbs form the buffer between the city's core and the rural area. Like many of the other city models, the industrial center is on the outside of the city, and the industrial center, most industrial growth has occurred recently.

3

The Spatial Organization of Human Systems

Chapter **11**

How a People Become a Culture

The study of culture is multi-dimensional. A simple definition explains culture as a group of people's combined customs, beliefs, and values. How it is studied, however, will really depend on what sort of lens you're using to examine it. Sociologists and anthropologists will use the lens of trying to understand the uniqueness of culture and its significance for a group of people. Historians will examine how a culture changes over time. Political Scientists will look at how culture influences the governmental systems of a group of people. From a human geography perspective, however, we're much more interested in understanding the distribution and spread of culture than its features. Understanding what culture is and how to break it down is necessary to track the spread of different cultural traits. For example, we need to know enough about the divisions of religions, like Protestantism versus Catholicism, to be able to compare their distribution and spread.

One important thing to clarify right away is that there are no "right" or "wrong" cultures. I won't try to persuade you of the inherent rightness of any cultural idea, especially regarding a culture's approach to understanding the divine and super-natural (religion) or how a culture organizes its structure or leadership (government). Essentially, religion and politics can get really touchy, really quickly, because many people attach their identities to cultural traits (especially religion), so I won't be promoting any cultural understanding over another.

Instead, we will look at cultures through the mindset of cultural relativism — understanding cultures for what they are, not identifying what they are not. Put simply, human geographers won't say one cultural trait is wrong because it conflicts with their cultural values. Instead, we identify those traits to understand them better within a geographic framework.

Another important way geographers examine culture is through the connection between people and landscapes. These are best examined through Place characteristics, as we've already discussed in Chapters 2 and 4. In Figure 11-1, the coloration and materials match the landscape and reflect the cultural values and traditions of the people who live there, combining to give the area a unique feel and identity. It helps bind people to a part of the Earth by strengthening their connections with the physical landscape.

FIGURE 11-1: Traditional art represented in Gyeongbokgung Palace in Central Seoul, South Korea

Process of Cultural Development

A cultural trait can be just about anything. A style of music, games, food, or clothing — it's all culture. We separate culture from things an individual does or likes by examining the spread and how widely practiced those things are.

For example, you might've grown up playing a variation of the Duck, Duck, Goose game. However, in Minnesota, some know that game as "Duck, Duck, Gray Duck," supposedly reflecting a Swedish version of the game transplanted to Minnesota by the Scandinavian settlers who migrated there. Because the Swedish migrants were highly concentrated in that one particular area, the game also spread in the area to even the non-Swedish children and became a game embedded in the culture of the entire state. While it might've started with a few people, it spread, becoming a common practice shared by many in a geographically fixated area, becoming a cultural trait.

Composition of culture

As discussed in the opening of the chapter, the best way to define a culture is a series of shared values, customs, and beliefs that a group shares. If you were to ask what the cultural makeup of a State is, say Brazi, there is no simple answer. Many pockets of different cultural influences are found all around the country, so the best way to answer that type of question is, "It depends." The cities differ from rural areas. Some regions have more Indigenous influence, while others have more European or African influence in the cultural makeup.

It is important to avoid stereotypes. For example, saying that Brazilians love soccer and speak Portuguese may be true for many Brazilians but definitely not true for all.

Defining culture

As we've already discussed, defining a culture is difficult, though it's simply the shared beliefs, values, practices, and customs of a group in a given area. However, along with a culture come subcultures and countercultures.

>> **Subculture:** Subcultures are the smaller cultural groups related to the main cultural group but unique enough to have traits that are distinguishable enough to be identified as their own group. Subcultures are a culture within a culture. For example, Hasidic Jews are a cultural group within the Jewish cultural community. Their beliefs align strongly enough with others within the Jewish culture to be considered one group by outsiders, but within the Jewish cultural groups, there is enough distinction between Hasidic beliefs and the more mainstream beliefs to be considered its own group.

>> **Counterculture:** These groups of people openly reject mainstream cultural trends. For a historical example, the 18th-century Russian ruler Peter the Great was very much against Russia's old traditions. After a trip to Western Europe, he sought to try to bring Russia to the level of the empires in the

West. Much of that depended on dragging Russia's ruling elites kicking and screaming out of their traditional ways. Peter was so involved that he would reportedly grab nobles in the streets and crudely shave off their beards (symbols of Russia's old traditions). More recently, "Goths" and other "non-conformists" define themselves by their diversion from popular trends.

So, let's break down the components of a culture:

>> **Beliefs:** A belief is a common idea or ideology. These can be religious or something like a belief in superiority (such as a class system). For example, in the Hindu Caste System, society is structured into a multi-tiered structure with a ranking hierarchy. Certain people are inherently born into different castes, allowing them different life opportunities based on their birth status. The Harijan are at the bottom of the system, and only low jobs like street sweepers are available to them.

>> **Values:** Values are things that members of that particular culture find important. In much of Europe's culture, leisure time is highly important. As such, most countries require employers to provide upward of a month of vacation time per year. In the United States and Japan, the value of hard work drives many to spend long hours on their trade, often well outside their contracted time.

>> **Customs or practices:** Customs or practices manifest the beliefs and values of a culture. These could be celebrations, habits, or even simply daily tasks that people do. For example, the Five Pillars of Islam are made up of the profession of faith (the *Shahada*), the five daily prayers (the *Salah*), the period of fasting during the month of Ramadan (*Sawm*), the practice of giving to less fortunate (*Zakat*), and the custom of taking a pilgrimage to Mecca (located in Saudi Arabia) at least once during their life (the *Hajj*).

HABIT OR CUSTOM?

Donald gets up every Saturday morning and eats his cereal with ice cream instead of milk to celebrate the beginning of the weekend. Even though this is something engrained into his routine, because only Donald does this, the habit is not widespread throughout an area's entire population, making it the habit of a particular person, not a cultural trait. If everyone in a particular area also ate their Saturday morning cereal with ice cream, then it would be widespread enough within an area to say that it is part of the culture, making it a custom. Things like chewing on nails or putting on your right shoe before your left are also habits and not necessarily customs that help define a cultural group's unique characteristics.

A cultural norm begins when those habits become standard practices with shared characteristics for most people in a given region. Cultural norms are the intricate details that make up a culture, combining standard behaviors and practices accepted within a culture. Those who don't follow these cultural norms stick out. For example, smiling at a stranger in Russia goes against the cultural norm. While smiling at strangers is considered polite behavior in many places, it is considered an indicator of mental disability in Russia. Also, groups of Americans are thought to be rude by some cultural groups because Americans break the local cultural norms by being too loud.

TECHNICAL STUFF

Exposure to new sets of cultural norms drastically different from what you're used to can be jarring. I remember my first experience riding in a car in China (while jetlagged and sleep-deprived). In the US, traffic laws are at least mostly followed, but in China, those laws are treated as guidelines. In the 30-minute drive to my new apartment, imagine my hazy horror of a drive in a new country where we spent most of the time driving in the lanes of oncoming traffic. That was my first (admittedly of many) experiences with culture shock while traveling in other countries.

Cultural manifestations

There are many ways that culture manifests itself, and I imagine if you take a walk around your community, you'll see quite a few of them. The following are some main ways a culture can be recognized or presented.

>> **Cuisine:** Talk to someone from South Korea about food, and a discussion of kimchi (fermented cabbage) is bound to come up. Kimchi is present in many of the most famous dishes associated with South Korean cuisine. Cuisine reflects a people's agricultural culture and access to different foods. The abundance of Indian food in Great Britain reflects its cultural mixing with the culture of India.

>> **Education:** How a culture educates and prepares its younger members to participate in society reflects that culture's values. The German system of high schooling reflects its strong trade programs. Instead of the one-size-fits-all structure of high school in the United States, German children are often sorted among many high schools. Students are sorted between a more generalized college pathway and a pathway that leads to trade school based on their availabilities and interests. This highly structured system allows students and parents to make more decisions about their career paths. In the United States, students are most often centralized into one high school where they receive the same core classes and then can tack on electives to specialize their education.

>> **Courtship:** How someone finds their significant other varies wildly from culture to culture. Some cultures still practice arranged marriages where the individuals don't even meet until their wedding day. In some places, particularly in Scandinavia, it is common for two people to live together, buy a home together, even raise children with one another, and never formally go through the marriage process. The weddings themselves also have a different feel depending on the culture. Don't believe me? Go to a wedding with a heavy Polish influence.

>> **Celebrations and festivals:** Holidays are often linked to religious practices. Modern Christian holidays are based on an interesting mixture of ideas. To attract many Italians, Christianity had to make room for their spring festival for rebirth and fertility (thus the symbolism of eggs and rabbits, a species known for their reproduction). For religious significance, the rebirth symbolism was attached to the rebirth of Jesus. Christmas was incorporated into the Germanic mid-winter festival (thus all the pine trees). If you really want to understand some of the origins of Christianity, do a bit of a search on Yule logs.

>> **Sports:** Recreational activities are often attached to a group's physical location. One of my favorite sports takes place in Scotland. In the Scottish Highlands winters, there is ice, and there are rocks. So, what are you going to do? You slide the rocks across the ice, trying to get them closest to a target. And there you go! The sport of curling!

>> **Dance and music:** The liveliness and color of many cultures in South America can best be attributed to the rhythm and movement of the music. The upbeat tempos and power of the instruments are associated with a strong tradition of dancing. It's much different than the two-step dancing you'll find in rural regions of the United States that are beat-based. Age groups often affiliate themselves with the style of music that was most popular during their formative years (teenage and early adulthood).

>> **Art and entertainment:** One of the things that I always loved doing while living in China was watching television. I couldn't understand hardly a word of it, but from what I could gather, the television shows can best be sorted between war (depicting World War II mostly), talent shows (mostly signing), children's TV (I watched these the most because they were the easiest to understand), British Premier League soccer re-runs, news, and foreign movies (usually really, really old ones I had never even heard of). I was living there when there was a desire for outside entertainment. The top musical group my students talked about was an Irish band called Westlife (which I had never heard of till moving to China).

The geography of language

Arguably one of the most important manifestations of culture, language is one of the easiest ways to start identifying the membership of a specific person in a particular cultural group. For example, the French culture is highly connected to the speaking of French.

Languages are complex and can reflect geographic processes such as cultural diffusion (the spread of culture) or political forces, especially the processes of colonialism and imperialism. Language is the series of verbal and nonverbal means by which members of a culture communicate with one another.

TIP

We'll discuss cultural diffusion in more detail in Chapter 12.

For example, most people speak at least three different languages. They speak English, reflecting their past as a holding of the British Empire and cultural imperialism. Many speak Swahili, a commonly diffused language in much of East Central Africa. Lastly, many Kenyans speak a more local ethnic language. The Bantu language is the largest branch of the Niger-Congo language family, the largest language family of the three main languages spoken in Kenya. Within the Bantu language, the largest language subfamily is the Kikuyu language, primarily spoken around Kenya's capital of Nairobi. Within Kikuyu, four dialects are connected to four regions.

A proto-language is a common language spoken centuries and centuries ago, to which many languages can trace their roots. Languages with a common proto-language will have a few similarities. English is part of the Indo-European language division (see Figure 11-2). From there, multiple splits are traced by grammar structure, commonalities in sound and alphabet, and common cognates (similar-sounding words). English is part of the Germanic language family (as opposed to the Balto-Slavic, Anatolian, and so on). Within the Germanic language family, English is part of the Western Germanic subfamily, including Dutch, German, Flemish, and Frisian dialects. Finally, within the English family, English dialect variations are spoken in Australia, South Africa, the United States, the United Kingdom, and many other places, including the form of English spoken in Kenya.

Because many States may include multiple languages — Kenya, for example, has 68 — they often use an official language or a *lingua franca*. An official language has been established in governmental circles. It is also the main language taught to students in government-run schools. In Kenya's case, the lingua francas are English and Swahili. A *lingua franca* is the commonly used language of social interactions in an area. Around Nairobi, most everyone may know English and Swahili, but the language most often spoken among friends, at home, or used while shopping might be Kikuyu.

There are many commonalities and differences between languages, and geographers must be able to map out these differences, as seen in Figure 11-2.

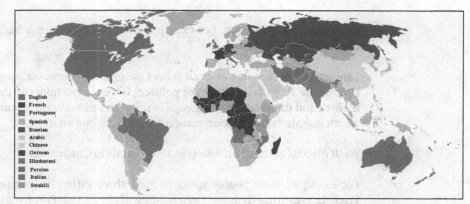

FIGURE 11-2:
A broadly generalized map showing the distributions of language families around the world

English
French
Portuguese
Spanish
Russian
Arabic
Chinese
German
Hindustani
Persian
Italian
Swahili

By mapping out languages, we can start identifying what are called *isoglosses* — clearly defined borders between different language families or branches. Slovakian is part of the Uralic language family, which is fairly neatly contained within the borders of the State of Slovakia (at least on this map). The countries surrounding Slovakia speak a primarily Indo-European language.

However, if you look at many other parts of the world, the isogloss boundaries do not conform to the political boundaries nearly as well. In Africa, for example, multiple States comprise two or even three language families. The number of languages can complicate connecting the people of a State, so many still use the European language left over from the colonial era as an official language. In Kenya, we already talked about using English for this purpose.

The geography of religion

As a broad oversimplification, religion is a belief structure with a common idea of morality and an established concept of an afterlife, including the designation of a deity (or multiple deities), the celebration of important dates related to the belief structure, and the connection of members through fellowship.

TIP

I do not intend to present any particular religious approach as being any more correct than any other religion. Religion is a deeply personal matter often heavily tied to a person's sense of self. An attack on a religion can be seen as a direct attack on a person. Also, I don't have the space to thoroughly discuss all ideas and concepts connected to one religion.

WARNING

Religions are deeply personal relationships, usually established based on faith. That is why attacks on religion around the world are taken so seriously, even if an offense was unintentional. Cultural relativism is especially important. When looking at another religion, it is best to understand it for what it is, not what it is not.

What might be okay in one religion may not be in another. Eastern Orthodox Christianity has a deep-seated tradition of iconography (the visual depiction of religious figures), but the same practice in Islam can be seen as deeply offensive. So, we must be sensitive to other cultures and spend time listening and learning.

Geographers are most interested in the spatial distribution and diffusion of religions over space and time. Looking at which religions spread where and when can help us better understand culture as a force connecting people through common beliefs. We'll detail some of the concepts connected to religion so that you can understand the complicated nuances when trying to understand the spatial distributions of religions.

First, let's start with some simple divisions. We divide all religions between universalizing and ethnic religions.

>> **Ethnic religions:** Ethnic religions are ones an individual is born into, like Hinduism or Judaism.

>> **Universalizing religions:** Universalizing religions are those that actively seek to recruit and convert new members, like Islam and Christianity, and are not necessarily connected to nationality or ethnic background. People can be born into families that practice a particular religion and spread that way or through the use of missionaries to gain converts.

This division makes a huge difference regarding how widespread the religion gets and how many members it has. Judaism has had a long and complex history. Mostly concentrated around Europe and the Middle East, the religion has spread through the physical movement of members (relocation diffusion). The religion actively encourages its members to marry other Jews to help ensure the religious succession of new members. A long history of persecution has moved Jews around the world, so they are now found in pockets of concentration around the world. Judaism does have mechanisms to incorporate new members who were not born Jewish, but their reach does not compare to the universalizing religions. Whereas the spread of Judaism is slow and concentrated, the spread of Islam and Christianity can be comparatively described as rapid and extensive.

Figure 11-3 shows a simplified look at the spatial extent of the major world religions. It gets fairly jumbled in some areas, and at this scale, it does not provide a lot of detail about some of the smaller pockets of religions, but it still gives a good idea of what the main faiths of people are around the world.

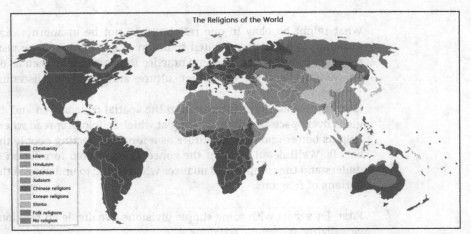

The Religions of the World

Christianity
Islam
Hinduism
Buddhism
Judaism
Chinese religions
Korean religions
Shinto
Folk religions
No religion

FIGURE 11-3:
Major world
religions

Unknow author / Wikimedia Commons / Public Domain.

Much like language, religions can be categorized in many ways, which is especially complicated for geographers because they must understand the complexity and history of religions. For example, mapping out the spread of the Islamic religion gets very complicated very quickly because Islam contains two main branches: Shi'a and Sunni. I won't get into the history of these two branches because you would need an entire book to do it justice. For simplicity's sake, know that much of the split between the two has to do with the succession after the death of Mohammad and the leadership of the Islamic faith. If I were to map the spread of Islam, the distinction between its two branches would be vital for understanding internal matters within Islam.

Further investigation of most religions reveals various sects with varying popularity and acceptance amongst the religious community. For example, the two main branches of Islam are the Sunni and Shi'a, though there are a number of other sects with fewer followers. For example, the Whabbi, Sufi, and Salafi are sects with varying degrees of similarity to Sunni or Shi'a. Some scholars consider them to be completely different branches.

Further muddying our understanding is that some extremist groups claim to be sects but may be more or less rejected by the main denominations. The Islamic State of Iraq and the Levant (ISIL — also sometimes known as the Islamic State of Iraq and Syria ISIS) claims to be the true branch of Islam and seeks to establish a new caliphate (religiously dominated kingdom).

REMEMBER

ISIL is largely rejected and shunned by much of the Islamic community, especially because of ISIL's perceived extreme views and attacks on peaceful communities (including against other Muslims).

WARNING

If all of this seems very complicated, you're right. Many details of language and religion can be intricate and difficult to understand. To get the most out of this section, focus on the idea that there are divisions within divisions (and so on) that can make for some seriously complicated spatial distributions. When someone says something along the lines of "Islam is the main religion in the Middle East," just know that that is only true to a point. That statement is overgeneralized because of the issue of scale and the complex mosaic of details. In general, you should avoid sweeping overgeneralizations.

Figure 11-4 shows a large mosque in Central Nairobi, an otherwise heavily Christian region.

FIGURE 11-4:
Jamia mosque in downtown Nairobi, Kenya

Language is further complicated by increased multilingualism and the spread of a global lingua franca, especially English, French, and, increasingly, Mandarin Chinese. Religion is spreading further and faster than ever with modern communication and transportation, but so is secularism (non-church or non-religious), which even further complicates efforts to represent cultural beliefs in spatial form.

Development of shared culture

Culture can be tricky. You might think pinpointing where someone is from would be fairly easy based on their habits and customs. However, with how much people move around and personal and virtual cultural exchanges, it can be difficult to trace cultural traits to specific locations. This can be especially complicated because of some of the finer details of cultures. Traditional cultural traits can be diminished or even go extinct through migration. For example, the heavy influx of Spanish speakers is replacing English as the dominant language in Miami, Florida.

That is why folk cultures are particularly interesting to geographers. Folk cultures are smaller and usually more geographically isolated (by distance or development).This often leads to the development of place-based cultures, where much of the culture is connected to the physical landscape. Things like language (especially in terms of vocabulary), housing, values, clothing, and so on can be especially dependent upon the physical landscape. For example, the Inuit of the northern United States and Canada have multiple words for "snow," but a Native tribe in the Amazon may not have any words for it because they have no experience with it.

TECHNICAL STUFF

Have you noticed that people worldwide increasingly listen to the same type of music, wear the same clothing styles, buy the same products, and speak the same languages? If you travel enough, you'll notice many big cities are starting to have the same feel. That is because of what geographers refer to as the popular culture. Globalization has increased the speed by which cultural traits can now spread. A K-pop band can record a new album one week in Seoul; then, their music is being listened to by teenagers worldwide the next week. Globalization is helping to speed up the process by which cultures become extinct as young people become more interested in the global culture than their own. When we think of extinction, we might immediately think of animals, but this can also refer to languages, religions, and whole culture groups. Cultures are wiped out as they are absorbed into the global culture.

These place-based cultural traits work to bind people together with their shared understandings. These folk cultures are so tightly bound that if you remove the people from their location, they might experience a form of existential crisis because their identity is so strongly attached to the physical environment. During Stalinist Russia, there was a policy of relocating the Native populations of the far North and far East of Russia to cities as part of a wider program of "Sovietization" and "Russification." Many studies have been done on the effects of these programs, especially on communities like the Chukchi. Removed from their homelands, many Chukchi fell into deep depression as a result of the disconnect. It was so bad for some that they were only too glad to return to their remote homelands (which were often much colder and much more devoid of modern comforts) to try to restore their cultural connections.

Similar experiences were had by Native communities in Canada, the United States, and Australia, where organized governmental programs removed Native peoples from their homelands. These disconnections from the physical landscape that bound many of their cultural connections together created internal disconnects that led to deep psychological distress for many.

It is with this understanding that recent initiatives to incorporate communities in South America, Central Asia, or other remote parts of the world into the popular culture have been cautioned against. Thinking everyone wants new technologies and Western-style housing comforts or wants to be incorporated into a global society is a form of ethnocentrism highly prevalent in the Global North. Indeed, people often want some of these things to an extent, but sometimes, they just want to be left to their own communities. This is a very complicated way to say that there is a complicated balance between not forcing culture onto others while still promoting development and advancement in quality of life.

Learning from the mistakes of others can be an important part of progress in these regards. After having been culturally ravaged by the efforts of "Americanization" and Indian boarding schools, Native communities within the United States are in the process of restoring their unique cultures. One of the most important aspects is reteaching the languages that have otherwise been removed from these Native communities. Many Native schools on reservations are trying to reincorporate lessons on language and tradition to rebuild a sense of community through common culture.

Along with languages, religions have frequently become phased out in favor of larger religions. Somewhat deliberately, throughout the processes of imperialism and colonialism, the religions of those doing the empire-building were imposed on the people they were in the process of subjugating. Often part of the process of "civilizing" people, imperialism and colonialism also had the convenient benefit of folding the newly subjugated people into the social structure that helped establish the colonizer/conquerer at the top of the social structure.

The process of cultural imperialism was one of the methods of subjugation forced on populations to help cement relationships between a people and the conquerer. This still takes place today, though maybe not as deliberately. However, the popular cultures of today are slowly creating a new globalized culture with shared customs, values, and beliefs through the exchange of ideas and increased interaction over the Internet. Multinational companies are one of the main mechanisms because they seek to swallow up market shares, often at the expense of local businesses. Fast food can be one of the most visual signs of this, as its presence in cities worldwide quickly overshadows the cuisines served in locally owned businesses.

Subculture, counterculture, and our culture

Humans like expressing themselves individually, but social beings need to fit in. This can lead to the development of subcultures or countercultures. One of the most striking examples is the "Emo" culture of the 2000s onward. Many people felt disconnected from the main culture or rejected the values and beliefs of popular culture, so they banded together to form a new sort of culture within a culture. With their own norms, including distinct forms of music, dress, and language, these self-acclaimed "non-conformists" actually developed a culture of their own by conforming to new cultural norms. Through these processes, a countercultural group ended up developing a subcultural group.

Generational groups, like the Teddy Boys of the United Kingdom in the 1950s, have often been a way for one generation to distinguish themselves from the generation of parents. Often a form of protest, many of the traits of these subcultural groups are meant to be a rebellion against the cultural values of the one they're trying to distinguish against. New music, clothing styles, customs, and even generation-specific slang can be means of fitting into the new culture and signifying cultural group membership. For the Teddy Boys, American rock and roll and very distinct clothing styles helped distinguish this subcultural group.

Making a mark on the geographic landscape

Now that we've looked at the complexity of culture and established why culture can be difficult to understand, let's spend some time on where geography fits into the study of culture more specifically. Defining culture and understanding the nuanced differences between cultures is really something better left for a sociologist or cultural anthropologist. What geography can do is focus on the connection between place and culture. The most obvious way we can do this is by researching the spatial distributions by making and analyzing maps. We've already talked about this quite a bit, especially in the context of how difficult it is to make maps of cultural traits because of their internal complexities.

The cultural landscape

One of the other things that geographers are particularly interested in is the cultural landscape. This relationship between culture and the physical environment can come in the form of how a particular culture uses or reflects on the environment.

The urban landscape is one of the most extreme representations of the cultural landscape. Some cities try to suppress and maintain the natural environment to the point that they create a totally new landscape from what was originally there (true to a degree for every human environment). Go to a window and look outside. While doing this, imagine how that environment looked before humans, which might not be too difficult in rural areas. However, if there is extensive agriculture, it may not be easy. In an urban environment, this activity might be outright impossible. Humans have gone to great lengths to terraform and conform the environment to their vision, making the original form inconceivable.

When I lived in Saint Paul, Minnesota's central business district, the only view from my apartment window was buildings, roads, and parking lots. My only view of "nature" was the sky and the ornamental trees (many of which were non-native to that part of the country). Even in Omaha, where I now live and work, the landscape is dotted with trees and buildings over what should be a tallgrass prairie. I always find it ironic that Nebraska markets itself as the "Arbor State" because of its role in creating Arbor Day, yet it is a landscape that should be mostly void of trees. Even the rivers and creeks of the area had to be "tamed." Creeks prone to flooding now sit at the bottom of large human-made embankments or encased with concrete, restricting their ability to meander and carve out new paths. This process is not new by any means, but it has certainly been sped up with modern machinery and increased human desire to "tame" nature. Efforts to tame the landscape will be tested as the effects of climate change continue to have an increasingly invasive approach on human landscapes.

The hyperfocus on development and a "keeping up with the Joneses" mentality between cities is also developing shockingly similar landscapes, sometimes, to the point that you can look around and see no distinguishable features to help you identify even what part of the world you're even in. This is a concept human geographers refer to as placelessness. Standing in Shanghai's financial district, it is hard to distinguish it from the financial district of New York, London, or even Nairobi. The spread of global chain stores like Subway, H&M, and Apple makes it even more difficult as they can diminish the impact of local culture on the landscape in favor of globalized popular culture.

Now, I am not saying that you can't still see the unique culture of a place reflected in the landscape. It might just take a little more searching and imagination.

Reading a cultural landscape

Consider Figure 11-5, which shows a cityscape with subtle hints of its location but is otherwise impossible to place, giving it a sense of placelessness.

FIGURE 11-5:
Placelessness
embodied in
photographic
form

When looking at Figure 11-5 as a geographer, there is not much to go on to tell us where this photo was taken, but we can glean the following information:

>> A paved street is fairly narrow and devoid of cars, save for a single delivery truck. This shows us that this culture is not as desperately tied to their cars as, say, Americans.

>> The brick roads tell us that the city is older because using bricks was a common method of road construction in Europe and older portions of the Americas.

>> The people are hard to pick out, but there does not look to be much diversity, nor are there heaps of people, so this helps tell us it is not a city that benefits from large amounts of immigration or tourism.

>> The buildings are a mixture of older, stylized flair of a multitude of European-based architectural movements combined with blander, nondescript buildings of a more modern appearance.

>> This is likely a downtown area in a European city that was designed before cars were heavily considered, given the narrowness of the streets. This helps us narrow the picture down to Western Europe, where many examples of cities were partially destroyed or damaged in World War II.

>> The one store name we can read, Harenberg, is of the structure of a Germanic language or at least connections to one.

Other than the observations above, the landscape is flat, and we can't see any other Place characteristics (utilizing the definition of Place from Chapter 2) to help us identify this as the city of Bonn, Germany. Now, see Figure 11-6.

FIGURE 11-6:
Image of a place that is less nondescript

This photo gives us more to go on:

» The river has a concrete embankment to prevent flooding and help secure the roadway along the riverbank.

» The river is and most likely was a focal point of this city because this main fortress sits close to the river.

» The fortification walls tell us this is a fairly old city that went through the experience of feudalism.

» A large rectangular building in baroque style signifies a European influence.

» The tall onion-domed towers' architecture points to an Eastern influence. This helps narrow down a river city in Russia (where Eastern influences and European influences come together) with obvious importance throughout many eras (given the varying ages yet still large stature of the buildings).

Based on these observations, this can only be a large city in Western Russia. This is the city of Moscow.

Don't feel bad if some of these were not as easy to pick up. Training yourself to read the cultural landscape takes a lot of practice. I would suggest traveling around your community to see what structures and physical features help give away its identity. Maybe it is the variety of religious places of worship, a plethora of restaurants serving foods from all around the world, or large green spaces that help preserve some of the place's natural beauty. Each part of a human landscape helps tell the tale of a culture's relationship with the environment and each other.

The landscape of Place

We've already discussed some ways geographers are working to map out the spatial extent of cultural traits. As we've already said, this task is not easy, given how complicated culture can be. Cultural borders are often complicated and rarely conform to humans' established political boundaries. One of the most fun parts of being a geographer is traveling to places to "ground-truth" an area to better understand the actual culture by walking the streets, talking to the people, and analyzing the cultural landscape.

Through ground-truthing and further study, we're constantly working to build an even clearer map of the world's cultures. If you want to get a feel for one of the methods of seeing the influence of culture in the mapping of place, pick out a US state, look at a map, and notice the place names. For example, many Wisconsin cities are linked to the Native origin of the state with names. However, places like Sheboygan (a name with a Native origin) are just down the road from Kohler and Fond du Lac (cities with European names — German and French, respectively), reflecting the processes of European settlement.

Elsewhere, New York was named by settlers after the city of York in Northern England. The entire province of Nova Scotia translates, more or less, as "New Scotland."

The study of toponomy and place names can be quite revealing when trying to understand the influence of culture on an area. Toponomy isn't an exact science by any means, but it's a start. And, again, it's always a great excuse to travel and do some ground-truthing of your own to better understand a place for yourself.

» **How culture is received and incorporated into society**

» **Why cultural diffusion can lead to fear and misunderstandings**

Chapter **12**

How a Culture Spreads

I n previous chapters, we discussed culture and how geographers specifically contribute to larger discussions about culture. This chapter focuses on how culture spreads (cultural diffusion), the geographic factors affecting its spread, and how people commonly react when exposed to new cultures. Today, most cultures are mixtures of many cultures. In fact, human geographers would be hard-pressed to identify a culture that hasn't been touched by others. Instead, we focus on the rate at which cultures spread and intermingle.

I like to challenge my students to come up with a cultural trait that is truly "American." Consider this:

» The government is a mixture of the Roman Republic with principles of democracy developed by the Greek City-States. Add in some philosophical developments of English and French Enlightenment thinkers, and you've got the American principles of government.

» Our economy is based on the principles of capitalism developed by Scotsman Adam Smith.

» The main religions are Roman Catholicism, Protestantism from Northern Europe, or Judaism and Islam from the Middle East.

» The main languages of English and Spanish are both European.

» Our foods are all inspired by dishes in other countries to the point that we can really only claim Thanksgiving dinner of Turkey and potatoes as "American" in origin.

» Most of the popular music styles have origins in Europe and Africa.

» The most popular sports in America — basketball, baseball, hockey, and football — are American but owe much of their early beginnings to the Canadian part of the Americas. Soccer's origins are disputed, depending on which country you ask in Europe.

Pieces here and there of our culture are unique to the United States, but it is not terribly far off to call the US a European culture — or, more accurately, a globalized culture. There is nothing wrong with that, either. Much the same could be said about many of the cultures around the world. The world is increasingly tied together by common cultural traits through economic, political, and social ties.

These cultural commonalities can be largely attributed to what geographers know to be the time-space convergence — the general idea that distances between places decrease due to advances in transportation and communication technology. Distances that used to take days, weeks, or even months to cover can now be reached in hours or seconds via airplane or the Internet. Air travel has drastically increased the connections between places. It is now possible to take a direct flight from New York to Singapore — the longest commercial flight covering nearly 10,000 miles — in 18 hours. Communication that used to rely on physical connections can now be done instantaneously over the phone or Internet-based communication networks like WhatsApp or Zoom.

The potential for culture to spread has drastically increased as well. Thanks to the Internet, humans have more access to information now than at any other time in history. We have tremendous capability to access information about other parts of the world and access to each other than ever before. Whether we take advantage of that wealth of information or just scroll through silly animal videos is another matter.

All the same, the time-space convergence has sped up the spread of popular culture and severely imperiled the world's folk cultures. Cultural isolation is increasingly rare, if not impossible. Technology's influence in helping spread culture cannot be understated.

TIP

I used to teach at an International School and often had students from all over the world with nearly impeccable English. When I asked them how their English got so good, they rarely mentioned their hard work in studying. Most would credit popular television shows like *Friends* or *How I Met Your Mother* for their mastery of nuances within the language.

The spread of culture is not without its negatives to go along with its positives; both are discussed later in this chapter. What is true, however, is that when we apply the principles of uniformitarianism (processes happening today have always happened), we can help better understand how culture has spread in the past by examining how culture spreads now.

Processes of Cultural Diffusion

Though the timing and mechanisms of cultural diffusion may have changed, the processes remain much the same. Whether it is the 9th-century spread of Christianity or the increasing popularity of Korean pop group BTS, culture can still be understood to spread in much the same patterns.

In each instance, cultural diffusion of a new trait can be understood to have originated from a cultural hearth. Jazz music is often thought to have originated in New Orleans and diffused outward. Modern Catholicism, a now global religion, traces its hearth, unsurprisingly, to the Vatican in Rome. Hollywood is heralded as the global center of cinema but is actually rivaled by film industries in Nigeria and India.

World cities are often cultural hearths. The concentration of people, the spread of ideas, the need for innovative solutions, and the competition for large markets can help facilitate the beginning of new cultural traits. Cities like New York, Paris, London, Tokyo, Hong Kong, and Milan have frequently been the hearths for cultural traits in entertainment, technology, fashion, and business that have helped make them global leaders. Their world-renowned reputations help attract new migrants to help further facilitate the development of new cultural traits.

Wide classifications of diffusion

The diffusion of cultural traits is commonly looked at through the lens of expansion diffusion. This means that a cultural trait has expanded to new areas and regions but remained strong in the source population around the hearth (an area around which a cultural trait originates). The English language, for example, originated in the hearth of modern England from Germanic Angle and Saxon influences. The language then diffused to Wales, Scotland, and Ireland but remained strong in England. Even as it has become the primary language spoken in countries like Canada, the United States, Belize, Australia, South Africa, New Zealand, Kenya, and almost countless other places worldwide, English has still remained strongly entrenched in the culture of its original hearth, England. Most forms of diffusion will fit under this wide classification, and we'll touch on it more later.

I would also like to consider proposing the idea of borrowing from biogeography and the distribution of species by understanding the spread of culture from the viewpoint of allochthonous endemism.

Allochthonous endemism is a term used to understand the spread of species to a region and the subsequent extinction of populations in the hearth. Allochthonous endemism could also be used to understand cultural diffusion as an alternative to expansion diffusion. Let's just call this "allochthonous diffusion."

For example, eating lutefisk at Christmas is a strong cultural tradition in many Norwegian ethnic communities in states like Minnesota and North Dakota.

If you've never had the displeasure of trying lutefisk, you should know that it's a gelatinous dish made by soaking white fish in lye and then rinsing it off. Sounds super appealing, right? My advice is to use all the butter you can if you ever find yourself at a Christmas lutefisk dinner at a Norwegian Lutheran church in the Twin Cities.

Eating lutefisk has remained engrained in the traditions of Norwegian immigrants to North America, even though the practice has died out in many places around Norway (because, well, gelatinous fish).

Contagious diffusion

Anyone who has ever lived in a college dormitory can tell you exactly how it is. First, your roommate gets sick, which means there's no hope for you to avoid getting sick, too. Then, the people you hang out with get sick. Meanwhile, the people in the rooms closest to you get sick because they are in such close proximity. Soon, the school must quarantine the residence halls because everyone is sick, and they're trying to prevent it from spreading even further.

A cultural trend spreads similarly. First, one person becomes aware of a new cultural trend. The people immediately around them spread it to their close friends and family. It spreads further and further in almost a compounding manner as more and more people are exposed to it.

Looking at the ripples when you toss a pebble into water is another way to describe the pattern of contagious diffusion. The ripples spread out and grow the further you get away from the original splash. In this case, the splash is the cultural hearth where a new cultural trait originates.

The only major difference about contagious diffusion now, as opposed to maybe two hundred years ago, is how culture spreads across space. Before widely distributed telecommunications — when diffusion depended on person-to-person contact — the spread of new cultural traits would spread from the hearth to the next closest cities in an expanding ring. However, today, cultural trends can jump around the world with ease because the Internet exponentially compounds the spread.

Christianity is a cultural trait that spread through contagious diffusion (recognizing, of course, that many factors influenced its spread). For this example, we'll use the Mediterranean region of Europe as the hearth, though we could use Jerusalem, Constantinople (modern-day Istanbul), or Rome:

>> From the Mediterranean region of Europe, Christianity generally radiated northward into the other Roman-influenced regions like modern France and Spain.

>> Eventually, it spread into the frontier regions of Britain and the Germanic portions of Central Europe.

>> Its spread south was restricted by the growing popularity of Islam in Northern Africa and Western Asia.

>> Christianity could more easily expand further east once the Russian princes could finally push out the last remnants of the Mongolian hordes.

>> The far north of Europe was finally converted to Christianity, which also helped stop the Viking raids that had been terrorizing the rest of the continent.

>> Once Europeans expanded beyond their continental borders during the Age of Exploration, they brought their religion to the shores of the Americas, Asia, Africa, and Australia.

What started as a slow ripple centered in Southern Europe and Southwest Asia eventually grew to influence all parts of the globe.

TECHNICAL STUFF

Pinpointing where Christianity began can be tough. Yes, the religion is based on the teachings of Jesus in the Roman province of Judea and subsequent spread by his disciples. The modern Christian church, however, is traced to the Council of Nicaea in 325 CE in the Eastern Roman Empire city of Nicaea. The different denominations like Roman Catholicism, Lutheranism (from Germany), the Anglican Church (from England), Greek Orthodox, Russian Orthodox, Ukrainian Orthodox churches, and even the Church of Jesus Christ of Latter-Day Saints (Mormons) trace their ideas of Christianity from the modern-day United States. Explaining Christianity's origin is very difficult because you must examine it on a branch-by-branch (or even sect-by-sect) basis.

Figure 12-1 shows the diffusion of the four major religions. The more localized ethnic religion of Hinduism remains fairly contained to the Indian subcontinent, while the universalizing religions of Islam and Christianity have spread through much of the world.

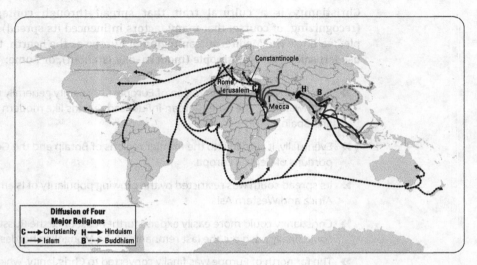

FIGURE 12-1:
Diffusion of the four major religions

Hierarchical diffusion

Have you ever noticed that when a new product is released, the rich and famous are often the first to have it and often appear in advertisements for it? Typically, celebrities don't endorse products because they truly believe in the product. (They might believe in the product, but they're more likely getting paid lots of money to tell you how much they like that product). More so, companies will spend lots of money to get a celebrity to endorse their product because they understand the patterns of hierarchical diffusion.

The general idea of hierarchical diffusion is that a trait will first pass from a high-ranking person or city to another high-ranking person or city before making its way down to lower-order people or cities. A high-ranking person is someone with significant political or social status who is highly recognized and admired. They're the type of people who set cultural norms. If they start wearing their hair a certain way, others will as well. The "Rachel" haircut, popularized by Jennifer Aniston's character from *Friends* is a good example of a high-ranking person using hierarchical diffusion to popularize a hairstyle.

A higher-order city is a world city with significant influence. Of course, when we talk about world cities, scale is important. On a global scale, world cities like New York or Tokyo immediately come to mind, but cities like Cape Town,

South Africa, or Lagos, Nigeria, probably don't. However, when discussing the hierarchical spread of cultural traits across Africa, Cape Town and Lagos are most definitely in the conversation.

Figure 12-2 shows the Victoria and Albert Harbour in Cape Town, South Africa. One of the more posh parts of Southern Africa, downtown Cape Town has a vaguely European feel from its connection to Europe during the colonial and imperial eras and the tight cultural connections that have remained.

FIGURE 12-2:
The Victoria and Albert Harbour in Cape Town, South Africa

REMEMBER

If you remember from Chapter 9, the Gravity Model can be applied to understand the interactions of places based on their physical distance from one another, but also their significance. Each city will have some form of interaction with other cities, but nearer cities will have stronger connections with each other than more distant cities. A small city will interact more with a large city far away than with a small city an equal distance away.

A city's physical distance and pull must be accounted for when looking at where cultural traits will spread. A new cultural trait is much more likely to spread from London to Istanbul, Turkey, before spreading from London to Antalya (a smaller but still significantly sized city in Turkey).

So, if we looked at this process in England, it would look something like this:

>> A new cultural trait spreads to London from the cultural hearth of Hong Kong.

>> From London, the trait spreads to Birmingham and Manchester.

>> Subsequent spread to smaller cities like Sheffield or Bristol continues on down to Plymouth or Bournemouth.

>> The trait spreads to smaller cities like Canterbury or Dover until it finally reaches small villages like Barnsole.

>> Eventually, the whole of England has been exposed to the new cultural trait.

The speed at which this happens, however, completely depends on distance. The impact of distance depends on technology for transportation and communication.

To give a historical example, we'll go back to Christianity. In the earliest stages of Christianity's diffusion into the Americas, missionaries (people who actively sought to spread the religion) would most actively try to convert high-ranking political figures (sometimes not using the best of methods). These missionaries knew that if they could convert a high-ranking political or social leader, converting the rest of the people would be easier because they could rely on the support of the converted leader. The converted leader's inner circle would be converted, followed by extended family members, and continuing outward until the whole population was converted.

Figure 12-3 shows the Gandantegchinlen Tibetan Buddhism Monastery in Ulaanbaatar, Mongolia — the center of Buddhism in Mongolia. The religion was more or less shut down due to governmental pressure from 1939–1989 but was eventually reopened after the fall of Communism. Hierarchical forces can also slow down diffusion.

Relocation diffusion

As complicated as hierarchical diffusion may be, relocation diffusion is fairly straightforward and simple. It's the spread of culture by the physical migration of people. Things get more complicated when we look at what happens after they migrate. Whether the culture further spreads out after the migration depends on many factors. If there are strong forces of chain migration and many people from the same culture move to the same general area, then there is a good chance that the influence of their culture in the new area will be fairly strong. It's kind of like how Boston has a strong Irish identity because there was such a strong tradition of Irish migration to the city. The first-generation migrants (foreign-born) hold onto their culture (especially language and traditions). Subsequent generations of those first migrants are less and less likely to maintain those strong cultural bonds the further removed they are from that first set of migrants who moved into the area. This is because later generations have more intermixing with people of other backgrounds and fewer connections to their ethnic culture. This is the process of acculturation. Acculturation is explained further in the next section.

Let's use Judaism as an example. As an ethnic religion that does not actively seek out new converts, Judaism builds its population of followers mostly by births. Because Judaism is so strongly tied to individuals and does not move as easily as just an idea, the diffusion of Judaism depends on the physical movement of people from one area to another. Many Jewish people moved to the United States East Coast, especially after the 1920s. In cities like New York, large Jewish communities were built, and they maintained their cultures and traditions. The likelihood of marriage between members is also higher, so the community grew by more births. However, in the US Midwest, the Jewish community is not as big outside major cities like Chicago or Minneapolis. Connections between Jewish people and others who share their beliefs are not as strong, so there is less opportunity to expand their culture through intermarriage. Jewish people may be more likely to marry people who are not Jewish, making it less likely their children would also be Jewish.

Relocation diffusion can be one of the biggest reasons for allochthonous diffusion. Most people living in Utah are strongly tied to the Church of Jesus Christ of Latter-Day Saints, commonly known as Mormons. The origins of the Mormon faith trace back to the Eastern and Midwest United States before its followers eventually found their way to Salt Lake City, Utah. The religion became more or less extinct in its original location but built up in the new location near Salt Lake City. From there, the religion diffused once more to be located around its original hearths of Missouri and Ohio.

Stimulus diffusion

Ask any Italian about "Italian food" in the United States; they might have some very choice words for you. The general idea of what makes Italian food might be present in Italian food in America, but if you are an American who goes to Italy, you might be hard-pressed to find familiar dishes you associate with being Italian. Cuisine is the best way to exemplify these concepts since cuisines outside their original source location are almost always different than the original source location. While living in China, I never found the kind of foods I knew from Americanized Chinese restaurants because the whole-fish, deep-fried songbirds, incredibly spicy food from the South, and the Muslim-influenced food from the West would not jive with the diets of most Americans.

TIP

Many cultures have their own unique ways of doing things, such as this South Korean restaurant, which provides a glove so your hand doesn't get greasy. (see Figure 12-4). In China, this involved putting corn on pizza. Pizza with corn ranks far lower than pineapple pizza ever will, in my opinion.

FIGURE 12-4:
A pizza menu in Seoul, South Korea. (Photo courtesy of Jill Muegge.)

Courtesy of Jill Muegge

The general idea of stimulus diffusion is that a cultural trait moves and then changes to adapt to local tastes. The essence of the cultural trait remains the same, but it takes on a bit more of a local flavor. Music may be similar in essence but with a more localized feel. Also, some Catholic traditions are different in Central America than in Rome. The main tenets are the same but with regional differences in their impact on daily life and how they are represented in the culture.

Some of the greatest examples of stimulus diffusion, besides food, are exemplified by the creolized languages that can occur from adopting portions of the language. A creolized language — the most famous of which are Louisiana Creole and Haitian Creole — is formed by the partial blending of multiple languages. The Cajuns of Southern Louisiana speak a language branch similar to Louisiana Creole. French's basic structure and vocabulary are present. However, the Cajnun language has a unique simplicity and accent, making it difficult for many native French speakers to understand because the Haitian and Louisiana Creole languages intermixed with African influences form a fully unique structure based on a combination of multiple languages.

REMEMBER

The spread of cultural traits and their subsequent changes help form some unique understandings and perceptions of what people think of the rest of the world. Because most cultural traits will undergo some sort of change to adapt to the local tastes of a place, many cultural traits exemplify stimulus diffusion.

Reactions to Cultural Diffusion

Culture is always spreading, and will continue to diffuse. These are simple facts. Whether you like it or not, there will always be new cultural trends and fads that will change the very fabric of a region, country, or even the whole world. A recent cultural study in the United States found that preferences in world cuisines shifted in 2023 from Italian to Mexican foods. What new cultural trends will come around are hard to predict, but what will remain is how people react to the new changes. Will it be openness or denial?

Acceptance and openness to new ideas

When presented with new cultural traits, some people will more willingly adopt and incorporate them into their own identities. The most receptive people tend to be younger generations in regions dominated by popular culture. The least receptive would be older generations in folk cultures. Younger people have had less time to become set in their ways. Psychologically, they're still in the phase of learning and establishing their personalities, and if they're living in a culture most influenced by globalization, then they're already being exposed to a plethora of diversity in cultural influences. Throughout history, there are plenty of examples of culture not being accepted, but the globalizing of cultures we're seeing today is plenty of evidence that cultural convergence is possible.

Figure 12-5 shows Piccadilly Circus in Central London, the posh epicenter of London consumerism. Piccadilly resembles the essence of Times Square in New York with a British feel to it.

FIGURE 12-5:
Piccadilly Circus
in Central London

Becoming a global culture

A meme circulating around the Internet jokingly says being British means driving a German car to pick up Indian takeout so that you can go home to sit on your Swedish-made furniture to watch an American television show on a Japanese television. Go to the area around Piccadilly Circus (pictured in figure 12-5), and you'll see this displayed in full force. Though not true for every British person, this meme points out that their access to other cultures more or less defines regions incorporated by popular culture. This meme could easily be used to describe the culture of any number of countries worldwide. The globalized transportation and communications networks are also helping to develop a globalized culture — cultural convergence.

As more people interact and share ideas, our cultures will increasingly resemble one another. This can be represented by shared cultural traits such a religion, language (increasingly relying on English as the global lingua franca), approaches to new technology and openness to new ideas, and a globalizing liberalism in terms of personal freedoms and identity.

This trend toward cultural convergence has had an alternate effect that may not have been an intended consequence as cultures spread and adapted to one another. We're presently living in the most peaceful time in human history. Yes, there are presently (as of 2023) major wars in Eastern Europe, Central Africa, South Asia, and between Israel and Hamas, civil strife in more than a dozen countries, and abuses of the rights of citizens in too many more, but it is still less than what we've experienced in prior decades. It's been almost 80 years since the last major global conflict, and examples of mass persecution leading to large death tolls have significantly reduced.

THE GOLDEN ARCHES THEORY

Thomas Friedman proposed why this is happening in his 1999 book *The Lexus and the Olive Tree: Understanding Globalization*. His general contention is that the world is undergoing a capitalist shift where there is a desire to modernize and access consumer goods (characterized by the Lexus automobile), stay culturally unique, and preserve cultural identities. One of Friedman's main arguments is the "Golden Arches Theory," which basically contends that no two countries with a McDonalds would attack each other. While there are, unfortunately, too many examples from recent history, including Russia's 2022 invasion of Ukraine, that prove the premise wrong, it does point out some interesting ideas.

The crux of the argument is that cultural convergence has brought us together so that countries whose cultures have aligned would have a more friendly political stance toward one another. Perhaps Russia was just detached enough from the rest of Europe for the powers of geopolitics (and Putin) to push them toward risking an already thin connection with the West. Or, perhaps Russia believed its ties with the East, China, and central Asia would be enough to keep their networks strong.

In any case, Russia's invasion pushed McDonald's (along with many Western brands) to close down their stores in Russia. China's growing cultural and economic ties to the West, especially markets in the United States, are thought to be one of the main reasons it has not risked further confrontation over the disputed island of Taiwan.

(continued)

(continued)

The following figure shows a McDonald's in Hangzhou, China.

Out of many, we are one: Multiculturalism

E pluribus unum, along with being the official motto of the United States (not "In God we trust" as is incorrectly believed), really embodies this next geographic cultural term — multiculturalism.

Multiculturalism more or less translates into "out of many, one." If you walk around Berlin, New York, Paris, or almost any big city, you'll see that it can be difficult to nail down their culture. The people look and speak like they come from all over, and many sounds, sights, and even smells make it difficult to identify the city you're in. Some parts of each city have a unique look and feel — so much so that you might think you're in a different city altogether. However, all the unique cultural contributions build up the city's overall feel.

Multiculturalism represents a "salad bowl" analogy of cultural integration. You may know the older "melting pot" analogy, though this idea breaks down in the idea that each culture blends to become a greater whole — a brothy soup. The salad bowl analogy, however, recognizes that each cultural contribution contributes to the whole (the "salad"), but you can still see each unique part (tomatoes, croutons, cheeses, and so on). This multiculturalism salad analogy can be used for a city at a more local scale, but it can also refer to the cultural makeup of a country or even the globalized popular culture as a whole. The salad bowl and the melting pot analogies represent the ideas of acculturation and assimilation, respectively, which is discussed in more detail in the next section.

Multiculturalism connects to the "out of many, one" idea. The United States uses *E pluribus unum*, as its motto because the country was built on the idea of the contributions of all, not the exaltation of one. That is why there is no official language or religion. The United States is meant to allow people worldwide to come and contribute to the country's identity and cultural makeup.

Figure 12-6 shows the Neukölln borough in Berlin, Germany. Neukölln's identity has been shaped by ethnic Germans and migrants from all over the world. Foods and shops catering to the area's large Middle Eastern population give it a unique feel, contributing to the city's overall identity.

FIGURE 12-6:
The Neukölln borough in Berlin, Germany

Taking on a new culture: The degrees of cultural integration

While living and teaching in China, my coworkers took their own approaches to living in another country. Most of us were Americans living in a country vastly different from our own, and the degree to which we sought to blend in with the Chinese culture varied from person to person. Some tried to blend in as much as possible, at least as much as an American could. They ate exclusively at Chinese restaurants, went to great lengths to learn the language, and lived in other parts of the city far away from the "foreigner" districts.

Some of us dabbled in Chinese culture but would return to KFC and our pirated copies of American television shows for comfort and a taste of home.

Others tried to retain their own culture by exclusively eating at Western-styled restaurants, not making much of an effort to learn Chinese (to the point of sometimes getting weirdly angry at people for not knowing English), and not going out in the city much without a native Chinese speaker.

I have just explained assimilation, acculturation, and rejection (which is discussed in the next section). In the expatriate community of China (not just the teachers I worked with), there was an interesting mixture of adventurers looking for a new experience, people who were socially awkward and didn't quite seem to fit in back home, and people who were looking to start over altogether. These three examples demonstrate some different types of cultural integration that go on when you have cultural convergence — multiple cultural ideas coming together.

Cultural assimilation was the first group of people. Often, they had a spouse who was Chinese, sometimes even children, and they were looking to make China their home. These people were looking to be absorbed into the culture and try to make their cultural values and practices indistinguishable from the majority culture (that of Beijing or Shanghai). With such strict regulations on who could move to China and such pride and strength in supporting cultural values, the country tends to assimilate those who move there. When I lived in Shanghai and Beijing, there was only a very small foreign-born population (as compared to the total population), and there was not great support for non-native speakers (especially once you got out of the touristy areas). It was either adapt and make do, or don't and suffer a bit. You had to learn to speak Chinese or risk being taken for a ride (literally sometimes) by cab drivers. Negotiating prices (or even understanding them) was hopeless as well.

Assimilation is necessary for survival for many migrants. Whether to be able to get work, go to the shops, or even just blend in, assimilation (at least in public) sometimes means giving up a piece of your own culture. This is especially common among the children of first-generation migrants. They want to fit in with their peers and not be singled out as an "other," so they might go so far as to reject the culture of their parents and wholly assimilate. Some countries will go to legal lengths to force assimilation. One of the most common ways is establishing an official language. The process of an official language requires that all legal processes occur in that language. Canada's official languages are English and French, meaning that all governmental acts (such as. governmental processes or official forms) must be in either French or English (usually both). South Africa, on the other hand, has 11 official languages, reflecting the country's diverse ethnic makeup.

Acculturation is much more common for first- and second-generation and temporary migrants, such as green card workers or time-contract geography teachers in China. Acculturation is adapting one culture by borrowing and absorbing bits and pieces without attempting to be completely assimilated within a culture. This often involves learning the local language and eating the local foods, but once you return to the comfort of your home, you revert to your original culture. Many migrants to countries like France, the US, the UK, or Germany act like the majority culture while out in public but switch to their native practices once they get home. I have many students you would never know almost exclusively speak languages like Somali, Karen, or Spanish at home. They've adopted multiple cultural traits and acculturated to the point that they balance multiple identities.

Denial and shutting out changes

Believe it or not, people are not always the most receptive to trying new things or being open to new cultures. Whether they are set in their ways, don't understand or comprehend, or are scared of losing their own culture, some people will go to great lengths to try to avoid change. The opposite of convergence, cultural divergence is the degree to which cultures remain separate and unique.

Cultural divergence results from physical distance, technological disconnection, and the efforts (usually political) to prevent convergence. These efforts are usually political because changes in cultural values and beliefs could be seen as a threat to the ruling class. An example is the diffusion of liberal ideas of gender roles. Historically, men have been the dominant political force across the world. Ideas of gender equality and the elevation of women's status to that of equal to men have been perceived as a threat to the power of men across space and time. The results come in the following forms:

>> Limiting political power (especially voting rights)

>> A gender pay gap

>> Limited access to birth control

>> Pronatalist laws and policies meant to increase births (further tying women to the home and out of the public sphere as they are traditionally the caregivers)

>> Limited support for women who are caring for young children

In some countries, for example, a pregnancy can still be grounds for termination by an employer. The global popular culture is increasingly adopting women's rights as a major cultural value, and as such, many countries are cracking down on changes in culture because they can lead to further developments in the social and political structures.

However, the Internet has exposed people to cultural values and beliefs more than ever. Even countries like Saudi Arabia, whose laws restricting the rights of women were some of the most strict in the world, have had to start slowly rolling back some of their restrictions. In 2018, Saudi Arabia removed a restriction on women's driving rights. They're still far from equality, but at least they're moving in that direction. On the other hand, Iceland also passed a law in 2018 that effectively banned unequal pay between men and women, forcing companies to submit proof that men and women are being paid the same for similar jobs.

These battles over gender rights are further extended now with the increased visibility of the transgender rights movements. Much of the battle over trans rights is a cultural battle that is more along generational lines than ethnic.

Cultural wars: A clash over identity

In my opinion, one of the weirdest arguments against new ways of thinking is what I call the "back in my day" argument. Just because things aren't how you remember them doesn't make how things are today incorrect. Ethnocentrism and xenophobia are the two main ideas at the center of cultural clashes (two or more cultural groups coming into contention with one another).

Ethnocentrism uses one's self as the center to measure things against and things that deviate too much are considered "wrong." Cultural relativism is the idea that you need to view another culture for what it is and not what it is not. Each culture needs to be understood to have its own beliefs, values, customs, and practices — understood in the context of the culture itself. A cultural practice only seems to be a misfit when you place it out of context. Each culture has its own framework for doing things, and what may appear "weird" to one person is completely normal to someone from that culture. To the person part of that culture, doing it another way is what they would consider weird.

Ethnocentrism is ignoring cultural relativism and assuming that one's own culture is the only correct way of doing things. Deviations from their own norms are considered out of place and incorrect. Ethnocentrism is disappointing because it comes from a lack of knowledge.

In the Western world, there is a lot of fear, mistrust, or even hatred toward Muslims. Islamophobia is often rooted in news and media coverage of wars or terroristic attacks that often go to great lengths to ensure they identify their religious affiliation. This is always weird since they don't identify the religious affiliation of attackers who are non-Muslims. I find it particularly frustrating that Islamophobic or anti-Muslim have never had a meaningful interaction with or even met a Muslim. Muslims are against the "Islamic terrorists" because the terrorists unfairly characterize faithful followers of Islam.

People from North Africa, the Middle East, and the rest of the Muslim world have not had much direct interaction with people from the West until relatively recently. While many Muslim beliefs and customs differ from those of traditional Western cultures, those differences do not make them any less valid. Much of the hatred and fear is related to xenophobia or the fear of foreigners. As more people become familiarized with Islam, they are more likely to find commonalities and realize that people, no matter where they're from, are not all that different. We're all just trying to make it on our way, and most of us don't want to make life any harder on anybody else if they can help it.

Figure 12-7 shows the cityscape of Amman, Jordan, where people are just going about their day and not paying me any mind as I mapped the city with my feet. Look at this scene's similarity to Figure 12-6 in Berlin. This is just further proof that we really do have much in common.

FIGURE 12-7:
Cityscape of
Amman, Jordan

Chapter 13

Establishing a State

I n the late 1800s, German geographer Friedrich Ratzel theorized that a State acts much like any other living organism, growing and protecting itself to ensure its survival. This idea formed the basis of his Organic State Theory. So, while human geography is centered on studying human activity, Ratzel's theory compares how a State performs to the actions of a rational human. The development of this theory marks the de facto beginning of the study of political geography (geopolitics) — how States interact with each other based on their geographic locations.

Political geography combines the studies of history, government, social structure, and many other fields and examines them all within the context of place. This chapter focuses on how geography affects the development of States (in political geography, the term "State" is used synonymously with "country") and how the geography of a State can, in turn, affect those trying to rule it. All the while, the role of humans remains the center of the study. Throughout this chapter, we will look at general political geography terms and trends, why States are formed, different types of borders, and how a State's size and shape can affect its control.

Stating the state of the State

In human geography and other related academic fields, we sometimes use a different vocabulary than you might hear on the news or in general conversation. We will go over some of the terms used in human geography to help make the rest of this chapter (and later chapters) make more sense.

A "State" is synonymous with "country." Confusingly, "state" can also be used to describe a smaller subdivision of a State. For example, in Canada, these smaller subdivisions are called *provinces*, but countries like Germany, Brazil, and the United States just call them "states."

A people's right to rule

Without getting too much into the realm otherwise occupied by history and political science, when we're looking at the political landscape of the world, a region, or even an individual State, we must always remember that in human geography, we focus on connections between human systems and their physical locations. Most people have spent at least a little bit of time looking at a world political map and noticed the patchwork of States, though it is incredibly helpful, if not necessary. Instead, we like to focus on the relationships between States as a function of their locations and the processes through which one State "stakes its claim" over an area against the competing claims of other States.

Let's talk about the concept of sovereignty to help clarify these ideas. The modern idea of a State has its roots in the Treaty of Westphalia, signed in 1648 to the end of the Thirty Years' War. Before this treaty, most regions were primarily organized as a series of kingdoms ruled through a system of lords and kings. The treaty marks the beginning of the era of modern States with established sovereignty, meaning each State has an established area with defined boundaries in which they — and they alone — have the right to make laws without outside interference.

In geography-speak, a territory describes a portion of a State. The people who live in the territory usually do not have the same citizenship rights as those who live in other parts of the State. American Samoa, for example, is controlled by the United States but does not have the same structure as a fully organized state.

Becoming a State

Once an area has achieved sovereignty, it is understood that they have risen to the level of Statehood. This idea of establishing States defined by their people and boundaries — and not necessarily by who happens to be sitting on what throne — originated in Europe with Westphalia and spread throughout the world during the colonial and imperial eras.

It is not always as simple as declaring Statehood and starting to rule right away. Often, this process involves bloody wars of independence, like was the case for Mexico to gain freedom from Spain. Or, this process can be made up of complicated negotiations and political dealings to gain recognition from other established States. This process can be greatly compromised if there are competing claims with other States over portions of land or even a State's right to exist, as is the case of Kosovo in southeast Europe. About 100 countries have recognized its status as a sovereign State, while the rest are undecided or against recognition. These disagreements make trying to say how many States are in the world especially complicated. The United States recognizes 195 States in the world as of 2023.

Once a State has achieved sovereignty and recognition, it can fully function and participate like any other State, possibly involving diplomacy, where it actively makes treaties and establishes economic or political relationships. When the State deals with only one other State, that arrangement is referred to as a *bilateral treaty*; and when three or more States are involved, it's called a *multilateral treaty*. If a State is firmly established, it can join the United Nations (UN).

TIP

The United Nations is discussed in more detail in Chapter 15.

Whether a multilateral or bilateral treaty or a membership in a large organization like the UN, all these efforts by States help them try to secure their economic and political interests.

TIP

If you want to learn more about how States interact, I recommend checking out *Political Science For Dummies* by Marcus A. Stadelmann (Wiley).

Dividing the States on a global scale

We won't get into much detail about the types of governments and their approaches to ruling over people; political geographers are more interested in the trends and patterns of those governments' locations. To help understand these patterns, we generally describe States as either *unitary* or *federated*.

>> **Unitary States:** In unitary States, the power is centralized to one main governmental body. There may be smaller dispersed governmental bodies (like a provincial government), but in a unitary government, their main role is to help ensure decisions made by the central government are carried out. A good example of this is China, where government power is centered in Beijing, and the provincial governments are more or less just responsible for ensuring that the decisions made in Beijing get carried out locally.

>> **Federated States:** In federated States, some of the power (typically national issues and how the State interacts with other States) is reserved for the central government. The rest of the power is divided between smaller subdivisions. In Brazil, for example, the central government in Brasília handles the large issues, but other decisions are relegated to its 26 states.

Figure 13-1 shows the distribution of federal and unitary States.

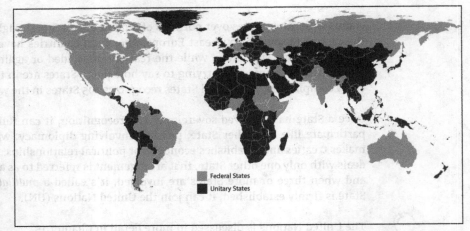

FIGURE 13-1:
Distribution of
federal and
unitary States
in 2023

Federal States

Unitary States

One nation under all

As discussed previously, Ratzel came up with the idea of a State operating like a living, breathing organism. Now, Ratzel had nothing to do with the following analogy, but bear with me here. A living organism comprises many parts, all working in unison. If one or two parts malfunction or don't work well with the rest of the parts, the organism as a whole starts to break down. Think of the State as the body and the people as the internal organs. If the organs start to break down, the body breaks down.

The word "nation" is often used interchangeably with "country" or "State." Human geographers avoid this interchangeability of terms because, in our world, a nation and a country are two very different things.

Human geographers use the term "nation" to describe a people with a common culture, heritage, and history. Consider the United Kingdom, for example, as a State of many nations — a multinational State, if you will. The State itself comprises the English, Welsh, Irish, Scots, Cornish, and other ethnic groups who trace their origins back to what is now the United Kingdom. Each group has its own unique traditions, history, and even language (in some cases) that distinguish it from the others. At one time or another, many of those groups have been at war with one another. Think of Scottish hero William Wallace, famous for standing up and waging war against the English king Edward Longshanks.

Also, remember that the UK has a large immigrant population whose experiences far differ from those of British people whose roots go back generations in what is now the United Kingdom.

In rare cases, a State can be almost entirely comprised of people from one nation, which we would call a Nation-State. These are increasingly rare and only found in smaller countries or countries without large-scale immigration (like South Korea).

National determinism and the drive for self-government

Another misconception is that nationalism and patriotism can be used interchangeably to describe a person's love for their country. That, again, would be incorrect in the world of human geography. The love of one's country can be defined as patriotism. However, nationalism is the idea of elevating and preserving the status of the members of a nation. Nationalism often involves promoting the interests of an individual nation, often at the expense of others. In Adolf Hitler's Nazi Germany State, for example, nationalism was a means of promoting the rights of his idealization of the "German nation" above all else. Hitler's vision is an example of *hypernationalism* and highlights one of the potential dangers of promoting nationalism in a country — an ideal of membership in the nation that classifies everyone else as "others" or outsiders. In extreme cases, this can lead to persecution and violence against people who are considered not to be a part of the nation.

Hypernationalism is discussed further in Chapter 14.

REMEMBER

Nationalism should not be used synonymously with the word "patriotism." Nationalism applies to only the members of the nation. Patriotism is all-inclusive and seeks to unify all members of a State, regardless of their nationality.

Nationalism does not always devolve into violence and can actually be an effective means for bringing people together to form a new State. Nationalism can also refer to the desire to unite the members of a nation under a single unified government with sovereign government rights. Again, nationalism can often walk a fine and dangerous line if it tries to exclude members. An example of a nationalistic movement that did not involve violence is the Catalonian region of Spain. The Catalans — Spain's largest ethnic group — have long spearheaded a movement to separate Catalonia from Spain to form a new State. In 2017, the region voted for independence and to become a sovereign State — a move that eventually was declared unconstitutional by the Spanish government, leading to the vote being thrown out. However, if the Catalans had successfully built a State free and independent of Spain, the people who lived in the region who weren't ethnic Catalans might not have felt connected to whatever new government had been formed.

Nationalism has affected other independence movements, including the American Revolution in the United States of America, fought by the people living in the

13 colonies who wanted the right to self-govern. However, even once independence was gained, women and people of Native or African descent were excluded by the new government, even though they made up sizeable portions of the 13 colonies' population.

The American Revolution is an example of a separatist movement, which can involve armed conflict, depending on the strength of the country that otherwise claims control over the area. That is not always the case, as in much of Eastern Europe in the late 1980s and early 1990s. Following a prolonged invasion of Afghanistan and a period of economic instability, the Soviet Union could not prevent the breakaway of its satellite States and republics. States in Eastern Europe and Central Asia that had been under Soviet rule for more than 50 years broke away rather quickly and relatively nonviolently. This process started in November of 1989 with the fall of the Berlin Wall and escalated to the eventual dissolution of the entire Soviet Union in December of 1991.

Separatist movements can be because of nationalistic reasons or for other reasons. Between 1989 and 1990, the Soviet satellite State of Czechoslovakia began to expel the communist government and create a new democratic government. In 1993, Slovakia and the Czech Republic were formally created, largely because Slovaks were concerned the Czech-majority government would involve themselves in their own interests too much. The Velvet Revolution, as it is called, was nonviolent but still resulted in the successful break of Czechoslovakia from the Soviet Union and then the division into Czechia (its modern short name as of 2016) and Slovakia.

A nation with no State

With only about 190 countries and literally thousands of different national and ethnic groups, it is not currently possible (or even theoretically possible) that all nations have a country of their own. Instead, we are left with a situation where we have many multinational States and Stateless nations. Multinational States can still operate just fine without conflict as long as they are not passing laws or doing anything that might disadvantage or cause resentment among particular subgroups. If a multinational State does either of these things, it risks encouraging those subgroups to form a new State of their own.

In some cases, ethnic groups are spread out between many States and begin nationalistic movements to create a State of their own. Middle Eastern Kurds are spread between many States, especially concentrated in Iraq, Turkey, and Syria. They have experienced persecution throughout their history, most notably in Iraq, where the Saddam Hussein–led government used chemical weapons against them. They have tried to form the Nation-State Kurdistan to avoid further persecution. However, to accomplish this, the States where they are presently located would lose some of their territories to form the new Kurdish State. So, the Kurds have been actively persecuted to prevent them from becoming powerful enough to accomplish their goal of establishing their own Nation-State.

Stating the Shape of a State

When a political scientist examines the political structure of a State, they look at things like how power is distributed and the connection between the people and the government. A historian might examine how attitudes toward power distribution have changed. A geographer, however, will focus on the relationship between space and power distribution, particularly how power is contained. What prevents one State from exerting power over another area? The easy answer: borders and boundaries.

TECHNICAL STUFF

The terms "border" and "boundary" can be used fairly similarly. A boundary just refers to an imaginary reference point where the extent of one government ends and another begins. These might (or might not) be formally established. A border is a formal separation of power where the extent of power for one entity ends, and another begins. Imagine you are traveling from Cairo, Egypt, to Tripoli, Libya. At the border, you have to go through passport control because you are leaving one State's governmental control and passing into another State's controlled area. The Libyans also need to check your passport to ensure you meet the requirements to be there, given the requirements to enter Egypt (visas and background checks) might differ from the requirements that Libya has.

Political borders may not be something you think about in your everyday life, but they can greatly impact you personally. Things like whether you're allowed to participate in the government through voting may depend on what side of a line of a map you live on. The drinking age might be 21 for people in one area, but in another area, it might be only 19. Even the websites you're allowed to visit may depend on where you live. Again, the only thing that separates them is a line on a map that might have been drawn more than 200 years ago. How your life is so greatly dictated by a human-drawn line on a map is a weird concept. Existentialism aside, borders in geography are of great importance to our study. They help us understand the decision-making process that has gone into the separation of powers over space.

There are borders and boundaries at all scales that will affect you somehow. It really is much more complex than you might think, so let's use the United States as an example. At the most local level, a person living in the United States lives within the boundaries of a city, township, or county.

TECHNICAL STUFF

And right away, we get a bit of complexity because some US states use boroughs or parishes instead of counties. Cities and townships simultaneously are part of counties (which are the next largest political unit except in major cities that sometimes expand to include multiple counties or even smaller cities that exist in two counties). I decided to include counties as a base level because many people in the rural US don't live in any type of city, and the county level is the smallest it gets for them. See, it's already getting complicated.

The next level, the state (in this case, not the same as a country) level, can greatly affect people's lives. In the United States, this can affect whether you pay a state income tax and at what rate. It can also greatly impact which college or university you might attend since the in-state tuition can frequently be a main decision-maker for college-bound students.

The next scale is the national level. Which country you live in can have huge implications for your life. Just think of all the ways your life might be different if you didn't (or did) live in the United States.

The study of borders is especially exciting and interesting because borders constantly shift, change, or lose significance altogether. The next section examines borders' power in shaping States and how they can be grouped based on some commonalities. One thing I encourage you to do while you're reading this is to think about how your life has been affected because of the borders you live within.

Building borders and staking a claim

The process of delimiting borders is complex and can often lead to conflicts between the two (or more) sides trying to establish the boundaries between them. If done well, however, borders can help unite the people of an area by their shared concept of ownership over an area. The justification and process used to determine borders are important to differentiate since they each can have different implications for States or smaller-scale political units.

The reason for demarcating (actually going through and drawing up a border on a map) a border is to separate different political units. The process is where things can be especially tricky. Sometimes, there are natural breaks due to large bodies of water (rivers, lakes, seas, or oceans) or mountain ranges that are helpful physical boundaries that might have already kept groups of people separate. The Himalayas, for example, have served as a good restrictor to the spread of the State of India and act as a good dividing line between them and China.

In areas where there are no natural breaks and intense conflict between the groups that the border divides, there are sometimes physical manifestations of the relationships. Fortified borders are a way to mark borders and protect the inhabitants within them. The Great Wall of China is perhaps the most famous example of a fortified border. It was meant to be a dividing demarcation line between the Chinese and the Mongolian tribes. History would show that as a defensive fortification, it served a much better role at marking the extent of China's territory than it ever did, preventing the incursion of the Mongolians southward. Walls have long been used as a form of fortifying borders, but since the advent of airplanes and modern weaponry, their ability to prevent people from gaining entry to an area is often negligible at best.

Deciding where the borders go: Cultural and ethnic borders

As complicated as delimiting borders may be using physical features, that might actually be the least complicated justification for where political borders have been demarcated. Attempts have been made to consider ethnicity when creating multinational States and establishing borders to prevent future tension. These ethnic boundaries are made increasingly more complex by the forces of migration. Following the destruction of the Ottoman Empire at the end of World War I, the State of Armenia was established to provide ethnic Armenians with a homeland of their own. The Armenian State was especially important given the treatment of the Armenians by the Ottomans during the war, which many have classified as a genocide. However, borders in the southern Caucuses had to be drawn up to make the State of Armenia. One of the major issues was that the ethnic Azerbaijani were also going through the process of State formation, and borders had to be drawn up that reflected the ethnic makeup of that region. An exclave (more on these later in the chapter) of Azerbaijan had to be created, separated from the rest of the country by Armenia. Consequently, many ethnic Armenians from the region of Nagorno-Karabakh found themselves as a part of Azerbaijan. These borders have resulted in conflict between Azerbaijan and Armenia, continuing even into the 2020s.

Figure 13-2 shows the contested region of Nagorno-Karabakh, which is claimed by both Armenia and Azerbaijani.

Though not as contested perhaps — but as equally complicated as ethnic borders — cultural borders are another justification for establishing a border. Sometimes, they can help decide the delimitation of borders, as in the case of the Republic of Ireland, or they can be used internally to help create administrative units, such as in Canada.

Let's start with the Canada example. The internal borders of the provinces and territories reflect ethnic and cultural boundaries. The territory of Nunavut in the country's far northeast is comprised predominantly of Inuit First Nations. The borders help establish their separation from the rest of Canada. The province of

Québec is another area that adds complexity to Canada's internal makeup. Though conjoined with the rest of Canada since its very beginnings, Québec maintains almost a fierce independence from the rest of Canada as the French-Canadian province (as opposed to the mostly English-speaking provinces). That does not mean all people within Québec speak French as their primary language, nor are the French Canadians of Canada wholly located within Québec. In this case, the borders mostly help signify the cultural prevalence of French Canadians who have a provincial government that advocates on their behalf. The ethnic and cultural linkages to the French heritage of the province remain strong — to the point that Canada has only narrowly averted referendums to establish Québec as a sovereign independent State.

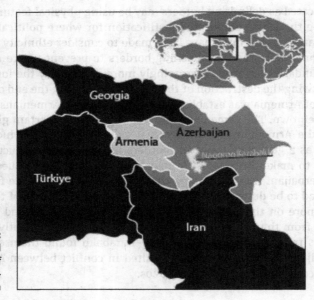

FIGURE 13-2: Contested region of Nagorno-Karabakh

Another interesting cultural border is the border that demarcates the division between the Republic of Ireland and Northern Ireland. When the Republic of Ireland began splitting away from the United Kingdom following World War I, one of the biggest complications was the question of Northern Ireland. While the people of the Republic of Ireland are mostly Catholic, most people living in the six counties in the northeastern part of the country are Protestant. It was decided that those six counties would remain a part of the United Kingdom while the remaining 26 counties would establish the Republic of Ireland. Again, this does not mean that all Protestants were contained within newly formed Northern Ireland and that all Irish Catholics reside strictly outside Northern Ireland. The established cultural borders have been at odds with the ethnic borders of Ireland, and since its very creation, the Sinn Féin party (among others) has been advocating for — as the name translates to — "ourselves alone." The Sinn Féin have sought to unify the Irish people under a single government, sometimes using direct measures to achieve this goal. In the 1980s, during what was called "The Troubles," supporters of a unified Irish State openly fought against British soldiers, leading to the Northern Ireland capital of Belfast essentially having to be fortified due to the violence.

Subsequent borders: An afterthought

I don't want you to think that creating borders always leads to conflict. There are plenty of examples of the formation of borders that did not result in conflict, though unfortunately, they sometimes do.

Probably one of the most traumatic examples of when the creation of borders led to conflict was what happened after the creation of the States of India (a majority Hindu country) and Pakistan (a majority Muslim country) in 1947. During the creation of this subsequent border, Muslims from India moved to Pakistan, and Hindus in Pakistan moved to India before the borders became more difficult to cross. An estimated 15 million people migrated during this event, with an estimated 1 million dying. The border is still highly contested, with the region of Kashmir being one of the focal points of argument between the two countries.

When a subsequent border is created — a border created after an area has already been settled — there might be an attempt to account for ethnic or cultural divisions, like what happened with India and Pakistan. During the Colonialism and Imperialism Ages in the Americas, Africa, Asia, and Australia, the borders were established by the colonizers/imperializers (mostly European) with little thought of the people living there. The creation of these borders has had reverberating impacts even into the present. Even if an attempt is made to account for ethnicity and culture, widescale resentment and conflict — both within and without the newly created countries — can occur. In the India and Pakistan example, the British judge who drew the lines never visited the proposed borderlands and only stayed in the country for about six weeks. It is no wonder the borders are so contested since so little time went into accounting for local sentiments.

TECHNICAL STUFF

We'll go over imperialism and colonialism more in Chapter 15, but the Age of Colonialism refers to the process of moving people from the source population (the home country) to a new sink population (the host area). The sink population remains committed to the home country and still sees themselves as citizens of it. Imperialism is the process through which an imperial power subjugates the people of an area for the economic benefit of the imperial power. Only as many people move from the imperial power to the subjugated area as are needed for the effective administration of the new imperial holding.

Superimposed borders: An outsider's thought

The India–Pakistan border is an example of both a subsequent border and a super-imposed border. A superimposed border is created by an outside entity or power, often without much input from the people who live where the borders are being drawn. Superimposed borders are one of the enduring legacies in political geography from the Colonialism and Imperialism Eras. They're often fairly easy to see on a map, with many straight or geometric lines that cut across natural landscapes. Think of the border between the United States and Canada. Except for along the Great Lakes and St. Lawrence River and a singular oddity at the top of Minnesota, the border dividing the two countries is a straight line along the 49th parallel (49° North Latitude).

Unfortunately, this is not an isolated incident. Much of the conflict in the Middle East has been attributed to the borders drawn by British diplomat Mark Sykes and French diplomat François Georges-Picot. The Sykes–Picot lines, as they have come to be known, split nationalities into multiple new countries under the mandates of mostly French or British stewardship. Some countries that were created were marginally homogenous from ethnic and cultural standpoints (though they were, most importantly, religious) — emphasis on the word "marginally" (and not completely) by any stretch of the imagination. Iraq is one of the most complex countries created by the Sykes–Picot lines. Comprised of ethnic Arabs who are predominately Sunni Muslim and ethnic Arabs who are Shia Muslims, with large concentrations of Kurds, Yazidis, and about a dozen other ethnic groups, the country has long been challenged by the presence of Stateless nations in an unstable multinational State. Saddam Hussein briefly unified the country in their shared terror of him, but once the common enemy was removed during the Second Gulf War, many of the ethnic and cultural conflicts reignited.

One of the most infamous examples of superimposed borders resulted from the Berlin Conference during the mid-1880s. Many negotiations between European powers (mainly the British, French, Germans, Portuguese, and Italians) met and carved up the continent of Africa. Each secured their mandates based on their individual goals, then subjugated African areas for imperial rule.

TECHNICAL STUFF

The Berlin Conference will be touched on again in Chapter 15, but its legacy is what we can see in the post-imperial landscape represented by the political borders. When the European powers divided up territories, they primarily considered natural resources and strategically important locations and gave little to no consideration to African cultural or ethnic groups. As of 2023, 54 countries are a part of the continent of Africa, but there are more than 9,000 ethnic groups. That's a lot of multinational States and Stateless nations. The borders were established by these European powers, who spent the better part of a century weakening their social, economic, and political structures before giving up their African holdings following World War II. The resulting State borders have almost no coherence in terms of their ethnic or cultural composition and can largely be blamed for the prevalence of civil wars on the continent (not to mention competing influences from outside governments and corporations that have been at play since the end of formal imperialism).

Antecedent borders: A forethought

Rarely, borders are created that precede people moving into the area. Antecedent borders are especially rare because most areas had people in them long before the modern State was developed. So, some examples of antecedent borders have to be stretched a little to make them work. Let's look at portions of the border of the sub-Saharan country of Algeria. Yes, its borders were also superimposed during the Berlin conference. The borders were established before any human settlement — at least in the southern section of the country, which reaches deep into the Saharan desert. Many areas of southern Algeria are still void of human settlement because of the harsh living conditions of Earth's largest hot desert.

With some stretching, we can say the state borders in the Eastern US are another example of antecedent borders because many of them were initially established by elements connected to the British Government. Also, the settlement of the western states by the United States government could be considered antecedent borders.

The land that now makes up the United States was inhabited long before the English, Spanish, Vikings, or any other Europeans ever got anywhere near the continent of North America. Once the United States gained its sovereignty from the British, it began the process of Westward Expansion, expanding into territory already inhabited. However, the US government viewed this land as theirs for the taking. The land was "claimed" through treaties, warfare, and sometimes outright deception. The process of Westward Expansion meant first securing the rights from Spain, Mexico, France, Great Britain, and Russia. Then, the United States had to go through the process of quelling and subjugating the many Native Tribes and formalizing the transfer of lands through a series of treaties with individual tribes. Once the lands had been secured and the Native peoples confined to their respective reservations, the States were drawn up and opened for settlement to people from the East.

If you really look into the definition and explanation of the process, it could be argued that the United States' process of "taming the West" was actually through means of colonization. The state borders were established before large-scale colonization began, but the original inhabitants had to be dispossessed for that process to be undertaken. The borders preceded the settlers (though not always) and thus could be made to fit the model of antecedent borders.

TECHNICAL STUFF

The "frontier" is a tricky concept to explain. Think of it as an area beyond the borders or outside the control of a State. In American history, the frontier was the land on the edges of the existing states. This land was mostly being settled by people from the United States, who pushed the frontier further and further into lands inhabited by the Native peoples of North America until the Pacific Ocean stopped them. Once the Kingdom of Hawaii was subjugated, the only area left to expand was the territory-turned-state of Alaska. That is why Alaska is sometimes known as the "last frontier."

Relict borders: A forgotten thought

As States grow and develop, their borders shift or are erased completely to reflect their changing political situation. Though the borders may be gone from an area, their legacy can remain long after they're gone. This is a concept called *relict borders* — where a border is removed, but there is still a noticeable separation in the culture or landscape that serves as a reminder that a boundary once existed. One of the classic examples of this phenomenon is the difference between West Berlin and East Berlin. Even though the Berlin Wall came down in November 1989, there are still fairly stark reminders in Berlin of the division that existed in the city for almost 45 years.

Now a popular tourist destination, Checkpoint Charlie in Central Berlin (see Figure 13-3) marks one of the crossing points where East Berlin and West Berlin once came together. Now, the street that intersects with the site is named Mauer Street, or "Wall Street," reflecting the historic presence of the Berlin Wall.

The city of Berlin was largely destroyed during World War II, and one of the ways that the legacy of the border between the two parts of the city is still reflected is in the buildings. Many of the buildings in East Berlin are concrete monoliths reflecting the Soviet style of architecture. In West Berlin, modern-styled, steel-and-glass buildings commonly reflect their longer connections to the rest of the Western world. Even at night, there is a visible impact. East Berlin still predominantly uses streetlights with sodium vapor lamps with a more orange glow. West Berlin uses more LED and fluorescent lamps that have more of a white look to them. Searching for images of night imagery of Berlin from above shows the contrasts between East and West Berlin even though the border no longer remains.

Maritime boundaries: A watery thought

The issue of borders is not only restricted to land but can also lead to complications at sea. Many States rely on the sea for fish to help feed their population or for resources that can be accessed with offshore drilling. On top of that, the oceans and seas of the world are important transportation systems for the movement of mass numbers of goods around the world. Historically, countries like Japan and the United Kingdom built vast navies to secure their shores and exert their influence across the seas. It was not until fairly recently a global system was implemented to determine how to establish maritime borders.

FIGURE 13-3:
Checkpoint
Charlie

The United Nations Convention on the Law of the Seas (UNCLOS) was originally signed in Montego Bay, Jamaica, in 1982. As of summer 2023, 151 parties (mostly States) have ratified the treaty. One notable exception is the United States, which signed the treaty but has been unable to ratify it in the Senate. The treaty establishes a zone of 12 nautical miles out from the baseline (normally the low tide line) that is classified as a State's territorial waters in which they can exert full control. Kind of. If the State happens to be in a strategically important area, like Egypt with the Suez Canal, it must still allow ships to pass through its waters to get from the Red Sea to the Mediterranean Sea — as long as they are acting in good faith, not hostility. There are more levels of control that a State can exert, but the furthest extent of their influence is 200 nautical miles from the baseline. States have the right to determine the harvesting or mining of resources from this Exclusive Economic Zone (EEZ).

If two (or more) States are closer together than 400 nautical miles, then the States' sea rights are equally divided. All this assumes that States are willing to play nicely together and recognize the claims of others. UNCLOS has led to some heated conflicts between States over tiny, otherwise insignificant islands. Whoever controls the islands also gets to claim the waters around the islands. Although there are many examples of these types of competing claims, one of the most important areas to watch is around the Spratly Islands in the South China Sea. China, Vietnam, Taiwan, Malaysia, and the Philippines are all contesting ownership over the islands to secure the fishing, oil, and gas rights. China has even gone so far as to make islands on top of coral reefs to exert more control over the islands as a whole. Maritime borders can lead to conflict, even if it is not necessarily about the land. Cooperation is necessary to prevent open warfare.

Looking to the future of borders, we can expect much of the same sort of conflicts and realignment of borders to reflect changing power dynamics. As climate change increasingly impacts the polar regions, States are already making moves to secure their interests in the very furthest reaches of our planet. More of the Arctic has become accessible with the receding sea ice. Russia has a vast fleet of nuclear power ice breakers to help them have the most access to the Arctic waters — partially in the hopes of maintaining their interests in the northern waters.

TECHNICAL STUFF

The terms of the Antarctica Treaty very clearly limit the ability of States to claim the southern continent.

In the more distant future, there is already discussion about the final frontier — outer space. The 2015 sci-fi movie *The Martian* discusses how maritime law for open seas and borders applies to space. Whether agreements will be passed for exploring and claiming outer space is a discussion beyond human geography.

The impact of the State's shape

After World War II, there was a shift from the focus of geopolitics for political geography to a more quantitative approach to understanding the relationship between space and power. The Theory of Territorial Morphology was developed to explain how the State's physical shape influenced how it could be ruled or interacted with by other countries. The theory divided States between compact, elongated, perforated, prorupt, and fragmented (see Figure 13-4).

REMEMBER

The post-war period marked a change in political geography. Remember Ratzel's theory that was discussed at the beginning of the chapter? Later, German geographer Karl Haushofer took Ratzel's idea of *Lebensraum* (translates to living room) and used it as a justification for the expansion of Nazi Germany during World War II. Geopolitics became taboo, so the field shifted toward a more quantitative approach to studying the relationship between space and power.

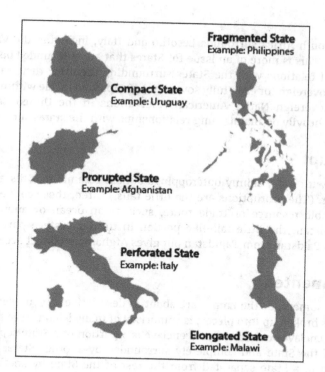

FIGURE 13-4:
Territorial
morphology
examples

Fragmented State
Example: Philippines

Compact State
Example: Uruguay

Prorupted State
Example: Afghanistan

Perforated State
Example: Italy

Elongated State
Example: Malawi

Compact

These States are fairly round and not at all oblong-shaped. Nowhere along the border should it be much further to the center of the State than anywhere else along the border. The center is one of the best areas for a capital because it will have the easiest access to all parts of the country. Defense can be more easily organized due to the ease of connectivity. Though not exclusively, many compact States are also Micro-States, meaning they're exceptionally small. The Vatican is the smallest country in the world at less than one-fifth square mile.

Elongated

As the name suggests, these States are long and skinny and can be quite difficult to defend because they could theoretically be cut in half by an invasion, making communication between the two halves difficult. Transportation is straightforward enough because they often only need one major route along the length of the States.

Perforated

The word "perforated" means "pierced with holes." No, this does not mean that there is a hole in the Earth's crust. It just means that there is a State within the

State. South Africa surrounds Lesotho and Italy, including the Vatican and San Marino. This is more of an issue for States that are surrounded because they rely on good relations with the States surrounding them for their safety and trade. Semi-sovereign (or even fully sovereign) groups who reside within States, like the quasi-sovereign Native American reservations in the United States, similarly depend heavily on maintaining relationships with the states surrounding them.

Prorupt

States with long, skinny outcroppings almost resembling tails are classified as prorupt. (The proruptions are the little tails.) Often, these connect the States to a valuable resource or trade route, such as an ocean or another country. In Afghanistan, the little tail-like portion in the far eastern part of the country divides Pakistan from Tajikistan but gives Afghanistan direct access to China.

Fragmented

Again, sometimes the names are about as descriptive as you need. A fragmented State is broken up into pieces, is comprised of many islands (see the Philippines), or has enclaves or exclaves. An enclave is a portion of a State separated from the rest of the State and completely surrounded by another State. An exclave is a portion of a State separated from the rest of the State by another (or multiple countries) but not completely surrounded by a single country.

Earlier in this chapter, Figure 13-2 shows that Azerbaijan has an exclave that it is cut off from by Armenia. The Azerbaijan region of Nakchivan is landlocked but not completely surrounded by Armenia, which complicates ruling the State because the Azerbaijan region does not have easy access to all parts of the State. Landlocked States — exclaves of States that do not have direct access to the sea — rely on their neighbors for trade and access to other countries.

Chapter **14**

What a State Faces from Within

A State has gone through the process of gaining independence, establishing its boundaries, and negotiating and delimiting its borders. Sounds like an ideal situation, and everything should be easy sailing into the sunset with no foreseeable problems for the new State, right? Unfortunately, it's not even close. In fact, this is now the beginning of the struggle to maintain a State. Whatever unifying factors might have carried the perspective State through the independence struggle quickly diminished, and the question the new State rulers are left with is how to move on from here. If the new rulers consolidate their rule and ignore the people's wants, they can fall out of favor. If they are too slow in implementing ideas, the people could become restless and demand change quicker than the government can establish itself. Throughout history, many new governments have taken over and failed, and a new government (or even the original government) has stepped back up to establish stability.

Political geographers are particularly interested in how governments meet the needs of the people. Whether through a federated or unitary government, a government must represent the people's will. Otherwise, it risks alienating its people and creating unrest. Sometimes, central governments share governance over particular affairs to avoid upsetting a regional group.

Sometimes, a smaller regional government is developed — a statutory delegatory process called devolution — whose power is derived from the central government. This smaller government operates at a subnational level and is still dependent upon the larger central government for many things, though the regional government can handle local issues of cultural or ethnic significance. States will utilize devolution to grant regional rights while still maintaining overall control. States are constantly in a balancing act between nationalistic, patriotic, and devolutionary forces, which they must try to contain in order to maintain stability within the State. The United Kingdom is a great example of a State connected through devolution.

As we've discussed in other chapters, human geography focuses on how space impacts the political decisions of governments and people. American geographer Richard Hartshorne developed the ideas of centrifugal and centripetal forces. Centrifugal forces potentially divide a State and could tear it apart. Centripetal forces unify the people of a State. Both concepts are examined further in the coming section, but you might already be thinking about your own country and coming up with a list of centripetal and centrifugal forces.

DEVOLUTION IN THE UNITED KINGDOM

One thing to remember about the UK is that it is a State comprising many nations, the largest being the English, Welsh, Scottish, and Irish in Northern Ireland. Scotland, Wales, and Northern Ireland have their own parliaments that handle local matters.

Each parliament defers to the English parliament in London for important issues affecting the whole of the United Kingdom (particularly defense and large economic initiatives). Each government has a degree of self-rule, but within Scotland's parliament in particular, there is much debate on whether or not Scotland should declare their independence from the rest of the United Kingdom.

A referendum to that end just barely failed in 2014. Rumors of another referendum over Scotland's displeasure with the United Kingdom pulling out of the European Union are plentiful and could happen as soon as 2024. So, while the devolution of governments has kept the United Kingdom together until now, it remains to be seen whether it will be enough to hold it intact into the future.

Centripetal Forces — Uniting a People

Fun experiment: Fill a bucket with a handle about halfway full with water. Grab the handle and start swirling the bucket around like a windmill. Unless you did it wrong, you should still be dry! Thanks to centripetal force, gravity should have held the water inside the bucket as you twirled it. Similar to water in a twirling bucket, physical and nontangible forces are constantly working to divide the people of a State, but if you can control those forces, the people will stay together.

Liberalism: A people and their freedoms

In general, freedom is defined by individualized rights afforded to citizens of a country. In political science, these are referred to as the spread of liberalism.

TIP

Because it's a complicated topic, we don't have the space here to map the spread of liberalism because liberalism comes in multiple forms. See *Political Science For Dummies*, by Marcus A. Stadelmann (Wiley), to learn more about different government philosophies.

While we cannot delve deeply into liberalism, we can look at how it spread over time and space. Liberalism is understood to be a cultural trait (how people allow themselves to be governed), so we can map its diffusion like any other cultural trait.

REMEMBER

Cultural diffusion was explained in Chapter 12 as the spread of cultural traits from one place to another.

Liberalism includes freedom of speech, peaceful protest, voting and participating in elections, and a free, independent press. These freedoms are especially complicated because each spreads to different places at different times. Sometimes, a country may have the right to vote, but its freedom of the press and protest are restricted. (A quick Google search will tell you which countries restrict a free press.)

Another complication of mapping the spread of liberalism is that it does not spread to all people at the same rate. The right to vote was included in the US Constitution, but it didn't afford that right to everyone. Though the US Constitution was written in 1787, the right to vote regardless of race was not enacted until 1870 with the passage of the 15th Amendment. The right to vote for women was not protected until the ratification of the 19th Amendment in 1920. So, while the United States has had the right to vote since 1787, that right should've come with a "for landowning white men only" asterisk.

Liberalism, very much like many other cultural traits, has historically spread through contagious diffusion. Freedoms are, at times, sort of like a new toy. If one of your friends gets a new toy, then you also want it. If one country has the right to vote, then the States interacting with it will see the benefits that right affords its citizens and want it, too.

For example, the US was one of the first States to establish a right to self-rule and freedom from a monarchy. The French monarchy provided the colonists with guns, ships, supplies, soldiers, and even commanders during the American War of Independence. When those French soldiers returned to France, they still lived under a king, which seemed odd since they had just helped one State free itself from a monarchy. It is little surprise that the French Revolution began roughly six years after the American Revolution ended. Nearby Haiti secured its freedom from France in 1804, and neighboring Mexico achieved independence from Spain in 1821. (Note: Mexico's independence has zero connection to Cinco de Mayo, which actually celebrates Mexico's victory over the Second French Empire at the Battle of Puebla in 1862.)

TECHNICAL
STUFF

Iceland's *Alþingi* (anglicized as "althing") parliamentary government dates back more than 1,000 years, making it the oldest continual form of democratic governance.

Liberalism can be a particularly strong force that binds a country together under a shared sense of freedom. Without it, however, a country could become discontent with its government for not providing the people with the same freedoms as neighboring States. This potential for discontent is why the government of the Democratic People's Republic of Korea (DPRK) — otherwise known as North Korea — takes such great measures to restrict communication between its people and the rest of the world. If the people of the DPRK became aware of how restrictive their government was, they could rise up and overthrow the government in favor of a new one, offering them higher degrees of individual freedom.

We know a growing discontent among the people can be dangerous to an oppressive government, and we need only look to the 1980s and the decline of the Soviet Union to prove it. One of Mikhail Gorbachev's reforms was the idea of *glasnost*, or "openness," leading to the spread of more information and the introduction of Western culture and rock n' roll (*a la* Billy Joel). The people of the Soviet Union were increasingly disenchanted with their own government and wanted more of what the West had to offer. When you add in the disastrous invasion of Afghanistan, the Chernobyl nuclear disaster, and an economic crisis, it's not hard to see why the Soviet flag was lowered over the Kremlin in 1991.

Federalism: Local power under a larger whole

The concept of federalism (or a federated State) also can be a particularly useful tool for holding a State together. As discussed in Chapter 13, federal States are countries where power is shared between smaller governmental units and the main central government. This is in contrast to power being almost completely focused in the central government and smaller governmental units primarily used to carry out directives from higher up.

Federalism allows for a degree of adapting government actions to the will of people living in a State. The people's will is expressed by local governmental bodies that are given direct control over an area via representatives sent to the central government to advocate on their behalf. In presidential republics, these people are usually called senators or representatives. In parliamentary systems, these people are usually members of parliament (or MPs) or something similar.

GERRYMANDERING

In short, political districts are complicated. To get even more technical, they're super complicated. An entire division of political geography is devoted to establishing political districts in the United States. The process is called gerrymandering since the districts often appear as wild shapes to (try to) meet the needs of the individuals who drew the regions. These geographic units are usually organized to determine the geographic regions of representatives for the US House of Representatives. I say "usually" because some states only have one representative, so gerrymandering is unnecessary.

We can thank Elbridge Gerry, a founding father of the US and former Massachusetts governor, for the term "gerrymander." Gerry was an eccentric figure — or, as biographer George Athan Billias said, "a nervous, birdlike little person" — who signed a redistricting bill in 1812 in which Massachusetts Republicans redrew the voting districts to their favor in the upcoming election. As the story goes, at an influential Boston dinner party in 1812, the new districts were referred to as a "salamander," to which another dinner guest responded, "No, a Gerry-mander." Shortly thereafter, the *Boston Gazette* published a political cartoon featuring "a new species of monster: The Gerry-mander."

Each state in the US has two senators who are not tied to any particular region of the state; rather, they are meant to represent the state as a whole. Representatives, however, are meant to represent the regional interests of a state at the national level. Political districts are meant to be contiguous (connected to all parts of themselves) and roughly equal in size. They are not supposed to be designed to give any particular group (especially political parties or racial groups) a designed advantage.

(continued)

(continued)

In theory, this sounds like a great way to hold the State together by ensuring that people within a region have a voice on the national stage. In reality, the process is highly political and can often be contested in the courts to determine whether the established districts are fair. The following figure shows the changing political districts of North Carolina over time.

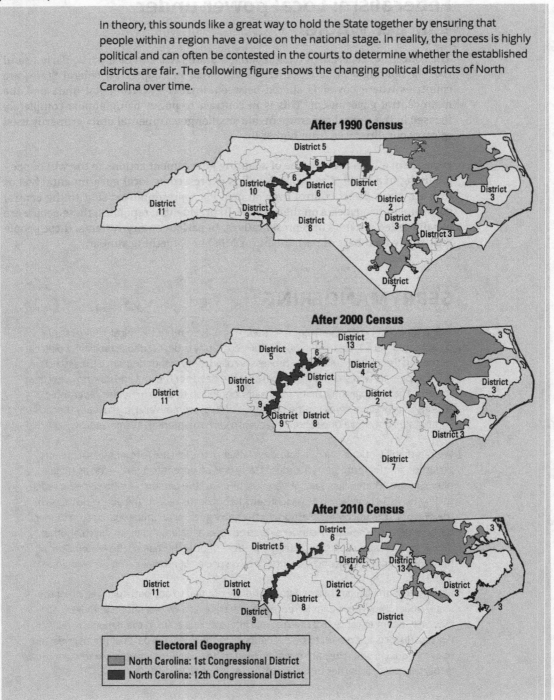

Electoral Geography
North Carolina: 1st Congressional District
North Carolina: 12th Congressional District

This sort of system is a powerful centripetal force because it allows the interests of people throughout a State to be voiced and included — if only for the sake of being able to speak their piece. When the people feel like their interests are being advocated for and the government works for them, it can help keep a State united. In unitary States, people might think the government only works for its own interests, neglecting the interests of less-populated areas. If everyone in a State feels connected to one central government, they might not be as divided by regional interests and allegiances. Problems like these vary from State to State. For example, a federal State like Russia is highly centralized, and most states (known as oblasts) hold allegiance to Moscow. However, oblasts like Chechnya or Dagestan have attempted to get more autonomy from Moscow.

TECHNICAL STUFF

Oblast translates to "region" or "province" in English and represents the administrative divisions of Belarus, Bulgaria, Kazakhstan, Kyrgyzstan, Russia, Ukraine, and the former Soviet Union.

TRIBAL SOVEREIGNTY

Along with territories, some States, namely the United States and Canada, have a further special political designation for their Indigenous communities. The United States and Canadian governments have established treaties with the Indigenous Native communities that afford the sovereignty to the reservations. When the United States or Canadian governments communicate with the tribal governments, they do so as one sovereign State with another. This is different from the relationship the United States has with its states, or Canada has with its provinces. As sovereign governmental units, reservations can make their own decisions on issues (like taxation, the establishment of casinos, and tribal schools and courts) that are autonomous from the states or provinces that surround them.

These relationships differ from tribe to tribe because they were negotiated individually with tribes by forming the treaties dictating the relationship between them and the government. The United States handles its relationship with Indigenous communities through the Bureau of Indian Affairs (part of the Department of Interior; thankfully, no longer through the Department of War), and Canada handles their relations through Indigenous Services Canada (ISC) and Crown-Indigenous Relations and Northern Affairs Canada (CIRNAC). Interestingly, The Oneida tribe, part of the Iroquois Confederacy, actually declared war on Germany during World War I. The Six Nations of the Iroquois Confederacy even issued its members a passport (known as the Haudenosaunee Passport) but have had issues with other States recognizing their passports. In 2010, the Iroquois national lacrosse team attempted to travel to the United Kingdom for the World Lacrosse Championship, only to have their visas rejected by the UK government because they did not recognize the Iroquois-issued passports as legal.

(continued)

(continued)

I mention Indigenous rights in the context of centripetal forces because it is still a method used to maintain the territorial integrity and borders of the State while supporting the sovereignty of groups within the State. Through the stipulations of the treaties, the Iroquois, for example, can still vote in US elections, serve in the military, and have many of the same rights as other US citizens. Also, they have sovereignty on their reservations to make decisions independent of the United States. It allows a form of unity while maintaining a sort of separation. It's complicated, but if you live in the United States or Canada, I would encourage you to research further or even reach out to your closest Indigenous group and learn more about their sovereign status.

Infrastructure: Connecting people, literally

When most people see a road, a line of rail tracks, or a row of power lines, that's all they might see. For a political geographer, however, they represent the networks that help connect the people of an area. Think of a region, state, or province of your own country. Now, remove all the infrastructure that connects it to the rest of the country. For example, let's say Indiana didn't have many roads, electricity, or Internet access, meaning they couldn't communicate with the rest of the country or drive to another state like New York. Maybe people in Indiana start to resent people in other states. It probably wouldn't be long before Hoosiers started questioning why they should remain part of the United States.

Infrastructure problems can be a real and constant struggle for fragmented countries. With proper transportation and communication network infrastructure, they might be able to overcome the physical obstacles created by the State's borders.

REMEMBER

As covered in Chapter 13, a fragmented State is a country that is broken apart and separated from itself by water or other countries.

One of the most helpful pieces of infrastructure that States can invest in to connect the people of their State is a highway or high-tech rail system. In the United States, this is the interstate road system. Many other countries — especially in East Asia and Europe — use a combination of high-tech passenger rail and highways. Many African States are working on improving their transportation infrastructure, often with China's aid. Kenya completed the Madaraka Express Passenger Service train in 2017, connecting the port city of Mombasa to the internal capital of Nairobi. Though it is not the bullet train you might find in Japan or France, it does shorten a trip that might take all day by car or shared van (called a matatu) to five hours. This train has helped improve connections between the capital and the coast and helped relieve congestion on the main road connecting the country's two largest cities.

Infrastructure must be equally distributed around the country. Otherwise, a centripetal force can be turned into a centrifugal force. This is a problem in countries like Thailand, where the primate city is Bangkok. If the resources (like electricity, phone/Internet service, or running water) were concentrated in Bangkok, the people in the rest of the country might resent the government for not providing them the same services.

TIP

Primate cities are explained in Chapter 9. To review, however, they are cities that are exceptionally larger than the next largest cities in an area in terms of population or economic, cultural, or political influence.

Regional autonomy: Separate but united

Bringing together a diverse population — especially when one group has a clear majority — is one of the biggest concerns for multinational States. Countries that cover large land areas, like Russia, Canada, the United States, and China, are particularly susceptible to this problem. Pragmatically, it makes sense to involve all groups to ensure they feel included, but that sometimes is just not practical. Failure to consider the concerns or perspectives of minority groups can leave them feeling left out or even persecuted.

One way to deal with this problem is to create autonomous regions or territories or develop a system by which groups self-govern. This solution can sometimes be a difficult but necessary step for States because it decentralizes power from the main government and allows for regions to operate semi-independently from the main central government. By developing autonomous regions, a government allows a portion of its land area to operate under a different set of rules than the rest of the State. Management can be difficult because autonomous regions allow some deviation from the goals and directions established by the central government, though doing so can help ameliorate conflict and discontent.

You might be asking why States would even bother having regions that might not even want to be part of the country in the first place. There are a variety of reasons a State would allow such an arrangement. The State may want access to the resources or the land itself and is not necessarily concerned about including the people living there. The State might be looking to secure its borders against potential invasion, so it's more interested in having the physical space. Or a State might be trying to prevent a rival power from moving into the area, creating a proximal threat to their territorial integrity.

Some countries have established territories to include minority groups but still allow a level of self-determination to mold the government to match cultural values. Territories allow for a degree of separation from the decisions made in the capital of the main country. Many countries, like Denmark, Canada, and the

US, still maintain territories, which can continue to be controversial. Let's use Denmark as an example. Denmark still maintains the island of Greenland as an overseas territory. Despite Greenland being roughly 50 times larger than Denmark, Denmark has a population of close to 6 million people, while Greenland's population is less than 60,000. Attitudes are split in Greenland as to whether to remain a territory and enjoy the benefit of Denmark's connections to the European Union and protections offered by being included in the North Atlantic Treaty Organization (of which Denmark is a part) or become independent and try to make decisions that more directly impact them.

Insofar as a territory is concerned, the question is whether to join a country and lose its semi-autonomy or declare independence and gain full autonomy. The US commonwealth of Puerto Rico has a political party — the Puerto Rican Independence Party — that campaigns for securing independence (as is fairly obvious, given the party's name).

Patriotism and nationalism as a unifier

One of the biggest challenges of keeping any State together is that they are mostly composed of different national, ethnic, and cultural groups with their own wants and desires. These groups can be especially difficult to accommodate if one nation has an overwhelming majority of the population, especially in States with a democracy because most operate on an all-or-nothing mentality. If 50.01 percent of people agree with something, it passes, but that still means 49.99 percent could be opposed. So, even with a democracy, States need to account for the wants and wishes of all people within the State or risk alienating the minority.

Multinational States can unite their populations using many different methods, including

>> Granting a degree of regional autonomy (especially easy in a Federalist or republic-styled government)

>> Developing special relationships of sovereignty (as seen with Native American Reservations in the United States or Canada)

>> Dividing up different voting districts or representative districts to allow for regional differences to be represented in the national government

>> Using the idea of a higher purpose to connect all nations (especially patriotism)

When you hear someone say they're "nationalistic" or "pushing for nationalism," you can replace that with "patriotic" or "patriotism." If they actually do mean they're "nationalistic," that is not nearly as simple. (See Chapter 13 for more on this.)

Patriotism can be a very helpful and positive way of unifying a divided country. And luckily, one of the most effective methods of building patriotism is already an easy sell to the population to buy into: sports! When Nelson Mandela become president of a deeply divided Republic of South Africa, he inherited deep ethnic, cultural, and racial divides — even more so than exist today. When South Africa hosted the Rugby World Cup in 1995, Mandela recognized a great opportunity to unify the country. In South Africa, the Black South Africans predominantly played soccer, and rugby still very much represented the culture of the White South Africans (known as the Afrikaans). Mandela threw his whole support behind the team and encouraged all South Africans to do the same, driving the South African team to win the World Cup in the process.

States often rely on patriotism to carry them through rough times or gain support for otherwise unpopular moves. Sometimes, they'll even try to manufacture patriotism by faking an event called a false flag operation, which can be dangerous if the public finds out the government has deceived them. At the beginning of the invasion of Poland by Nazi Germany, for example, German soldiers went into Poland and stole uniforms. They then staged an attack on Germany in the stolen uniforms to try to make it look like Poland was attacking them to encourage the public to patriotically support the pre-planned invasion of Poland. Many far-fetched conspiracy theories claim that Pearl Harbor and even the 9/11 attacks were false flag attempts by the government to get the US involved in wars.

DO YOU BELIEVE IN MIRACLES?

The US men's hockey team's defeat of the Soviet Union in Lake Placid, New York, in 1980 was credited with helping to rebuild US patriotism after the horrors of the Vietnam War and the Iran Hostage Situation, the embarrassment of Watergate, and a whole host of other setbacks. ABC Olympic announcer Al Michaels's iconic "Do you believe in miracles" call remains one of the most enduring moments in televised sports.

Centrifugal Forces — Pulling a State Apart

Just as there are geographic forces that can bring the people of a country together, there are also forces that can pull them apart. We call these centrifugal forces. Scientists often use centrifuges to separate elements. The centrifuge spins, forcefully separating elements. Much like a centrifuge, a centrifugal force in political geography separates pieces of the State, intentionally or unintentionally.

TECHNICAL STUFF

A citizen is a person who has been given full rights and privileges as afforded by the government of a geographic area. One of the most common forms of citizenship is through birth; if you are born in the State, you are automatically a citizen. Some States have citizenship through blood, in which you must demonstrate a certain amount of lineage to obtain citizenship. Citizenship through blood can be highly exclusionary. In Germany, for example, a large population of people of Turkish descent were brought to the country after World War II to fill a large labor gap. Though their families have been there for years and generations, many still have not obtained German citizenship.

Nationalism out of control

Nationalism is potentially one of the most dangerous political forces within a country. Depending on how membership is defined, nationalism can unify a State's people, but it can also do so at the expense of people who live in the State by turning them into an "other." In some States, the nation comprises people born there, turning people who moved there from somewhere else into "others." Or, they are citizens, which "others" people who live there without citizenship. Perhaps they define citizenship by cultural traits (especially language, religion, or even political affiliation), ethnicity, or ancestry, which is highly complicated, and, of course, excludes people who don't fit that particular definition.

Jumping from nationalism to ethnocentrism usually isn't a big leap, meaning using your own beliefs and customs as a measure to compare other groups. Ethnocentrism can lead to a sense of righteousness regarding a person's own culture or way of thinking over those whose customs or beliefs differ. From ethnocentrism, stereotypes and racism can develop, leading people to believe in their superiority over other groups, leading to the elements that form the foundations of racism and hypernationalism.

REMEMBER

Nationalism and patriotism are NOT the same things. Patriotism is love for one's State. The idea of nationalism refers to the promotion of the interests of one particular nation (group of people with a common heritage, history, and culture), often at the expense of the rights of others. This is why the idea of "American nationalism," in particular, makes no sense since the United States is a multinational State made up of many groups with different experiences throughout its history. Often, American nationalism is closely linked to "White nationalism," which is the promotion of the rights of Americans of European descent at the expense of the rights of people of other skin colors or ethnicities.

Racism: A construct that can deconstruct

If you remember back to our discussion of demographic geography in Chapter 5, the concept of race is the perceived physical differences between groups of people. Race has been a very common means of othering people in States to deny them political rights.

In South Africa, the system of Apartheid was constructed to divide the level of rights a person was entitled to. Black/Native South Africans (people of Indigenous South African descent) are by far the largest portion of the population but were given the least amount of rights and freedoms under the Apartheid system. Coloured and Indian South Africans were given more rights and freedoms, but not as much as White South Africans (people of European descent).

TECHNICAL STUFF

According to the Apartheid Museum, people in South Africa "were classified into one of four groups: 'native,' 'coloured,' 'Asian,' or 'white.'" For more, see https://www.apartheidmuseum.org/exhibitions/race-classification.

Mixing between people of different races was strictly regulated, and some forms of interaction (marriage, for example) were strictly forbidden. Apartheid was officially abolished in the mid-1990s, but the legacy of the policy is still deeply ingrained in South African Society. The discrimination of individuals and their relegation based on race is unfortunately common throughout the world. The United States, for example, has many laws and even amendments aimed at attempting to prevent the limitation of rights based on race. The rise of White nationalism in the US, however, shows that there is still a troubling amount of work to be done to remove racism from American society.

TIP

For more on racism in American society, I would suggest reading *Black American History For Dummies*, by Ronda Racha Penrice (Wiley).

Hypernationalism

I know I've said it before, but I will keep saying it to ensure it sticks: Nationalism is very dangerous. In the best of cases, if a leader does not know what they are actually doing, nationalism might only lead to unrest. Unfortunately, if a leader does know what they are doing, nationalism can be directed with horrifying results. When nationalism is weaponized to the effect of turning "others" into "enemies of the people," you can expect to see some historic levels of violence.

A government that utilizes hypernationalism usually seeks to solidify its power or unify its people. By doing so, a government can encourage violence against others, regardless of whether that was the intent. For example, in an economically desperate country experiencing never-before-seen depression, a charismatic leader comes to power by blaming the "others" for the country's problems and promising to rebuild the State to its former glory. Their political speeches are laced with hate, calling out these others for creating the situation the State faces, even though the others are not at fault. The leader's fiery rhetoric propels them to the pinnacle of power in the country, which they then wield against the people they have risen to power by vilifying.

Unfortunately, that is not just a hypothetical example and has been repeated multiple times throughout history. Adolf Hitler used that exact process to rise to power by targeting the Jewish community and communist political ideologies. Pol Pot targeted academics, anyone with foreign connections, and ethnic minorities in Cambodia. During the Rwandan genocide of the 1990s, the Tutsi ethnic group was targeted by the Hutus, resulting in upward of 800,000 deaths in just 100 days. Unfortunately, these are just some examples; plenty of others could be used.

As a part of the othering of hypernationalism, efforts are usually taken to dehumanize or vilify individuals. During the Rwandan genocide, the Tutsis were frequently referred to as the "tall trees" or "cockroaches." Nazi German "scientists" also put a lot of effort into the field of eugenics in an attempt to support their claim of superiority. Eugenics is a pseudoscience that has been discredited. The study focuses on finding biological and genetic support for the superiority of an ethnic or racial group. Throughout its history, eugenics has been used to justify colonization, imperialism, slavery, ethnic cleansing, and even genocide.

TECHNICAL STUFF

Genocide and ethnic cleansing are similar; the difference comes down to the intent. With ethnic cleansing, the goal is to remove all "others" from an area, leaving only the desired population. Ethnic cleansing can involve mass murder, forced relocation, and all types of violence. On the other hand, genocide is the destruction and elimination of the "others." The United Nations established a definition for genocide in 1948 following World War II and the Holocaust. The definition includes the use of mass murder or traumatic mental or physical harm, putting the group in conditions that would lead to their destruction, limiting their ability to reproduce, and targeting children for removal to prevent generational longevity. Along with the Holocaust, the Cambodian, Armenian, Rwandan, and Bosnian genocides are the most accepted examples (though even some of these are refuted by some groups). Beyond these, many other current and historical examples could be seen as fitting the criteria to be classified as genocide.

With all this focus on the alienation and vilification of others, one of the inevitable results is violence against them. You can't continually refer to them as enemies, villains, criminals, and so on and then be shocked when violence breaks out. Whether the leader directly called for violence no longer matters; anything that happens as a result of their rhetoric is squarely on them. Most often, the targets of the othering are Stateless nations or what we could classify as "marginalized communities."

Stateless nations, like the Jews during World War II, do not have a political apparatus to advocate on their behalf and are at the mercy of the State in which they are living. The State of Israel was established in 1948 for the Jewish people. By doing so, however, the Palestinians who lived in the area have become a Stateless nation themselves. Marginalized communities are groups that are targeted because of their differences from the norm (cultural, religious minorities, race, gender, or sexuality).

REMEMBER

Hitler did not only target Jews. He also targeted socialists, homosexuals, people with mental or physical disabilities, ethnic minorities like Slavs or the Roma (Gypsy is the pejorative term for the Roma), and many other communities. He actually ended up targeting so many people in his attempt to unify Germany that it is rumored the reason he never had children was because he was afraid they would not meet the standard of the "ideal" German that he had created. Worse still is that the intrastate (within a State) issues tend to become interstate (between States) issues and can lead to spillover, affecting even more people. Hitler's ideas spread with the German army during World War II to lead to the deaths of millions across Europe (and the whole world, really, with the expansion of the war into the Pacific and Africa). The Rwandan genocide spilled over into neighboring countries. The Democratic Republic of the Congo is still dealing with turmoil from the conflict almost 30 years later.

REMEMBER

Obviously, these are all bad things. In terms of the unity of a State, I hope you'll be able to recognize that any "unity" that comes from hypernationalism is not at all worth the means it took to get there. There are plenty of examples of politicians utilizing nationalism that flirts with hypernationalism to rally support. My advice: Be very, very, very skeptical of these individuals. No examples come to mind of a State built on hypernationalism where the people live together in harmony and unity. For one nation to rise within a State, it must do so at the expense of others.

A desire to break free

I hope you're starting to figure out by now that definitively identifying something as a centripetal or centrifugal force is very difficult. In Japan, nationalism may be fairly effective at keeping the country unified, but historically, it led to an expansion of its empire to include much of the Pacific. A combination of terror and patriotism unified Stalin's Soviet Union but did so by suppressing the nationalist ambitions of Ukrainians, Latvians, Estonians, and a solid number of other groups.

In this last section, we'll review a little as we tie some concepts back to the idea of holding a state together using geographic forces.

Devolution: Dividing to unite

Devolution can be particularly helpful for holding multinational States together. The delegation of power to local governmental units allows the localized government to be more reactionary to the needs of their specific population. Let's use a "hypothetical" example:

1. The Parliament of the United Kingdom enacted a fairly unpopular referendum with the rest of the States.

2. For argument's sake, let's just say the UK decided to exit the European Union, calling the action "Brexit."

3. A couple of years later, Scotland, which barely survived a referendum to remain part of the UK, decided to leave the UK to remain aligned with the historic members of the Auld Alliance, the French, and share in the benefits of being part of the EU.

4. Once Scotland decides to leave the UK, Northern Ireland holds a similar referendum, deciding that the complexities of their shared border with the EU's member States of the Republic of Ireland are too much of a hassle.

5. Wales, recognizing the newfound independence of their neighbors, Scotland and Ireland, also decides to hold a referendum of its own to secure its right to self-determination, free from England's influence — something it's had to endure since the age of the Tudors.

TIP

Snarky sidenote, but really not too far from the truth: To see more about how the UK became unified in the first place, feel free to watch *Game of Thrones*, er, I mean *War of the Roses* and *The Tudors*.

Even though that was a speculative example, just how far-fetched it is remains to be seen. To say it is in the realm of possibility is not an overstatement because we've seen it before, and it's called Balkanization. Balkanization somewhat mirrors what happened to the former State of Yugoslavia in 1991, when it broke up, forming multiple new States: Croatia, Slovenia, Bosnia and Herzegovina, Montenegro, North Macedonia, Serbia, and Kosovo (contested). This process is called Balkanization because it describes what occurred in the Balkan region of southeastern Europe between 1817 and 1912 and again after 1991, when the Balkan State broke up, forming multiple new States (see Figure 14-1). As you might imagine, this is not a clean and easy transition. There is a high probability of conflict as new borders are formed. In the case of Yugoslavia, that is, unfortunately, what ended up happening as the new States sought to grab as much land as possible and draw borders that completely included their ethnic populations (Croatia as a State for the Croats, Serbia as a State for the Serbs, and so on).

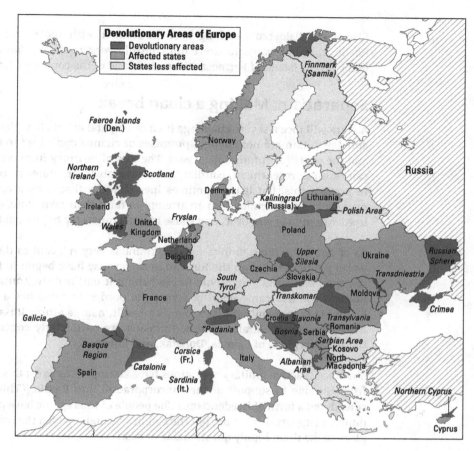

FIGURE 14-1:
The devolution
of Europe

Devolutionary Areas of Europe
- Devolutionary areas
- Affected states
- States less affected

Irredentism: Connecting all under one

Irredentism is the attempt to include all members of an ethnic group in the developed Nation-State. For consistency's sake, we'll stick with the Yugoslavia example from the previous section. During the State formation phase of Yugoslavia's break up, States were formed with borders attempting to account for ethnic and cultural divides as much as possible.

In an area as culturally and ethnically intermingled as the Balkans, this was a process that was doomed to result in arguments and conflicts. The newly founded State of Bosnia and Herzegovina included many ethnic Serbs and Croats within their newly delimited borders. Both of the newly formed States of Serbia and Croatia ended up in conflict with the new State of Bosnia and Herzegovina as they also tried to expand their borders to include exclave communities of ethnic Croats and Serbs who now lived in the new State.

Elsewhere, Pakistan has long been in conflict with India over the region of Kashmir. China wants to exert full control over the ethnic Chinese population living on the island of Formosa (the main island of the contested State of Taiwan).

Separatism: Making a clean break

A State will face a severe challenge if all centripetal efforts have failed, patriotism and devolution are not enough, promises of change don't lead to enough action, and the centrifugal forces have won. The loss of territory from centrifugal forces can result in resentment, conflict, and even global war. States go to great lengths to prevent this, but it is sometimes inevitable. In that case, breakaway regions may declare independence in an attempt to form their own State, or the forces of irredentism may win over, and those regions might try to join another State.

As of 2023, the Russian invasion of Ukraine is very relevant to the discussion of world politics. Although the Russian invasion may have begun in February 2022, the conditions and geographic forces behind it outlined the conflict long before Russian soldiers came pouring across the border. Ukraine has a long, complex history that we won't get into, but as a result, a large ethnic Russian population lives throughout Ukraine. Ethnic Russians are particularly concentrated in the Ukrainian regions of Crimea, Donetsk, and Luhansk.

Since 2014, active military operations have attempted to wrest these regions away from Ukraine in support of their incorporation into Russia. (This could also be considered a form of irredentism.) The people of the regions have passed referendums to support this action, but the conditions under which the referendums took place make them highly questionable at best.

Ethnic Russians' attempts to break away from Ukraine and become part of Russia would classify as a separatist movement. Russia supplying ethnic Russians in Ukraine with weapons and technical aid did not change that classification much. When Russia itself invaded Ukraine proper — not just the parts of Ukraine where there was some movement to separate already — this conflict became classified as an interstate conflict.

TIP

Interstate conflicts are discussed more thoroughly in Chapter 15.

Separatist movements can get very messy quickly because of the interests of the States trying to maintain control of the region, and prospective breakaway regions often receive aid and encouragement from the State they wish to join. In the case of independence movements, the situation really does not get any less tricky because the potential breakaway region hopes to split from its current State and create a whole new sovereign State of its own. Other states may still get involved if they hope to weaken the original State or if they hope for future considerations from the new State. This can be a gamble because if the breakaway region fails, any States that supported them risk losing the victor's favor.

TECHNICAL STUFF

During the American Civil War, France and Great Britain aided the Confederacy in the South with materials and supplies. Both hoped to have continued access to the agricultural products from the Southern states, and Great Britain hoped to weaken its former colony. When the Confederacy lost, their promises to pay back what they borrowed essentially became worthless, and many of those who supported them were left with little hope of regaining what they were owed.

These complex State relationships and their geographic realities are further examined in the next chapter.

Chapter **15**

Withstanding Outside Forces on a State

As you learned in Chapter 13, German geographer Friedrich Ratzel's Organic State Theory says a state acts much like any other living organism might. Ratzel's theory might not be the most well-known political geography theory, but it does start the conversation about how geography affects a State's decisions. However, determinism — States are destined to do X, Y, or Z simply because of their physical location — contradicts Ratzel's theory by simplifying a State's actions down to a product of their location.

Clearly, Britain did not grow to encompass nearly one-quarter of the world because that was its Island State destiny. It grew to such mammoth size as many other empires did — by consciously subjugating and exploiting other States. Nor did Adolf Hitler invade Poland and Germany's other neighbors because their physical proximity made war inevitable. Hitler's ambitions and horrific motives drove the Nazi German State to swell beyond its borders.

Also, something else plays the largest role in a State's decision-making process: the human element. Ratzel argued that States — much like humans — make decisions based on their best interests. And location plays a factor in those decisions. One of Zimbabwe's biggest trading partners is the Republic of South Africa, not because it has the best economy or access to all of the goods that Zimbabwe needs, but because they are neighbors. There are, however, cultural connections between the two, dating back to their time as part of the British Empire.

This chapter further investigates how location plays a role in a State's decision-making. However, even though physical location plays a role in a State's decisions, many other factors contribute to that process. Chapter 13 focused on State formation and borders, and Chapter 14 discussed the geographic forces affecting a State from within. This chapter focuses on the outside forces that affect a State.

States Playing Nice (or Not)

While we could spend a lot of time discussing the complexities of describing international agreements and the processes through which they're negotiated, we will stick with how geography can contribute to a State's decision-making about these agreements.

TIP

If you'd like to learn more about formulating these agreements, I'd recommend *Political Science For Dummies* by Marcus A. Stadelmann (Wiley).

State relations

The most basic method of interaction between States is through bilateral and multilateral agreements. Bilateral agreements are between two States, and multilateral agreements are between three or more States. These agreements can take many forms, such as mutual defense military alliances, trading agreements, amity (friendship) agreements, and the like. In this chapter, we focus on economically or militarily focused agreements.

The economic ties that bind

States trade rather extensively with each other to obtain products that they otherwise might not have had access to. When Christopher Columbus first landed on the island of Hispaniola, he met the Taino and Arawak peoples who lived there. The Arawak and Taino had jewelry made of gold that had been traded, most likely from Mesoamerica a couple of hundred miles away. Columbus mistook this to mean that there was gold in the area and could not fathom an intricate trade system across the Americas. Columbus enslaved the people and worked them to death, to the point of genocide. Also, Mansa Musa, king of the Mali Empire in West Africa in the early 14th century, is regarded as the richest person . . . ever. He built up his kingdom by trading ivory, gold, salt, and people who had been enslaved.

Things like gold, salt, oil, or uranium do not have an inherent value to them. They're not necessary for human survival (in fact, all can kill a human if consumed in high volumes or mishandled), but they have value because one group has them and another does not. Therein lies the essence of the necessity of trade: One State has an excess of something another State wants. A tit-for-tat relationship can be formed, where a State exchanges resources it's flush with in exchange for resources it isn't. Or, a State can use currency to purchase what it doesn't have from another State. Also, we know that tracking and regulating trade has long been of great importance because the earliest examples of writing from Sumer in the Fertile Crescent of Mesopotamia were almost all about tracking grain amounts and trade.

These trade relationships usually develop out of proximity and convenience. At one time, China relied on Australian iron ore because Australian ore was closer to Japan and, therefore, more accessible. Modern shipping and telecommunications have made long-range trading relationships more possible, so States are not as reliant on proximity alone. Trading blocs and economic unions are becoming increasingly necessary regionally to compete on the global economic stage. As an oil-producing country, Saudi Arabia is not super influential, but when you add Venezuela, Iraq, Kuwait, and the other members of the Organization of the Petroleum Exporting Countries (OPEC), they can be influential enough to impact global gasoline prices. The European Union partially originates in the European Economic Community (EEC), formed in 1957.

Economic cooperation is one step toward political cooperation because trade processes began linking countries, limiting the likelihood they would want to go to war with a trading partner. In the 1990s, Thomas Friedman theorized that no two countries with a McDonald's had ever gone to war with each other. The Golden Arches theory has, unfortunately, been proven incorrect — most recently, when Russia invaded Ukraine in 2022 (though since then, McDonald's has closed its restaurants in Russia).

TECHNICAL STUFF

McDonald's opened its first restaurants in the Soviet Union in 1990, serving a record 30,000 customers on its opening day. Because Russia invaded Ukraine, McDonald's shuttered its businesses, leaving 62,000 employees behind when it closed more than 800 restaurants. At first, the move was called temporary, but the move was made permanent later. The move cost McDonald's as much as $1.4 billion. Many other brands, such as Coca-Cola, Levi's, Starbucks, Ford, and IKEA, have pulled out of Russia since the war began.

Friedman tied this theory to a larger observation that countries are caught in a struggle between prosperity and maintaining their identity. This theory examines the nature of economic connections between countries and their influence on a country's decisions. This theory has been used to explain how Russia could invade Ukraine since Russia's economic ties to the West were not as strong, and Russia viewed its existing ties as expendable. Russia hoped the economic bloc it had cultivated in Central Asia and the connections with China would be enough to tide it over economically if Western businesses and governments further cut ties with Russia. Russia didn't expect how quickly the Western European States and the United States would shut Russia out of the world economy. The biggest struggle for Europe has been shedding its reliance on Russian oil and gas. Otherwise, Russia has lost access to global markets, foreign products, and outside investment, taking huge chunks of its economy. Some theorize countries like China, which are more economically interconnected than Russia, will have to seriously consider the economic impacts if they ever choose to engage in a conflict that evokes a response similar to the world's response to Russia's attack on Ukraine.

The enemy of my enemy

At the end of World War II, uneasiness fell over Europe when States in both the East and West began squaring off. France knew that if the Soviet Union decided to attack, there was not much they could do to prevent the Soviets from marching through the streets of Paris. The same was true with the British, Danes, Turks, and even the Americans. All knew it would be very difficult for them to resist on their own. But, if they could all band together, they would have a much better chance of staying safe against the growing Soviet threat from the East. These countries aligned philosophically and geographically, so the next logical step was to align militarily. The North Atlantic Treaty Organization (NATO) was born out of these ideas. Not long after, the Soviets formed the Warsaw Pact with their neighbors — Albania, Bulgaria, Czechoslovakia, East Germany, Hungary, Poland, and Romania — the Cold War alliances.

TECHNICAL STUFF

A personal pet peeve of mine is when people — particularly newscasters, academics, and politicians — use the term "third-world countries." The "first world" referred to countries aligned with the US and NATO. The "second world" was the Soviet-aligned States. The "third world" was aligned with neither, usually because they were geographically far out of the way or lacked political or economic influence enough to be too much of a concern to either side. The "third world" term has taken on a derogatory meaning and refers to a global system that no longer exists. So, please, stop using it. And if you do hear someone using this term, I give you full support to correct them with your knowledge of political geography. More correct terminology is covered in the developmental geography section of Chapter 18.

NATO is an example of what geographers call a Collective Security Union — a system of alliances meant to combine the strength of the individual members. One of the best examples was the system of alliances in Europe before World War I. Due to cultural and regional connections, the German Empire aligned itself with the Austria-Hungary Empire. Serbia gained the support of its ethnically Slav cousins, the Russian Empire. France and Britain threw aside almost 1,000 years of rivalry to ally themselves against the growing threat of Germany (and then tied themselves to Russia for good measure). Complicating things, the kings of Russia, Germany, and the United Kingdom were all cousins, but that's for another book. The idea was that the two super blocs of Germany and Austria-Hungary on one side were to prevent war with France, Russia, and the United Kingdom on the other. There was just one problem. As Captain Blackadder put it in the British television show *Blackadder Goes Forth*, "It was bollocks."

It turned into a World War spanning Africa, Asia, Europe, and including States from the Americas and Oceania, instead of being only a regional war between Serbia and Austria-Hungary. So, while Collective Security Unions prevented large-scale war during the Cold War, they also expanded a regional war into a global war during World War I.

Imperialism and colonialism: The ghosts of systems past

Remember when we talked about relict borders in Chapter 13? (Relict borders are boundaries that no longer exist, though they still very much play a role in an area's cultural, societal, or political makeup.) Relict borders also connect to the study of outside forces on a State. To understand why a State is the way it is, you sometimes need to understand its history of colonialism or imperialism (or even some more recent reiterations). Though the British Empire's hold on Hong Kong may have officially dissolved in 1997 with the return of the Pearl of the Orient to China, the legacy of the empire remains in something as simple as which side of the road drivers drive on. Hong Kong drivers drive on the left side of the road, a holdover from 156 years of colonial rule. However, the British ruled the original American colonies for even longer, and yet we drive on the right, so the example isn't perfect.

REMEMBER

Colonialism is the movement of people from one State and the establishment of settlements in another area as a continuation of the culture and power of the original State. Imperialism is the establishment of a bureaucracy that administers an area on behalf of the imperial government or sovereign. Examples of Colonialism include the 13 colonies of North America, the French of New France (Canada), the Spanish into all of Central and South America, and the Dutch into South Africa. The age of colonialism kicked into high gear after Christopher Columbus's expeditions in the late 15th century and early 16th century.

Imperialism was the subjugation of an area by an imperial power, usually for economic gain through the imperial power's control of natural resources. British India is the classic example. A relatively few British imperial diplomats, along with a cadre of military and business aides, subdued the populations of what are now India and Pakistan using their industrial weaponry and shrewd manipulation of local populations. Once India was secured under British control, they encouraged the population to grow cotton to be sold to the British at very low prices. The cotton was shipped to the United Kingdom, woven into thread, and made into clothing in the factories. The clothing was then sold to the citizens of the British Empire, including the people of India. The profits were then used to buy more cotton, make more clothes, and so on. These profits were extremely beneficial and lucrative for the State, which was subjugating the other States.

Even though the ages of colonialism and imperialism may have officially ended, we still see the influences of these systems on States around the world — so much so that human geographers now talk about neocolonialism and neoimperialism (new colonialism and new imperialism). Neocolonialism is the usage of cultural, political, and economic influence to dictate the policies of other States. This is done especially to influence the leanings of States that used to be within the holdings of an imperial State. An example is the French still exerting influence over their previously held States in northern Africa, such as Morocco, Algeria, or Mali, or the draw of people from Central or South America to attend university in Spain.

Neoimperialism is seen as a continuation of the imperial era, though it is being done by the less-traditional powers using economic politics instead of the gunboat politics that typified the imperial era.

TECHNICAL STUFF

Gunboat diplomacy uses conspicuous displays of naval power to imply a direct threat of warfare if the stronger State doesn't secure terms it finds agreeable.

One of the best examples of neoimperalism is the banana republic — the political concept, not the mall-based clothing store. A banana republic refers to States — mostly in Central America — where the United States took measures to influence the political structures to solidify American business interests. It worked like this:

1. A US-based company would enter a country and buy huge swaths of land to start growing crops (especially bananas, hence the name) with the promise of bringing jobs and development.

2. After a time, the ideals of liberalism would spread, and the workers would start demanding things like a minimum wage and other workers' rights.

3. Governments would rise to power in the States to advocate for these rights, often with the support of a communist government like the Soviet Union, which would be looking to gain power and influence in the region.

4. The government would win power and begin implementing reforms that raised business costs or threatened it completely for American companies.

5. The US government would intervene on behalf of the businesses and its own interests (and against the interests of its rivals), often to oust the government and install a government more aligned with the US government.

REMEMBER

Unfortunately, many of the most brutal dictators in the history of the Americas rose to power this way. Don't believe me? Do a quick Internet search on the Western Hemisphere Institute for Security Cooperation (also known as the School of the Americas). Though the institute had other roles, if you look through the school's roster of graduates, you might find some less-than-desirable affiliates (including infamous Panamanian dictator Manuel Noriega). Many States still bear the scars of this system. You might also notice that many of the migrants now seeking to enter the United States are from many of the countries that received the aid of a School of the Americas member.

The systems of neoimperialism and neocolonialism have been especially connected to the economic and political developments of the Cold War and beyond. During the Cold War, the spread of American influence was meant to stave off the influence of socialism and Soviet-aligned governments. The Soviet Union also spread its influence to thwart the alignment of other States with the US, leading to proxy battles over the souls of countries like Greece, Turkey, Vietnam, and South Korea. More recently, the strategy has been an effort to secure access to markets and raw materials — all part of the grander schemes collectively known as geopolitics discussed in the next section.

Geopolitics

At one time, political geography focused on an area's strategic value to a State — its geopolitical value. Some criticize the field of geopolitics because it has been linked to the processes of imperialism and used to justify the control of one State by another. Understanding geopolitics is helpful because it can provide insights into how States made certain historical decisions and can clarify recent events. When Russia invaded Ukraine in 2022, at least a couple of academic and popular media sources applied geopolitical theories developed more than 100 years ago to explain the strategic implications of Russia's influence or control over the State of Ukraine — both for Russia and NATO States.

Friedrich Ratzel is widely regarded as the father of geopolitics original theory. Ratzel and Swedish politician Johan Kjellen (who coined the term "geopolitics") were influenced by Charles Darwin's relatively recent idea of survival of the fittest. They believed that neighboring States would eventually conquer States that failed to expand. Ratzel and Kjellen's interpretation were picked up, along with Ratzel's idea of living space (lebensraum) by German geographer Karl Haushofer. Nazi Germany used Haushofer's writings to justify its territorial expansion (for its lebensraum). The Nazis believed Germans were the master race, which is where

Darwin's survival of the fittest idea came into play. In fact, geopolitics became a sort of taboo subject for a while because one of its major theories could be linked to the origins of World War II. During the Cold War, geopolitical thinking resurfaced but was linked more to the ideas of Halford Mackinder and less to Friedrich Ratzel.

In the late 1800s, Sir Halford Mackinder was possibly one of the most "British" Brits. Mackinder was a University of Oxford professor, geographer, and staunch supporter of the British Empire. He once climbed Mount Kenya because he understood that men of his station were expected to do that sort of thing. As a founder of the Geographical Association, he developed his Pivot Point theory in his *The Geographical Pivot of History* article, published by the Royal Geographical Society in 1904. He argued that the control of the world could be decided by who controlled what he called the *Pivot Point* (essentially modern-day Russia and Central Asia). Figure 15-1 shows Mackinder's rendering of the Pivot Point as the crucial point of control dictating world politics. Mackinder believed this area contained the necessary resources to fuel that control and had access to what he called the *Inner Crescent* (Europe, the Middle East, and South and East Asia). He said whoever controlled the Pivot Point could control the world. He published a follow-up paper in 1919 that renamed the Pivot Point the Heartland (thus the Heartland Theory). After observing the changes in warfare during World War I, Mackinder said control of Eastern Europe was crucial:

1. Whoever controlled Eastern Europe would be able to contain and control the Heartland.

2. Whoever controlled the Heartland could control the World Island (Europe, Asia, and Africa).

3. Whoever controlled the World Island could control the world.

So, control of Eastern Europe became crucially important to anyone who dreamed of controlling Eurasia or Europe.

See what I mean about Mackinder's theories having a more recent application? If you're not catching my drift, do an Internet search for Mackinder + Russian invasion of Ukraine.

Mackinder's theory was meant to advise the British government on taking Russia's growing threat seriously — especially if Russia were ever to pair up with the most powerful industrial State in the Inner Crescent, Germany. That nearly came to pass just before World War II. Mackinder's theory was tied to imperialism and the importance of maintaining a land-based position in the industrial era.

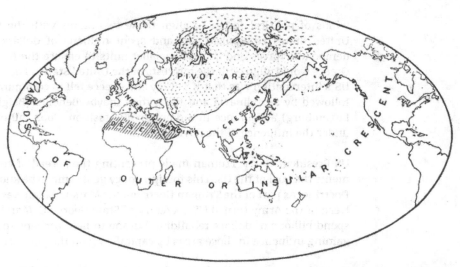

FIGURE 15-1: Mackinder's rendering of the Pivot Point as the crucial point of control in dictating world politics. (Image source: public domain.)

Halford J. Mackinder/Wikimedia Commons/Public Domain

Mackinder died before being able to amend his theory to account for post-war era changes. During World War II, naval and air power — particularly aircraft carriers — proved crucial in maintaining an area's superiority. The theory and framework through which geopolitics was understood needed to be adjusted for the new reality of the United States as the new dominant sea power and the Soviet Union as the new land-based power in continental Europe.

Mackinder's theories would be dropped in favor of American political scientist Nicholas Spykman's ideas. Spykman criticized Mackinder's assessment of Russia's potential and argued the importance of controlling what he called the *Rimland* (roughly the same theory Mackinder called the *Inner Crescent*.) His theory came to be known as the *Rimland Theory*. The general premise was that whoever controlled the Rimland could keep the Heartland (Russia/Eurasia) in check and maintain control of the World Island. Crucial to this was control of Eastern Europe, the Middle East, and Eastern and Southeast Asia. The American foreign policy ideas of containment and domino theory come out of this theory.

TECHNICAL STUFF

The policy of containment is another way to refer to the Truman Doctrine and was a US foreign policy to provide political, military, and economic aid to democratic or newly independent States threatened by communist forces, thereby containing the spread of communism.

In 1947, much of the world was still very much in turmoil. The destruction and subsequent economic recession resulting from World War II led many newly established States into times of uncertainty. The Soviet Union sought to solidify its influence in Eastern Europe and possibly expand beyond. The futures of Greece and Turkey were highly in doubt, and socialist organizations were pushing the winds of political forces to align those two States with the Soviet Union. The United States recognized this and spent millions of dollars to prop up pro-democratic forces and combat socialist units to ensure the future of Turkey and Greece would align with the interests of the United States. The justification for the US's intervention was that if Turkey and Greece fell to communism, they could be followed by Scandinavia and Italy, then maybe Benelux (Belgium, Netherlands, Luxemburg) and France in a domino-like fashion. Soon, all of Europe could be under the influence of the Soviet Union.

US President Harry Truman made preventing the spread of communist governments the goal of the US. This foreign policy goal came to be known as the Truman Doctrine. As part of the Truman Doctrine, the Marshall Plan was devised by former Head of the Army turned US Secretary of State George C. Marshall. The US would spend billions of dollars rebuilding Europe to help prevent socialist forces from gaining influence in those areas by capitalizing on the poor economic situation.

Beyond the supportive effects of rebuilding a devastated Europe, the additional goal of the Marshall Plan was to contain the spread of the Soviet Union and then attempt to combat their influence in the Rimland. The plan was so successful at containing the spread of communism in Europe that a similar plan was implemented in Asia, especially toward Japan and South Korea. The push toward the Rimland, however, failed spectacularly. The US and its Western European allies would not regain influence in the European portion of the Rimland until after 1989, when the Eastern European countries began dismantling their Soviet-aligned governments in favor of more pro-Western democracies.

TIP

I would suggest reading up on covert operations directed at Ukraine and Albania or the 1968 Soviet invasion of Czechoslovakia as a part of the (Leonid) Brezhnev Doctrine. Tim Weiner's *Legacy of Ashes: The History of the CIA* is a very good place to start.

In regions like Asia, Africa, and the Americas, the domino theory and containment were also active in the Cold War in guiding US policy for Rimland areas. Aid to the nationalist government of China was unsuccessful in preventing the establishment of the People's Republic of China by the Chinese Communist Party in 1949. So, with that portion of the Rimland beyond US influence (not necessarily aligned with the Soviet Union, but definitely not aligned with the US), the US had to direct its attention to ensuring that more States did not fall under the influence of communist governments.

This directive led the United States into the Korean War on the Korean peninsula, which ultimately resulted in the stalemate between the Democratic People's Republic of Korea (North Korea) and the Republic of Korea (South Korea) that continues to this day. Also, the United States was drawn into what used to be called French Indochina, now Vietnam, to attempt to prop up South Vietnam against the Soviet Union and China, which supported North Vietnam. The Vietnam War eventually resulted in the complete control of the country under the leadership of the communist North Vietnam. The fallout from the Vietnam War is partially credited with leading to the transitions of neighboring Laos and Cambodia (albeit temporarily in Cambodia's case) to communist governments.

Beyond Asia and Europe, Soviet and US interests butted against one another in many other parts of the World Island as imperialistic empires dissolved their hold. In Angola, the communist-aligned People's Movement for the Liberation of Angola (MPLA) fought against the anti-communist forces of UNITA (National Union for the Total Independence of Angola). UNITA was first supported by the US and later by the neighboring Republic of South Africa. The Soviet Union supported a number of revolutions in the Americas but was most successful in helping the communist State of Cuba to solidify its control of the island.

THE GRAVEYARD OF EMPIRES

Of all of the places in the world that have become notoriously strategic locations, Afghanistan has perhaps been the most elusive to capitulation. Located at the transect of the Middle East, Eurasia (with the added bonus of access to the soft underbelly of central Russia), and South Asia, Afghanistan has been eyed by many superpowers throughout the years. All have failed to subdue the historically resilient people in the epically rugged landscape.

In the 1800s, the British Empire sought to bring the region under its influence to prevent interference from the Russian Empire in the rule of the "crown jewel" of Britain's Empire, India. Russia recognized that British presence in Afghanistan would seriously threaten its position in Central Asia, especially after it was made clear in the Crimean War of the 1850s that Britain would intervene to weaken Russia. Russia's and Britain's rivalry over Afghanistan became known as the Great Game, ultimately establishing Afghanistan as a sort of buffer zone between the two competing Empires. Along with events in Africa and World War I, the Great Game contributed to the beginning of the British Empire's decline.

Almost exactly 100 years later, the Soviet Union tried its hand at subduing Afghanistan with much the same result. For almost ten years, the Soviets poured men and materials into Afghanistan. Though the Afghans were seriously overmatched, a combination of terrain, the Afghan's resolve, and an incredible influx of weaponry orchestrated by the American Central Intelligence Agency (CIA) tipped the war in the Afghan's favor. In 1989, criticism of the Soviet government's involvement in Afghanistan, as well as their handling of the Chernobyl Nuclear Disaster, marked the beginning of the Soviet Union's decline.

(continued)

(continued)

In 2001, the United States was the next State to attempt to subdue Afghanistan. After the terrorist attacks of 2001, the United States waged war against the Al-Qaeda terrorist organization and the Taliban government — accused by the US of aiding and supporting terrorists within its borders. After 20 years, thousands of lives (mostly Afghan fighters and civilians), and more than $8 trillion spent, the United States also withdrew in early 2020.

The fall of the Berlin Wall in 1989 and the events leading up to the fall of the Soviet Union in 1991 led to a shift in the geopolitical strategies of the world's megapowers. After 1991, there was only one real clear world superpower — the US. Russia and the United States coexisted relatively peacefully in the post–Cold War Era. Europe was beginning its transition to the European Union, and China was beginning its meteoric rise as an economic and subsequent military world leader.

The September 11, 2001 terrorist attacks on the United States by the ghost of a past acquaintance — Osama Bin Laden — led to a monumental shift in the world, including geopolitics. Much of the discipline shifted to understanding the nature of shatter belts, choke points, and territorial disputes (explained shortly). Even so, the ideas of Mackinder were never too far out of the minds of the United States and Russia. After 1991, it was understood that much of the Eastern European States of the Rimland was meant to be a neutral buffer State between Russia and the NATO States of Western Europe.

One by one, many States that formerly were aligned with the Soviet Union joined NATO. Poland, Czechia, and even the Baltic States of Estonia, Latvia, and Lithuania, which border Russia, were eventually added to NATO. In 2008, US President George W. Bush announced the intention to add Ukraine and Georgia (the Caucasus State, not the US southern state). Vladimir Putin recognized further NATO expansion into the Rimland would just about encircle Russia on its Western borders. The Russian support for ethnic Russian separatists in Ukraine in 2014 and Russia's subsequent invasion in 2022 can be interpreted as Russia's efforts to prevent the loss of the whole of the Rimland to their NATO rivals.

Modern geopolitics

Instead of writing guidebooks for world domination, geopolitics has shifted to understanding the geographic implications for strategically important areas and the geographic natures of territorial disputes. Geopolitics explains why so many conflicts occur in the same places while not as many in others. The study of how geography connects to conflict can be broken down into different scales — choke points, shatter belts, and territorial disputes.

CHOKE POINTS

At the most local level are choke points. These geographically significant areas typically funnel transportation and communication routes through a comparatively narrow corridor, such as mountains on either side, the narrowing of a body of water, or an isthmus (a narrow strip of land with sea on either side). Following are some examples:

» **The Bosporus Strait in Turkey:** All Mediterranean and Black Seas shipping must pass through this narrow strait. With control of the strait, Turkey can dictate who goes in and out.

» **The Malacca Strait near Indonesia:** This strait controls access between the Indian Ocean and the South China Sea, one of the busiest shipping channels in the world.

» **The Cape of Good Hope around southern Africa:** The cape was highly contested between many European empires until the Suez Canal was built, replacing the Cape of Good Hope for significance.

Control of places like the Panama Canal, the Middle East, or even the Strait of Gibraltar meant control of major transportation routes.

TERRITORIAL DISPUTES

Just as the term implies, a disputed territory is an area whose control is being contested either by two or more States, or between a State and the people living in the territory. The Strait of Gibraltar is a tiny area of land of less than 3 square miles that has been a huge point of contention between Spain and the United Kingdom for quite some time. The United Kingdom presently controls it and thus has the most direct control over the European side of the strait. Morocco controls the other side from North Africa. Spain has advocated for control of the region without success.

Beyond control of strategically important areas, territorial disputes can come up over the ethnic or cultural makeup of an area — like Pakistan's claims to Kashmir and Jammu, which is presently administered by India. Territorial disputes can be historically based, like China's claim over the region of Tibet. National pride can also factor in, as States do not want to be seen as weak, so they will fiercely defend territorial claims — even if it is just a set of rocks in the East Sea (also known as Dokdo or Takeshima) that South Korea and Japan are contesting.

Finally, territorial disputes can be over access to critical resources like oil or fishing rights. The South China Sea is highly contested by nearly half a dozen States that all want the area because of the presence of fishing and oil reserves.

WARNING

Because many of these disputes are tied to national pride, they can quickly lead to contention. Notice I have gone to great lengths to not assign ownership over any area to one side or the other. Some of these disputes have been going on for centuries, and I'd rather not complicate them further. For this reason, when I teach about the topic, I like to use the Whisky War as an example. The "war" between allied States Denmark and Canada involved either country visiting the island, removing the other country's flag, and leaving a bottle of liquor for when their foe arrived to remove their flag. Unfortunately, the "war" ended in 2022 when the two countries decided to split the island. Most territorial disputes are not as cordial as the Whisky War and lead to deaths and family separations, making them no laughing matter.

SHATTER BELTS

If choke points are local and territorial disputes are national, then shatter belts are a regional-level way of understanding modern geopolitics. A shatter belt is a highly contested and volatile region because of its strategic location and complex ethnic composition. Areas like the Middle East, Southeast Asia, the Balkans, or East Africa could be considered shatter belts.

A shatter belt is an area that is strategically important enough to cause severe geopolitical consequences if one power gains influence over it. So, any incursion by a great power into a shatter belt area is fiercely met by one or more competing powers. Let's use the Crimean War as an example. At its basic understanding, the war started between Russia and the Ottoman Turks over the strategically important Crimean peninsula. Control would have given Russia the ability to dominate the entire Black Sea. Understanding this, France and the United Kingdom allied with their historic adversary, the Ottomans, to prevent Russia from gaining control.

This sort of posturing continues today in places like the Middle East, where global powers like Russia and the United States are meddling in the affairs and aligning with regional powers like Iran, Saudi Arabia, and Israel to maintain just enough conflict to prevent any power from gaining control over the area. But the meddling doesn't go far enough to spill into a regional or global war like what happened in the Balkans during World War I.

We Are the World

Geopolitical strategies aside, there are actually efforts being made to bring the world's states together. Though this may be surprising to hear, we live in the most peaceful period of human history. That is not to say there is no conflict; there most certainly is. However, the frequency of large conflicts and the number of casualties have severely decreased. The fear of nuclear weapons and mutually assured destruction has prevented conflicts (thus far), and precision weapons have decreased non-combatant deaths. Humans live longer and have greater access to resources on average than at any other point in history.

REMEMBER

Remember that poverty and disparity in access to things like healthcare and clean water that are otherwise lost in the aggregate are still very much issues. Much of this can be credited to an increase in what we call transnationalism. This is the spread of ideas and people across borders to the extent that it is helping to unite the world through their interconnectedness. This peace has been furthered by increasingly global cultural, political, and economic structures. The spread of culture has already been covered in previous chapters, so we'll skip that and instead devote the last section here to political and economic structures.

Supranationalism

It became evident after the Second World War that a forum needed to be established for States to air their grievances, settle disputes, and establish an organization to settle global problems. With these things in mind, the United Nations (UN) was formed to do all this and more. Though it does not have the power to pass legislation on behalf of States and does not have a standing army of its own, the UN is largely credited with preventing World War III and raising the standard of living globally.

I won't go too far into the structure of the UN because that is better kept for a political science book. However, what the UN does have at its disposal is the ability to condemn the actions of States and pass non-binding resolutions. The Cuban Missile Crisis in the 1960s was largely diffused when the United States was able to present evidence to the world on the UN's floor that the Soviets were placing nuclear weapons in Cuba. This evidence led the Soviets to come to the table to de-escalate the situation with the United States and remove their missiles from Cuba (if the US also removed theirs from Turkey). The United Nations Convention of the Law of the Seas (UNCLOS) helped establish a framework for dealing with the geographic problem of water rights.

At a smaller scale than the UN (since it literally contains just about every State), many Intergovernmental Organizations (IGOs) help States work together to address many issues. One that has already been talked about extensively, the North Atlantic Treaty Organization (NATO), provides security for its members. The Southern Common Market (known as Mercosur) provides economic cooperation among its members in South America. Each IGO offers differing levels of cooperation among its members, but each has the common goal of fostering cooperation and strengthening each of those involved.

OPEC (Organization of Petroleum Exporting Countries) is an economic organization that also influences the political decisions of its member States.

The European Union is the most intertwined IGO, though each of the members still maintains a degree of sovereignty. The EU established a common market, complete with a common currency (the EuroDollar) and a transgovernmental body based in Brussels, Belgium, that legislates on behalf of the union.

The EU is attempting to strengthen its bonds economically by removing trade barriers. Culturally, they have removed border control between member States through the Schengen Agreement, allowing for the free movement of people between States.

The Erasmus Agreement has allowed citizens from any EU State to attend university in any other EU State free of charge.

You're unlikely to see many European students at a college or university in the US. Why would they spend thousands of dollars on US education when they can go to European universities for free?

The EU has established itself to the point that it has solidified itself as a dominant economic power — something that none of its individual members could be.

The World Systems Theory

The spread of transnationalist ideas has led to increased economic cooperation. We've already discussed the disproven theory that no two States that had a McDonald's have ever attacked each other. While this theory doesn't hold true, it highlights an interesting connection between economic and political structures.

Immanuel Wallerstein developed his World Systems Theory, which further examined the relationship of States on a global economic scale. The basis of his theory was that all States were interlocked under an exploitive relationship that relied on one another. The wealthiest States (what he called the *Core*) exploited the less wealthy States (the Periphery) for cheap labor and materials. The Periphery needs the Core for investment and high-technology goods. In the middle — what Wallerstein calls the Semi-Periphery — are the States that exploit the Periphery but are also exploited by the Core.

These relationships are examined further in Chapter 18, which deals with economic and developmental geography, but you should understand that these relationships have developed an interconnected economic structure that has helped bind States politically.

4

The Spatial Organization of Human Economic Systems

» **The impact of technology on humans' ability to support themselves**

» **The connection between economics, farming, and agricultural practices**

Chapter **16**

The People Need Food

Have you ever been sitting at the dinner table in the middle of the winter, eating fresh vegetables and wondering how the heck you can get fresh vegetables at that time of year? Or, have you ever thought about how tomatoes are considered a staple to Italian dishes, even though tomatoes are native to the Americas, not Europe? If you've ever had thoughts even remotely like these, then I am proud to inform you there is a field of geography for you — agricultural geography! Agricultural geography usually falls under the larger discipline of economic geography and rural land use and is one of the most in-demand fields of geography.

With population changes, economic development bringing more people to the cities, and climate change putting additional stress on food production, agricultural geography deals with topics of global importance. Humans produce more than enough food to meet the needs of every person in the world. However, where that food is produced does not always match up with where the people live, creating food insecurity. Hunger is not a production problem; it's a distribution problem. So, just like everything else, geography can be used to help address hunger.

This chapter examines agricultural geography through historical, economic, social, political, and environmental lenses. Just like any other geography field, agricultural geography doesn't happen in a vacuum. The Russian invasion of Ukraine in 2022, for example, has predominately been examined for its political implications, but Ukraine's position as the "breadbasket of Europe" has massive economic and agricultural implications as well. Ukrainian farmers had to shift to soldiering, the wheat fields of Ukraine transitioned to battlefields, and the ships were stuck in port. Global food prices in some areas have been impacted as food becomes scarcer because of decreased supply. It's basic supply and demand but with very real human costs for the areas relying on shipments of Ukrainian grain.

Origins of Agriculture

Not to sound too overzealous, but it is impossible to overstate the development of agriculture in terms of the development of human society. Okay, I might get a little bold and argue that agriculture is the most important development in human history. Yes, agriculture is even more important than creating the Internet or sending humans into space. And before you get too judgmental, just know that I made this argument even before I moved to the state of Nebraska.

The Neolithic Revolution

To get to agriculture's origins, we have to look at a region that is not known for its agricultural fertility: the Middle East. If you ask most people about the Middle East's place identity, they might bring up things like the deserts, oil, or religious-fueled conflict. The idea of it being the "birthplace of human civilization" is not usually high on people's perception of the region, but that's exactly what it is.

Archeological evidence suggests that humans began farming in the region known as the *Fertile Crescent* (the modern-day Iraq area between the Tigris and Euphrates Rivers) about 12,000 years ago. Before that, humans had been hunter-gatherers, meaning they were nomadic or semi-nomadic, moving from one area to another in search of food or following large herds of animals. The nomadic life wasn't glamorous. A broken bone could spell doom for someone who spent all their time moving from one place to another. Some social anthropologists have actually suggested that humans might have lived pretty good lives due to their communal reliance on each other, diverse diets, and active lifestyles. On the whole, the First Agricultural Revolution (also known as the *Neolithic Revolution*) sparked a societal shift that set humans on a course that would lead them to develop to the point we are today.

Evolutionary evidence suggests the first human-like species (*Homo habilis*) evolved as long as 2.4 million years ago. The first *Homo sapiens* (modern humans) began showing up about 200,000-300,000 years ago. Between that time and 12,000 years ago, humans were hunter-gatherers. Don't get me wrong; plenty of rudimentary inventions and technologies were developed during that time. But in the 12,000 years or so since the invention of agriculture, humans have been developing at breakneck speed.

With the development of agriculture came the need to keep track of materials and food stores. Thus came the development of writing. The Sumerians of the Fertile Crescent are credited with originating writing with a style of writing called *cuneiform*. We know that the development of agriculture corresponds with the development of writing because some of the oldest examples of writing are about the storage of crops.

Along with writing comes the need to develop a class of educators who can teach the next generation how to read and write. Mathematics also grew out of the need to calculate storage, crop yields, and track sales. The development of economic systems flows from the development of math to determine the process of transferring agricultural goods in exchange for services or currency. A whole class of artisans developed, specializing in making agricultural tools (and later, weapons of war) from copper, bronze, and, eventually, harder metals like iron and steel. You can get the picture from here regarding the development of society and the growth of social structure.

TECHNICAL STUFF

Interestingly enough, history itself can be attributed to the origins of agriculture. Anthropology and history both study the historical development of human society. The difference between the two is that historians rely on the written record, while anthropologists work with archaeologists to uncover and interpret the development of society by analyzing artifacts. With the development of writing, the written record removed all the guesswork, and historians use that to piece together the path of human society using documents and historical accounts. So, it's not wrong to say that human history begins with the development of agriculture. The rest was just anthropology.

On a more geographic path of significance, the Neolithic Revolution tied people to a specific place. Instead of moving around all of the time, people stayed put on the land they were familiar with farming. Cities started developing as people congregated in one place to farm or support the farmers. The oldest known cities, like Jericho in modern-day Palestine or Çatalhöyük in modern-day Turkey, are located in the Fertile Crescent. The rise of the earliest cities corresponds to the advent of cultivating crops in the area.

The advancement of warfare also arose during the Neolithic era. This is not to say that there was no conflict before then, but with the concentration of people came the concentration of wealth and resources. Divisions arise between the haves, the have-nots, and the wants. City walls were erected, and a warrior class was formed to protect the cities' wealth.

As previously noted in Chapter 1, mapmaking and cartography developed along with agriculture. Of course, many cave drawings and prehistoric petroglyphs are thought to be maps of hunting grounds or important locations. Surveying and mapmaking developed along with agriculture and the rise of kingdoms to help people understand what is where, but perhaps more importantly, who owns what for the sake of taxation.

Complex social roles in the Neolithic Revolution

A change in social roles also started developing with the advent of agriculture. Along with vertical social stratification, there was also a horizontal level of stratification (such as multiple types of jobs classified as "middle class"). The processes of the enslavement of people and tying individuals to the land were formalized once groups of people settled. Early on, the processes of slavery were not tied to any characteristic (such as race), and often, enslaved people were taken as spoils of war or kidnapped and had their freedom sold away. That definitely does not make it any better, but it is not until the Columbian Triangular Trade (discussed later in this chapter) that the ideas of race are strongly attached to the processes of enslavement.

As already discussed, the development of agriculture led to the vertical division of labor (farmers, laborers, governmental workers, and so on), leading to the development of a class system based on the perceived value of one's work. Many early classes were built around the concepts of the perceived contributions of the uneducated laborers versus the educated administrators. Along with this came a division based on land ownership. The settlement of people in one area led to wealth accumulation by select individuals. This wealth was most typically tied to a specific family and passed from one generation to the next through a process known as *primogeniture*.

Wealth or land ownership was passed to the first-born son or daughter based on whether a society was matrilineal-based (descent traced through the mother, like the early Cherokee Nation of North America) or patrilineal-based (descent traced through the father, like much of the royal lines of Europe). Subsequent children born after the first-born child usually had to use their family's wealth or position to gain a position in academics (become a scholar), the religious order (become a priest, for example), or receive a commission in the military. Women in patrilineal societies were expected to marry and contribute to their husbands' families.

Another result of the agricultural revolution is a change in women's roles. In hunter-gatherer societies, women indeed had different roles (typically, they were foragers) than men, but their contributions were seen as just as valuable as those of men in many cultures. In many agricultural societies, women were confined to the home while men tended the crops. As the crops were the generators of wealth, men's work was perceived to be much more valuable than the work of women. Never mind the fact that women secured the home and supported the raising of children. Because their role did not necessarily generate income, their position was considered subservient to men. Women were especially hampered in early agricultural societies due to their role as mothers and caregivers. More children were needed to provide labor for the farm. Life expectancies were lower in some areas because diets were worse because of less diversity in the foods and a lack of protection against famine in the case of crop failure. Because of this, women were expected to have more children to ensure the security of the lineage or to allow enough laborers for the fields.

Hearths of agriculture

Agriculture did not just happen everywhere, all at once. There were particular technologies or the domestication of certain types of plants or animals that happened at different times in different areas. Human geographers look at the different plants, animals, and technologies, study how they spread, and try to understand their impact better. One of the best ways to do this is to attach agricultural developments to changes in the quality of life for people living in areas where those developments take place. The domestication of horses, for example, brought a form of transportation but also a means of plowing up large sections of fields to produce more food. Once introduced to the Americas, horses allowed the Plains Indians of what is now Mexico, the United States, and Canada to drastically extend their annual migration patterns. This section will examine important centers of origin (as seen in Figure 16-1) for different technologies and domesticated agricultural products over time and space.

Agriculture classifications

Now that we've more or less established that the invention of agriculture is quite possibly the most important milestone in the development of human civilization, it's time to look at how it spreads, develops, and connects to the distributions across space. In the coming sections, we'll look at how agriculture has changed since the Neolithic Revolution and how those changes affected human society in different parts of the world.

First, we need to discuss how agriculture is classified spatially so we can differentiate between subsistence and commercial agriculture.

TIP

We'll talk more about these differences when we talk about farming in More Developed Countries (MDCs) and Less Developed Countries (LDCs) in Chapter 17.

For now, all you need to know is that subsistence farming is a form of agriculture where farmers usually live off of the products they grow and care for. In commercial agriculture, farmers grow crops to sell and then use the profits from the sale to live off (including buying food).

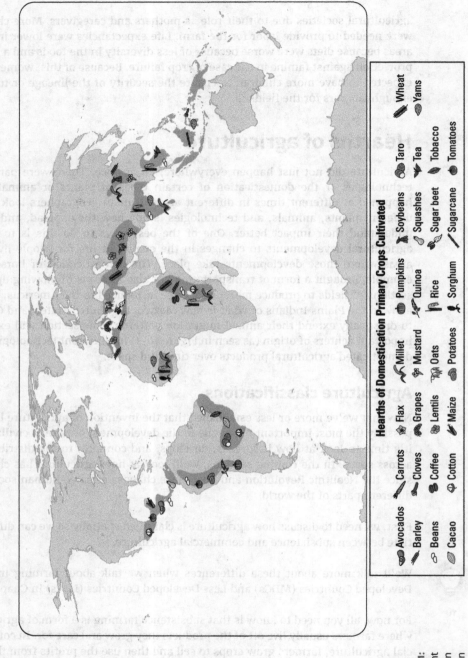

Hearts of Domestication

	Primary Crops Cultivated	
Avocados	Flax	Millet	Pumpkins	Soybeans	Taro	Wheat
Barley	Grapes	Mustard	Quinoa	Squashes	Tea	Yams
Beans	Cloves	Oats	Rice	Sugar beet	Tobacco	
Cacao	Coffee	Lentils	Sorghum	Sugarcane	Tomatoes	
Carrots	Cotton	Potatoes	Maize			

FIGURE 16-1:
Early plant
domestication
by region

The two classifications we can use to describe different spatial agricultural practices are intensive and extensive.

>> **Intensive agriculture:** Intensive agricultural practices are forms of farming that take place in a comparatively small area with a higher concentration of labor and resources in any particular place. Farming practices like dairy farming, vegetable farming (truck farming or market gardening), or wet rice cultivation are examples of intensive processes. Concentrating the farming practice into a more limited area allows farmers to maximize yields in a smaller area, requiring more labor by the workers involved. Dairy cows need to be milked and fed daily, whereas beef cattle may only be provided supplemental browse (feed) when they're in their grazing pastures, requiring much less work than it takes to milk each dairy cow individually.

>> **Extensive agriculture:** By comparison, extensive agriculture utilizes farming practices over a larger geographic area and requires less work than a comparable amount of land devoted to intensive agriculture. Things like field crops (wheat, corn, oats, potatoes, and so on) require much more space to grow but less tending than fruit orchards or vegetables like peppers. The profits are usually much lower for extensive agricultural products, but farmers can still make up their incomes by the sheer volume of products being produced.

In both forms of agriculture (intensive and extensive or subsistence and commercial), access to technology can significantly increase the efficiency of a farm laborer. The next section will look at more recent agricultural revolutions. With a focus on the changes in technology and how that affected agricultural production, the changes in farming have had reverberating impacts across society.

Agricultural regions

Unlike today, with the Internet and modern transportation, new technologies and goods did not travel nearly as quickly as things do now. Agriculture actually developed independently in five hearths (centers of origin) and diffused to the rest of the world. Although the five regions are in five very different parts of the world, one thing they have in common is that they're all within or very near the tropical region of the world. Following are the five hearths and the key root vegetable or grain tied to them:

>> **Fertile Crescent (discussed earlier in this chapter):** wheat, barley, and oats (all grains)

>> **Sub-Saharan Africa:** yams (a root), sorghum (a grain), and cowpeas/black-eye peas (a legume)

>> **Mesoamerica and South America (centered on modern-day Central America and the Northern Andes Mountains):** peppers and squash (vegetables)

>> **Yellow River Valley of East Asia (specifically, modern-day China):** rice (a grain) and soybeans (a legume)

>> **Southeast Asia:** mango and coconuts (fruits) and taro (a root vegetable)

TECHNICAL
STUFF

The only variation was in Mesoamerica. Its earliest agriculture was tied to peppers and squash (vegetables). Later, however, the growth of civilizations in the Americas was supported by the cultivation of potatoes (a root) and maize (a grain).

WARNING

It is well known that Italians have perfected the making of dishes supported with tomato sauce. The Irish have a multitude of ways to cook potatoes. Americans have a massive reliance on beef. And in China, corn is used on just about everything (including, to my displeasure, pizza). Ironically, none of those foods come from the place where they're now ingrained in the culinary traditions of the culture. Tomatoes did not first grow in Italy. Like potatoes and corn, tomatoes are products of the Americas. The beef cattle that are now used to make those all-American hamburgers are descendants of cows originally from Europe and Africa. So, just remember that "traditional dishes" may not be as traditional as they might seem.

One of the defining features of agricultural regions (in addition to the plants people could grow) is the animals that people could domesticate. Dogs were the first animals to be domesticated. They were thought to have first been domesticated in Siberia in what is now Central Russia, as far back as 27,000 years ago. Along with being companion animals for security, dogs were thought to have been used as pack animals and hunting aides. Dogs were the only species to have been domesticated before the Neolithic Revolution and have been faithful companions ever since.

Elsewhere in the world, the availability of easily domesticated animals was a necessity for developing cultures. Especially useful traits were their strength, docile temperament (that prevented harm to their handlers or each other and decreased their chances of getting away), and ease of reproducing.

Many animals fitting those criteria came from the Middle East. Sheep, goats, and later, cattle were thought to have been first domesticated in the Middle East. As good sources of protein and other products (like leather, wool, or milk), these animals contributed to the rise of early civilizations near the Mediterranean Sea and Indus River valley in modern-day Pakistan. In South Asia and modern-day India, chickens and cattle were domesticated and incorporated into people's diets about the same time pigs were also being domesticated (roughly 8,000 years ago).

Because of their geographic connections, there is strong evidence to suggest that once these animals were domesticated, their use by humans diffused throughout Africa, Europe, and Asia. One of the most important animals to be domesticated in Afro-Eurasia was also one of the most recent. Archeological studies suggest that humans did not master the usage of horses until as recently as 6,000 years ago in Central Asia. Horses revolutionized humans' ability to hunt and travel but were not used in wide practice as draft animals until the Second Agricultural Revolution.

The Aborigines of Australia were without domestic animals until the dingo's arrival (a species of dog thought to have migrated to Australia about 5,000 years ago). It was not until Europeans arrived in large numbers in the 1700s that many other domestic animals were introduced. North America was in a similar situation. The Natives of Northern and Central America relied on dogs and turkeys as their main domestic animal. The nations of North America were proficient farmers (maize especially) and hunters.

One of the biggest misconceptions about the Americas is that they were still "wild" when the Europeans first arrived in large numbers in the early 16th century. In fact, there are many examples of settled areas with well-established agricultural systems. The Mayans of Central America are believed to have cut down so much rainforest for agriculture that they shifted the precipitation patterns and led to their downfall. The Aztecs completed massive engineering projects around what is now Mexico City to allow them to farm on irrigated platforms on Lake Texcoco. Even the prairies of North America were a manicured landscape. Natives intentionally set fire to the prairies to allow for new growth. Bison were attracted to the new grasses growing in the burned areas, making hunting easier for the Plains Nations. Horses eventually would aid in their hunting, but they would not arrive in the Americas until a few individuals escaped the corrals of Spanish conquistadors in the early 16th century.

TIP

Your fun fact for the day is that American feral horses (known as mustangs) are actually descendants of Spanish horses.

The rest of the animals of the Americas were too temperamental or downright dangerous to domesticate in large numbers. With large predators like wolves, mountain lions, and bears, animals like deer, elk, or bison had strong fight-or-flight responses. They still do, in fact, which is something that tourists to National Parks like Yellowstone still seem to forget, sometimes with tragic results. Please do not ever try to pet the fluffy cows!

In South America, the native peoples of the Andes Mountains were fortunate enough to have alpacas and llamas. Though not especially strong animals, especially when compared to oxen or horses, their sure-footedness made them ideal to help carry heavy loads through uneven mountain passes. Outside of the Andes, there are known prehistoric communities of people, including evidence of rather large areas like Kuhikugu in central Brazil, whose growth was thought to have been linked to cassava growth. Not as much is known about early agricultural societies in South America, so if you're looking for a research interest to cultivate, there's a great one to consider.

Agriculture Grows and Spreads

In the United Kingdom in the 17th century (1600s), another new technology was being developed that would revolutionize the agricultural world again: steam. Although steam power is predominantly discussed in the origins of the Industrial Revolution, the British quickly understood its potential in agriculture as well. Early steam engines were not small by any means and didn't produce nearly as much power as modern engines. Engines were most effective in large vessels such as trains and ships, but eventually, they were streamlined to the point that they could be used to power farm equipment like tractors.

The Second Agricultural Revolution

The products and machines of the Industrial Revolution were not the glamorous and intricate machines we see now, but that does not make them any less significant. We'll discuss this in more detail in Chapter 19, but for now, we'll focus on agricultural products.

The inventions of the Second Agricultural Revolution were primarily restricted to Great Britain, the English-speaking world, and the States near the United Kingdom in the revolution's earliest stages before eventually diffusing to other parts of Europe. The creation of steel was one of the most impactful inventions of the Second Agricultural Revolution. Steel is not a metal that occurs naturally in nature; rather, it is created using a blend of mostly iron ore and coal — two elements found in abundance and with relative ease on the British Isles.

Steel allowed for much sturdier, stronger, and more productive tools. A man named John Deere from across the Atlantic Ocean in the United States recognized its potential and patented the design for a steel plow in 1837. The steel plow was far stronger than prior plows and was designed to clog less often, so digging up fields could go much faster. This was especially helpful in breaking up the tough sod of the American prairies. With the invention, a single farmer with a plow and a team of draft animals could till up a much larger area than workers using traditional hand-held hoes. A single plow could complete the work of a team of men much more efficiently and made it much less necessary to need a whole team of men at all times to tend fields.

While the steel plow was helping Americans cultivate the Great Plains, another invention in the American South also changed the agricultural landscape there. Cotton was one of the most profitable products grown in hot and humid climates. As a very labor-intensive process, the agricultural practice of plantation farming required large amounts of manual labor. This came mainly in the form of enslaved people from the continent of Africa and subsequent generations.

The Cotton Gin, invented by Eli Whitney, greatly increased this process by quickly separating cotton from the seeds, an otherwise labor-intensive process. With it, cotton plantations rapidly expanded because they could focus the labor of the enslaved workers on growing and maintaining the plants. The complete opposite effect of the steel plow, mechanical reaper, or seed drill, the cotton gin actually expanded the need for agricultural labor. For this reason, the Southern states fiercely opposed the abolition movement since their entire economic system depended on unpaid forced labor. Many states of the Confederacy mentioned the preservation of slavery as the reason for their secession at the beginning of the American Civil War — not state's rights, as often cited (unless that refers to a state's right to have slavery).

THE EVOLUTION OF FORCED LABOR

Slavery had long been used as a form of labor. However, it was really not until modern Europeans got involved in the trade of enslaved people that people from a particular region of the world were enslaved based on their race and used for free labor. During the Roman Empire, for example, enslavement could be an inherited trait or a way to pay off a debt. If a family fell on hard times, a family member could be sold into slavery until the debt had been repaid. In other parts of the world, the capturing and enslavement of people from nearby communities was a fairly common practice but happened on a more local scale.

With the conversion of much of Europe to Christianity, the religious ideologies prevented the enslavement of fellow Christians, so Europeans began looking to the continent of Africa for a supply of people for the slave trade. During the Middle Ages, there was not as much need for slavery because predominantly agricultural societies relied on the labor of a class of people called *serfs*. Whoever controlled the land also ruled over the people who lived on it — the serfs. This was a sort of tricky way around the restrictions on slavery because the people were not technically owned, but the land

(continued)

(continued)

they lived on was, and the serfs were indebted to the lord (or Earl/Duchess, Duke/Duchess, or Count/Countess,) who owned the land. The serfs were not technically enslaved, but they were not exactly free either since there were many restrictions placed on them.

Cities were filled with tradespeople and were relatively small until the Second Agricultural Revolution. Large concentrations of people required a large amount of food, which was impossible until the mechanization of agriculture in the 1700s. London's population in 1500 was estimated only to be about 50,000 people. By comparison, the city of Cahokia (near modern-day Saint Louis, Missouri) had a population of about 25,000. Once Europeans started looking to branch out during the era of colonization, they were in desperate need of labor and looked to the continent of Africa to supply that labor.

The processes of indentured servitude (a process by which someone had their way paid to the colony in exchange for a set number of years working off the debt) were used early on but were quickly replaced by the Transatlantic slave trade (part of a larger system known as the *Columbian Triangle Trade*).

Columbian Triangle Trade describes the process through which people were captured and enslaved in Africa and brought to the Americas (South, North, and Central). There, they were forced to produce agricultural products (mostly things like sugar, cotton, and tobacco) that were then shipped to Europe. They were then turned into products like processed sugar, cloth, and cigars sold in Europe and to the colonists living in the Americas.

The profits made were used to purchase goods (especially guns, clothes, and manufactured items) that were then used to purchase more enslaved people in Africa. When most countries officially banned the Transatlantic slave trade in the early 1800s, slavery was maintained as an institution in the Americas through the enslavement of the children of the enslaved people already there (and forced reproduction in many cases).

By the time the United States banned slavery in 1865, much of Europe had already ended the practice. Between then and now, slavery has gradually been removed from the economic institutions of countries in the rest of the world. Additional measures from the League of Nations and its modern reiteration, the United Nations, have more or less removed the formalized processes of enslavement from states worldwide.

Other inventions like the seed drill, chemical fertilizers, and mechanical reapers (used to cut wheat and other grass-like field crops) were used to great effect in the UK. These, along with advancements in the Enclosure Movement, led to a great transition in the social structure of Great Britain and set it on the path toward becoming the world's superpower. Serfdom had ended in England around the mid-to-late-16th century. Instead, farmers worked on common lands, using a percentage of their crops to help pay the landowners' rent. These commoners had traditional rights to use the land to collect firewood or graze animals.

The Enclosure Movement

The Enclosure movement refers to transferring these common lands into private ownership. Fences were placed to demarcate land, restricting the ability of commoners to continue farming. With most lands transferred into private ownership by the 1800s, many rural workers were left looking for work. This process started during the 1500s and is one reason countries like England began colonizing other parts of the world:

>> With agricultural land becoming increasingly scarce, England began looking to their developing 13 colonies in North America for available agricultural land.

>> The French did the same with New France (now the Canadian Province of Québec).

>> The Spanish and the Portuguese looked to Central and South America to expand their holdings.

>> The Dutch established New Amsterdam (now New York) and the colonies along Africa's Southern Coast.

TIP

The British eventually absorbed both New Amsterdam and South Africa. The Dutch colonists remained in relatively large numbers in South Africa. These colonists were known as the *Boers*, meaning "farmers."

Colonization was also necessary for these European countries since more food because of the Second Agricultural Revolution meant more people.

In England, the Enclosure Movement led to a mass exodus of people to the cities, arriving with little education and only having experience in agriculture. Newly developing industrialized factories were snatching up the incoming urban migrants and putting them to work in the industrial sector (with very little pay and sometimes horrid living conditions, as observed by Karl Marx, but that is for another chapter). The increased food supplies from the mechanization of farm labor led to a population boom. Between 1600 and 1800, London's population grew from only about 200,000 to close to 1 million. Within another 50 years, London's population would top 2 million. The great population shift to the cities that began in England due to agriculture continues today. In 2014, the United Nations reported that more than 50 percent of Earth's population lives in cities.

Cities became more involved with agriculture during the Second Agricultural Revolution by centralizing slaughterhouses and meat-packing plants in urban areas. With refrigeration still largely reliant on ice availability, getting meats to urban markets without spoiling required the animals to be transported alive. There, they could be slaughtered for local consumption, or the meat could be placed on refrigerated rail cars to be shipped to other areas.

For example, much of Chicago's growth can be attributed to its importance as a centralized location for meat packing between the largely agricultural areas of the Great Plains and the more urban markets of the United States East Coast. However, one of the disadvantages of this system is that regulations and protections for workers arrived more slowly than increases in agricultural production rates.

TIP

For more on the absolutely appalling conditions of early-industrial meat-packing facilities, I recommend you read the book *The Jungle* by Upton Sinclair. It helped shed light on the result of lax restrictions on meat-packing plants and helped lead to the increased regulation of the industry. As much as many people don't like having governments regulate industry, they're also responsible for ensuring you don't have rats mixed in with your hamburger.

The Third Agricultural Revolution

Whereas the Second Agricultural Revolution was primarily contained to what is now classified as the Global North (mostly More Developed Countries) and not of great benefit to the Global South (Less Developed Countries in Latin America, Africa, and Asia), the Third Agricultural Revolution expanded the availability to mechanization, farming techniques, and chemicals to almost all corners of the world. This agricultural revolution was a big step toward addressing the global issue of food insecurity. The revolution was so revolutionary that American scientist Norman Borlaug received the Nobel Peace Prize for his contributions to the world's food supply.

Before World War II, most of the world practiced labor-intensive subsistence farming. Much of Europe, northern North America, and select countries throughout the rest of the world began reaping the benefits of the agricultural revolution. (Get it? Reaping? As in, like, wheat?) Tractors were relatively scarce outside those areas, so much work was still done by hand. Chemicals like pesticides, herbicides, insecticides, fungicides, and fertilizers were successfully used to help ensure crop stability as much as possible. Though the United States had experienced the Dust Bowl in the 1930s, social welfare programs were being developed to aid farmers if their crops failed.

The same could not be said for the Global South. If a bad storm came through and destroyed crops, families would have to hope for the generosity of neighbors to help persevere. Without strong markets and stable governmental support, prolonged droughts could lead to massive famines. In fact, starvation and cutting off a civilization from its food supply has been used as a tool of warfare throughout human history. After the United Nations was created, there was a mechanism for identifying and directing food aid to areas hit by famine. By far, however, the best method of securing a state against food instability is the development of a strong agricultural core.

That is exactly what the Third Agricultural Revolution worked to address. Mechanization had taken hold, and the science of farming was about to take hold and expand in a big way. Along with increasing yields in the United States, Canada, and Western Europe, it was time for agricultural technology to expand significantly. At the center of it all was a hearty resistance form of winter wheat that Borlaug had developed. What makes winter wheat unique is that it is planted in the fall, remains dormant over the winter, and begins growing right away in the spring. The plants he selected and replicated were specifically high-yield and disease-resistant, meaning that much less of the farmer's labor would go to waste on unproductive crops. Farther, because the plants began growing right away in the spring, they were ready to harvest earlier, allowing the farmer to plant a second crop during the same growing season. When implemented along with machinery, chemicals, and modern irrigation methods, the *Green Revolution*, as it has been called, effectively ended food insecurity for the most part in some of the most famished regions of the world.

The research completed as part of the Green Revolution showed that a farmer could effectively double their potential output when employed as a whole package (structurally with crop rotation, chemicals, machines, and proper seeds). Borlaug first implemented these ideas in Mexico. Before the introduction of the Green Revolution, Mexico had widespread food insecurity. Within a relatively short time, the agricultural output had increased to the point that Mexico had enough food that it could begin exporting to other countries. Borlaug's work in India and Pakistan is where he gained the most recognition. Credited with saving a billion people from starvation, Borlaug was nominated and received the Nobel Peace Prize for effectively securing the food security of both states against famine.

SOVIET COLLECTIVIZATION

Sometimes, agricultural revolutions are not super successful and can actually have horrific results. This is definitely the case with the attempts to implement collective farming in the Soviet Union and Communist China. In the Soviet Union, this included removing farms from private ownership and turning over the means of production to the laborers. Tractors were distributed, cattle were allotted, and productivity numbers were forged. The forced attempt at collectivization resulted in more than 5 million deaths between 1930 and 1933. Academics are reexamining the ethnic and religious factors leading to the persecution of Ukrainians — who suffered some of the worst effects of the Great Soviet Famine — to determine the applicability of referring to this period as a genocide. The term Holodomor means "death by hunger" in Ukrainian.

This debate was furthered by the Russian Invasion of Ukraine in 2022 because Russian President Vladimir Putin has tried to justify the "special military operation" as simply trying to reclaim land rightfully belonging to Russia. Ukraine has pointed out that the relationship has not been a historically pleasant one for Ukraine and has used this historical imbalance as a means to encourage resistance to Russia among the Ukrainian people.

Communist China's form of industrial-agricultural communism (as opposed to the industrial-centric communism experiment in the Soviet Union) meant that all resources were shifted toward increasing crop yields. These agricultural shifts were part of the Great Leap Forward proposed by the Chinese Communist Party. This included rounding up academics and other city-dwellers, plopping them in the fields, giving them some tools, and setting a quota for how much food they were expected to grow. Between 1959 and 1961, in what is thought to be the greatest human-made disaster of all time, an estimated 15–30 million people died from hunger.

GMOs and selective breeding

Along with chemicals meant to increase crop yields, another element arose during the Third Agricultural Revolution that would drastically change the way our food is grown. Selective breeding or genetically modifying crops (GMO means genetically modified organisms) to produce subsequent generations with the most desirable traits is not new in agriculture. In fact, modern corn is believed to be the result of thousands of years of selective breeding. As a derivative of the teosinte grass, individual plants that produced larger seed pods were harvested and selected for replanting. Over years and years of choosing the plants with the most desired traits, we were left with corn with much larger edible seed pods (the corn cobs) than the original grass-like species it evolved from.

Also, animals that grew biggest and healthiest were selected to breed and pass on their genes, giving farmers the highest probability that the animal offspring would be healthy and grow large. Often, animals sold to butchers are priced on their size, so it benefits farmers financially to reproduce animals of good stock. Part of this process includes feeding the animals. It does a farmer no good if an animal gets sick because a dead animal is a wasted investment, so it is in the farmer's best interests to create conditions for their animals to be as big and healthy as possible.

TIP

There has been much debate about the merits of feedlots versus free-range movement of livestock animals. Chapters 17 and 18 cover this in more detail, but using growth hormones with animals to help them grow bigger and stronger began in the Third Agricultural Revolution.

Agribusiness

Bridging the gap between the Second and Third Agricultural Revolutions was the rise of agricultural businesses, or *agribusiness* for short. The businesses themselves actually developed quite organically. (Organic. Get it? A little bit of agricultural humor there.)

During the Second Agricultural Revolution, it became harder and harder for individuals to compete in an increasingly global market. Adding to their troubles, food counts as a *need*, not a *want*. So, if we apply basic economic principles, people want to pay as little as possible for food because it's one of the biggest expenses for a family. With the market stacked against them, farmers had to come up with ways to compete against the mega-farms that had started popping up during the Second Agricultural Revolution, which were supported by wealthy investors who could afford the newest machinery. How pricey, you may ask? Let's put it this way: If you're driving a fancy Italian-made sports car down a country road, there is a very, very low probability that yours is the most expensive vehicle on the road. Today, many tractors or combines can be priced in tens or even hundreds of thousands of US dollars.

To tip the market in their favor, farmers in different regions banded together in rightly named co-operatives (or "co-ops" for short). Instead of one person buying an expensive tractor, a group of individuals pooled their resources to buy a tractor together that they would all have access to. The same would be done for trucks to transport their products or grain silos to store food until enough could be collected to load onto a train to ship to the market.

One major problem still needed to be solved, especially for extensive agricultural practices: Who do they sell their products to? Intensive agriculture is still predominantly used for personal consumption or sale to most local markets.

(Farmers' markets are still very popular means of selling products from intensive farming operations.)

However, for the large field crops, farmers will produce far more than a single family could even consume in a year. That is where companies like CHS, General Mills, Hormel, and Land O'Lakes come in. To farther prove the popularity of these sorts of companies, do a quick Internet search of the food products that those companies produce to see how big an agribusiness business can be. Furthermore, for the example above, I only listed agriculturally-based companies from the US state of Minnesota listed as Fortune 500 companies.

To explain how agribusinesses work, I will use the famous potted meat product, SPAM, created by Hormel Foods in Austin, Minnesota. Along with their company-owned farms, Hormel has contracts with hog farmers around the region. They breed and raise the hogs and then sell the adult hogs to a Hormel-owned slaughterhouse that prepares the meat to be sent to the Hormel factory, where it is processed and branded as SPAM. This arrangement is good for the company because it can rely on the farmers for a steady supply of meat, which it can regulate to ensure quality standards. It is also good for the farmers with a consistent market for their products.

Monoculture

One of the downsides of this system is the shifting of agriculture to farmers, who only raise one sort of crop or livestock for commercial sale. This is what is known as *monocropping* or *monoculture*. In theory, this is good because the farmer doesn't need to buy all the different types of equipment for different sorts of agriculture. But it can make the farmer more vulnerable.

Let's use another Minnesota company, Jennie-O Foods, as an example. In 2022, the highly infective avian flu (a disease passed to both wild and livestock birds) passed through the Midwest United States. Farms that were found to have infected turkeys had to go through the process of "depopulating" their flocks. That's a nice way of saying they had to cull the entire flock since there was no way to ensure that none of their remaining birds were infected. Entire farms had to wipe out their stocks. The Avian flu also hit the chicken industry hard. This was an issue for the farmers, but at least there are things like farm insurance and federal assistance to help them get through it. This drastically increased the cost of poultry products for consumers since the supply of turkey and chicken was drastically reduced due to the flu.

Agricultural Location

Later chapters look more closely at the specific types of agriculture and where they're distributed. For now, let's establish general trends to understand the relationships and explain why they are located where they are. Why are many vegetable farms near cities and large ranches or grain fields far out in the countryside? What's nice about these theories is that they're fairly universal and not necessarily tied to any one location, though there are always exceptions. However, these theories help us understand wider trends and relationships.

Bid-rent theory

A farm's physical location significantly affects whether the operation is extensive or intensive. This relationship between the type of agriculture and proximity to an urban area is called *bid-rent theory*. The basic premise of this theory is that the closer a plot of land is to a city, the higher the expected land cost. The farther you are from an urban area, the cheaper the land. So, closer to the city, it is likely that farmers practice more labor-intensive forms of agriculture with higher possibilities of profit (especially fruit, vegetable, and dairy farming) to help pay for the higher land cost and less ability to purchase large land areas. Extensive farming practices are more likely to occur farther from an urban area because land is cheaper and more plentiful.

TECHNICAL STUFF

To test this theory, visit a website that tracks available real estate and find the cost for a one-acre plot of land near the largest city in your area (or hectare for those 150+ States that use the metric system instead of the Imperial system used in the US). Then, try to find the price of an equal-sized piece of land as far from a big city as possible. Depending on where you are, the price difference should be considerable. Now, think of this from the perspective of a farmer. You're not going to want to buy large chunks of land close to the city to use for livestock ranching (something that takes considerable space). The costs of land alone would make it very difficult to secure a profit. Instead, you will want to buy land farther away from the city, where land is cheaper and profits are more attainable.

Transportation is another factor. The relationship between transportation and location, as combined with the bid-rent theory, is farther examined in the Von Thunen model of agricultural land use in the next section.

Von Thunen

Though possibly a bit outdated, given that it was created in 1826 and still calculated for transportation by ox cart, the model of Agricultural Land Use created by

Johann Heinrich von Thunen is one of the best at demonstrating the relationship between the location of different types of agriculture and the proximity to the market (see Figure 16-2). I won't get into all of the details of the model, but Von Thunen had to account for some of the things that farmers would try to maximize their profits. Land cost, the amount of land needed, and how long it takes for products to spoil must also be considered.

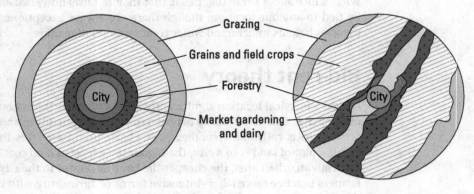

FIGURE 16-2:
The Von Thunen model of Agricultural Land Use with an adaptation for a river

- Grazing
- Grains and field crops
- Forestry
- Market gardening and dairy

City

City

REMEMBER

The model shown previously in Figure 16-2 represents a variation that accounts for the presence of a river. Because rivers provided a comparatively quick and easy route for transporting goods, they could be located farther away from the market as long as they were still along the river.

When all transportation factors are accounted for, you get a model with the market (the main urban center) in the middle. Another assumption that the Von Thunen model must make is that the model exists in a completely flat location without changing geographic features from one area to another. The model represents a situation that cannot apply anywhere in the world because it can't account for things like elevation or boundaries. The value of the model comes in the ability to apply it to examples and see how closely they align with this idealization of the relationship between location and agricultural practices.

Around the market are the rings of intensive farming practices. In this case, they're market gardens (fruits and vegetables) and dairy farming. Because these products spoil more quickly and are harder to transport, they must be located closest to the market. Farther out in Von Thunen's model is a forestry ring. In newer interpretations of the relationship between agriculture location and transportation, the forestry ring is eliminated. In Von Thunen's time, however, the forestry ring was necessary for firewood and building materials. Because wood is heavy, the forestry ring needed to be close to the city, but wood does not spoil like other agricultural products, so it can be located farther out.

Beyond the forestry ring is the field crops ring for grains, especially wheat, oats, barley, corn, rice, and rye. Very much in the extensive agriculture category, these crops require large amounts of land but do not yield as much bulk per plant as most of the vegetables in the market gardening ring. The harvested crops are still relatively light, especially compared to dairy products and larger vegetables. So, transportation is easier, especially given they won't spoil quickly if kept dry.

The furthest out is the grazing area, which is another extensive form of agriculture. Grazing animals (sheep, cattle, goats, and so on) require huge amounts of land, so they're placed furthest away from the market. This location still fits within Von Thunen's concerns with transportation because even though they're the heaviest of all agricultural products, they can walk themselves to the market with the right encouragement.

Aquaculture

In much of the world, fish are a very large part of the diets of millions of people. With fisheries stocks largely depleted in many areas, it is increasingly necessary for fish and other seafood to be raised much like other forms of livestock (as shown in Figure 16-3). Given that they're waterborne, this presents challenges, but the creation of sea-based pens and holding cells allows farmers to raise fish along the coastal parts of the world. The concentration of fish in a single area presents issues for the ecosystem, but if managed properly, aquaculture has been proven to be an effective means of raising seafood. As of yet, aquaculture is still predominantly practiced in the More Developed Countries of the world because Less Developed Countries still rely on offshore fishing to supply their seafood needs.

FIGURE 16-3: Icelandic fish farm near Isafjordur

Chapter **17**

The People Need More Food

In the previous chapter, we examined how technology, economic factors, and a little bit of luck influenced the origins and distribution of agriculture. In this chapter, however, we will look a little further at how global economic systems influence the distribution of agricultural practices, but we're also going to look at one of the most important factors: the climate. Plants and animals are finicky creatures. If they're pushed too far out of their comfort levels, they could go into shock and potentially die. This is why some things cannot be grown or raised in certain areas. In Iceland, for example, the growing season is too short, and the summers are too cold, so its fruits and vegetables must be grown, quite ingeniously, I might add, in geothermal heated greenhouses.

Continually rising temperatures from climate change are also a key concern. As a mammalian species, humans are the most adaptable species in the world, allowing us to exist in just about every corner of the planet. Our food, however, cannot. The things we depend upon most are at risk from warming temperatures. For this reason, among others, US Secretary of Defense Lloyd J. Austin declared climate change a threat to national security in 2021.

TIP

The connection between environmental degradation and increasing international turmoil is further examined in the book *The Coming Anarchy: Shattering the Dreams of the Post Cold War* by Robert Kaplan. It is definitely worth a read if you want to understand further the connection between political situations and agriculture.

Not to be too gloomy, but the predicament we find ourselves in with climate change is not inspiring. One of the biggest concerns is that there will be a significant disparity in our ability to manage and mediate the effects of climate change. Countries that spread north (in the Northern Hemisphere), south (in the Southern Hemisphere), or have higher elevation areas have some potential to move agricultural centers further toward the poles or higher elevations to buy themselves some time. The States in the temperate and tropical regions oriented as east/west States relatively along the same lines of latitude have less ability to redistribute their agricultural cores. These States have little wiggle room to move their agricultural production and less economic or political support. States located near the equator, where there is already a higher concentration of impoverished States, are especially vulnerable. Because the tropics are home to such a high concentration of globally marginalized communities (based on race, economic status, religion, and so on), environmental justice is a concern.

TIP

We'll talk more about these topics later in Chapter 20, "The People Need a Healthy Environment."

Agricultural Distributions

Let's examine agricultural practices and where they're predominantly located. Now, I want to lay out a couple of ground rules before we get started:

>> I will not be claiming that the distribution of agriculture is purely determined by climactic and environmental conditions. To do so would discount the influence of historical factors such as colonialism and imperialism and the systems of exploitation that exist in the modern global economic structure. If I were to say that farmers in Haiti mostly practice subsistence farming centered around the growing of cassava, plantains, corn, and rice because of their warm Caribbean climate, that would only be partially correct. That statement would ignore the effect that years of French colonialism and an especially brutal system of slavery had on the State, among many other factors.

>> Given the amount of space I have in this chapter, many of the descriptions will be generalizations. Like many other topics we've already covered, agricultural geography could fill multiple books. So, when I say something like, "Plantation agriculture predominately takes place in LDCs," take note that I said, "predominantly." Plantation agriculture occurs in MDCs but less often, and other forms of agriculture might even occur right next to a plantation.

So, with these things in mind, let's get to it!

REMEMBER

More Developed Countries (MDCs) are the traditional core States of the world with advanced economic systems and higher concentrations of wealth. Less Developed Countries (LDCs) are the peripheral and semi-peripheral States with lower concentrations of global wealth.

Agriculture in LDCs

Remember that agriculture is distributed quite differently at different scales, so the generalizations made in this section are meant to give an idea of what each practice is and where it is most commonly practiced. Some other generalizations about agriculture in LDCs are

>> Subsistence agriculture is more common in LDCs than in MDCs. Subsistence agriculture happens in limited cases in MDCs, and many farmers within LDCs farm commercially.

>> Depending on the State, many farmers could be subsistence farmers. Visit the Central Intelligence Agency's *World Factbook* at www.cia.gov/the-world-factbook/. On the Economy tab, look at the numbers for the labor force by occupation. The higher the percentage, the higher the likelihood that subsistence farming is common. For example, in Norway, a fairly well-developed MDC, less than 3 percent of its labor force is involved in farming. In Papua New Guinea, an estimated 85 percent of the population works in agriculture. There may be similar amounts of farmland being cultivated in MDCs as there is in an LDC, but there will be fewer farmers working each bit of land in an MDC. The concept of agricultural density explains this phenomenon by examining the number of farmers in each unit of farmland. MDCs have lower agricultural densities because of the heavy reliance on machinery.

Nomadic herding: Going where the green grass grows

In areas where the climate can support plants fit for animals to graze on but is too dry (or the growing season is too short) to support the cultivation of large field crops, you'll most likely find some sort of nomadic herding going on, especially concentrated in grasslands, semi-arid, and subpolar regions. Nomadic herding is found specifically in the tropical savannas of central Africa, the temperate grasslands of central Asia, the tundra/high alpine biomes of Northern Eurasia, and high alpine zones.

Livestock are the main products (lots of sheep, goats, and cattle in warmer climates, and reindeer/caribou in the northern climates). Farmers herd their animals from pasture to pasture based on the rains or availability of fresh browse. Their migrations typically follow a seasonal path that nomadic herders will retrace year after year. Reindeer herders follow their herds throughout the winter. The reindeer can dig through the snow to reach grasses they sniff out. Farmers in the alpine areas practice a very specific form of migration called *transhumance*, meaning they move their herds up or down in elevation throughout the season because different alpine regions' climates and biomes depend on the elevation.

TECHNICAL STUFF

In its noun form, "browse" refers to the leaves, twigs, and buds of woody plants eaten by deer and other animals. In its verb form, "browse" describes the activity, as in, "Reindeer browse for fresh browse to sustain them." Eating browse is an important part of deer and other animals' diets, especially during the winter when food is scarce.

Shifting cultivation: Burn baby, burn!

As mentioned before, things like fertilizers and other chemicals help plants grow. However, these chemicals are prohibitively expensive and costly to ship, making them unattainable for many farmers. In the world's tropical regions, they're also essential when trying to convert virgin jungle into arable land. The solution? Add nitrates to the soil (which is an essential element of fertilizers). But without the capital to afford synthetic nitrates, farmers have to resort to biological nitrates, which is just a fancy way of saying they must burn things — the forests themselves.

This is why shifting cultivation is more commonly known as *slash-and-burn*. The general shifting cultivation process goes like this:

1. The farmer moves into an area of jungle and cuts down a section where they want to plant crops.

2. The farmer burns the chopped-up vegetation to add nutrients to the soil.

3. The land is farmed for 3-5 years until the soil becomes unproductive because of exhaustion from overuse and lack of replenishment.

4. The farmer repeats this process in another section of the forest.

This form of agriculture is exclusively practiced in the tropical jungles of the forests and depletes much of the equatorial rainforests. Brazil has one of the highest rates of deforestation in the world because of shifting cultivation that rose during the presidency of Jair Bolsonaro. In 2023, Luiz Inacio Lula da Silva (known as "Lula") reassumed the presidency (after having served as Brazil's president from 2003–2010) and has made a priority of reining in the harmful practice.

Plantations: Corporate monoculture

Plantation agriculture is another cause of deforestation. Plantations are large monoculture farms typically owned by large multinational companies that grow crops to be sold to foreign businesses. They focus on cash crops that grow well in tropical and subtropical regions that can't be grown in abundance in the countries where the businesses are headquartered. Crops like cocoa, coffee beans, cotton, rubber, and palm oil are grown in large plantations.

Let's look at rubber. Rubber is actually the latex sap that occurs naturally in many plants, but most commonly and abundantly from *Hevea brasiliensis* trees (also known as rubber trees) that grow in tropical regions, such as Thailand (see Figure 17-1). However, the world's top-tier tire companies are located in places like France or the United States. The companies have to contract with the plantations to grow and process the raw latex that can then be shipped out to factories to be molded into tires. There are a lot of other steps, but the main geographic considerations are that MDCs in temperate zones rely on plantations located in tropical zone LDCs to supply them with the raw materials.

FIGURE 17-1:
A rubber tree plantation in Thailand

9kwan/Adobe Stock Photos

Although this process brings in capital and investment from the MDCs, it can also lead to the exploitation of the LDCs.

In global economic terms, plantation agriculture is part of the precondition to the take-off stage for a State's economic growth (discussed more in Chapter 18 as part of economist W.W. Rostow's Model of Economic Development). The influx of investment into a country is a mechanism in Rostow's model for transitioning from a mainly subsistence-based structure to a commercial-based economic system. Companies will invest money to build roads, pay workers, develop ports, and so on.

In his World Systems Theory (again, covered in Chapter 18), sociologist Immanuel Wallerstein argued that MDCs exploit the labor and resources of LDCs. One thing is certain: Plantations convert large swaths of land that could otherwise be used as croplands into land devoted to cash crops that will mostly benefit people in outside communities. One of the biggest criticisms of plantations is that they use up a lot of arable land in LDCs prone to food insecurity on crops that can't even be eaten.

REMEMBER

In Chapter 15, we talked about Banana Republics. That whole explanation was about how the plantation system can significantly interfere with the governmental structures of LDCs in favor of business interests. I'm not saying that always happens, but it does.

Wet rice cultivation: As intensive as it gets

Rice is one of the most common cereal crops grown worldwide, but is strictly tied to environmental conditions. Because it needs to grow in water, the places it can grow are limited. In North America, wild rice grows along the shorelines of lakes in the United States and Canada but is harvested as a wild crop, not necessarily grown. Southern and Southeastern Asia is the hearth for rice as an agriculturally cultivated product. Figure 17-2 shows a terraced rice paddy in Vietnam.

Planting and growing wet rice corresponds with the monsoon season. During the dry season, farmers prepare the grounds and begin growing the rice seedlings. Once the monsoons come and the rice paddies fill with water, they transplant each plant to the rice paddy to continue growing. The growing of rice requires constant attention to control the moisture they're growing in, weeding, and protecting against pests. (Controlling the moisture includes allowing the fields to dry out and then flood again.)

Once the rice is matured, it must be harvested, dried, husked, and processed for eating or grinding into rice flour. Like I said, it's a process.

REMEMBER

If you plan on growing your own rice, you'll have to read more on the process. My generalizations vary by region. But, hopefully, you have a bit more appreciation for how much work goes into growing these crops. Most rice farming is now done with the aid of machines, but in subsistence-based communities around the world, they're still growing it using these traditional methods.

FIGURE 17-2:
Terraced rice paddy in Vietnam

Sirisak_baokaew/Shutterstock

TECHNICAL STUFF

Since its domestication in China, rice has spread to many parts of the world. As a cereal crop that can grow in warm climates, it is a staple part of the diets of billions of people worldwide. As a species of plant not particularly fond of cold and frost, the far Northern and Southern States must import their rice. The further away you get from the equator, the more likely your cereal grain diet is more based on corn or wheat than rice. In China, most of the main dishes you might have experienced are either rice- or noodle-paired. In traditional Chinese cuisine, rice is grown as the main crop in Southern China. In Northern China, however, wheat is grown to make noodles. Geographers call this divide between the two main grains "the noodle line."

TECHNICAL STUFF

Monsoons are created in the tropical zone by shifts in the Intertropical Convergence Zone (ITCZ), a jet stream consisting of high-altitude moisture created by the rising evaporation coming off the bodies of water along the equator (Indian, Atlantic, and Pacific Oceans). When those bodies of water warm up, they cause the ITCZ to shift as they displace the jet steam. In Asia's case, for example, this causes the ITCZ to shift directly over India and Southeast Asia instead of just wrapping around the Indian Ocean. When this happens, the ITCZ acts as a superhighway for warm, moist air to be transported over Southern and Southeastern Asia that falls as massive amounts of precipitation as it cools. Thus, the monsoons! When the oceans cool down again, the ITCZ corrects south, and India and the rest of Southeast Asia enter their dry season.

Agriculture in MDCs

A product of the industrial era, modern farming in the world's MDCs has benefitted from widespread mechanization. Large teams of workers are no longer needed in many forms of agriculture, as much of the work is now done by machines. That does not hold true for all forms of agriculture at all times. Many forms of agriculture, including the large field crops, require seasonal laborers (mostly migrant workers who move from region to region throughout the year) who fill labor voids.

Especially during planting or harvesting, agriculture still depends on large amounts of low-paid labor to sustain its operations. In some cases, orchards and vegetable farms that are more intensive require larger amounts of labor all year.

REMEMBER

When we're talking about agriculture in MDCs we're mostly referring to Western and Northern Europe, Northern North America (US and Canada), Japan, Australia, New Zealand, and even semi-peripheral areas like Chile, Argentina, Mexico, Turkey, and South Africa.

Dairy farming: Bringing home that cheddar

Though I may have never worked on a dairy farm, frequent trips to Wisconsin have made me appreciate them. There's nothing like a good fresh cheese curd or a solid piece of cheddar (white, not dyed) with the salt crystals still in it. Milk and cheese products come in all sizes, flavors, and degrees of aging. One thing remains the same about dairying around the world: It's an intensive process.

Whether it is a dairy cow, goat, or even camel, the animals need constant care to milk, feed, and keep healthy. In LDCs, families may still have a dairy animal at home, but they're increasingly acquiring their milk like people in MDCs — at the grocery store or market. Getting milk this way presents its own set of challenges since milk goes sour, and cheese goes moldy very quickly if not pasteurized, cooled, and preserved. That is why, even today, dairying occurs somewhat near urban centers. The days of morning milk deliveries are mostly gone, but the core necessity remains to get milk products to customers as soon as possible to prevent as much waste as possible. There is not too much to say about the spatial distributions of dairy processes other than that.

Certain regions in States are known for their milk production. In the US, it is the states of Wisconsin, Vermont, and California. Plenty of milk production occurs outside those areas, but because dairy cattle can live in colder regions as long as they have access to feed, it makes sense to have dairy farms in areas that aren't potentially usable for field crops — more on that in the next section.

Mixed-crop and livestock: The crop that feeds

Like dairying, mixed-crop and livestock agriculture is widely distributed across MDCs. Because the geographic locations in which these types of agriculture are fairly unremarkable, let's instead spend time talking about what it is so you can think about how you've seen it in your own part of the world. Animals like cattle need a lot of food, and if you can believe it, their diets are managed to ensure steady growth and health.

Though some animals are raised on large open ranges, many are in smaller enclosures with less ability to move around and graze. Instead, they must be supplied with a steady amount of feed.

Most of the corn grown in MDCs is used as feed corn for livestock. Even cattle raised in grasslands often spend time in a feedlot right before slaughter, where they are given lots of feed to try to add as much weight as possible. Growing the livestock with the crops has its added benefits as well. During the fallow (non-growing season), animals can graze the fields and eat any leftovers. Also, their waste helps replenish nutrients in the soil.

Livestock ranching: Home on the open range

Ranching and grazing animals is reserved for more extensive open areas where other forms of agriculture are difficult. Grasses are one of the most adaptable plants on Earth and can grow in areas where few other plants can survive. This is a very good thing for sheep, goats, and cattle because they need a lot of it. Many animals will spend most of their lives grazing pastures before being sent to a feedlot. Their diets are supplemented as needed, especially since a full-grown cow can eat as much as 35 pounds of grass a day.

This massive amount of feeding is why much livestock ranching occurs in the open grasslands of Australia/New Zealand, the prairies of the United States, Mexico, and Canada, and the pampas grasslands of East Central South America. Again, grazing and ranching occur in many other areas, but these are the main MDCs in which it occurs. That is because of the concept of bid-rent theory, which examines the cost of land in relation to the distance from an urban area. Grazing animals need lots of land, which can be quite expensive, so the most cost-effective place to do it is far away from urban areas in these open grasslands. Because grazing and ranching take up a large area, this is a great example of an extensive agriculture practice. Farmers have to do a lot of work maintaining their herds, but raising the livestock to sell them off is a longer process.

One of the most unique forms of livestock ranching is done in Iceland. Too cold for much else, most of the agricultural land is devoted to herds of sheep, a breed of horse found only in Iceland, and hay. Farmers in Iceland release their sheep during the summer to graze the island's tundra grasslands as they see fit. With no natural predators, cars, trucks, and tour buses are the only real danger. Before winter, all the farmers in Iceland collect their sheep, sorting out theirs and arranging for sheep belonging to other farmers to be picked up. (They're marked with ear tags.)

If you ever travel to Iceland, please drive cautiously and look out for sheep wandering along the side of the roads.

Mediterranean agriculture: Eat your fruits and veggies

For once, we have an agricultural practice with a spatial description that is really easy to describe. Kinda. Along with around the Mediterranean (in Europe, the Middle East, and North Africa), Mediterranean agriculture is also common in Southeastern Australia, Southern California, South Africa, and along the Pacific Coast of Chile in South America. Their locations correspond to the Marine West Coast and chaparral climate regions. Created by the proximity to cooler bodies of water, these areas don't receive huge amounts of precipitation, but they're not exactly deserts either. They benefit from warm-to-hot temperatures year-round and only experience mild temperature shifts and precipitation throughout the year.

These areas are ideal for what is called *truck farming*, or the growing of fruits and vegetables. There are also a great number of olive or date orchards in the Mediterranean region.

And I don't want to offend anyone because this can be a matter of national pride, but these are some of the world's best regions for wine grapes. Don't believe me? Go to a liquor store (if you're old enough, of course!) and check the wine labels. You'll see that lots of wine comes from Spain, Chile, Argentina, Australia, California, France, Italy, and South Africa. Now, before I get a bunch of strongly written letters about the merits of wine from other regions, I'm just pointing out the main areas. The quality of wine is affected by many factors, such as the amount of moisture, temperatures, and even soil quality. Grapes grown in wetter, colder areas tend to be sweeter, which is reflected in the wine. Those dry, tart wines are more suited for the grapes grown in the Marine West Coast climate region. Though I'm not writing *Wine For Dummies*, I think a good way to remember the location of Mediterranean agriculture is that it's associated with wine country. And if you want to read more about wines, be sure to check out the actual *Wine For Dummies*, by Ed McCarthy and Mary Ewing-Mulligan (Wiley).

The grapes grown in the chaparrals of Italy are some of the best in the world (see Figure 17-3). Wine has been a drink for thousands of years but is now at risk due to warmer temperatures and shifts in precipitation patterns due to climate change. If you're a wine drinker who turns your nose at the idea of climate change, you might want to rethink that stance.

FIGURE 17-3:
A vineyard in Tuscany, Italy

Dan74/Adobe Stock

Instead of offending wine lovers further, let's return to truck farming. This is often an extensive form of farming that takes place closer to urban centers because fruits and vegetables go rotten more quickly if they're not kept cool and moist. With modern refrigeration, it is now possible to keep fruits and vegetables much longer, and they can be shipped worldwide. However, one big problem facing Mediterranean agriculture is global warming. If you've noticed that the cost of fruits and vegetables is increasing, it's not just because gas is more expensive. As droughts become more common, yields go down, and farmers and markets must charge more to make their margins.

Because they're semi-arid regions to start with, the chaparrals where Mediterranean farming takes place are being affected by desertification, turning the land into an unfarmable desert and severely limiting the amount of land available for growing these crops. These topics are discussed further in Chapter 20.

Grain and field crops: Watch your carbs

Finally, let's talk about field crops. They're about as extensive as it gets and almost impossible to grow in MDCs without tractors and modern machinery because, without them, you just won't be able to compete with the large corporate-owned farms. Nowadays, farmers work on behalf of a major corporation or sell through a co-op. Competition is tight, and profit margins are so high that small-time family farms are becoming increasingly rare in MDCs. In fact, the only way to get into farming on your own, most commonly, is to inherit a farm. Just visit a real estate website and find the cost of a 160-acre plot in the United States or Canada, and you'll see what I mean.

Growing grain and field crops usually occurs far outside major urban areas. Farmers profit in quantity, especially corn, oats, soybeans, wheat, potatoes, and so on. The crops are then sold to agribusinesses that make the products into consumer goods (chips, cereals, breads, flour, and the like). Agribusinesses sell the products to distributors like grocery stores. Because of the operation scale, your dinner plate might actually represent multiple agricultural regions at multiple scales. Likely, the ingredients in your meals came from around one State or even multiple States.

One of the major benefits of field crops is that once they are dried out and stored properly (sometimes even frozen), they can be kept for a very long time. Though they are not heavy individually, they can be heavy in bulk, making transportation much trickier. Either way, they can be shipped longer distances and kept longer, allowing them to be grown further out without as much risk of spoilage.

Modern agricultural practices

One of the world's largest issues today is food insecurity. Wars have been waged over it. States are struggling with planning for future population growth, and overall, there are massive questions connected to climate change. Food insecurity is a matter of access to food, but also access to fresh food. In the world of processed foods and high-calorie sweets, there is sometimes access to food, but that food is unhealthy. That is where the field of geography can come in. We can use geographic inquiry to identify areas that need more high-quality food options, adjust transportation networks, or create more food options.

Identifying food deserts is one of the biggest topics of study for agricultural and urban geographers. A food desert is an area that does not have ready access to fresh food products (dairy, fruits, vegetables, and meats). Stores selling these items must be easily accessible by walking or public transit. There are usually other qualifiers, but being easily accessible is the main one. Food must be accessible to everyone, regardless of whether they have a car. Some food deserts have gas stations/convenience stores that sell snack foods or fast food, but the foods offered in those types of stores are often high-calorie and high-sugar and can lead to health problems like diabetes and heart disease. Some of the highest concentrations of diabetes and heart disease in the United States, for example, are on many Native American reservations because of the lack of stores with fresh food options.

This also brings up how social justice is involved in understanding geography. Because many of the communities most affected by food deserts have been marginalized by their economic, ethnic, or racial class, another dynamic is added to the discussion. Let's say you're a student sitting in class, and you feel hungry. You'll find it very hard to pay attention to anything else. According to Maslow's Hierarchy of Needs, food is a physiological need, and if your hunger persists daily, you'll eventually fall behind. If you fall behind too far, you might lose out on different opportunities that might not be available later. Eventually, you might lose job opportunities because employers look for potential employees with certain skills or who have achieved high levels of academics. When hunger affects everyone, there is a governmental supply problem, but when it affects people of one community (racial, ethnic, or another social group), then it becomes a social justice issue.

TIP

Check out *Psychology for Dummies*, by Adam Cash (Wiley), for more information about how physical conditions can affect a person's cognitive abilities.

Once geographers have identified the food deserts, it is up to the policymakers to take that information and get to work, either by advocating for more stores with fresh food products or developing community gardens where residents can grow their own. Urban agriculture has been experiencing a huge boom in the last 20+ years, especially in cities hit hard by economic recessions. Vacant lots and portions of community parks have been redeveloped into urban farms.

Also, agricultural geographers look at food production and demographic growth and plan for the future. Without proper food security, the political situation in a State can quickly deteriorate, so it is important to begin planning now to try to ensure issues don't arise later. If the caloric output of a State's agricultural infrastructure does not meet its present or future demands, then that becomes a transportation issue, and geographers can work with policymakers to route enough food to meet the people's demands. These sorts of systems are working to tackle food insecurity on a global scale, but there are still plenty of issues.

WARNING

Again, I can't stress this enough: The issue of global warming is a massive X factor in all of this, and trying to estimate what will happen in the future is difficult. If agricultural productivity decreases after plans are set, then, obviously, those plans won't work anymore.

The changing agricultural landscape

Love 'em or hate 'em, genetically modified organisms (GMOs) are here. Although there is a lot of conflicting scientific information about their harmful impacts or safety, they're used in abundance worldwide. Essentially, GMOs are plants that have had their genetic code altered to grow stronger, bigger, and faster. They can be disease or pest-resistant and help increase yields. They allow for less chance of crop failure and produce higher yields to help support growing populations. The biggest question about GMOs is whether there are any harmful side effects for the humans who eat them. As of yet, there is no conclusive evidence within the scientific community that they do.

Livestock regularly receive growth hormones to help them grow large enough to meet the demands for meats worldwide. There has been a lot of criticism about how agricultural livestock are handled (most recently made famous in the *Food Inc.* documentary). Livestock growth hormones, however, are the most effective means of supplying human consumption needs.

Traditional farming practices have enjoyed a resurgence as a means of providing a "healthier" lifestyle. I only put "healthier" in quotations because the science is split as to whether the organic foods and the grass-fed movements have any health benefits. Both are fairly intensive processes, as they require more attention than their alternatives.

ORGANIC MOVEMENT

Let's start with the organic movement. Instead of using large amounts of chemicals, the organic method tries to limit those and uses alternative fertilization and pest control methods. One of the more interesting examples is the Vergenoegd Winery near Cape Town, South Africa, which employs a large flock of ducks that are released every morning to help control the snail population around the grape vines. They produce a brand of wine called "Runner Duck" that highlights this creative solution to a problem that would otherwise have to have been controlled using chemicals. With so much individual care required (whether done by humans or ducks), farms must be smaller or use more labor (or both).

GRASS-FED AND FREE-RANGE

The "grass-fed" or "free-range" movement also looks to revert to more natural livestock-raising methods. The fresh-caught fish movement is similar, and again, it's fairly intensive. Organic agriculture and grass-fed livestock farmers usually end up having to charge higher prices for their products because of the increased amounts of labor needed to produce non-GMO livestock. With more time and input spent raising their products, they also need more profits to justify the expenditures. With little oversight, however, some of the purported GMO- or chemical-free products may not be completely free of them. Farmers might have just restricted their usage below a certain threshold so they can put those claims on the label. There have also been instances of producers labeling their products "organic" or "wild-caught" without actually following those practices and charging more anyway. One of the best ways to ensure you know what you're eating is to either grow it yourself or talk with the farmer. Farmers' markets have still been great ways to bridge the gap directly between producers and consumers and are popular all over the world.

Green agriculture

One of the offshoots of the new agricultural developments is the turn to "green agriculture." Again, geography has been at the forefront of helping agriculture be sustainable. As we've already mentioned, desertification is a big issue (not just with Mediterranean agriculture, but almost all regions). One of the big issues is the amount of time fields spend without anything growing in them. When the fields are just exposed soil, there is a high potential for wind and soil erosion. A lot of soil eventually ends up in the sea or waterways and essentially becomes unusable for farming. To combat this, farmers increasingly turn to no-till agriculture, where the ground is not tilled — exactly as the name implies. Instead, cover crops (clovers or even grasses) hold the soil together, and crops are planted directly into them instead of churned-up soil. This form of agriculture is not feasible everywhere but can potentially limit the amount of topsoil being eroded away.

Crop rotation and cover crops are being used to let the soil replenish nutrients, so not as many chemical fertilizers are used. Legumes, like beans, can actually replenish nutrients in the soil. For example, farmers can help regenerate their fields if they rotate between planting corn, periodically leaving the field fallow (unused or used for livestock grazing), or planting cover crops like clover.

Lastly, the most exciting development in agriculture from a geographic perspective, is the use of mapping. With drones fitted with special cameras, it is now possible for farmers to get an accurate understanding of what treatments their crops need. Infrared cameras are especially helpful. Healthy crops will give off a signature that can be observed and mapped using Geographic Information Systems (GIS). The farmer can then figure out what treatments (herbicide, fertilizer, extra watering, and so on) are necessary for the areas giving off an unhealthy signature (see Figure 17-4). GIS benefits the environment by limiting the potential of chemicals running off into water supplies by better directing what areas need spraying and reducing the amount of chemicals needed. The farmers benefit because they only apply the treatments to the areas that need them, not entire fields, lowering their costs.

Unfortunately, GIS technology is still rather expensive (though drones are much cheaper than helicopters, satellites, or other remote sensing methods). Consequently, their benefits are reserved mostly for MDCs. But, with the increasing availability of drones and computer mapping software, the benefits of geography-aided agriculture will diffuse to all corners of the world.

FIGURE 17-4:
GIS in agriculture

Monopoly919/Adobe Stock

Chapter **18**

The People Need Economic Opportunities

The status of States and regions around the world is a mosaic of happenstance and design. Far from being a lottery of location, the levels of development for different States worldwide result from many geographic features. Purely attributing development to location ignores the human elements, but purely attributing development to human ingenuity ignores the geographic factors.

What it means to be "developed" is relative and difficult to understand. I still cringe when I hear a politician, newscaster, or even teacher say "first-world country" or "third-world country" to describe a State's level of development. I doubt many who so confidently use these phrases have stopped to ask, "What about the second world?" If their curiosity led them to that question, they would find that the "second world" was the States aligned with the Soviet Union during the Cold War (as opposed to the States aligned with the United States and their NATO allies in the "first world" and the non-aligned States in the "third world"). References to third-world and first-world align with a world system that no longer exists. Then, there is also the group of people who refer to parts of the world as "developing countries" or the "developed world." The only problem with that is that it makes no sense at all. All States and regions are constantly developing, and no area ever stops developing. Hence, "developed" is in the past tense.

So, if the most common ways of referring to levels of development are nonsensical, what terminology should you use? Each discipline may differ slightly, but human geographers refer to countries as "More Developed Countries" (MDCs) or "Less Developed Countries" (LDCs). We've mentioned MDCs and LDCs throughout this book already, and for consistency, I've been using those terms.

An MDC is an area that has already achieved a high level of development in relation to the world average but still has the potential to develop further. LDCs are perhaps below the global development standard, but they also have the potential to develop further. MDCs and LDCs are measured using the Human Development Index (discussed later in this chapter), which is meant to be a more scientific measure than the perceptual measure of "developed" or "undeveloped."

Like many other issues we've discussed, it's important to remember the idea of scale. If you were to purely examine the State of China from perceptions based on the central business district of Shanghai, you might assume that the whole of China is comprised of a very highly developed urban metropolis with access to many global brands. There is a huge disparity between the urban centers in Eastern China and the more rural areas in the Western provinces. There are high concentrations of wealth in one area and extreme poverty in others. Making assumptions based on limited information can lead to very flawed understandings. Throughout this and the following chapters, I will do my best to explain the concepts and provide examples. Just know that these examples won't mutually apply to all areas or even the same area at different times.

The Precursors to Development

One thing to understand is that humans have always been developing — just at different rates and in different ways. One thing that drives me nuts is when my students say something like, "Back in the day, they didn't have a high level of technology." I have to remind them that in 40 years, they'll look back at the level of technology they viewed as "high tech" was actually quite archaic. Heck, can you believe that in the 1990s, we thought the concept of caller ID was so valuable that it was a service you actually had to pay for? Now, I appreciate that my cell phone tells me the unknown number calling me in the middle of teaching a class is a telemarketer so that I can confidently block it. All this is to remind you that everything humans use to help them complete a task or go about their lives is the result of "technology development." The wheel of technology that led to great levels of development just happened to be "back in the day."

Development is the result of geographic and human factors. Without getting too far into the history or economics of human development, we will focus on geography's influence on human development, recognizing that different areas develop at different rates from a number of different factors. The influence of time-space compression and digital technology has led to some interesting development trends. Villages in rural Western Kenya skip right past the usage of fossil fuels for electricity generation and go directly to solar power. Development is not a linear path and means different things for different areas. Universally, when looking at development, the factors of land (physical space and resources), labor (human resources), capital (tools and infrastructure), and entrepreneurship (ideas) have been the drivers of development across time and space.

REMEMBER

Time-space compression is the geographic factor that causes the relative distance (in terms of the time it takes to connect two areas) between areas to shrink with further technological development. Throughout history, imagine communication between Sydney, Australia, and London. In the last 200 years, communication has transitioned from taking weeks to months by ship-borne letters to instantaneous video calls. Travel has also compressed from weeks-long journeys via ships to a 22-hour flight (depending on layovers). Currently, you have greater access to parts of the world than at any other point in history. Even that is prone to change!

Natural resources

From a geographic perspective, one way to focus the examination of industrial development is to use physical attributes. Specifically, I'm talking about the natural resources necessary and available for industrial development, regardless of whether they are renewable (such as wood that can be regenerated within one human lifespan) or nonrenewable (such as oil or coal, which takes longer than one human lifespan — thousands of years — to regenerate.) Industrial development needs resources (as discussed later in this chapter and Chapter 19) and ways to transport those resources and products. Resources without a means to get them to a factory or processing center aren't any good to a business, and products without a means of getting them to consumers are no good to a company. On top of all this is the necessity to make a profit to make the company sustainable. It is an intricate geographic balancing act of reducing the cost of obtaining (and transporting) resources and products.

Theory of Industrial Location

This is the exact relationship Max Weber studied way back in 1909. He developed his Theory of Industrial Location (which contributed to the development of the Model of Industrial Location), which seeks to understand the interaction between the locations of natural resources, production facilities, and markets. He looked at how transportation networks have affected their respective area based on relation to their locations. If the raw materials were far more difficult (and costly) to transport than the finished product, the production facility needed to be located closer to the raw materials than the consumers.

Figure 18-1 shows Weber's Model of Industrial Location, which represents the optimum location of a production facility (P) in relation to the Market (M) when the weight of finished products and the location of raw materials (S) is considered.

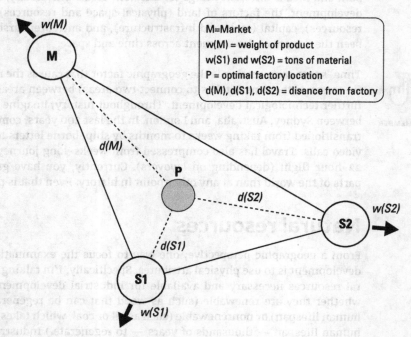

M = Market
w(M) = weight of product
w(S1) and w(S2) = tons of material
P = optimal factory location
d(M), d(S1), d(S2) = disance from factory

FIGURE 18-1:
Weber's Model
of Industrial
Location

In his model, he had to work on the basic assumption that a business was looking to maximize its profits (by limiting costs). Thus, he sought to show the relationship between the physical location of different apparatuses of the manufacturing of goods and the potential impact transportation distances could have on profits. This is why this is also called the *Least Cost Theory*.

If the natural resources necessary for industrial development are too inaccessible for them to make a profit, then the business won't exist. And, of course, if the resources don't exist in a region, industries revolving around those resources can't exist.

Agglomeration is an interesting way for businesses to reduce their costs. Agglomeration is when many similar industries gather in the same area to take advantage of the networks established by the other industries. Imagine Corporation A established a production facility to create a widget for the residents of a city. Corporation A helps build the roads connecting its facility to natural resources, and they've contracted with companies in the area to make and maintain their widget-making machines. Corporation B decides to build a production facility right next to Corporation A. This is so they can take advantage of the existing transportation networks, material supply chains, and pool of knowledgeable laborers to make and operate their machines. Then, Corporation C moves in to take advantage of a growing industry. Soon, you've got your own little Silicon Valley of widgets. By the way, Silicon Valley is a great example of agglomeration (in this case, specifically something called a *growth pole* or *technopole*).

The process may start with a high-technology research institution, Stanford University, in this case. Technology companies began locating themselves close to the university to take advantage of the pipeline of graduates, spawning a huge development boom. Other industries moved in to support the new industries, and suddenly, there was a massive influx of investment into supporting these new industries. Silicon Valley (home of many major tech companies) became a technopole as other tech companies located themselves close to one another to take advantage of the existing infrastructure. Although businesses might compete in some respects, they can also collaborate. A lot of labor transfers occur as employees switch between companies.

TECHNICAL STUFF

We can view industries as either bulk-gaining or bulk-reducing. A bulk-reducing industry makes a finished product smaller and lighter than the original input. For example, think of a 2x4 piece of wood made from a much larger piece of wood — a log — which is made smaller by shaving away portions, leaving a piece of wood smaller than the original. A bulk-gaining industry makes a finished product larger than the original inputs. For example, a steering wheel is fairly small and easy to transport, but when you add it to the rest of a car, the finished product — a car — is much bigger and more difficult to transport than the steering wheel.

Natural resources and colonialism

If resources are easily accessible in one region that are not available in another, they will be coveted. That's as true today as it was hundreds of years ago. Unfortunately, this leads to the tragedy of wants and needs and the lengths States — or even individual groups — will go to secure those resources, even if the resource is the land itself. When we look at the ideas of colonialism and imperialism from an economic development standpoint, we see one political entity (whether an official State entity or operating on behalf of the State under a charter) looking to develop at the expense of another.

REMEMBER

In Chapter 15, we discussed the differences, but here's a quick refresher. Colonialism is the actual movement of people from one area to the next to make a new area an extension of the "old country." For example, Dutch colonists moved to South Africa and established it as an extension of the Dutch realm. Imperialism is establishing bureaucratic control over a region for fealty and exploitation. For example, the British established a domain over India to control its people and resources.

Colonies are meant to extend the amount of land under the direct control of a government and increase the access to resources contained within the land. Imperialism aims to extend access to resources and develops governmental structures to maintain that access through systems of control. And yes, there are some benefits for those in the lands being colonized or added to imperial domains, but they are often negligible compared to the benefits of the States that are colonizing or establishing imperial control.

For example, before the introduction of the British Raj and subsequent incorporation into the British Realm, India had gone through periods of empire and decline, much like Britain itself. Using its industrial advantage, the British took control of India. (There were some major complications, but for that, I suggest reading up on the history of the British Raj.) The British used India to grow cotton (and tea once it successfully smuggled tea plants out of China). The raw cotton was shipped to the British, spun into thread and cloth, and then sold back to the Indian people. This system helped make the British incredibly wealthy without having to upgrade the standard of living for the Indian people.

Meanwhile, in Elizabethan and Edwardian Britain, the standards of living soared as people had greater access to goods from all around the world — goods that were otherwise out of reach for those who lived in most of the far-flung regions of the British empire. At one point, Britain held domain over almost one-quarter of the world's land area and was the uncontested ruler of the seas between 1812 and 1914.

The ironic thing about colonialism and imperialism is that they increased the dependency of the colonizing and imperial States on their domains for the resources they needed for the industries they developed.

As a relatively small land mass in a colder region of the North Sea, Britain did not have access to a plethora of raw materials. Besides resources like tin, iron, coal, and sheep, few resources were abundant. Furthermore, Britain's population grew so rapidly that by the time the 20th century rolled around, it barely had enough agriculture on the island to support its population — a fact that became abundantly clear during World War II when Germany blockaded the island to starve them out of the war. Many British industries were dependent on the resources sent from the empire.

The same was true with France, which depended on its holdings in Africa, Indochina, and many other imperial powers. It's also one reason for Japan's expansion leading up to World War II, as it sought to obtain secure access to the resources it needed for industrial growth. For this reason, imperial powers held onto their overseas holdings as long as possible, and the decolonization period slowly occurred after World War II. Cut off from their raw materials and reeling from the destruction and losses of the most destructive war in history, many countries, including Britain, went through a period of economic depression until the United States provided assistance through the Marshall Plan.

Neoliberalism and the modern global economy

Though the mechanisms of colonialism and imperialism may no longer be enacted, their essence remains. Instead of being the tools of governments, colonialism now takes the shape of economic expansion and multinational corporations. Don't get me wrong, there are a lot of positives about globalization and the expansion of markets, but you always have to ask what benefits for whom. Banana Republics (discussed in Chapter 15) are when a foreign corporation effectively manipulates a State's economic and/or political systems to allow it to control a labor market. That still happens frequently, though perhaps not as overtly.

Neoliberalism refers to the economic doctrine of promoting privatization, deregulation of corporations, and establishing the free market. That sounds good, but again, say it with me: For whom? In the United States, if you like the 40-hour work week, overtime, minimum wage, restrictions on child labor, and healthcare and retirement benefits that come along with being employed, then thank government regulations. Regulations are what prevent corporations from taking advantage of their employees. The argument against them is that the more regulations there are, the fewer profits a company can make and the fewer employees they might be able to hire.

Privatization is the concept that businesses are better off when run by corporations, not government services. For example, in a perfect capitalistic society, multiple healthcare providers compete to provide the best service for the lowest price while still earning the highest profit (to be competitive with others trying to provide the same service). The problem is that that may not be possible geographically. In privately owned hospitals or medical centers, the longer you're there, the more money they make. And if there is no competition (like in rural areas), they could theoretically charge anything they'd like.

The patent system also removes competition by protecting the intellectual ownership of a new idea. Because healthcare is a necessary service, the argument is that it should be de-privatized and government-run. As institutions funded by fixed tax dollars, the argument is that it would be in the best interest to get you as healthy as possible as quickly as possible to get you out of there. The argument against deprivatization is that there is a lot of waste in government-run programs and less freedom to choose providers whose quality of service may vary. Typically, the States that do choose to have government-run healthcare systems have much higher tax rates, but going to the doctor is much less of a financial burden than in a place with a private medical system like the United States.

There are pros and cons to both systems. It's up to each State to decide what's best for them. (And again: Best for whom?)

TECHNICAL STUFF

Much as the name implies, a multinational corporation is a business that has multiple entities in multiple States. Often, the headquarters are in one State, but the production facilities might be in another. They might have stores in multiple States and customers around the world. Multinational corporations provide unprecedented access to goods worldwide through global trade networks.

Free trade means many things in so many places. In essence, free trade is the removal of barriers to trade between countries and limiting restrictions for foreign businesses. One of the classic examples was the North American Free Trade Agreement (NAFTA), which made the movement of goods between Mexico, the United States, and Canada easier. As a free-trade union, it was meant to promote economic cooperation within the region, leading to the rise of factory towns in Northern Mexico called *Maquiladoras*. American-owned businesses relocated just across the Mexican border, where they could take advantage of Mexican labor forces with limited regulations (limited control of minimum wages, working hours, and working conditions), creating literal sweatshops without air conditioning.

REMEMBER

NAFTA was replaced in 2018 with the United States-Canada-Mexico Agreement (USMCA) with the hopes of balancing trade deficits and readjusting the balance of labor caused by NAFTA.

Products were assembled in Mexico and shipped to the United States and Canada, where they could fetch the highest profits. When Mexico implemented more regulations, corporations pulled out and moved production facilities to China and other less developed manufacturing centers. Now, corporations use the mechanisms of neoliberalism to impose a neocolonialism-like approach to persuade States not to enact policies that would otherwise encourage businesses to relocate elsewhere. However, consumers in MDCs benefit by having access to cheaper products made in LDCs.

Factors of production

In the simplest economic terms possible, a region must develop its industrial infrastructure to access land, labor, capital, and entrepreneurs. Again, these are all geographically based issues because they obviously need to be located within some geographic confines that make them accessible and interconnected enough to actually benefit a prospective industrial area. Historically speaking, the industrial era more or less corresponds to the development of the modern State development period, though in some regions, there is overlap with the imperial era, so we'll discuss how the scale of imperialism and colonialism aided the development of industry. States that developed industrially first had the easiest access to land, labor, capital, and entrepreneurs.

Before getting into a discussion of the geographic understanding of these four factors of production, we need to add some disclaimers. It's not always easy to get land, labor, capital, and entrepreneurs to give rise to the inevitable forces of industrialism. In some cases, all elements were present in an area, but outside forces (like imperialism or colonialism) prevented their development beyond a certain level. It can be very deterministic to say that all you need are the resources because it discounts the influence of outside forces. Industrialization and development were used as a justification for imperialism and colonialism with the idea that the industrial powers could show the native inhabitants how to use the land "properly." This land usage approach is ethnocentric and does not align with history. For example, Singapore achieved a high level of industrial development despite lacking at least one of the geographic factors of production (land abundance). Singapore's success is an example of possibilism, which says, given the chance, any State can reach a high level of development despite its geographic limitations.

Let's get back to land, labor, capital, and entrepreneurship (henceforth to be known as the "factors of production").

>> **Land:** Land is easy enough; it is the physical space and access to necessary natural resources (discussed later in this chapter) necessary to support industrial growth. Simply put, you can't build a factory without enough space and nothing to build it with.

>> **Labor:** Labor is also fairly straightforward. You need a working class of people to work in your factories. They need adequate education to work in the factories and be supported enough to continue working there. Labor is often one of the largest expenses for any business because you have to pay them a livable wage, so they can actually afford to continue working for you. Also, you must provide healthcare so they remain healthy enough to continue working for you. You also need to provide incentives like retirement packages to keep them working for you. During the COVID-19 pandemic, I was shocked by how many business owners griped that "no one wants to work anymore." There were plenty of people who wanted to work; they might just not have wanted to work for them because those businesses didn't provide the labor conditions or pay necessary for their business to be attractive to prospective workers.

>> **Capital:** Capital is a bit more complicated and hints at some structural geographic factors that need to be in place. Very few people have the necessary money just sitting around to start a new business. A banking structure must have the mechanisms to offer loans to prospective business owners to start or expand their company. A governmental system strong

enough to support industrial growth is required to provide the safety and trade networks necessary to sustain an industry. If you ever ask why a State has not achieved a high level of economic development, one of the best places to look is at the governmental and banking structures.

>> **Entrepreneurship:** Entrepreneurship depends on an individual (or individuals) having an idea for an industry. Steve Jobs did not have the idea for the computer (the first computer is attributed to British mathematician Alan Turing, who used it to break the German code during World War II), but he came up with how to make the personal computer accessible to individuals. Apple was built on this idea and has expanded to be one of the most valuable industries in the world because of it.

Markers of development

As areas develop, there are ways of measuring their impact on people. We looked at the total fertility rate and life expectancy in Chapter 5. Those are great measures because they can tell us a bit more about how technology is being used to improve the quality of life for the people of a society. Life expectancy is easy to understand, but you might be confused about the total fertility rate.

When the United Nations did a study on improving the quality of living in some of the poorest countries in the world, the main piece of advice they came up with was to invest in education for women. One common — and very false — claim is that men do more work than women.

One of the main divisions geographers are interested in is the difference between formal and informal labor. Formal labor is the traditionally understood employment where an employee is hired, goes to work, and receives a paycheck. Informal labor is not similar in that it provides a traditional salary, but it is no less valuable than "formal work." Don't believe me? Just tell a stay-at-home parent that what they do is not considered work. (Really, don't do that — especially since that is not at all true. Homemaking is a different type of labor that is no less valuable to the continuation of the home life than earning a wage. The only difference is that homemakers are not paid for their labor).

In many parts of the world, adult homemakers (primarily women) may also participate in a form of entrepreneurship, tending a garden, making goods, and selling their products to produce supplementary income. The more children a homemaker has to supervise, the less capable they are to participate in this informal economy. However, if a woman is treated equally regarding access to education, she can participate in the formal economy and earn a wage on equal terms as a man (though, globally, women are still paid less than men for comparable labor). So, a lowering of the total fertility rate actually corresponds to an increase in the participation of women in the workforce. Women in the workforce lower the average family size as they prioritize careers over large families. When that happens, a family will have access to two incomes and fewer family members to support it.

The Human Development Index

The Human Development Index (HDI) is the "more scientific" measure of development I mentioned earlier. Along with the life expectancy, the HDI is factored using the mean years of schooling attained by adults over 25 (to measure education levels for older generations) and expected years of schooling (to measure education levels for younger generations). The importance of women receiving schooling and participating in the formal economy is reflected in two of the four measures used by the United Nations to measure development levels. Obviously, if men receive a disproportionately higher amount of education than women, it will bring the average for both scores down and affect the HDI levels overall.

Literacy rate is one of the more common measures used for development (but not the HDI). The literacy rate has long been the standard for measuring education, though it has positives and negatives. On the positive side, it's been tracked for a long time, so you can see change over time. On the negative side, it leaves out a base level of education. Reading and writing do not signify a high level of education in today's digital age. Another issue is that the high levels of immigration do not account for large numbers of people who are not literate in the primary language.

In Germany, for example, plenty of people who are literate in their home language have migrated to the State from elsewhere but would not be counted as literate in Germany because they cannot read and write fluently in German. The measures of how many years of schooling are used for HDI instead of the literacy rate reflect the diversity of education needed to be competitive in the modern labor market.

Along with life expectancy, expected years of schooling, and average education attainment, the measure of Gross National Income (GNI) per capita is used to measure the HDI. GNI offers an interesting look into the quality of living for people in an area: The more money a person has, the more access to goods and services they have. GNI is calculated by the costs of sales of goods and services (including foreign contributions, unlike Gross Domestic Product [GDP]), divided by the population. In States where the GNI is high, an average family has greater access to wealth than areas where GNI is low. Of course, there can be disparity within States, regions, or even singular cities, but GNI at least gives us an average view that we can use to compare areas to one another.

Developmental Geography

Saying that all States — or even all parts of one State — evolve at the same rate and in the same manner is false. The development mechanisms are different everywhere throughout time, but we can model them based on some commonalities and patterns. Economics blends with geography to examine how the influences of space factor into the sequences, causes, and effects of development. By viewing development with a spatial lens, it is possible to examine the interactions of states and the role that geography has in development.

Again, the disclaimer here is that it is important to remember scale. To say that Malawi in Southern Africa is an LDC is only true to a point. The State may be classified as an LDC, but there are still areas with high concentrations of wealth. Similarly, you could say that the United States is an MDC with areas of extreme poverty. Depending on your analysis scale, you get a different understanding of development. If you measure the development of an area based purely on one part, you will get an incomplete understanding of the development of that region. And even if you do a thorough analysis, you will only understand that place's development at a singular time. The messy thing about development is that places keep developing.

Theories of development

When examining the relationships of development, it is important to understand that economic advancement does not happen independently of other internal and external forces within a State. It is important to note that political — and even societal changes — often accompany or precede economic system changes on many scales. For example, as a person goes through the stages of growth, they rely on the help and support of others while also competing for higher positions. It could be argued that Ratzel's Organic State Theory could be applied to understanding the actions of States, especially regarding the cutthroat economic atmosphere in the world's economic system.

TECHNICAL STUFF

These understandings and relationships are expressed in the Stages of Economic Growth Model proposed by W.W. Rostow and the World Systems Theory developed by Immanuel Wallerstein.

Rostow's Stages of Economic Growth

Everybody knows that the United States is the best country in the world, and every other country wants to be like it. At least, that's what W.W. Rostow, a high-level aide in many US government roles, operated under. In 1960, the United States was in the thick of the Cold War and looking to assert its political, cultural, and economic superiority over the feckless communists. Under these conditions, Rostow developed his ideas in his 1960 publication, *The Stages of Economic Growth: A Non-Communist Manifesto.*

TIP

Hopefully, you're picking up here that Rostow viewed himself as a champion of capitalism and the free market. Rostow built his model with the idea that States progress through stages of economic growth similar to the experience of the United States with the ultimate destination of being a highly consumeristic capitalistic democracy. One of the problems right off the bat is not all States will follow the same path toward development as the United States. However, that's the joy of models. They don't always have to be fully applicable.

In reality, Rostow's model helps examine a general process and characteristics of States at differing levels of economic development. Rostow split them into five stages:

>> Traditional Society

>> Preconditions for Take-Off

>> Take-Off

>> Drive to Maturity

>> High Mass Consumption

These stages are explained below:

>> **Traditional Society:** These are States (or regions) that are largely economically isolated and rely on largely informal economic structures. Subsistence agriculture is common, along with barter trade systems. Most goods are produced and consumed locally, with few outside products available.

- No States fall within this classification, but some rural areas in localized portions of the Amazon Basin, Southern Pacific Islands, and minimal areas elsewhere do.

>> **Preconditions for Take-Off:** In this second stage, an outside entity (a corporation or State) has recognized the potential of a particular region, given its wealth in natural resources. With limited capital to exploit the resources on their own, foreigners establish industries utilizing local labor to capitalize on cultivating or extracting wealth from the natural landscape. Agriculture transitions to plantation-styled systems owned by foreign companies. Foreign-owned factories and industries slowly develop to incorporate the area into the world's economic system.

- Portions of modern-world States operate under this structure in LDCs. The economic processes associated with imperialism are a better example.

Britain built railways and ports in India to better exploit the region's cotton capabilities. Also, France developed rubber plantations in Indochina (especially Vietnam). More recently, American-owned businesses developed the oil palm plantations of Indonesia, and Russia developed the Central African Republic.

>> **Take-Off:** With strengthening political systems comes the increased desire to gain control over a State's economic systems. In the Take-off stage, a State develops its own industrial systems and begins shedding the yoke of foreign-controlled businesses. Developing an entrepreneurial middle class in the capitalistic system develops domestic businesses to mimic foreign businesses. Industrial-age education systems are developed to train the next generations of factory workers, and agricultural transitions to mechanized urbanization are increased. The cornerstone of the State's economy transitions from the primary sector (agriculture and natural resource collection) to the secondary sector (manufacturing). The environment takes a hit as resource exploitation further expands and industrial pollution increases. (Many foreign businesses try to stick around as long as possible, but there's even more local economic development now.) Under these conditions, Adam Smith made his observations in *The Wealth of Nations*, and capitalism is born (Karl Marx also made these observations in his *Communist Manifesto*, birthing socialism).

- This is the Industrial Revolution. Each State that has gone through an Industrial Revolution has done so at a different mark in history. Whether it is the United Kingdom about 300 years ago or China within the last 100 years, the Industrialization of a State involves many social and political growing pains.

>> **Preconditions for Take-Off:** A healthy primary and secondary sector allows for developing a diversified economy with a growing tertiary sector (services). Democratic political systems begin stabilizing to support a growing middle class. Some individuals question the State's new identity and cling to more traditional cultural ideologies, but capitalistic profits drown them out. Banking and business services push the State into the world economic structure — not as sources of raw materials but as increasingly capable competitors. Shedding the last remaining hesitations is all that is needed to shed the remaining hesitations. The State becomes the United States reincarnate.

- Like China, there are many high LDCs. They still have a large manufacturing core but an increasing middle class interested in white-collar jobs. Governments regulate industries further, and foreign-owned businesses search for new places to exploit — I mean "develop." This is a scary time for a State as it looks to dive fully into the world economy and leave its traditional agrarian roots behind.

>> **High Mass Consumption:** A minimal portion of society remains employed in agriculture or manufacturing. Manufacturing and agriculture are still there but are highly automated through mechanization. The bulk of jobs are now in the tertiary, quaternary (development and passing of knowledge — teachers, researchers, and *Dummies* book authors), and quinary sectors. (Connected to the tertiary, the quinary sector represents the decision-makers and policymakers — politicians, healthcare developers, and the experts who train the next generation of experts.)

- The pinnacle has been reached. You have made it to the level of an MDC similar to Sweden, Canada, and Australia. Strong democratic political systems support a capitalistic, free-market economy. Industries produce high-technology goods that are the envy of the world. Agriculture is highly mechanized and employs a very small portion of the population. Even farmers buy their food at a grocery store. There is high access to wealth and strong connections to other MDCs.

Wallerstein's World Systems Theory

Whereas Rostow employs a capitalistic democratic approach to development, Immanuel Wallerstein is not as much of a cheerleader for the economic and political doctrines and views the economic connections between States through a Marxian lens. Rather than viewing development through the stages of growth, Wallerstein marks it through exploitation. Wallerstein's theory also incorporates history, though with the continued view that development is the relationship between the Core, Periphery, and Semi-Periphery (see Figure 18-2).

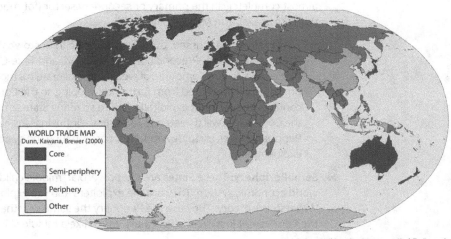

FIGURE 18-2: A representation of the status of States in about 2000 according to Wallerstein's model. (Image source: Public domain.)

WORLD TRADE MAP
Dunn, Kawana, Brewer (2000)
- Core
- Semi-periphery
- Periphery
- Other

Lou Coban/Wikimedia Commons/Public Domain

In Chapter 2, you learned that Marxist geographers are interested in the power dynamics and the geographic measures used to maintain control for one particular group over another.

Wallerstein applied his theory throughout history (though developed around the same time as Rostow) to mark the changes in development over time and place. Noting that the incorporation of regions into the world economy also incorporated them into a system through which they fill a role with other States.

» **Core:** In modern terms, Core States are MDCs. They exploit the Periphery and Semi-Periphery for cheaper labor and their raw materials. Core States are highly involved in the economy's tertiary, quaternary, and quinary sectors and rely on the other States to produce their lower-order consumer goods. Manufacturing is focused on quality over quantity. Their high-order goods are sold in the Periphery and Semi-Periphery to the limited populations that can afford them.

  - A watch made in China (a Semi-Periphery State) might be perfectly adequate. It will do what it needs to do for a reasonable price. A watch from Switzerland, however, will be a status symbol and much more expensive, even though it does basically all the things the Chinese watch can do. People in China who can afford a Swiss watch will also want it as a status symbol.

» **Periphery:** These States are LDCs placed among the first three stages of Rostow's model. They are largely viewed as the providers of raw materials and cheap labor. The MDCs exploit LDCs, which provide cheap materials for people in MDCs to live comfortable lives. People in Periphery States work almost completely in the primary or secondary sector (for much lower salaries than are available in MDCs, I might add).

  - As was already discussed, the areas identified in Rostow's first three stages (Traditional Society, Preconditions for Take-Off, and Take-Off) don't have high access to large amounts of wealth. In Wallerstein's model, they're purposefully prevented from further developing so the Core States can continue the cycles of exploitation. With so many States in the Periphery, the Core States will threaten to relocate their businesses elsewhere if the Periphery States try to develop, thus perpetuating the systems of exploitation.

» **Semi-Periphery:** These States are the proverbial "middle children" of the world economic system. They are the exploiters and the exploited in Wallerstein's theory. They use the Periphery the same way the Core does, but the Core uses it just like the Periphery, much like a middle child will pick on a younger sibling after being picked on by an older sibling. Regarding social and political organization, the Semi-Periphery shares many similarities with the Preconditions for Take-Off stage in Rostow's theory.

- For a long time, I used Russia as an example of a Semi-Periphery State, but that does not work now since the Core has cut it out of the world economic system. Russia exploited Central Asia and constantly fought for membership among the Core States of the West, which still relied on it for oil and gas. China is a better example now. Core States are threatening China with the same fate as Russia if it decides to move against areas the Core has designated as off-limits.

Development for all?

As we've already mentioned, development is not always uniform and does not always reach everyone equally. Economic geographers try to identify areas of disparity. By matching things like income levels with demographic factors, we can better understand the nature of inequality. Research on the topic can be produced and used to combat inequality and advocate for development. On a global scale, this can take the form of identifying global issues and how the international community can work together to address these issues. On a more local scale, this can take the form of community development to support groups. Many blighted areas are often connected to marginalized communities (racial, ethnic, and so on). This topic is particularly interesting to Black geographers who examine the relationship between space, race, and development. Looking at where and on whom governments spend money can reveal larger social issues.

The inequality between men and women in labor markets is an economic geography issue that is particularly interesting to feminist geographers. Women's work has long been treated as less valuable than men's work, as reflected by their pay for similar jobs. Gender discrimination, such as being fired for becoming pregnant, is still common in more parts of the world than we would perhaps like to admit. Organizations like the International Monetary Fund (IMF) and the United Nations Development Programme collect data on women's participation in the workforce, education attainment levels, and information on women in high-level positions to calculate the Gender Inequality Index (GII). LDCs still typically score lowest on the GII, especially in sub-Saharan African states. GIIs are mostly equal in MDCs, especially in Western Europe and Scandinavia. Iceland, for example, has even gone so far as criminalizing pay inequality based on gender.

One of the most effective means of combatting disparity is issuing microloans. Instead of writing one big check to a governmental organization, a microloan is paid directly to an individual or small business. These can be especially helpful for women who participate in the informal economy and may not be otherwise eligible for government programs. Microloans can purchase tools and equipment to build up a business. Microloans are especially helpful for entrepreneurs looking to start up a business and participate in the formal economy. Microloans have been especially helpful in promoting community development when women are involved. Men are more likely to migrate to urban centers for better opportunities when their economic outlook improves (through more training in a particular skill set, for example). Women are more likely to remain in one area and improve their economic standing there.

Understanding development indicator data

In terms of indicators, census data can help us understand concentrations of wealth. On a country level, we can use the Gross Domestic Product (GDP) to understand the value of goods and services produced within a State. The Gross National Income is the combination of the value of goods and services produced domestically plus the foreign contributions (for example, products sold out of the country). When we look at these indicators per capita (the values divided by the population), we can better understand the wealth available to individuals when comparing one place to another. The concentrations of wealth generally correlate to a place's standard of living.

Not too difficult of a concept. The more money you have access to, the higher your quality of living (in terms of being able to afford healthcare, groceries, and luxury items). This process is especially complicated because of the differing costs of living in various parts of the world. You won't get much of a house for $300,000 in Oslo, Norway. In Thailand, however, you could afford a fairly nice house in a private community near the beach for the same money. That's why many people from MDCs retire to an LDC to make their fixed incomes much more powerful. That is why we adjust our indicators for purchasing power parity (PPP). Simply adjust for the differing costs of living in different areas.

One of the other means of monitoring the status of an economy is by watching the unemployment numbers — the number of people without a job. If the number goes down, economics are good, and companies hire more people. If the number of unemployed people goes up, businesses don't have as much confidence in the economy and are not hiring as many people or are laying people off. Unemployment will never be zero because people are between jobs (looking for a new job or taking a break to raise a child, for example) and some are unable to work due to disability. The dependency ratio is the number of non-working people whom those with jobs must support. This ratio generally focuses on people under 15 who are too young to work or those over 65 who are too old to work. However, this ratio can include the unemployed as well.

Over-employment — particularly among the younger generation — is increasingly being examined by geographers. Over-employed people have had multiple jobs. With increased living costs and salaries lagging in some places, many people have to work more than a traditional 40-hour work week to make ends meet, leading to the rise of the gig economy. Contract workers work short jobs for a business without being formally employed, giving rise to people taking on work gigs rather than full-time employment.

Corporations in MDCs are especially favorable to contract workers since corporations only need the contractor to complete a single task, and the employer doesn't have to contribute to healthcare or retirement contributions. Contract work provides workers with the extra cash they need to reach the quality of living they want.

WARNING

Gig work can be very stressful since there is no guarantee that a contract will be renewed or that a new and similar contract will present itself. Saving and planning for the future is difficult if you don't know whether contracts will be available from month to month or even from one day to the next.

» Inventions that spurred economic growth

» How location affects industry locations

Chapter **19**

The People Need Goods and Services

Take a second to reflect on how strange the world that we live in is right now. You can hop onto the Internet and use a company like Amazon to buy a product that might have even been produced in another part of the world, and it shows up in just a couple of days. You may have even bought this book online, and there you go! Only a couple of hundred years ago — a blip on the scale of human history — products were made locally, and anything from elsewhere was considered a luxury item. The kings and queens of Europe once held lavish parties to show off their supplies of sugar, something that now costs only a few dollars at a local grocery store. Cooking pots were prized possessions that were passed down from family to family. People just have more access to "stuff" now than they ever had in the past.

Go to your local library, find newspapers from 100 or more years ago, and read about the international travels of the paper's readers. Today, newspapers don't consider international travel by average people to be newsworthy, but your Instagram feed sure does. While it used to be actual news to report when people were traveling, it is so mundane now that it's easy to forget that we have incredibly easy access to the world. I have traveled to six continents — something that would have been deemed borderline-legendary 300 years ago. I could've made an entire career off of writing my travel memoirs (many people did!), but now it is common to the point of not being unique.

REMEMBER

Stop and think about where we are and where we've come from. This chapter examines exactly that and tries to put the ideas of development, industry, and history in a geographic context.

Industry of the Past

We often take for granted how easy it is to walk to a store and buy the things we need. Though money may dictate the quality and quantity of the goods or services we buy, we have unparalleled access to goods and services like never before. Need a product? Pop on the Internet. Need someone to come fix something? Call them up!

For much of human history, manufacturing goods and providing services was either done by tradespeople (crafts were almost completely male-dominated professions) or handled by individuals. Towns would be lucky to have a blacksmith to create tools from metals, a carpenter to do woodworking, seamstresses to make clothes, and so on. It wasn't until the growth of cities that we saw many of these crafts expand and grow the availability of goods and services. More people created more competition. More urbanization meant more specialization. A carpenter could be really good at their job, but they still relied on blacksmiths to make their tools so that they could do their jobs. When multiple blacksmiths became available in the same area, competition between those blacksmiths started. Many crafts established guilds to prevent one business from undercutting another, thereby affording protection. Sort of the precursor to today's labor unions, a guild was an organization of craftspeople (from the same craft) who set quality and price standards for their services to ensure one craftsperson didn't drive out the others by offering inferior services at lower prices. They did this through condoling membership. Many crafts had a rigid hierarchy of assistants, journeymen, and eventually masters.

TECHNICAL STUFF

Many people's names (especially in Europe and the Americas) can be traced back to a distant relative's job. For example, the surname Baker or Becker (German equivalent) signifies that somewhere down the line, someone in the family was a baker. Surnames were often connected to whom a person's father was (for example, Hanson means Son of Hans), but sometimes people were known by their profession. John the Baker might have become John Baker. Some common English surnames connect to professions, such as Taylor, Miller, Cooper, Carpenter, or Shoemaker.

The guild system worked because the tradespeople controlled the manufacturing modes. Guilds were local, and tradespeople catered directly to the needs of their community. If a tradesperson didn't have the skill to make a certain tool, that community wouldn't have that tool. Simple as that. We know there have been trading systems throughout Afro-Eurasia (Africa, Europe, and Asia) for thousands of years because many goods showed up in places that didn't match the style or materials of the area they were found in. The same can be said for the Americas and Oceania (separately, not together). It wasn't until the Age of Exploration that the exchange of goods became global.

This localized system of manufacturing is called the *Cottage System*. Work was done at home or in a small shop by specialized manufacturers. The production speed, quality, and quantity varied from producer to producer, and consistency was minimal. Renowned artisans would place their mark on their goods as a sign of the quality of the product. The value of Japanese samurai swords from hundreds of years ago is still determined by the quality and whether a sword can be traced to a particularly famous swordsmith. The localization of production was connected to feudal societies (land ownership by birthright — think kings, queens, dukes, lords, and so on) — where local goods were produced with local resources.

This all changed with the mercantilist shift connected to the Age of Exploration and the Age of Colonization. It has already been discussed in the sections on agriculture as part of the Columbian Triangle Trade. Raw materials were brought from the Americas to Europe to be made into manufactured goods that could be sold worldwide. The modes of production did not change much from mercantilism, but it expanded the middle class and the range of specialties as more materials were now available. The drive for these raw materials (particularly beaver pelts) was one of the driving forces for the expansion of Europeans. Beaver pelts were waterproof and made for quite fashionable hats in the cold and soggy parts of Europe. Beavers were nearly brought to extinction on the American continent, though beaver skin hats helped show producers the buying power of a rising middle and upper class, leading producers to look for ways to capitalize on their productive potential.

Industrial revolution(s)

The world's industrialization story is a matter of site and situation. Simply put, the site is where something is (the physical placement or location of something). The situation, however, refers to what something is next to. Being in close proximity to important resources and markets is critical insofar as the ability to industrialize is concerned. In Chapter 18, we talked about the four factors of production (land, capital, labor, and entrepreneurship). The State that industrialized first, the United Kingdom, did so because it had the most advantageous site to take advantage of its situation. As seen in Figure 19-1, Britain acted as the hearth of industrial development, from which the economic process could then be diffused.

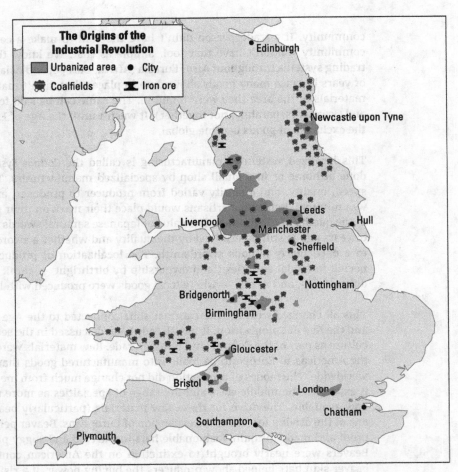

The Origins of the Industrial Revolution

- Urbanized area
- ● City
- 🚃 Coalfields
- ✕ Iron ore

Edinburgh
Newcastle upon Tyne
Leeds
Liverpool
Hull
Manchester
Sheffield
Nottingham
Bridgenorth
Birmingham
Gloucester
Bristol
London
Chatham
Southampton
Plymouth

FIGURE 19-1: The hearth of the Industrial Revolution in Britain

Generally accepted to have begun in Britain around the 1760s, the Industrial Revolution drastically changed how goods were produced. But why Britain, you might ask? Why that site (if you're using your geographer lingo)? Look at the situation! Britain was the first State to put together the four factors of production to allow for the mass production of goods. In the industrial era, that meant the ability to master machines and metal — steel, in particular.

Steel is not a naturally occurring metal. To produce it, you need to mix iron ore, coking coal, and limestone — three abundant elements on the British Isles. Not only are they abundant, but they're also close to the surface. Being an island with a healthy canal system, Britain also has easy access to water routes to transport heavy materials. The production of steel made it possible to build bigger and stronger buildings, bridges, and eventually different vehicles (trains, ironclad ships, and much later cars). The supply of steel opened up a lot of possibilities. Much of the Industrial Revolution is a tale of inventions and diffusion.

Along with industrialization came a renewed interest in science and inventing. Many of the inventions of the 1800s helped not only production but also everyday people go about their lives.

Building industrial might

Many things like the wheel, pullies, or cables were not new. With steel, however, they were reborn stronger. Ships are a great example. They've been around basically forever in human history in one form or another. When you make their hulls out of steel (still comically with sails until the creation of the first steamship in the United States by Robert Fulton in 1807), you have a vessel that won't break apart so easily if it runs aground. Steel effectively made cannons obsolete since the cannonballs were not strong enough to pierce their hulls. This created a whole new arms race to invent new weaponry to defeat the new armor (using steel to make the weapons, of course).

TECHNICAL STUFF

Funnily enough, the first steam engine was actually invented to pump water out of mines. Scottish inventor and engineer James Watt saw the potential to move vehicles and create industrial power. In 1804, British inventor and engineer Richard Trevithick used that design to create the locomotive. It would not be long until an extensive rail network crisscrossed the British Isles. That, plus the canal system, made transporting goods around the island much more efficient and quick than ever before.

On top of that, Britain built up an extensive merchant marine (cargo ships) to transport raw materials and finished goods around the world. They further built up their navy to protect these ships and defend their interests, propelling them to be the uncontested world power from about 1812 until World War I in 1914.

Electrifying the workplace

Perhaps one of the most impactful inventions of the Industrial Revolution, the electric light bulb, brought light to industrial Europe. Prior to lightbulbs, most lamps were oil-burning (think rendered animal fat, not petroleum) and gave off sooty soft light. In the mid-to-late 1800s, light bulbs — attributed to Joseph Swan (England), Thomas Edison (American), or Nikola Tesla (Serbian/American) — expanded the workday. Factories could now work around the clock, not needing to shut down at night.

REMEMBER

Remember, we're still in the time before many regulations, so we're talking about 12+ hour workdays for little pay. Men, women, and even children were involved in the work process.

Making long-distance communication possible

Today, if you want to talk to someone on the other side of the world, you only need to pick up your phone, send an email, or start a Zoom call. Communication is nearly instantaneous, even with some of the most remote portions of the world. Up until the 1830s, the only means of sending a message was via a letter (what we now affectionately refer to as "snail mail"). In the 1830s, Samuel Morse (American) began perfecting his method of sending messages through a signal passed through a wire, using a system of dots and dashes. (Samuel MORSE Get it? Morse code!) Soon, these wire cables were being strung across continents and even laid under the oceans.

TIP

If you ever want to get into some nerdy investigations, find some maps of the cables that have been sunk along the ocean floor to provide phone, Internet, and fiber connections.

The telephone did not come until 1876 when American inventor Alexander Graham Bell received the patent for his work. The telephone had an advantage over Morse because it allowed for direct voice communication, with much more commercial potential. Morse telegraph stations required knowledgeable operators to send, receive, and decode messages. The telephone could be used in households and allowed for easier person-to-person contact.

Healthy inventions: Supporting the working class

As was talked about in earlier chapters that tackled agriculture, the cotton gin, steel plow, McCormick reaper, and seed drill increasingly reduced the need for agricultural workers. These inventions gave cities the workers they needed to increase their industrial capabilities. One challenge that came along with the increased industrial capabilities was keeping people fed and healthy. Cities were dirty, disgusting places. Some less-celebrated inventions that came along during the Industrial Revolution were no less important than the powerful machines.

Pasteurization processes were popularized by the research of French chemist Louis Pasteur in the 1860s. Heating milk, cheese, or wine kills off bad bacteria and deactivates some microbes that cause spoilage. Pasteurization made many foods much healthier, which was good since the 1800s were not known to be a particularly healthy time.

It was not until the 1860s that scientists could fully understand the impact of bacteria on making us sick. A couple of accidental inventions gave us a better understanding of the need to keep cities clean and invent the concept of sanitation. London physician John Snow helped narrow down the source of an 1850s cholera epidemic to a single pump, highlighting the need for sewers and proper waste collection. Both were incredibly important, given that pitching waste outside or into a nearby river was the most common form of waste removal.

CHOLERA PANDEMICS

Cholera is a waterborne disease caused by human or animal waste contaminating drinking water. While a cholera infection is often mild or asymptomatic, it's sometimes severe and life-threatening and was particularly deadly in an era with almost no understanding of how to treat diseases. Leeches, anyone?

Cholera can be deadly on an epic scale. Since the 19th century, there have been seven cholera pandemics, the first of which spread from a reservoir in the Ganges Delta in India. Six subsequent pandemics killed millions of people worldwide. The most recent pandemic started in South Asia in 1961, landed in Africa in 1971, and eventually reached the Americas in 1991. Cholera is still deadly, even with today's medicine. Researchers have estimated there are 1.3 to 4 million cases of cholera each year and anywhere from 21,000 to 143,000 deaths.

Florence Nightingale's contributions came during a time of war — the Crimean War of 1854, to be exact. One of the main causes of death for soldiers was often disease, not battle wounds. She is often credited with inventing modern nursing. She pioneered nursing methods of changing bandages and cleaning wounds to ward off the negative effects of those pesky bacteria that the world did not quite fully understand yet. Many other inventions helped make the industrial world a cleaner and more comfortable place to live. Prevention was the best means of preventing death by sickness because penicillin — the main drug used to fight off bacterial infection — wouldn't be invented until the 1920s.

Industrial regions of the past

You might've noticed that I went out of my way to include the countries where various inventions and inventors came from. Clearly, the earliest industrialization occurred in the United Kingdom and the United States for myriad reasons, chiefly stability and sovereignty. Between 1650 and 1900, the UK was comparatively peaceful, aside from some trouble with a Frenchman in the early 1800s and a rebellious American colony in the 1770s. The political and social stability offered them the atmosphere needed for scientific exploration to take place. Things in the US were a bit different, given it was a new State looking to assert itself in the world system it was born into and grasping at industrialization (at least in the Northern states) to establish itself.

During the same period, France, Russia, and Austria (the Hapsburgs) had monarchical growing pains and had to fend off social unrest and reoccurring revolutions. Spain was reeling from the dissolution of its overseas empire as its American colonies declared their independence, one by one. Italy was not a unified State until 1861, and Germany was not unified until 1871. The rest of the world was either subjugated as a colonial or imperial holding, more or less delaying their industrial development to a point (with exceptions, of course).

The United Kingdom's industrialization was especially focused on urban centers near London and across the Midlands. Cities like Liverpool became transportation hubs to fuel the empire. Other cities, like Birmingham, Edinburgh, and Manchester, became important manufacturing centers. The thick smoke of the factories choked the sky over the United Kingdom. The industrial era actually sparked a sort of counter-revolution in the arts. Romanticist (an era of painting) painters from the United Kingdom, like John Constable, emphasized the English countryside and used the juxtaposition of the smoggy cities to criticize industrialization. In literary traditions, J.R.R. Tolkien criticized industrialization by embodying it as the race of orcs in his *Lord of the Rings* series of books. The hobbits connected to Constable's rural, peaceful idealization of what the world should be.

In the United States, the northern states embraced industrialization much more than the southern states, especially in the urban areas near Boston, New York, and Philadelphia. The famous Lowell Mills of Massachusetts helped transition the Northeast to the country's industrial center. The southern states based their economy on an agricultural system that relied on massive amounts of labor in the form of enslaved people.

In the 1800s, it was increasingly apparent that the system of slavery was made obsolete by industrial mechanization. Its inability to compete and moral objections to the practice combined to increase the calls for its abolition. Despite what some might have you believe, the American Civil War was fought over the issue of slavery. The northern states were shifting their economy, and moral objections to slavery were increasing. The Southern states were fighting to maintain their slavery-based economic system.

The "state's rights" you might have heard some claim were at the center of what sparked the Civil War really were about southern states' rights to base slavery on race. The war was, in essence, a struggle between modernity and traditionalism. The industrial might of the North ended up being one of the deciding factors of the war (in the North's favor). The North could outproduce the South, and the command of rail networks gave it a far superior ability to move men and materials. The logistical advantages of the rail network in getting goods and people to different destinations were made especially evident by the North during the Civil War. After the war, the United States expanded the network from coast to coast. The country's industrial core remained in the northern states but shifted toward the Great Lakes region to be closer to the coal fields of West Virginia and the iron ore fields of the Upper Great Lakes. Both the coal and iron could be shipped via the Great Lakes and still stay in ready access to the main market (New York).

The American Civil War highlighted the advantages of industrialization and the need to build up industrial capabilities to remain competitive militarily and economically. In the period after the American Civil War, industrialization expanded rapidly to many parts of the world.

In Europe, industrialization was diffused to a limited number of areas. The Rhine-Ruhr valley of what is now Western Germany benefitted from its close proximity to major population centers (Paris, Amsterdam, and Cologne), the Rhine River for transportation, and natural materials (especially coal). The Po River Valley near modern-day Milan in northern Italy had similar situation advantages that helped it transition to an industrial center. The diffusion of industrialization operated like contagious diffusion, radiating from the hearth in Central England. Starting in the 1840s, each decade saw an expansion further and further out into the urban centers of Europe.

Africa, South America, Asia, and Australia missed out on the first round of industrialization — with few exceptions. Some places, like Australia, South Africa, and India, built modern railways and harbors mostly for the benefit of the imperial British. As holdings of the British empire, there were some efforts to modernize them, but only to the point that it was beneficial to the business dealings of the empire itself. Railways were built from the interior to the nearest harbor, with little regard for the convenience of local populations.

One exception was Japan. The Meiji Emperor, who had come to power in 1868, was looking to bring Japan out of the feudal era and into the modern industrial era. The government of Japan engaged the United States and other industrial States to help provide expertise. Japan modernized its railroads, military, and means of production. To complement the economic changes, the Meiji government restructured Japan's political and social structure to give the emperor and central government more power, diminishing the power of local Daimyos (lords).

With many parallels to the United States, Japan's transition to an industrial society instead of an agrarian society also sparked a rebellion of sorts. This time, however, instead of being slave owners, it was a warrior class of samurai. The samurai depended on the old structure and were considered protectors of traditional values. They rose up against the new structure in 1877 in what is known as the Satsuma Rebellion. The rebellion was eventually crushed by the combined numbers of soldiers and industrial weaponry (cannons and rifles) that even the samurai could not withstand.

After the Satsuma Rebellion, Japan had established itself as an industrial power and would soon begin establishing itself as an imperial power. By using its industrial advantage, Japan began eyeing the Korean peninsula, Manchuria, the rest of China, and eventually the whole of the Pacific Ocean.

Before World War I, Eastern Europe was largely agrarian-based. Before the war, Russia flirted with industrialization and swallowed up much of Central Asia and Eastern Europe throughout the 1800s. In 1891, Russia embarked on an effort to connect its massive empire by completing the longest railway in the world — the Trans-Siberian Railway (totally worth a ride if you ever get the chance). Russia even tried asserting itself as an industrial power by taking on another industrial power, Japan. The Russo-Japanese War of 1904 was a disaster for the industrializing Russian Empire that ended with its Pacific fleet at the bottom of the sea and its army defeated. Internally, some factions were angry that Russia was not modernizing quickly enough, while others were equally angry that Russia was considering industrializing at all.

The story was very similar for Austria-Hungary, which ruled much of Central and Southern Europe, and the Ottoman Empire, which ruled the rest of Southeastern Europe and the Middle East. Russia, Austria-Hungary, and the Ottomans are known to history as "the three sick old men of Europe" for holding on to traditional political and economic structures and not embracing industrialism. In their defense, some sort of social unrest from their conservative or liberal factions occurred, regardless of what they did.

After World War I, the Ottoman Empire was dissolved and mostly split up among the victors. Austria-Hungary was dissolved into Austria, Hungary, and some other smaller Balkan States. Industrialism largely avoided these areas because of the political and economic turmoil associated with their reorganization. Russia had much, much larger issues. The fallout from Russia's disastrous victory in World War I kept it very busy.

TECHNICAL STUFF

The Russian Revolution involved Bolsheviks and Mensheviks (Communist), Royalists, supporters of the newly founded Russian Parliament, Anarchists, and even soldiers from States like the United States and the United Kingdom (look up the North Russia Intervention if you want an interesting read!).

The Bolsheviks eventually won out, and the Soviet government under Vladimir Lenin undertook his New Economic Plan, followed by Stalin's Five Year Plans. Lenin's and Stalin's plans undertook the industrialization of the newly formed Soviet Union (regardless of the costs). Theoretically, Soviet collectivization placed the control of the means of production with the workers.

In reality, the Soviet Union was an awfully corrupt oligarchy with narrowly divided power. Fear of Stalin was so high that production numbers were fabricated to the point that much of their industrialization existed purely on paper. Stalin used forced labor supplied largely by prisoners arrested on made-up charges. He also did this as a means to redistribute populations to access the mineral and natural wealth of the Soviet Union. He also used these forced relocations to quell ethnic displeasure with his programs. Many Estonians, Ukrainians, Latvians,

Lithuanians (and other ethnic groups) were shipped to the far-east part of Russia to work in Gulag labor camps, where they couldn't make trouble for Stalin.

The industrial power of Russia became a liability during World War II when the Soviets' industrial might dissolved into a myth when pitted against the highly industrialized German army. It took the Soviets years — and millions of lives — to use its production centers to eventually bury the German army with Russian industrial supremacy.

After World War II, the Soviets overtook most of Eastern Europe and imposed Soviet-style industrial development. Soviet factories were known for producing high quantities of low-quality goods.

Industry of the Present

Since World War II, the world has gone through some rather interesting shifts in terms of the distribution of manufacturing and industry. Some traditional manufacturing cores have undergone deindustrialization, and new areas of industrialization have popped up. Most manufacturing in the United States and Europe has shifted to mechanization and robots. The assembly lines with hundreds of workers that were made famous in the production facilities of the Ford Motor Company are a thing of the past. Instead, large workforces have been replaced with machines and just a few workers to ensure the machines are operating properly. The main advantage here is that robots don't need breaks, healthcare, or vacations and usually remain consistent. Highly engineered products like cars require a level of precision that can be nearly guaranteed with machines, cutting down on manufacturing errors. Much of this occurred because companies could find cheaper labor pools elsewhere, so they outsourced portions of their manufacturing, leaving huge parts of the UK and the US without many manufacturing jobs, causing severe economic hardships.

Many of those jobs that were once stationed in the Core (see Chapter 18) have now been moved to what American sociologist Immanuel Wallerstein classified as the Semi-periphery or even the Periphery. States are eager to attract these manufacturing contracts because they provide jobs and can help lead to infrastructure development to support the new industries.

Some states, like China, even establish economic zones to attract foreign manufacturing facilities. These Special Economic Zones (SEZs) usually offer manufacturers tax incentives and can act as growth poles. When a new industry is established in a specific area, that business acts as a magnet for new investment and the development of new businesses.

For example, in 1980, Shanghai, China, was what the Chinese call "a small fishing village" with an estimated population of between 5 and 6 million people. Shanghai's Pudong New Area (built around the colonial central business district) was designated as an SEZ for economic development. As a growth pole, the SEZ attracted foreign businesses to take advantage of the labor and tax incentives of manufacturing in China. Businesses grew to support the workers and manufacturing centers. Soon, schools, hospitals, and infrastructure were needed to support the influx of workers and their families. This led to an explosion of development and an estimated population of about 29 million people. It's not so much a "small fishing village" anymore, but it is now the third-largest city in the world.

In More Developed Countries (MDCs), much of the manufacturing has shifted around technopoles and post-Fordist manufacturing facilities. A technopole is very much like a growth pole, except the industry involved is more high-tech. San Francisco's Silicon Valley is one of the most famous examples. Silicon Valley is a collection of high-tech computer and Internet-based companies that needed access to the highly educated labor force produced by nearby institutions like Stanford University. Boston is a technopole for medical technology. In a relatively small area around Boston, several highly specialized institutions specialize in medicine, like Harvard University, Massachusetts Institute of Technology, Boston University, and Tufts University's School of Medicine. Many research and testing companies and teaching hospitals have been established in the Boston area because of its high concentration of schools from which they can hire graduates.

TECHNICAL STUFF

One of the defining features separating a growth pole or technopole from agglomeration is the creation of new economic opportunities. Agglomeration is when multiple factories are built near each other to take advantage of shared resources and transportation. A growth pole is created when those industries produce something that creates new businesses from its products or supports the industry.

Industrial Regions of the Now

The diffusion of industrialization has sped up in the post-World War II global market. Decolonization allowed States to expand beyond Rostow's Preconditions for Take-Off stage and into the Take-off, Drive to Maturity, or High Mass Consumption stages. If you want to put that into Wallerstein terms of development, Peripheral States have moved into the Semi-Periphery or Core. Present manufacturing by region can be seen in Figure 19-2.

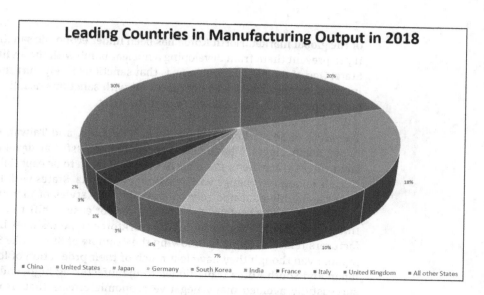

FIGURE 19-2:
Global manufacturing by region

Leading Countries in Manufacturing Output in 2018

30% 20% 18% 10% 7% 4% 3% 3% 3% 2%

■ China ■ United States ■ Japan ■ Germany ■ South Korea ■ India ■ France ■ Italy ■ United Kingdom ■ All other States

Simply looking at where your cars, electronics, and homewares are manufactured should give you a better sense of how widely manufacturing has expanded. Central America and East Asia saw incredible growth after World War II. Industries have expanded in parts of Africa and Western Asia, but much of their economies are still based on the primary sector. Some States, like the United Arab Emirates (UAW) and Saudi Arabia, have largely jumped from the primary sector (oil, including the secondary sector refining processes) straight to the tertiary, quaternary, and quinary sectors of the economy, almost completely skipping the manufacturing phases of the secondary sector.

Many lower-order goods (things we use daily like clothing, plasticware, and wider usage electronics like fans, low-cost furniture, and the like) are produced in LDCs where labor costs are lower, allowing those companies to sell products for a lower price and still make a profit. Think about it; if you need to buy plastic food containers, price will be a primary concern. While designer food containers are probably a thing, at the end of the day, they do the same job, and most people will want to spend as little as possible on them. Higher-order goods (like high-end electronics, designer clothing, and furniture) are probably also produced in LDCs on behalf of companies where research and development occur in an MDC. Also, the production might even take place in an MDC.

REMEMBER

We've talked about it before, but the idea of commodity dependence is that States need to maintain good relations with other states because of their economic connections. If the United States and China were ever to go to war, the United States would lose access to one of its biggest manufacturers of goods. China, on the other hand, would lose access to its biggest customer. This is why one of the biggest things a State can be threatened with is economic sanctions that might cut it out of the global market. North Korea has been under economic sanctions for years to try to prevent them from developing a nuclear bomb with the ability to hit another State. One of the biggest problems is that sanctions rarely hurt the people they're intended to hurt. The leaders of States hit with sanctions usually get by just fine, but the people are the ones who suffer the most.

The areas of South Korea, Hong Kong, Singapore, and Taiwan (nicknamed the "Four Asian Tigers") have been especially successful at developing high-skill labor forces since the 1950s. This has allowed them to be especially good at being flexible enough to change with consumer demands. States with labor forces that aren't as highly educated rely on assembly line styles of manufacturing. If the product becomes obsolete, the workers cannot easily shift to producing something new. China is transitioning its workforce to be resilient if foreign manufacturers relocate. China is following the example of States like South Korea and Japan. Even though they have lost much of their production of low-order goods, Japan and South Korea transitioned to manufacturing high-end electronics and successfully avoided many negative economic effects that usually accompany deindustrialization.

The interconnectedness of supply and labor relationships that have developed from an increasingly globalized economic market is known as the *New International Division of Labor (NIDL)*. Take a cell phone, for example. Inventors in the United States, South Korea, Japan, or Finland might have developed the phone's design. The resources for the phones might have come from the Democratic Republic of the Congo. The phones themselves might be assembled in China. Finally, they're sold to consumers for a fraction of the cost had they been completely produced within the State where the company is headquartered.

Periphery and Semi-Periphery States provide the primary and secondary sector economic functions, and the tertiary quaternary, and quinary economic sectors are concentrated in the Core and Semi-Periphery. To put that in simpler terms, resource extraction (shown in Figure 19-3), processing, and manufacturing are focused on the Periphery and some parts of the Semi-Periphery. The data collection and management (business analytics), research, and development are focused in the Core and some of the higher Semi-Periphery states.

Geographers don't like to speculate much (because when we're wrong, it makes us look bad), but there are some demographic indicators geographers can use to understand when further industrialization might spread next. We base these indicators on what has been attractive to industrial development in the past: rapid population growth but lower levels of education (meaning a large population that would still be good for factory jobs because demand is lower for service jobs until education infrastructure can improve). Also, stable government and ease of access to transportation markets are necessary.

Lou Coban / Wikimedia Commons / Public Domain.

FIGURE 19-3:
The division of the world between the Core, Periphery, and Semi-Periphery

With these ideas in mind, there is a lot of interest in the continent of Africa — especially the State of Nigeria. Nigeria has many of the population growth indicators there; it just needs a couple of other factors to fall into place to be attractive to foreign companies. All the same, European, Chinese, and United States investments have been pouring into the African continent, and most of the world's fastest-growing economies can now be found there.

Otherwise, around the world, many new industrial zones are located in large urban centers with a large labor pool. Almost universally, cities are understood to be where the jobs are, and rural-to-urban migration has been taking place as more and more people flock to cities looking for jobs.

People and Profit

The number one goal of any business is to make money. That's why they're there. Yeah, they might enjoy what they do, but the money drives them to do that instead of sitting on a nice beach all the time relaxing. Fewer costs mean more profits.

Looking at business location and profits is the simplest application of these concepts in human geography. We've already looked at this with German economist Alfred Weber, but his contemporary colleague and countryman August Lösch said a desire to maximize profit is the geographic factor driving business decisions. Lösch says businesses should be located where profits are highest. Think of a high-end electronic store in a city. It would make sense to locate it close to a major transportation highway, railroad, or airport so that transportation costs would be the lowest. Weber would agree (mostly).

Lösch would say the electronics store should be located where customers can most easily access it, even if that means driving up shipping costs. Profits will be higher because more people will buy the product. Businesses and industries are where they are to help them make money.

In the next section, we'll discuss a couple of other ways to help businesses maximize their profits or minimize their expenses.

Updated Manufacturing and Business Practices

Production facilities in MDCs have had to learn to be more flexible to meet the demands of diverse consumer markets. Take cars for example. When Henry Ford came up with the idea of vehicles being produced on an assembly line, he was quoted as saying a customer could have "any color so long as it is black." That's a little different than today, where you can go to the Ford website, design your car, and have it delivered to a dealer for pick-up.

Post-Fordism describes modern industrial production that has moved away from mass production in large factories with huge workforces, as pioneered by American automobile magnate Henry Ford, toward small, flexible factories that cater to specialized markets. Manufacturers need to be flexible and creative to remain competitive.

For example, boutique or screen-printing clothing stores might not make the actual shirts, but they add a design and stylization (buttons, ribbons, or ties), and can take a shirt that might have been produced for $5 in Vietnam, add their own flair, and sell it for $40 in Florida. In production terms, just-in-time delivery means manufacturers don't keep large supplies of raw materials or ready-to-go products around. They may not even make products unless there are open orders to fill. They'll also plan out shipments of raw materials based on when they'll need them (based on analysis of sales trends) so they do not need massive storage facilities. The efficiency of only ordering what you need and only making what you can sell is helping manufacturers maximize their profits.

At one time, manufacturers stocked stores with large amounts of inventory and then ordered more as needed. While this might still be the norm for many products, some industries are shifting to an inventory management technique called *just-in-time delivery*, where a store or dealership only has enough to meet demand.

For example, a car lot can cover a lot of space — space that is expensive in a city. It does not make sense to keep a lot full with 100 cars monthly if the dealership only sells 20 a month. Instead, a company will plan a continual rotation and distribution of new inventory to have products arrive when needed, with minimal time just sitting on the lot. I experienced this myself when I purchased a new vehicle in 2017. The dealer basically unloaded it off the truck from the manufacturing plant and gave me the keys. Just-in-time delivery relies on collecting large amounts of data on consumer trends from different areas.

If food producers send more products to a store than can be sold before they go bad, they are stuck with expired products that are potential profit losses. If producers can time their deliveries so products are shipped to the stores when they're needed, they'll sit on shelves as little as possible before being purchased — minimizing losses and maximizing profits. Companies that know how to master just-in-time delivery using geographic knowledge can gain a competitive edge that maximizes their money-making ability.

TECHNICAL
STUFF

Businesses must also consider what forms of transportation they use for resources and products. Each form of transportation has its positives and negatives. Faster transportation usually means it's more costly. Bulkier items also mean more expensive. Trains and ships are usually cheaper (but slower) alternatives to trucks and airplanes.

Figure 19-4 drives this idea home by demonstrating the changes in transportation times in just the last 500 years.

Transportation is about logistics and diminishing costs as much as possible. One way transportation services do this is by using break-of-bulk points. If you had a manufacturer in Seoul, South Korea, that was shipping products to different cities in Germany, it probably would not make sense to have a plane that went from Seoul to each German city. Instead, the Seoul manufacturer would send one big plane (as often as needed) from Seoul to one main city in Germany. (Let's be real; it's probably Frankfurt, given how big that airport is). At the Frankfurt airport, the products would be split up and sent to the individual cities. The break-of-bulk point, in this case, would be Frankfurt. Using this method, businesses can limit longer trips and utilize cheaper transportation networks in more local areas.

Airlines do the same thing with passengers. Think of each time you have to connect somewhere as a break-of-bulk point. Instead of with products, it's people!

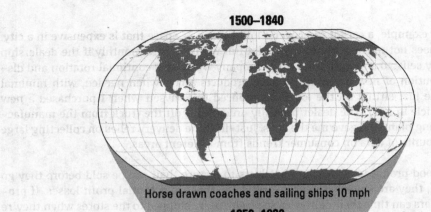

1500–1840

Horse drawn coaches and sailing ships 10 mph

1850–1930

Steam locomotives 65 mph
Steam ships 36 mph

1940s

Propeller aircraft 300–400 mph

1960s

Jet passenger aircraft
500–700 mph

FIGURE 19-4:
Changes in
transportation
times over time

Chapter 20

The People Need a Healthy Environment

We often hear that today's generation is disconnected or spends too much time on their phones. However, as a teacher who works with young people, I wholeheartedly disagree. Today's youth is far more knowledgeable about the world than many think and care deeply about the environment and social issues. The Fridays for Future movement, begun initially by Swedish activist Greta Thunberg, has gained a great deal of recognition and spawned a lot of interest among Millennials and Gen Z. Their social media activity and interest in events like the March for Science shows that young people are engaged, paying attention, and not happy about how some of our leaders have responded to this same issues. As certain political groups act against environmental-minded movements, they risk alienating a population of young voters.

I'll level with you: I have tried to balance my presentation of the environmental issues our planet faces. However, an overwhelming consensus among the scientific community clearly indicates that humans are doing irreparable harm to the planet's climate and ecosystems. Unless we do something rapidly, the effects may be catastrophic for human life on Earth.

CLIMATE CHANGE DENIAL AND SCIENTIFIC MERIT

If someone tells you climate change is not real, I give you full permission to tell them they have no idea what they're talking about.

I'd like to provide balanced coverage of climate change, but the truth is that the evidence itself isn't balanced. It's not as if the scientific community were equally split on the issue. The scientists who have spoken out against human-caused (anthropogenic) climate change usually lack the credentials to do so, haven't completed peer-reviewed research (research that other experts have checked), or their research is funded by fossil fuel companies — the ones who risk losing the most from actions to reduce climate change.

Only a small percentage of peer-reviewed research studies show that climate change is not connected to human activity. For every study that comes out with this conclusion, however, there are scores more that contradict their findings.

The only real reputable detractors from the scientific consensus are not arguing against human-induced climate change. Instead, they are arguing the rate at which human activity will affect the changing climate.

Climate has and always will change because of several natural factors. Many natural occurrences affect the climate, including Milankovitch cycles (the Earth's tilt, wobble, and path around the sun), changes in volcanic/seismic activity, wind and ocean patterns, and even natural shifts in plant life. Many of those things usually occur over thousands or even tens of thousands of years, but the speed at which those things are occurring now is faster than we've ever seen. Changes in temperature correlate almost directly to changes in atmospheric carbon dioxide. Lastly, that shift in CO_2 directly correlates to the beginning and diffusion of the Industrial Revolution.

Going Green

The politicization of the environment and science is probably one of the most unfortunate turns of world events in the last 30 years. The biggest problem is that the environment and science do not care what world leaders think or feel. It is what it is. And while we fight and bicker, many environmental problems are continually getting worse.

As I write this in July 2023, the world is experiencing its hottest month on record . . . ever. In all human history, July 2023 has been the hottest month that we know of. And predictions are not looking good for the future. People are literally dying, and yet, there are global factions that are preventing action to turn the tide on global environmental depredation.

TIP

Understanding the extent of a problem is the first step toward addressing the issue. While we know how extensive the environmental problem is — and we have the science to support that evidence — there are people still fighting about whether there is a problem in the first place! Some think or hope climate change will go away on its own. Sorry, but that is like trying to treat a cancer diagnosis with "good vibes." That's not going to cut it, nor is inaction going to fix climate change. Much like cancer must be treated aggressively when a problem creates far-reaching problems across the entire planet, we must take aggressive steps to combat it. Yes, some treatments will be painful, but they're necessary. Where the planet is concerned, going green is the treatment.

Geographic perspectives on sustainability

As we discussed in Chapter 6, there have long been concerns about how quickly humans are consuming resources. Whether it is Malthus's theories predicting impending misery or more optimistic views of perseverance through technological development, one commonality is that we know resources are dwindling.

SUSTAINABILITY

Before we jump into the next section about dwindling life on Earth, I want to unpack the word sustainability. That word gets thrown around a lot, but I don't think most people fully understand its meaning. Sustainability means the ability to keep doing something, and that is the goal when it comes to resources. So, sustainability in terms of how we use the planet means that the goal is to be able to keep living.

Some people want to continue using resources at our current rate. That, sorry to say, is unsustainable for many things (which is discussed later in this chapter). "Sustainable usage" means we get to keep using something; we just use it at a rate that allows us to continue using it indefinitely. Sustainable usage contrasts with the idea of conserving or preserving something. When we conserve or preserve something, we're trying to protect it at its current state or usage rate.

Dwindling life on the planet

While the reduction of natural resources may not be apparent to everyone in all aspects, one area is getting a lot of press — the reduction of the planet's flora (plants) and fauna (animals). Plant and animal life has been decreasing for a long time, and we've known about this problem for a long time. In fact, alarm bells began sounding clear back in the 1680s.

In about 1681, the dodo bird went extinct from a small island in the Indian Ocean. People at that time were beginning to understand fossils and the records of past species. But this was the first time in history that humans recognized that they had the potential to eliminate a species from the face of the planet. Since then, human activity has been responsible for the extinction of millions of species. Some even went extinct before we even knew they existed! The populations of animals like polar bears, northern white rhinos, and right whales have reached critically endangered levels.

REMEMBER

Not all animal extinctions are caused by humans. Some occur naturally. We refer to those natural extinctions as the background extinction rate. The problem is that the rate at which species are going extinct — and the sheer number of species going extinct — is much higher than the background extinction rate.

TECHNICAL STUFF

I have had the fortune of teaching biogeography to students interested in the conservation and animal sciences. One of their first questions is always, "What is biogeography?" My simplified explanation is that it is about "why stuff lives where it lives." Along with studying climate and biological systems, we look at the connections between plants and animals and the physical environment. Though it might annoy my colleagues everywhere who teach biology, I like to point out that the work of Charles Darwin was that of a biogeographer, not just a biologist. His work focused on how the evolution of different species (mockingbirds, not finches; that was his research assistant) was connected to the physical environment of each island in the Galapagos Islands archipelago. Biogeography provides a lens through which we can look at biological processes over space. When we match these spatial trends up against human trends, we get a clearer picture of the magnitude of ecological problems our natural world faces. Ecology, simply put, is the study of humans and the environment.

TECHNICAL STUFF

An archipelago is a group — or chain — of scattered islands. The Hawaiian Islands, British Isles, and Canary Islands are examples of archipelagos.

Today, biogeographers spend a lot of time tracking species and how their behavior has changed because of the warming planet. When an ecosystem changes, plants and animals have limited options: move (dispersal), change (adaptation), or perish. We've already touched on the whole perish thing —that's extinction. Increasingly, species move further north in the Northern Hemisphere (or higher in elevation) to reach cooler spots. For example, in North America, moose are moving further north to get away from ticks, whose range has extended due to the warmer summers and less cold winters, which are ideal for them.

Meeting human consumption needs: Fish and seafood

For many States around the world, their main source of protein comes from the seas. People need to eat whether they live in an MDC or an LDC. If the population of an area exceeds the carrying capacity and the physiological density is too great to support the population, people need to look elsewhere. If the area happens to be a coastal area, there's a great potential to harvest fish and other sea creatures to supplement what they can grow on land.

Fishing has become so ingrained in the fabric of some societies that it is reflected in its culture. The northeastern United States is famous for its clam chowders, crab cakes, and lobster. One of the United Kingdom's best-known dishes is fish and chips. Japanese sushi is perhaps one of the country's most famous — or infamous, depending on how you feel about raw fish — cultural exports. Villages in Iceland (like Flatley) have fishing so ingrained in their culture that it works its way into other parts of society, as the depiction of Jesus fishing in a traditional Icelandic sweater in Figure 20-1 shows.

FIGURE 20-1: The Icelandic culture of fishing

All along the shores of nearly every continent, you can find little fishing villages supported by the seas' bounty. Even some larger cities, like Shanghai, China, started with fishing as its economic foundation. So, where does fishing take place? Basically, anywhere there is water with fish!

Right away, we need to distinguish between commercial fishing and sportfishing. Sportfishing is the kind of fishing an angler does for fun (and perhaps competition), trying to catch fish for their dinner table, or simply because it's fun. By contrast, commercial fishers' livelihoods depend on what and how much they catch.

Most States heavily regulate their fishing stocks for both sportfishing and commercial fishing. Generally, sportfishing does not raise too many concerns about maintaining fishing stocks. Typically, some species of fish have size and creel limits (how many fish the angler may keep), and sometimes, there are limits on when and where specific fish species may be harvested. Size restrictions are put in place since a fish's size typically indicates its age. Depending upon the conservation plan in a particular area, anglers might (or might not) be allowed to keep fish of breeding age, or slot limits might dictate a specific size range (say, only large-mouth bass between 12 and 15 inches may be kept).

The same is true for commercial fishing. Fish populations are managed with size restrictions, the number of fish that can be harvested, and when and where those fish may be kept. One of the biggest problems with this system is the restrictions that States (or US states) apply only to its territorial waters. The United Nations Convention on the Law of Seas (UNCLOS) dictates that State restrictions only apply to waters within 200 miles of shore. In International waters, a different set of policies attempt to preserve marine life stocks, but that depends on whether a State honors those agreements. For example, the International Whaling Convention (IWC) restricts the harvesting of whales in international waters. Several States, Japan, Iceland, and Norway, to name a few, have decided not to observe the agreement and continue harvesting whales.

Another major concern for marine life is that populations have severely declined, especially in international waters. In the tragedy of the commons, States have been fishing international waters with a "If we don't catch the fish, someone else will" mentality. So, even though fishing grounds in international waters are much more difficult to get to, the number of fish and other marine life in these areas is still decreasing dramatically. Contributing to this is the further degradation and development of coastal areas. Many fish species use the corals and mangroves (a sort of swampy vegetated coastal area) to spawn. As global warming pollutes or heats up those waters or the corals and mangroves are destroyed, it is becoming increasingly difficult for marine life populations to recharge. Some countries, like Ecuador, have had great success in protecting coastal areas. As a result, the number of fish caught is actually increasing in areas with more fishing restrictions in coastal areas. As individuals, you can help. The Monterey Bay Aquarium in California has published a list of fish that are sustainably harvested and species whose numbers are dwindling and thus best to avoid. This allows people to make informed decisions about their choices and how they affect other systems, like fisheries populations.

Globally, fishing rights have actually been quite contentious. States with large populations, like China and Japan, depend on the seas to be able to feed their people. Chinese fishing vessels can be found off the coasts of many countries, some as far away as off the continent of Africa. They pay countries to use their territorial waters. In the South China Sea and East Sea, States have engaged in some pretty heated territorial disputes over what are otherwise just rocky out-croppings in the oceans. Control of those areas means control of the fishing in that area. This is nothing new and has led to many conflicts throughout history. During the Cod Wars between the United Kingdom and Iceland in the 1950s through the 1970s, the UK violated Iceland's territorial waters, so the Icelandic coast guard would just tow out the UK fishing vessels. Eventually, it became clear that Iceland would not back down, so the UK was forced to respect Iceland's waters.

Meeting human consumption needs: Timber

If you've ever flown over the more northerly parts of the planet (Canada and Russia especially), you might've noticed there are a lot of trees. And yet, the rate at which we're cutting down timber is quickly dwindling supplies. Huge amounts of forests are being cut down in Asia, Europe, and North America to meet the building needs of populations there. More regulations are needed for when and what forests can be cut in those areas, but large forest areas are being cleared out. Wildfires are among the biggest issues associated with North American and Australian forests. Countries like Canada and the United States have adopted a policy of stopping little fires as soon as possible so they don't become big forest fires. The problem is that the little fires are needed to clear out the underbrush and dead materials on the forest floors. That makes it much easier for little fires to grow and spread quickly into big forest fires. Instead of having occasional small fires, they're more prone to large fires (especially with a warming planet) that wipe out huge amounts of forest.

We've already touched on the Amazon Basin, where the main concern is slash-and-burn agriculture, and in Southeast Asia and Central America, where wide swaths of forest are being felled to make room for plantation agriculture. How-ever, we haven't yet touched on the large industries that profit from the trees themselves. This deforestation is important — no matter where it happens — because forests act as carbon sinks. Forests pull carbon dioxide from the air and inject it into the soil. The fewer trees there are, the less capable those forests are in removing carbon from the atmosphere.

Let's shift to the rare and exotic timber trade affecting much of the equatorial region. Two types of trees are especially sought after because of their rare color or unique qualities — teak and mahogany. Both are highly sought after because of their ability to resist water saturation — a quality acquired as tropical rainforest trees. If you go to a local hardware store and try to buy lumber made from local trees, it might only cost you a couple of dollars per foot. With rare woods, however, it could be exponentially higher depending on where you are. The trade of rare woods is an extremely lucrative business. The biggest issue with harvesting rare woods is that companies will cut down huge swaths of forest to get to the one type of tree they want to harvest.

Cutting trees down for firewood also affects many forests, particularly in the equatorial regions and areas where locals live more of a subsistence lifestyle. In the grand scheme of things, this is not as much of a problem as some of the other topics we've talked about, but it's still worth noting. Compared to industrial activities, such as Canadian forests being cut down for the Athabasca oil sands, firewood consumption is a local problem that becomes minimal on a more global scale.

TECHNICAL STUFF

The Athabasca oil sands are large deposits of heavy crude oil (bitumen) in northeastern Alberta, Canada. These oil sands contain a mixture of crude bitumen (a crude oil in a semi-solid, rock-like form), silica sand, clay minerals, and water. The Athabasca oil sands are home to the world's largest known reservoir of crude bitumen sand. Some extraction methods require large-scale excavation with massive hydraulic power shovels and heavy hauler trucks, destroying the forests and leaving toxic tailings ponds.

REMEMBER

Removing forests is always a concern for the plants and animals that live there. I could write much more on this, but as this is a human-centric book, I'll just leave it as a fact that many plants and animals are endangered because of the destruction of their habitat.

Meeting human consumption needs: Hunting

Since humans have removed many of the predators from the landscape, largely due to fear of harm to themselves or livestock, animal populations need alternative forms of regulation. In the United States, the only thing keeping deer populations in check is the hunting season monitored by the states. Weirdly enough, state natural resource departments decide how many animals can be harvested to prevent overpopulation and disease.

When hunting occurs outside these regulations, that's called *poaching*. Poaching of game in MDCs is an issue, but in other parts of the world, it can lead to the extinction of whole species. Rhinos and elephants have long been sought after for their tusks and horns. Elephant ivory is used in carvings and as a high-priced decoration. Rhino horn is actually more valuable than gold by weight. It is used as a perceived miracle cure in traditional East Asian medicines despite having no medicinal properties at all. The most poached animal in the world is the pangolin (see Figure 20-2), which is hunted for both the purported medicinal qualities of its scales and for its meat.

In many places, animals are hunted because they are considered a nuisance. Lions, tigers, or wolves that regularly attack livestock or people are often hunted down to prevent further attacks.

FIGURE 20-2:
A Chinese pangolin in the Leipzig Zoo. (Image source: public domain.)

Tou Feng / Wikimedia Commans / Public Domain

The over-hunting of species has gone on for hundreds of years. Whether it is the extinction of the great auk from northern waters for food or the drastic reduction of the North American beaver for its fur, humans have long over-consumed species, assuming they will never go extinct. The truth is, however, that hunting can be fairly helpful when properly managed. The sale of hunting licenses funds many countries' conservation efforts. Even in the United States, many state parks are supported by revenue from hunting licenses. In many African countries, like Namibia and South Africa, a large portion of game warden and park salaries are paid for with hunting license revenues. Some hunters are willing to spend thousands of dollars to shoot exotic species, so some countries will actually help select the animal that may be harvested — usually one that is no longer of breeding age or is too aggressive and dangerous to other animals.

Meeting human consumption needs: Minerals and mining

As we've already talked about in Chapters 18 and 19, many human economic systems depend on natural resources. The resources we extract — lithium, iron, coal, and so on — leave a scar on the landscape like the one seen in Figure 20-3. Some resources, like coal or tin, have historically been mined using shaft mines — holes dug deep into the earth, where the resources are located; the resource is dug out and sent back to the surface. Shaft mining is often much more dangerous and time-consuming, though it's still done, especially in LDCs. Countless mining accidents have occurred in places like China, Chile, and even in the US, leading to the deaths of workers. MDCs increasingly resort to open-pit mining, where huge amounts of earth are dug (or even blasted) away, allowing large diggers and trucks to access the resources much more quickly and safely. They'll literally move mountains to get to the resources, causing large areas to be destroyed to get the resources underneath.

FIGURE 20-3: North Antelope Rochelle Coal Mine in Wyoming, as seen from space. (Image source: public domain, NASA.)

NASA / Wikimedia Commans / Public Domain

In Northern Minnesota, for example, companies dig up the forest to get to the iron ore and taconite beneath the surface. Major pit mines throughout the Iron Range around Lake Superior in Canada and the US dot the landscape. The earth is dug up and sent to processing facilities to remove and refine the usable iron-based substance. This has been a controversial process, to say the least. On the one hand, the local economy depends on the jobs related to the mines. On the other, the large pits cut into the landscape. Once finished, the companies usually let them fill up with water to form new lakes. The dug-up earth and unused refuse are piled up, sometimes creating new hills. Runoff from these tailing heaps is a major concern because it contains metals and other substances that are usually far below the surface. Those substances can leak into the lakes and rivers in the area, harming one of the most pristine landscapes in both Canada and the US.

The Democratic Republic of Congo (DRC) has had severe issues associated with mining because it has one of the highest concentrations of rare earth minerals (REM), leading to a lot of foreign mining. These REMs are used for making things like smartphones, computers, and electric car batteries. Forests are cut down to get to them, but in this case, deforestation is one of the DRC's lesser concerns. The country has been in an on-again, off-again civil war for the better part of 60 years. One theory behind the recurring civil war is that the DRC is one of the richest countries in the world in terms of natural resources. Foreign companies help destabilize the government by bribing governmental officials and supporting non-government rebels, preventing the government from being strong enough to utilize the resources and allowing foreign companies to continue extracting the resources for big profits.

Desertification

Humans are an especially adaptable and resilient species. We can adapt like no other species on our planet. However, the plants and animals we depend on do not share the same traits as us. The Food and Agriculture Organization of the United Nations (FAO) estimates that for every 1°C-increase in global temperatures, we'll experience a 10 percent drop in agricultural output. This is because plants are finicky and grow best within an ideal temperature and precipitation range (the tolerance range of a species). If the species must endure conditions outside its tolerance range for too long, it cannot grow either.

Also, an increasing number of plants and animals die each year from excessive heat. Year after year of excessive heat and decreased precipitation can lead to a trend known as *desertification*. Simply put, this is the growth of deserts. Some of the most susceptible areas to desertification are the areas along the fringes of current deserts. On just about every continent, those are the chaparral and grassland areas.

As we discussed in Chapters 16 and 17, chaparral and grassland areas are where much of the planet's agriculture is concentrated.

Desertification is expected to increase food scarcity and insecurity because of overgrazing, increased temperatures and drought, and wind erosion. As you can see in Figure 20-4, the threat of desertification is widespread. Large-scale initiatives, like the Great Green Wall being constructed along the southern edge of the Sahara Desert, are needed to try to combat desertification. Windbreaks can help slow the dispersal of infertile sand into productive agricultural regions. Cover crops and no-till agriculture can help slow soil erosion and help ensure the productivity of existing farmland. While windbreaks and other initiatives like decreasing grazing in threatened areas aid in decreasing desertification, the largest thing that is needed is to try to slow the trends of temperature increase.

TECHNICAL STUFF

The Great Green Wall project was adopted by the African Union in 2007 to help stop desertification in the Sahel region, preventing the expansion of the Sahara Desert. A wall of trees is being planted across the entire Sahel region, from the City of Djibouti in the Republic of Djibouti in the East to Dakar, Senegal in the West, a distance spanning 4,831 miles. The goal is to restore 100 million hectares — that's around 250 million acres — of degraded land. More than 15 million trees were planted in Burkina Faso, 1.4 million in Senegal, and nearly 10 million in Ethiopia. As of 2023, about 18 million hectares (more than 44 million acres) have been restored, accounting for about 18 percent of its goal.

Green energies and resources

The United States Environmental Protection Agency (EPA) notes that roughly 25 percent of global emissions of harmful greenhouse gases come from the production of heat and electricity — the single largest source of harmful gases making their way into the atmosphere. Another 14 percent comes from fuel burned for transportation. Heat and electricity production and fuel consumption are easy enough to track. In fact, many weather apps include an Air Quality Index (AQI) reading.

TIP

AQI readings are based on the number of particulates in the air. Forest fires will most definitely affect the reading, but otherwise, the AQI reflects local emissions. Weather apps on smartphones regularly include AQI data.

Most climate scientists argue that the air pollution generated from using fossil fuels for fuel power and electricity generation is unsustainable, especially because the fuels themselves are nonrenewable. Once they're used up, they're gone. The rate at which we're using them will lead to life as it is now on Earth being unsustainable. Certain portions of the Earth — especially closer to the equator — are becoming so hot that life is increasingly less feasible there.

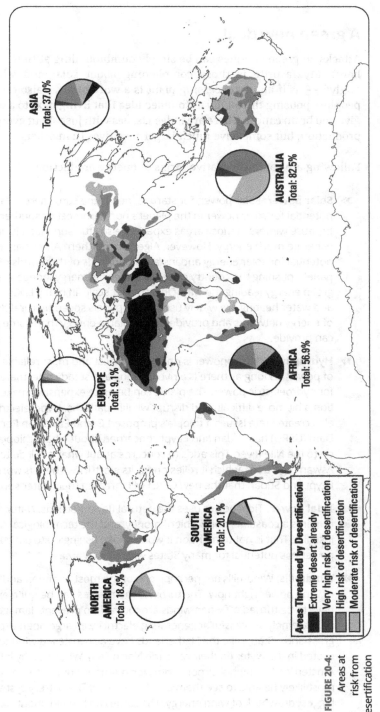

FIGURE 20-4:
Areas at
risk from
desertification

Areas Threatened by Desertification
- Extreme desert already
- Very high risk of desertification
- High risk of desertification
- Moderate risk of desertification

ASIA Total: 37.0%

AUSTRALIA Total: 82.5%

AFRICA Total: 56.9%

EUROPE Total: 9.1%

SOUTH AMERICA Total: 20.1%

NORTH AMERICA Total: 18.4%

A green new deal

Attacks on green energies can be simply dumbfounding at times (insert facepalm here). My favorite is those complaining about solar and wind farms being "ugly" — as if an oil processing plant is a work of art. I also cringe when I hear people espousing the totally unfounded idea that living next to a wind turbine will give you brain cancer. There are indeed issues with just about every form of energy production, but some have much larger negatives than others.

Following are some alternative forms of energy production:

>> **Solar power:** Solar power, for starters, needs the sun. There is far less potential for solar power in the planet's northernmost or southernmost places because winters in those areas experience so little sun that it is difficult to generate much energy. However, Algeria in northern Africa has realized the potential for solar energy and installed hundreds of thousands of solar panels, pushing the country closer to achieving energy independence with green energy leading the way. On a smaller scale, in many LDCs, solar lighting and water heating are widely used. Solar panels speed up rural development of energy networks and provide more reliable energy than some power grids can provide.

>> **Hydropower:** Hydropower is one of the oldest and most reliable generators of power. As long as there is a river flowing at a steady rate, there is potential for hydroelectric power. The plants can be quite expensive, make transportation a bit more difficult, and disrupt wildlife patterns. Hydroelectric plants can also create State issues. Ethiopia's proposed Grand Ethiopian Renaissance Dam (GERD) has Sudan and Egypt concerned about what Ethiopia's dam will do to the Nile River. This adds to concerns about what it will do to Egypt's own Aswan High Dam, which it relies on for its electricity. There is worry among Egypt and Sudan that the new GERD will threaten their water supplies.

>> **Tidal power:** Tidal power uses the natural flow of oceans. Naturally, this requires a coastline, quite a bit of money, and the technological capability to install it. That is not to mention it would make fishing quite difficult. Still, tidal power has potential for many States with coastal areas.

>> **Windmills:** Windmills are perhaps one of the most common and visible forms of wind power right now. The turbines themselves can be quite expensive and have to be turned off when winds are too high to prevent damage. They can be extremely successful at generating electricity in large open expanses, like grasslands. States like the Netherlands have also installed wind turbines rooted in the water (in their case, the North Sea). When you fly into Amsterdam's Schiphol airport from North America or Northern Europe, you'll most likely be able to see them out the window. The battery systems are the biggest drawback of wind energy. The same can be said about solar.

The batteries are used when there is not enough wind to generate electricity. If there are multiple days without much wind, alternative electricity production methods are still needed. However, this becomes less and less of an issue as improvements in power storage are made.

>> **Nuclear energy:** Nuclear energy falls in a weird middle ground. On the one hand, uranium — the primary fuel for nuclear plants — is technically a nonrenewable resource. However, because there is so much of it and we use so little of it, it's basically inexhaustible. The biggest issues with nuclear power are the cost of establishing a safe nuclear plant and the instability of it as a power source. When done correctly and safely, nuclear power is a very clean and effective method of producing electricity. Environmental factors can lead to some real human and environmental issues, as we saw in Fukushima, Japan, in 2011. Also, human factors come into play, as they did in Chernobyl, Ukraine, in 1986 or Three Mile Island in Pennsylvania in 1979. Then, there is the whole worry about the creation of nuclear weapons thing. The world community heavily sanctions Iran and North Korea in an attempt to prevent them from getting materials that they might use to make a nuclear bomb. Those sanctions also prevent Iran and North Korea from building nuclear power plants because they use many of the same components. Bombs and meltdowns aside, nuclear energy is perhaps the cleanest, most effective form of creating energy to date.

TECHNICAL STUFF

The Chernobyl disaster stands out because an accident led to a reactor explosion. The exposed core poisoned the landscape to the point that thousands of square miles of northern Ukraine will remain unlivable for more than 20,000 years.

Global Solutions to a Global Issue

The potentially most frustrating thing about the whole climate change situation is that we could do something about it. In the 1970s and 1980s, it became apparent that the Earth's ozone layer was depleting. The ozone layer helps prevent us from absorbing too much of the sun's radiation. Without it, there's a good chance that things like cancer would be much more common as humans would be exposed to more harmful radiation.

The main culprit behind the destruction of the ozone layer was chlorofluorocarbons (CFCs), which are commonly found in aerosols. The international community came together and signed the Montreal Protocol in 1987. The agreement went into effect in 1989 and limited the use of CFCs. And something shocking happened: It worked! The ozone layer replenished itself and is, more or less, acting normally once again. This further proves that when there is a global problem, global action can actually have an impact. And yet here we are, faced with an even bigger global problem, asking ourselves what can be done.

Climate change: A human issue

Natural climate change has been happening since the very origins of our planet. Many things naturally can affect the Earth's climate, including volcanic eruptions, Milankovitch cycles (changes in the Earth's tilt, spin, and path around the sun), changes in the albedo effect, and even the types and numbers of plants and animals.

As I said at the beginning of this chapter, if someone tells you climate change isn't real, try not to facepalm too hard. The only debate is the extent to which humans are influencing climate change.

Now, we will focus on the anthropogenic causes and implications of climate change — the human side of the issue. We know the Earth has gotten warmer and colder throughout its history. What is concerning is the rate at which the planet is presently warming. We've been able to track global temperatures through dendrochronology (the study of tree rings), the analysis of ice cores, ocean sediment, and even the historical writings of humans. From this, we can put together a fairly accurate understanding of the ebbs and flows of global climate patterns. What we're seeing now is that the Earth is warming at a faster rate than at any other time in human history.

Again, I'm taking a one-sided approach to climate change here (as opposed to trying to argue that climate change is not an issue or not human-connected) because that is the overwhelming consensus of the scientific community.

Climate change is exactly like what the name says: a change in climate. Global warming refers to a generalized increase in temperatures. Some scientists will use one term; others will use the other. Climate change is probably the most accurate since it reflects that some areas are actually predicted to cool down. These areas are minimal compared to the general evidence showing that temperature will increase everywhere. Still, some scientists are starting to use the phrase "Climate Disaster" to communicate what we're facing here.

Climate is a long-term trend. It's looking at a place and being able to say what the precipitation and temperature patterns will most likely be throughout the year. Weather is what it is currently doing outside. Raining, cloudy, or snowing? That's all weather. Meteorologists predict weather change; climatologists predict climate change.

THE CASE FOR CLIMATE CHANGE

Climate change–deniers look outside to see it's snowing and conclude climate change isn't real. Or they'll blame a large hurricane on climate change. That's not really how either of those things works. You really have to look at long-term trends to be able to start picking up any sort of change over time. That is where science comes in.

Just know that any politician who talks about climate change is only repeating what they've heard from someone else. And when most people say they've "done research" about climate change, you can replace the word "done research" with "read some stuff online." Actual research involves geologists, climatologists, biologists, astronomers, ecologists, environmental scientists, chemists, oceanographers, glaciologists, and many others. Geography ties all of those fields together. We take the information they collect and display it on maps to understand it spatially. My research on climate change has involved going to different parts of the world and talking with people in the area to gauge how they've recognized changes in climate patterns. Be it Kenya, Ecuador, Iceland, Germany, or even around the United States, the constant is that the lives of people are changing as the climate begins to shift.

Science shows a strong correlation between rising temperatures and changes in the amount of carbon dioxide humans produce. Countries like China, the US, India, and Russia are the top producers of CO_2. When we take into account the amount of CO_2 produced per capita, the picture suddenly changes a bit. The US is still high, but oil-producing States like Qatar, Canada, Kuwait, and the United Arab Emirates are revealed to be the top CO_2 producers.

Collectively, the work of those studying climate change is shared and evaluated by others. One of the most important parts of science is that other scientists must review it to ensure their conclusions are correct. The Intergovernmental Panel on Climate Change (IPCC) is the most notable organization involved in this process. The IPCC facilitates the sharing and review of data between scientists from all over the world. Scientists share their findings, discuss the results, and make recommendations at their meetings. Their tone has become increasingly alarmist as the data becomes increasingly clear we're headed toward catastrophe. Yet, few major actions are being taken. Individual States are taking on initiatives to lower their carbon footprint, but much more is needed to prevent what scientists predict is coming.

TIP

There is tons of information about climate change online, and if you're interested in learning more, the IPCC or the United Nations Environment Programme are great places to check for quality information.

Climate change: Global solutions

Globally, it seems people are waiting for one magic solution that will change everything (or they're completely ignoring it). The ways to address climate change can generally be divided between adaptation and mitigation.

>> **Adaption:** Adaptation involves different approaches to deal with the effects of climate change that are already happening, such as installing air conditioning, changing agricultural practices, and changing seasonal behaviors.

>> **Mitigation:** Mitigation, on the other hand, is the continued effort to stabilize and reduce the warming trend from increased greenhouse gas emissions. These efforts involve reducing the carbon footprint by switching to green energies and changing how land is used.

Restorative practices are one mitigation approach, including the idea of "rewilding." In the American prairie, for example, converting a human agricultural or residential landscape back to prairie allows the land to heal itself. The prairie grasses have much deeper roots than those found in our lawns or agricultural crops. The deeper roots increase the potential for carbon sequestration, thus helping an area that was otherwise part of the problem become part of the solution. Rewilding in the rainforests can also be successful. Costa Rica is one of the best examples. They adopted policies to help facilitate the regrowth of the rainforest, and they are now one of the lowest emitters in the Americas.

Costa Rica has seen its rewilding efforts pay off by attracting ecotourism (see Figure 20-5). Ecotourism is a tourism trend where people travel to especially pristine areas. Each year, millions of people visit the country's clean beaches, lush forests, and well-preserved national parks. The Galapagos Islands of Ecuador maintain one of the most well-preserved natural areas on the planet with the support of funds from ecotourism. On the reverse, however, is Iceland. Each year, a country of about 330,000 people welcomes well over 1 million tourists, who create trash that well exceeds the regular usage. Also, these tourist visits swallow up a significant amount of resources.

Environmental and climate justice

One reason it's imperative to address climate change as soon as possible is that the problems associated with increasing population will have the hardest effects on some of the most vulnerable populations. Impoverished areas are the most vulnerable because they have the least amount of resources available to help them adapt or mitigate. For example, building seawalls to protect against rising sea levels is expensive. For States, regions, or cities already struggling financially, it's all the more difficult to deal with yet another problem.

FIGURE 20-5:
Toucans in
Manuel Antonio
National Park in
Costa Rica

Even in wealthier countries, the most vulnerable groups are the elderly, people dealing with health issues and lower-income people. Increasing temperatures lead to further respiratory and infectious diseases. Ticks and mosquitos can extend their range, leading to increases in diseases like malaria. As temperatures increase, heat-related illnesses increase. People who cannot afford air conditioning are especially at risk. When temperatures reach dangerous levels in areas that have not historically been so hot, there will be an increase in deaths from heat exhaustion and respiratory illnesses.

Global efforts

Occasionally, the world comes together and actually recognizes that the environment must be given the same level of attention given to the economy. The first such major meeting took place in 1992 when world leaders met at the United Nations Framework Convention on Climate Change in Kyoto, Japan. The resulting Kyoto Protocol committed to reducing greenhouse gas emissions. Most notably, however, the United States did not ratify the treaty or adhere to its ideas. When one of the largest emitters in the world is not involved, the agreement's intended goals certainly take a hit.

In 2015, the world met again, this time in Paris, to discuss the growing climate crisis. Clearly, the Kyoto Protocol's goals had to be refined to meet the growing reality that the scientific data was showing. When the Paris Climate Agreement (sometimes called the *Paris Accords*) went into effect in 2016, nearly every state in the world either signed it or ratified it. Initially, Syria did not sign on but did so later. Nicaragua did not sign the agreement because it felt the agreement was too weak.

REMEMBER

The United States pulled out in 2017 because the agreement placed too many restrictions on it that President Donald Trump felt would hurt the economy too much — even though countries established their own goals, and many have proven to be able to do so while still maintaining economic growth.

When President Joe Biden took office in 2021, one of the first things he did was move the United States back on a path toward rejoining the agreement. Even when President Trump decided to remove the US from the treaty, many individual states — and even US cities — made climate-based initiatives of their own.

Beyond the international and national initiatives (of which there are far too many to ever list in a book like this), one of the most impactful guiding frameworks for trying to improve the planet is the United Nations' Sustainable Development Goals (SDGs). Adopted in 2015, these wide-sweeping initiatives look to further the UN's goals for peace and stability. Seventeen in total, the initiatives address social, economic, political, and environmental issues found in every corner of our planet.

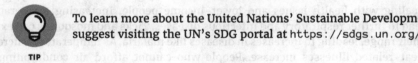

TIP

To learn more about the United Nations' Sustainable Development Goals (SDGs), I suggest visiting the UN's SDG portal at https://sdgs.un.org/goals.

5

The Part of Tens

How human geography contributes to many career paths

Where you can see human geography in action

Chapter **21**

Ten Human Geography Careers

O bviously, you've thoroughly enjoyed this book, and now you're wondering what careers you can pursue that hire people with training in human geography. Luckily for you, human geography is a very versatile discipline that offers many different career pathways people can pursue using their understanding of people and location. This chapter highlights just a few ways to apply your human geography knowledge.

The Academic Route

A lot of the knowledge included in this book has been made possible by hours of research and years of dedication from academic geographers. These people have obtained a master's or Ph.D. in geography and used their training in research and geographic concepts to understand the world better. They most often work for some sort of college or university. Along with teaching college-level classes, where they can share their knowledge with aspiring geographers, they also work on their research. Some academic geographers who work in big research institutions might spend as little as 40 percent — or even less — of their time teaching; they spend the rest of their time researching or performing other services (administrative or working on behalf of an organization).

The smaller the university, the more time academic geographers spend teaching. Their research involves going into the field, collecting data, compiling other resources, and publishing research papers. Academic geographers work with others in the same field and attend conferences to check, re-check, and share information to help us understand their research. Literally dozens of research paths are available to human geographers, allowing them to contribute to the body of knowledge in various fields, including political, agricultural, economic, cultural, medical, and environmental.

The Geospatial Route

The geospatial route is an increasingly common route for students interested in geography. Geospatial geography involves training and a degree in geospatial technologies like Geographic Information Systems (GIS) or remote sensing. From there, they can also teach at the university level. GIS courses are important for colleges and universities with a geography department. In fact, universities without a geography department often still have GIS courses because they are such a valuable tool for anyone interested in many other careers. Even students who go to school for things like agriculture must take GIS courses. Working for private companies or government organizations (especially city or county government offices) is another route for GIS students, where they help collect, organize, analyze, and share geographic information. For example, they might map sewer lines so cities can plan new systems or map census data that helps governments better understand their population and needs.

The Business Route

Have you ever noticed that certain businesses are located in specific cities or parts of cities? For example, new car dealerships are located in one part of the city, while only used car dealerships might be found in other parts. Businesses rely on human geographers to understand the market trends of different areas. If you put a store, like a fast-food restaurant, in the wrong place, it might be doomed to fail.

By understanding what people like about a certain type of fast food and where those people are geographically located, businesses give themselves a better chance of success. Along with business location, economic geographers work to understand local, regional, and even global trends to ensure that businesses make smart economic and geographic decisions. That can also involve establishing shipping and transportation networks to reduce costs and maximize profits.

The Medical Route

Remember during the height of the COVID-19 pandemic when all of those dashboards of interactive maps came out to track the numbers of new infections and other statistics? They are part of the medical geography subdiscipline of human geography. Much of medicine is devoted to understanding how new or existing diseases spread. With this knowledge, researchers can respond more quickly to potential outbreaks by sending resources and medical staff to help contain medical events like pandemics.

They can also study how diseases affect people based on different demographic factors (like age, race, or gender). Medical researchers can then institute plans to prevent people from getting sick in the first place. Medical researchers also position resources (vaccine clinics, hospitals, and so on) where those resources are more likely needed. These things require knowledge of medicine, geography, and population characteristics. So, if you're interested in medicine but can't stand the sight of blood, medical geography might be the perfect way to help people!

The Military/Intelligence Route

An often-cited quote about war being God's way of teaching Americans geography has been attributed to everyone, from Mark Twain to journalist Ambrose Bierce to comedian Jon Stewart. Regardless of who said it, there's some truth to it because many Americans often have never heard of a specific place (like Iraq, Afghanistan, or Vietnam) until an armed conflict or war teaches them the geography. Military operations depend on understanding the site and situation factors inside the conflict area (or potential conflict area). Transportation networks, resource locations, population characteristics, and even cultural characteristics can be important pieces of intelligence.

It is often said that during the Cold War, the United States actually had better maps of Moscow than the Soviets did. The Soviets distributed fake maps to create confusion in case of an invasion. The United States, however, made very detailed maps so that if there were an invasion, they could easily make their way around the Soviet capital. Military intelligence is all about what is happening where, and geographers are part of that. Geographers can also help assess the local, regional, and global implications of a conflict and help understand why it is happening in the first place.

The Education Route

Having a background in geographic skills and concepts is part of being civic-minded. For that reason, many states and countries mandate that students receive geography training. Well, somebody has to teach those courses, right?! That could be you! Teaching geography at the primary, secondary, and post-secondary levels helps students expand their social understanding. Helping curious people learn more about the world is what this book is geared to do. Speaking from ample experience, being a geographic educator is not always an easy gig, but it can be rewarding. Humans are naturally curious and want to know about their surroundings. Geographic educators help people of all ages scratch those intellectual itches.

The City/County Government Route

Local governments must collect vast amounts of data about their residents to know how to serve them best. What areas are growing the most? Which city areas are food deserts? What are the housing costs in different parts of the city? These are all questions that geographers can help answer by applying their understanding of human geography. Urban geographers are particularly interested in the walkability of cities, the locations of mass transit networks, blight areas, development, and gentrification. These are important things to know when planning things like schools, utilities, fire and police protection, and roads. University urban planning and geography departments are often closely associated because they focus on many of the same things. With cities changing so fast — urbanization in semi-periphery or periphery States or new urbanism and suburbanization in core States — urban geographers are in high demand to help city and county governments plan for the future.

The Marketing Route

Let's say you've created a cool, new widget you think could be a really big money-maker. Your next step is to do some market research to understand who will want your widget, where they live, and the best way to inform them of the product so they'll buy it. We've discussed how businesses make decisions based on where their customers are, but you also need to know what those customers want to buy.

At a school where I worked, a group of Brazilian students came to our school each December for a one-semester study-abroad experience. We always had to have coats, hats, and gloves ready for them when they arrived because winter clothes were not really something they could buy back home. Why would you sell winter clothes to people who live in tropical areas? Similarly, Minnesota is so cold in the winter that ice cream advertisements disappear for a few months and return when warmer weather returns. Both are examples of targeted marketing, where knowing consumer habits and trends help make business decisions. That's all human geography!

The Conservationist Route

I often tell my students that if they want to save a species, they can study it all they want, but it's not until you get people involved that you can actually do anything about it. Knowing the anatomy of an endangered species is cool and all, but knowing what makes it die off will make more of a difference in most cases. For many species, like the lemurs of Madagascar, nothing physiological or biological is causing their numbers to decline. It is, however, the destruction of their habitat by expanding human cities and farms. Understanding the root of problems allows conservation scientists to work with local communities to find the solution. Understanding the cultural, economic, and even political landscapes takes time, so many conservationists take a lot of time to approach a problem from an ecological perspective, considering both the human and environmental causes and effects of a problem.

Using a geographic perspective and a human geography lens, they can better understand the scope and context of the problem. Human geographers specializing in land use, economics, culture, and populations are especially helpful.

GIS is another high-demand area. Geospatial data on locations and movement (gathered with tracking devices) and the location of habitats and human systems can all be compiled and analyzed to understand trouble spots and plans to address high-concern areas. Human geography is literally at the forefront of efforts to save the world!

The Travel and Tourism Route

Knowing who travels when, where, why, and how can be important for companies and governments. Travel and tourism are the main money-makers for businesses in some areas. Tourists bring in lots of money from outside areas and can be a big boost to the economy. The areas that suffered most during the COVID-19 pandemic were the ones that relied on tourism dollars. Tourism requires hotels, restaurants, transportation services, guides, outfitters, and support services like medical and safety. Travel and tourism can act as huge growth poles. Sometimes, the economies of entire regions can be completely tied to tourism. Understanding what people like (beaches, mountains, scenic areas, amusement parks, and so on) can be especially helpful in attracting more tourists. In recent years, the study of ecotourism has grown because people want to travel authentically to truly experience an environment.

Governments also need to understand tourism. For example, Iceland — tiny Iceland, with a population of about 330,000 — receives about 1 million tourists every year (give or take, depending on whether there is a global pandemic). That huge influx of tourism creates enormous stress on hotels, roads, and even grocery stores in a country that is not used to having that many people. Understanding who comes from where can also be especially helpful to ensure guides who speak those tourists' languages can help ensure guests have a great experience. Not only does a country or area want you to visit, but it also wants to ensure that you keep returning to spend your money!

Chapter **22**

Ten Places to Visit to See Human Geography in Action

A s you read this book, I hope you learned that everything is geography, and geography is everything. You can go to many places to see and apply the principles covered throughout this book. Of course, you can always use the Internet to find fun and interesting geography applications, but there's nothing like going out in the field to see it for yourself. In this chapter, I tell you about some places you can go to see human geography in action and what you should be looking for to learn as much as possible. So, get out there and start writing your own Earth Story!

A Major World City

Major world cities might be the first to come to mind when you think of some of the best places to exchange ideas and culture. Cities like New York, London, Paris, Tokyo, Hong Kong, and Moscow represent great meeting places for people worldwide. In each of these cities, you'll find just about every culture worldwide.

A tapestry of languages and ideas, you'll find vibrant neighborhoods, boroughs, and even shops or restaurants in major world cities. All of this combines to give cities a feel that really is unmatched elsewhere in the world. Not only have the forces of migration and urbanization made these cities massive, but the cities have been influenced by migration and urbanization. Moscow, for example, acts as the nerve center for the entirety of Russia and the Slavic-speaking world, including much of Central Asia and Eastern Europe.

London, Paris, and New York are truly global cities where you'll be able to see how the processes of cultural diffusion have created a truly unique mixture of cultures that can only really be found in these metropolises. If you've never been to one of these cities, you can get a sense of their scale simply by looking out your plane's window as it approaches for a landing.

A Large Regional City

Chicago is not the capital of the state of Illinois, but I would argue it is much more important than the city of Springfield. I would even go so far as to say that Chicago acts as a quasi-capital for the entire Midwest region. Large regional cities, like Shanghai, St. Petersburg, Munich, or Sydney, that otherwise don't have any official importance from a political standpoint can have regional importance in their ability to still attract people from elsewhere.

For example, Sydney, Australia, is the capital of New South Wales State, but people move there from all around the world because its importance is far greater than that. You could argue that it is a world city, but what would not be debatable is its importance for the entire Eastern half of Australia.

Regional cities (often airline hubs) share similar cultural and urban qualities as world cities and have many of the same elements — only on a smaller scale. For example, Chicago is full of embassies and consulates from other countries but does not have the same international pull as New York.

Another Country

One of my favorite travel stories is my first real experience traveling out of the US. I immediately felt intense culture shock in the airport when I landed in China. I was jetlagged and hadn't slept for more than 35 hours, which made the experience of riding in the van from the airport to my new apartment quite surreal. It felt like we spent more time driving in the lanes of oncoming traffic than our own. Then, to be completely immersed in a culture entirely different from anything I'd ever experienced growing up in the Midwest could only be truly learned from living it.

Books, movies, and documentaries can never tell you what another country is like. The smells, sounds, and foods must be experienced firsthand. The concepts covered in this book will differ for every city you visit. My only advice here is to travel as much as possible and keep an open mind. Always make sure you experience a place for what it is and avoid constantly thinking about what it's not by comparing it to your home country.

A State or National Capital

State capitals or national capitals — it really does not matter. They all sort of have the same feel. The energy is different than in other large cities. A capital city's political influence attracts a certain type of person and business and has the same general vibe. Capitals are meant to represent their state or nation. Washington, DC, is meant to be a beautiful US shrine. As the center of its once vast empire, London has a similar but different air.

Capitals are not always the largest city for their region — like Lincoln is not the largest city in Nebraska — but they still act as a growth pole for businesses and industries relying on close proximity to the political nerve center. Capital cities typically have concentrations of highly educated people compared to other areas and can attract universities and outside professionals to increase opportunities for those who live there.

Visiting heads of state and local representatives can make life in capital cities interesting, especially for transportation. Just talk to someone from Washington, DC, about the annoyances of road closures for official motorcades. This also means capitals are lightning rods for their region. If the government does something unpopular, protests can be organized quickly. While walking the streets of Bogota, Colombia, on election day, it is not an exaggeration to say that I encountered more than 200 police officers in an area of about 1 square mile who were there to address any issues. (Luckily, there were none.)

A Rural Area

Renting a car and visiting the countryside can be one of the most interesting and authentic ways to visit a rural area. People not attached to any sort of tourism agency can give you one of the clearest ideas of what the people of a country or place think. Having a seat in a local pub and enjoying a drink (if you're of age, of course) can be a great way to start a conversation. (In my experience, people are overly enthusiastic to welcome an outsider and share ideas.)

Otherwise, seeing everyday people's everyday lives as they go about their days can be one of the most interesting parts of your trip. Watching farmers herd their sheep along the road in Iceland or kids waving at your car as you drive through rural Kenya can be just as memorable as the bright lights of the major cities. Obviously, rural areas offer one of the best chances to see the elements of agricultural geography and land use, but you should also recognize all of the elements from the Five Themes of Geography (see Chapter 3).

A "Natural" Area

Sometimes, you can learn more about a culture by looking at what it protects instead of what it has built. Some say there are no untouched places left on Earth. Consequently, many areas are undeveloped because people have consciously decided not to develop them. Visiting natural parks or recreation areas can be a great way to see what types of land a culture values and how it is used. Whether in a national park with pristine beaches that locals use to get away from the hot cities on a summer day or a forest filled with exotic areas, cultures can be measured by how they protect their resources.

Visiting national parks and recreation can be a great way to see how a local economy can be built up by protecting and supporting an area of natural importance. It can be a sad experience, however, to see how the overutilization and mass influx of tourism can take a place that is otherwise one of the most beautiful spots in the world and ruin the experience. Just try going to Yellowstone National Park in July, and you'll understand what too much tourism looks like.

A Small Town

One of the things that I find fascinating about small towns is the sense of community that does not exist in large cities. At best, I've known who my next-door neighbors were in the cities I've lived in. However, sometimes, I had no idea who was living on the other side of my apartment wall.

The communication networks and familial connections of small towns are entirely different and one of the things that prevent people from moving away. Another interesting phenomenon, especially in the United States, is how chain migration processes tend to be amplified. Perhaps 150 years ago, when someone moved from one country to another, they gave their new home a name that honored their hometown in the "old country." (For example, if they were from Prague, they might've named their home in a new country, "New Prague." Also, the new community might've retained some traditions reflecting their original ethnicity. For example, Pella, Iowa, still holds a tulip festival each year — a continued tradition harkening back to the Dutch roots of the original European settlers to the area. In many parts of the world, small towns are where you'll get the chance to experience folk cultures that are much more authentic than the popular culture in the larger cities.

An Isolated Settlement or Village

One thing that never ceases to amaze me is that I can be miles out in the countryside — thousands of miles from home — and I'll still be able to find some sort of connection with the people there. Perhaps it's someone in rural China wearing the jersey of their favorite NBA player or being in the middle of Siberia and speaking English with my cabinmate. These things remind me that Earth is not as big as we think. The fact that I was introduced to a song created by a Norwegian band by a Korean student while teaching in Minnesota sometimes makes it annoyingly clear that we are more intertwined now than at any other point in history. At least by traveling to small rural villages, you can see remnants of what makes us unique. Omul drying on racks along the shores of Lake Baikal reminded me that some things have remained in Siberia, even though many things have not.

An Airport, Train Station, or Bus Station

Next time you're at a train station, airport, or bus station, find the nearest departures board. The places you can visit from that station tell one story, but the frequency of buses, trains, and planes going to places tells a completely different story. For example, Omaha, Nebraska, has two weekly direct flights to Austin, Texas. However, it has well over a dozen daily flights to Chicago, Illinois, on multiple airlines. This example helps show the Gravity Model (see Chapter 9) in real time so you can see the connections between one place and another.

Looking for a flight to Turkmenistan? You'd be hard-pressed to find a direct flight from anywhere in the United States. In Istanbul, Turkey, however, you will see flights to places that most people in the United States have never even heard of, including direct flights to Ashgabat, the capital of Turkmenistan. The languages spoken over the public address also reveal much about the area's cultural landscape, including the amenities each airport offers. After a 12-hour flight to Qatar, I was thrilled to find a designated "resting area" with comfy chairs and required quiet. I was just about to fall asleep when the Fajr morning prayer came over the intercom to remind me I was in an Islamic country. Transport stations are interesting because you'll see people from all walks of life in a relatively small area. And they're all stressed, which leads to some very interesting interactions.

Your Own Community

Your community is one of the best places to see human geography principles. With the eye of a geographer, you'll see things differently. A bus stop soon represents urban sprawl and population distributions; the newly developed part of town is a sign of gentrification; and the farmers' market is market gardening. It does not matter where you are; you can apply multiple aspects of this book to understand your community from a geographic perspective.

Even this book itself results from geographic networks of transportation, economics, and culture. You really can't get away from it. But why would anyone ever want to get away from geography? Go out and enjoy the world with your newly developed perspective of human geography.

Index

W

Wahabbi, 180

walled villages, 159–160. *See also* nucleated settlements

Wallerstein, Immanuel, 292, 317–319. *See also* World Systems Theory

Wall Street, 160

Walmart, 135

warrior class, 267

Warsaw Pact, 250

water scarcity, 86

Watt, James, 327

The Wealth of Nations (Smith), 316

Weber, Alfred, 48, 305–306

Weiner, Tim (author), 256

West Bank, 117

Western Hemisphere Institute for Security Cooperation, 253

Westward Expansion, 221

wet rice cultivation, 292–293

Whiskey War, 260

"white flight" phenomenon, 149

White nationalism, 239

Whitney, Eli (inventor), 275

Wiegand, Steve, 129

windmills, 354–355

Wine For Dummies (McCarthy/Ewing-Mulligan), 296

Wisconsin, 188

women's roles, changes in, 268–269

world cities, 141–142, 194–195

world city models, 164–168

world community, 86

World Factbook, 289

World Health Organization, 49

World History For Dummies (Haugen), 129

World Island, 255, 257

world population density, 77

World Systems Theory, 262, 292, 317–319

World War I, 250–251

World War II, 87

Wright, Louis (historian), 76

X

xenophobia, 207

Y

Yellow River Valley, 272

Yi-Fu-Tuan, 46

Yugoslavia, 242–243

Z

Zakat, 174

Zimbabwe, 247–248

Zionist movement, 117

zone of independent workers' homes, 161. *See also* concentric zone model

zone of transition, 161

zoning restrictions, 150

About the Author

Kyle Tredinnick has been involved in geographic education since starting his career in education in 2009. Originally focused on history, he has become a geographic education advocate through numerous endeavors. After receiving a Bachelor of Science in social studies secondary education from Saint Cloud State University, he taught in schools in China and Minnesota before moving to Omaha, Nebraska, to continue teaching and complete a master's in geography at the University of Nebraska-Omaha. Kyle is working on completing a Ph.D. in geography at the University of Nebraska-Lincoln, focusing on geographic education, all while teaching for Omaha Public Schools and the University of Nebraska-Omaha Department of Geography/Geology.

Along with teaching, Kyle co-owns Geopolaris Education Publications and is involved with a number of geographic-based organizations. Along with having served on the Board of Directors for the Geographic Educators of Nebraska and the National Council of Geographic Education, Kyle has been fortunate enough to have the opportunity to work with a number of organizations, including National Geographic, The Goethe Institute, and the Fulbright Teachers for Global Classrooms program.

Kyle lives in Omaha, Nebraska, with his wife, Jill, and two cats. He enjoys traveling as much as possible and uses hockey (both watching and playing) to help balance a busy working schedule.

Dedication

For all of the family, teachers, and mentors who helped make me the geographic educator I am today.

Author's Acknowledgments

First, I appreciate my very understanding wife, Jill, who has been patient and supportive throughout my many "side gigs." Thank you so much for helping me through this extensive process.

As a teacher, I must acknowledge all of the teachers and advisors who believed in me and provided me with opportunities to push my potential. Dr. Kyle Ward (I won't acknowledge your current affiliation) was one of the first who really pushed me (and literally drove me to my first GeoFest). Dr. Christian Dando at the University of Nebraska at Omaha helped mentor and advise me as I transitioned to my role as a professional geographer. Mr. Harris Payne gave me ample opportunities to get involved. Dr. Kelly Swanson has been a great friend and guide in the world of consulting. Dr. David Lanegran helped oversee my conversion to geography and literally got my first job for me. And an excellent set of professionals who advised me while completing my Ph.D. program at the University of Nebraska-Lincoln: Dr. Patrick Bitterman, Dr. Becky Buller, Dr. Robert Shepard, Dr. Beth Lewis, and Dr. Sarah Bednarz.

Of course, I would like to thank my family and friends who so understandingly supported me and excused my prolonged absence while completing this project (though, really surprisingly, not that bad).

Making this project possible was my fantastic team of geographers. Dr. Swanson, Dr. Bitterman, and Dr. Shepard are getting a shout-out once again. The feedback you provided was massively valuable in helping make this book as helpful a representation of our craft as possible. I must also give a shout to Rick Kughen, the development editor. I apologize for the incredible amount of run-on sentences, all the incomplete thoughts, the frantic late-night emails (that you answered surprisingly quickly at all hours), and all the incredibly disconnected anecdotes that went into a project of this scale.

Finally, my students helped inspire me along the process. Your excitement and even the weird, snarky comments helped push me through completing this book.

Publisher's Acknowledgments

Acquisitions Editor: Elizabeth Stilwell

Project Manager: Rick Kughen

Development Editor: Rick Kughen

Technical Editors: Kelly Swanson and Patrick Bitterman

Production Editor: Tamilmani Varadharaj

Cover Image: © VioletaStoimenova/Getty Images